Love and Hate
in Jamestown

LOVE AND HATE
IN JAMESTOWN

*John Smith, Pocahontas,
and the Heart of a New Nation*

DAVID A. PRICE

ff

faber and faber

First published in the United States in 2003
A Borzoi Book published by Alfred A. Knopf
1745 Broadway, New York, NY 10019

First published in the United Kingdom in 2004
by Faber and Faber Limited
3 Queen Square London WC1N 3AU

Printed in England by Mackays

Grateful acknowledgement is made to the following for permission to reprint previously
published material.

Cambridge University Press: Translated excerpts from The Jamestown Voyages Under the First
Charter: 1606-1609 edited by Philip L. Barbour. Reprinted by permission of Cambridge
University Press.

RoundHouse: Excerpts from Jamestown Narratives: Eyewitness Accounts of the Virginia
Colony edited by Edward Wright Haile. Reprinted by permission of RoundHouse.

Trio Music Company, Inc., and Fort Knox Music, Inc.: Excerpt from the song lyric 'Fever' by
John Davenport and Eddie Cooley. Copyright © 1956 by Trio Music Company, Inc., and Fort
Knox Music, Inc. Copyright renewed. All rights reserved. Reprinted by permission of Trio
Music Company, Inc., and Fort Knox Music, Inc.

A CIP record for this book
is available from the British Library

ISBN 0-571-22098-3

2 4 6 8 10 9 7 5 3 1

Contents

Love and Hate in Jamestown

PROLOGUE

⟨⟨·⟩⟩

In the year 1606, on a Roman tennis court, the artist Caravaggio killed an opponent after an argument over a foul call. A middle-aged mathematician named Galileo Galilei, who had not yet built his first telescope, published a book of observations about the recent appearance of a supernova in the sky. Japan's first shogun, Ieyasu Tokugawa, had recently begun his rule. The Dutch painter Rembrandt was born. In Oxford, Cambridge, and Canterbury, forty-seven scholars appointed by the king were laboring over a new translation of the Scriptures, which would come to be known as the King James Bible. A new play called *Macbeth* opened in London. And in late December, in London's River Thames, three small ships were anchored, awaiting a voyage across the Atlantic.

Those three ships—the *Susan Constant*, the *Godspeed*, and the *Discovery*—went on to change the course of history. After a series of fruitless attempts by the English to create an outpost in North America, the voyagers of 1606 finally broke through. The colony that they established at Jamestown would open the way for later English settlements up and down the East Coast, and eventually for the United States itself.

The Jamestown colony was an entrepreneurial effort, organized and financed by the Virginia Company of London, a start-up venture chartered eight months earlier; its business model was to extract profits from the gold, silver, and other riches supposedly to be found in that region of North America. Also, because no one yet knew the extent of the North American continent, the company expected to find a trade route by river through Virginia to the Pacific. (Religious conversion of the natives was a distant third objective.) The enterprise was a joint-stock company, its equity held by a limited circle of investors. In a little over two years, the Virginia Company would have its initial public stock offering at twelve pounds, ten shillings a share. English America was a corporation before it was a country.

Few of the investors were actually on the three ships, fortunately for them. The colony's ultimate success would come at a fearsome price: disease, hunger, and hostile natives left behind a toll of misery and death. Most of the 105 or so adventurers who went on the ships would be dead within months, and that was only the first wave of mortality to hit the colony.

It's amazing the settlement survived at all. The alien territory of Virginia would have been a challenge to the best of explorers. But the 1606 expedition, by and large, was not made up of the best, or for that matter the brightest. Half of the colonists aboard the three ships were "gentlemen"—upper-class indolents who, as events unfolded, literally would not work to save their own lives. (The true meaning of the word "gentleman" in those days is suggested by the 1605 George Chapman farce *Eastward Ho*, involving adventurers making ready for a voyage to Virginia; one character instructs another, "Do nothing; be like a gentleman, be idle; the curse of man is labor.") Worse, the "gentlemen" of Jamestown comprised most of the colony's leaders, who came to revile and plot against one another as the sick and the starving were dropping dead around them.

The survival of the small English outpost was thanks mostly to two extraordinary people, one a commoner and one a royal. The commoner was Captain John Smith, a former soldier with an impatient nature and a total lack of respect for his social betters—or anyone else who hadn't proven himself through his merits. The royal was Pocahontas, the beautiful, headstrong daughter of the most powerful chief in Virginia.

The names of John Smith and Pocahontas have by now passed into American legend. Like the Jamestown story as a whole, their stories have been told over the generations with varying degrees of accuracy. The imaginative 1995 Walt Disney Co. movie, for example, endowed Pocahontas with a Barbie-doll figure, dressed her in a deerskin from Victoria's Secret, and made her Smith's love interest. Or, as Peggy Lee sang,

Captain Smith and Pocahontas
Had a very mad affair
When her daddy tried to kill him
She said, "Daddy, oh don't you dare
He gives me fever with his kisses
Fever when he holds me tight
Fever, I'm his missus
Oh Daddy, won't you treat him right."[1]

Trouble is, Smith and Pocahontas were never romantically involved. That isn't surprising; when Smith was in Virginia, Pocahontas was a girl of eleven or so. The real Pocahontas was a child of privilege in her society—that is, the Powhatan Empire—who was curious about the English newcomers, befriended Smith, and gave him and the rest of the English crucial assistance. Years later, looking back on her contributions, Smith would recall that her "compassionate pitiful [pitying] heart . . . gave me much cause to respect her."[2] He credited her with saving the colony. The English in Virginia, for their part, chose a strange way to repay her: after Smith left the colony, they kidnapped her and held her hostage for ransom from her father, Chief Powhatan. Yet during that time, she came to embrace English ways, married a thoroughly lovestruck Englishman named John Rolfe, and lived out the rest of her short life in his country.

Smith, at the other end of the social scale, was born in 1580 in rustic Willoughby by Alford, Lincolnshire, to a simple farm family, putting him just one rung above peasanthood. Soldiering was to be his ticket out. He was of slightly below-average height, even by the standards of his time, measuring in at perhaps five-foot-three or five-foot-four, but he was stocky and tough. He had dark hair and a full beard, and eyes that showed intelligence and confidence. In a portrait made later in his life, Smith meets the onlooker's gaze with neither haughtiness nor servility, but instead with unassuming equality—an unusual attitude in his class-conscious homeland. "He was honest, sensible, and well informed," Thomas Jefferson wrote of him a century and a half later.

The young John Smith attended grammar school in nearby Louth while dreaming of overseas adventure; at the age of thirteen, no longer content with fantasizing, he tried to run away from home in hopes of making his way abroad. His father, George Smith, had other ideas and succeeded in stopping him. At fifteen, bowing unhappily to his father's wishes, John Smith became an apprentice to a merchant. A year or two later, however, in a bittersweet turn of events for the young man, the path to the sea became open: Smith's father died.[3]

This time, there was no one to stand in John Smith's way. Bored with counting his master's money, Smith headed to the Continent and fought under a Captain Joseph Duxbury in the Netherlands, aiding that country in its war of independence against Spain. Life on the battlefield agreed with him. Returning to England a few years later, he had a plan ready: He withdrew to "a little woody pasture," as he called it, to make a single-minded study of all things martial. He was twenty years old.

In that pasture, Smith showed the first signs of what would become his lifelong preoccupation with practical knowledge. He practiced horsemanship. He read Machiavelli's *The Art of War*. He learned the life story of Marcus Aurelius, the Roman emperor and Stoic philosopher (and patriarch of the 2000 film *Gladiator*). Smith became an explosives expert, with the aid of a translated copy of Vannoccio Biringuccio's *Pirotechnia*. He memorized codes for sending signals over distances using torchlight. Although some of his study seems more on the side of erudition than practicality, Smith would have seen no bright line between the two: history, biography, and munitions were all pragmatic subjects that a military man needed to operate effectively in the world.

Smith was ready to embark on his chosen profession. He made his way back to the Continent. In the summer of 1601, he enlisted with Austrian forces in Hungary that were fighting the occupying armies of the Turkish Ottoman Empire, the Muslim superpower that had conquered much of Central Europe, North Africa, and the Middle East. In Hungary, Smith deployed his signaling torches, his explosives (he called them his "fiery dragons"), and other devices and stratagems to lethal effect, earning himself the title of captain. Here he experienced a taste of meritocracy: with individual excellence and contribution came respect and advancement. It made its impression on the young soldier.

His fortunes took a decided turn for the worse on a cold winter's day in 1602, when he was captured on the battlefield in present-day Romania. He was taken to an auction with others to be sold into slavery—"like beasts in a market-place," he recalled. Smith ended up on a Turkish farm under a cruel master, where his head was shaved

bare and a ring of iron placed around his neck. He found he was joining hundreds of slaves—European, Turk, and Arab—who informed
him that escape was impossible. That was all he needed to hear. He was
laboring in the fields one day when the master came by on horseback
to beat him; seizing his chance, Smith turned the tables, beating the
man to death with a threshing bat. Smith then put on the dead man's
clothes and took off on his horse for friendly territory.[4]

Smith wrangled a place in the Virginia expedition several years
afterward. The historical record doesn't reveal why he was picked. The
leadership of the Virginia Company probably saw him simply as a
hired military hand in case of an attack from the Spanish or trouble
with the natives. If so, he proved to be larger than that role. No matter
how or why he got the job, it seems obvious in retrospect that he was
unusually well suited to become the colony's leader, as he ultimately
did. His adventures in Hungary gave him the experience of dealing
with foreigners both as comrades and as adversaries. Those years also
shaped his distinctive worldview, one in which ignorance was to be
treated as a dangerous enemy, and in which people were to be judged
by their effectiveness rather than by their bloodlines.

Hence, unlike most Englishmen of his day, Smith believed it was
important to understand and deal with the natives as they actually were,
not as symbols of primitive evil or virtue. Accordingly, he studied the
Powhatan language and culture closely, and indeed, he left behind our
most detailed ethnographic writings on those people. With the benefit
of that information, he was able to keep Chief Powhatan at bay through
a mix of diplomacy and intimidation—not through massacre—at a
time when the Powhatan Empire outnumbered the English by well
over a hundred to one. It was this record that led several of Smith's
admirers among the colonists to write later, with only slight exaggeration, that "thou Virginia foild'st, yet kep'st unstained"—that is, he
foiled the natives in Virginia, but didn't stain Virginia with their blood.

At the same time, Smith faced the daunting task of whipping his
own countrymen into shape, particularly "the better sort" (as gentlemen were often called). They "exclaim of *all* things, though they never
adventured to know *any* thing," Smith groused, "nor ever did anything
but devour the fruits of other men's labors." The gallants, he added
with a sneer, were discontented because they didn't have "any of their
accustomed dainties, with feather beds and down pillows, taverns and
alehouses in every breathing place, neither plenty of gold and silver

and dissolute liberty as they expected." Once they were truly under Smith's thumb, as he moved from serving as a council member to colony president, he gave the "better sort" reason to squirm with his decree that "he that will not work shall not eat."5

All that was to come later. As the three ships sat at anchor in late 1606, there was little reason to assume that the mission would succeed. The crews could lose heart and mutiny, like the crew of explorer Sebastian Cabot almost a century earlier. The ships could go down in bad weather, as Sir Humphrey Gilbert's did during a 1583 attempt at colonizing. And, of course, the colony could establish itself and then fail for any number of reasons, like the Roanoke settlements of 1585 and 1587.

Those expeditions, organized by Sir Walter Ralegh, sent colonists to Roanoke Island off present-day North Carolina. Ralegh—or Raleigh, or Rawleyghe—became famous to succeeding generations for an alleged episode of chivalry involving Queen Elizabeth and a mud puddle. (Ralegh supposedly took off his best cloak and laid it over the puddle for the queen to step over.) In his own time, Ralegh was better known as an accomplished mariner and poet and as a handsome object of the queen's affection. Like Humphrey Gilbert, his half brother, he was also known for his enthusiastic butchery of the Irish as an officer in that country, not sparing women or children.

After he received encouraging reports from a brief reconnaissance mission to Virginia, Ralegh sent off his first colonizing expedition from England in April 1585; it left 107 men at Roanoke that summer. Ralph Lane, one of their leaders, was awestruck by, as he wrote, the "huge and unknowen greatnesse" of the continent. Things went awry early on; the colony lost most of its food supply when its supply ship, the *Tiger*, struck ground during a storm; salt water flowed in and spoiled the provisions. That meant the settlers would have to live off the land—or freeload off the natives. Lane opted for the latter, using the threat of force when charity wasn't forthcoming. (Perhaps fortunately for the natives of Roanoke Island, Ralegh himself never set foot in the New World.) After putting up with the English through the winter, the natives began starving them out. In June, after months of desperation, the colonists were rescued by Sir Francis Drake and taken back home.

The next attempt took a different and less militaristic tack, with Ralegh sending a group of 110 men, women, and children under the rule of a painter, John White. Two of the women, including White's daughter, were pregnant and soon gave birth to the first English children to be born in the New World. A month after the settlers arrived at Roanoke, White headed back to England for supplies. War between England and Spain kept White from returning until 1590. When he did, he found that the settlers—including his daughter and granddaughter—had disappeared without a trace. There were no bodies or any other signs of a struggle. The only clues were a tree carved with the letters "CRO" and a post carved with the word "CROATOAN." From this, White logically inferred that the group had moved to Croatoan Island, home of the Croatoan tribe. But bad weather, and the snapping of two anchor cables, foiled his plan to sail to that island to investigate; with his return to England went the last chance of finding the so-called Lost Colony. No Europeans would ever see the colonists again.[6]

Such was England's record of failure upon failure in attempting to create foreign outposts. In 1606, some 114 years after Christopher Columbus's world-altering discovery, England remained less than a third-rate colonial power. Indeed, the notion that English-speaking people would someday occupy and govern most of the North American continent would have seemed literally insane. The unimportant island nation of England was noted mostly for its irksome privateers—government-licensed pirates, in effect—who looted Spanish cargo ships.

England's record up to that point looked even less promising when measured against the already far-flung empires of Portugal and Spain. By 1606, Portuguese explorers had long since established sizable colonies within present-day Brazil, India, and Indonesia. The Portuguese had been administering the port of Macau, on the coast of China, since 1556 (as they would continue to do until 1999). From their colonies in coastal Africa, the Portuguese were playing a pivotal and inglorious role in the European slave trade, transporting Africans to European colonies in South America.

Then there was Spain, the other colonial superpower of the day. Decades earlier, Vasco Núñez de Balboa had marched through Panama to find the Pacific Ocean; Pedro Menéndez de Avilés had founded St. Augustine, Florida; law student turned explorer Hernando Cortés had conquered the Aztecs in Mexico; and Francisco Pizarro had crushed the Incas in Peru. Francisco Vásquez de Coronado had explored vast stretches of the present-day southwestern United States and stumbled upon the Grand Canyon. All told, Spain in 1606 dominated most of South America, Central America, Florida, Cuba, and the Philippines. Since 1580, in fact, Portugal itself had been under the Spanish crown, and it would remain so until 1640.

Along the way, the conquistadors built a well-deserved reputation for brutishness. After the Aztecs received Cortés as a god, he and his forces kidnapped their emperor, plundered their treasures, massacred their nobility, and destroyed their capital city of Tenochtitlán. Pizarro essentially repeated the pattern in Peru, taking a son of the recently deceased emperor for a ransom of tons of silver and gold. The *encomienda* system in the Spanish territories, which granted ownership of an area's natives to a favored Spanish settler or military man, then enslaved the people of those once-powerful empires.7

The leaders of the Jamestown venture—who needed no excuse to hate their Spanish enemies anyway—were disgusted by the Spaniards' record of bloodthirst. "No Spanish intention will be entertained by us neither to hereby root out the naturals [natives], as the Spaniards have done in Hispaniola and other parts," vowed colonist William Strachey. A group of colonists, defending the colony's "charitable" treatment of the natives, later wrote caustically of "others not pleasing, that we washed not the ground with their [the natives'] bloods, nor showed such strange inventions in mangling, murdering, ransacking, and destroying as did the Spanyards the simple bodies of such ignorant soules." The meager economic fruits of the Virginia colony could not be compared to the riches brought home by the Spanish, the group argued, because "what the Spanyard got was chiefly the spoyle and pillage of those countrey people, and not the labors of their owne hands." A 1609 tract of the Virginia Company pledged that the natives would be won over to English ways, "not by stormes of raging cruelties (as West India was converted) with rapiers point and musket shot, murdering so many millions of naked indians, as their stories doe relate, but by faire and loving meanes, suiting to our English natures." The company's governing council in London, in a 1610 report, ridiculed the Spaniards' purported religious justification for their doings:

> To preach the Gospel to a nation conquered, and
> to set their souls at liberty when we have brought their

bodies into slavery, it may be a matter sacred to the preachers, but I do not know how justifiable in the rulers, who for their mere ambition do set upon it the gloss of religion. Let the divines of Salamanca [Spain's University of Salamanca] discuss that question how the possessor of the West Indies [i.e., Spain] first destroyed and then instructed.[8]

As it happened, the Powhatans also hated the Spanish. A Spanish party had come to the Chesapeake Bay around 1560 and captured a teenage Powhatan boy; he was baptized and renamed Don Luis de Velasco. Don Luis was educated in Mexico and Spain, and then brought back to Virginia ten years afterward to establish a Catholic mission. Don Luis fled, returning to his own people, and the Powhatans took their revenge on the Spanish by killing the missionaries. The Spanish, tipped off to the events by a native prisoner, sent a gunboat in 1572 to retaliate and look for survivors. The Powhatans' memory of the affair was still fresh in the early 1600s.[9]

But if the English were opposed to the Spanish and their ways, and the Powhatans were as well, why did they become antagonists? Indeed, the Virginia Company, with its intended policy of "liberality" toward the natives to win them over, envisioned a sort of peaceful coexistence between the two groups. Toward that end, the colonists were to seek out only uninhabited ground for settlement. The clue to the trouble, of course, lies in the sympathetic phrase "ignorant souls." The English, while more humanely inclined than the Spanish at this stage, still saw the natives as savages—and that was their everyday term for them: "savages." (It was sometimes rendered as "salvages" in the chaotic spelling of the day.)

To understand what the English actually meant, though, one has to set aside the intervening four hundred years of American racial history. Seen through the prism of those four hundred years, the English attitude looks like racism; how could it not be? Improbably enough, though, the English of 1606 were not generally racist in their view of the Virginia natives—not in the conventional sense. The English did not believe that white people like themselves were innately superior and the natives innately inferior; savagery had nothing to do with biology. It also did not signify that the natives were necessarily fierce (some tribes were, some weren't). For the English, "savagery" instead referred to the cultural condition of primitivity. The opposite of "savage" was not "white"; it was "civilized" or "Christian."

This may sound, at first, like a distinction without a difference, but its implications were significant. It meant savagery was only the starting point for a people's progression toward modernity. It was a temporary condition, which did not render those within it less than fully human. Savages could not rightfully be enslaved. Violence could not be unleashed against savages without just cause. Reflecting the spirit of the time, Strachey wrote of the natives, "We are taught to acknowledge *every* man that beareth the impression of God's stamp to be not only our neighbor but to be our brother." John Smith later denounced an English mariner named Thomas Hunt for capturing twenty-seven natives in New England and selling "these poore innocent soules" into slavery in Spain.

The English did not exclude themselves from the progression: in the days of Roman conquest, as the English now saw it, the Britons themselves were the savages. The civilizing influence of the Roman conquerors, and later of the Christian gospel, had lifted the English up from that savagery. Supporters of the colony expected it to bestow the same benefits on the natives through a relationship of benevolent cultural imperialism—peaceable unless the natives struck first—and mutually beneficial trade.[10]

The lack of a racial component to the English attitudes is unsurprising, given that the English in fact regarded the natives as white people (unlike the Moors and black Africans they knew by reputation). The natives were born white, the English believed, and then their skin changed color—from the effects of the dyes that they used to decorate themselves and to ward off mosquitoes. (A colonist aboard the first voyage would recall, "Their skynn is tawny, not so born, but with dying and paynting themselves, in which they delight greatly." Another suggested, "They would be of good complexion if they would leave painting, which they use on their face and shoulders.") After an Englishman named William Parker was captured by the natives and reunited with the colonists several years afterward, an observer marveled that Parker had "grown so like both in complexion and habit to the Indians that I only knew him by his tongue to be an Englishman."[11]

While English attitudes were enlightened by the standard of the era, they were not totally benign from the natives' viewpoint. Far from it: the civilizing effect of the Romans' influence served, in turn, as a justification for the English to settle in Virginia in the first place. "Why, what injury can it be to people of any nation for Christians to come unto their ports, havens, or territories," William Strachey asked, "when the law of nations, which is the law of God and man, doth privilege all men to do so?"

It was no injury at all, he answered. The English settlers were merely doing for the natives what others had done for the English: "Had not this violence and this injury been offer'd unto us by the Romans, we might yet have lived overgrown Satyrs, rude and untutor'd, wand'ring in the woods, dwelling in caves, and hunting for our dinners as the wild beasts in the forests for their prey." Similarly, the Virginia Company argued that it was justifiable to occupy part of the local land, not only because there was plenty of unoccupied territory on the huge continent to go around, but also because "there is no other moderate and mix'd course to bring them to conversion but by daily conversation where they may see the life and learn the language of each other." In the end, the backers of the colony believed, the natives would be grateful: "Their children when they come to be saved, will blesse the day when first their fathers saw your faces."[12]

So it was that the members of the first Jamestown voyage boarded the *Susan Constant*, the *Godspeed*, and the *Discovery* on December 19 and 20 of 1606—most of them with pure hearts and empty heads, expecting to find riches, welcoming natives, and an easy life on the other shore.

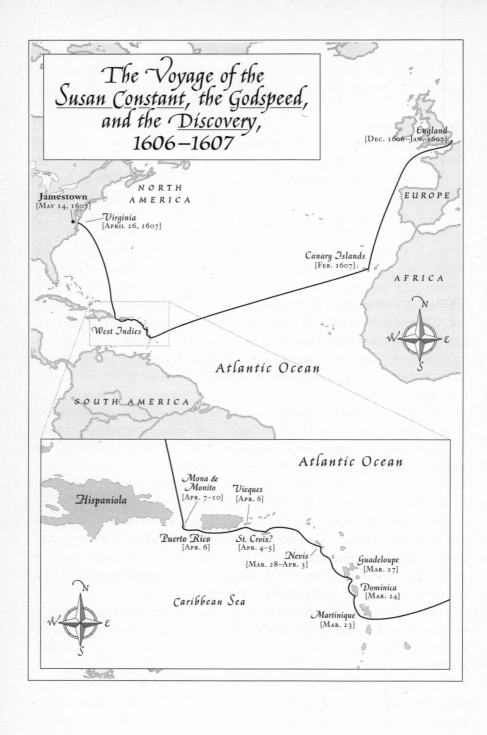

The Voyage of the
Susan Constant, the Godspeed,
and the Discovery,
1606–1607

England
[DEC. 1606–JAN. 1607]

EUROPE

NORTH
AMERICA

Jamestown
[MAY 14, 1607]

Virginia
[APRIL 26, 1607]

Canary Islands
[FEB. 1607]

AFRICA

West Indies

Atlantic Ocean

SOUTH AMERICA

Atlantic Ocean

Hispaniola

Mona &
Monito
[APR. 7–10]

Vieques
[APR. 6]

Puerto Rico
[APR. 6]

St. Croix?
[APR. 4–5]

Nevis
[MAR. 28–APR. 3]

Guadeloupe
[MAR. 27]

Dominica
[MAR. 24]

Caribbean Sea

Martinique
[MAR. 23]

2

THE CROSSING

⟨❧⟩

The departure of the expedition drew little attention at the time. The three ships left without fanfare from docks at Blackwall, located in what is now known as the London Docklands, just down-river on the Thames from central London. From there, they jour-neyed through the river's crowded shipping lanes toward the English Channel.

The flagship of the voyage, the 120-ton *Susan Constant*, was mod-est enough in size, around 116 feet in all. The others were smaller still: the *Godspeed* was roughly 68 feet long and had a capacity of 40 tons; the *Discovery*, about 50 feet and 20 tons. Yet even these figures make the ships sound larger than they were. The *Godspeed*, for instance, was 68 feet long *in theory*—if one measured from tip to tip. About a quarter of that length, though, was taken up by the spars overhanging her bow and stern, leaving an actual deck length of 52 feet or so. That figure, a more realistic measure of the ship's usable area for the voyagers, is equivalent in today's terms to the length of three parking spaces. The *Godspeed* was around 15 feet wide at its broadest point.[1]

How the men were able to cope with their cramped quarters over the four-month journey is difficult to conceive. The 105 or so colonists were joined by some 39 crewmen, with the result that 71 bodies some-how had to be jammed onto the flagship, 52 on the *Godspeed*, and 21 on the tiny *Discovery*. The ships had not even been built to carry passen-gers; they were cargo ships. Christopher Columbus, in his first cross-ing of the Atlantic, sailed with two-thirds the number of men in larger vessels. The *Endurance*, the vessel of Ernest Shackleton's ill-fated

Antarctic expedition, was 144 feet and carried 28 men. In a 1985 reenactment of the Jamestown voyage, on a modern replica of the *Godspeed*, those on board found the situation trying—and that time, there were only fourteen of them. "That, to me, is a really hard one to fathom— fifty-two people on that boat," said Neil Tanner, a crew member. "We talked about that a lot. With the fourteen of us, it was *crowded*."[2]

Apart from the cabins already in place for the crew, the ships undoubtedly had a few cabins jerry-built for some of the more elevated gentlemen of the mission. Foremost among these was Edward-Maria Wingfield, a charter investor in the Virginia Company. Wingfield was wellborn (his father was a godson of Queen Mary) and was accompanied on the voyage by at least two servants. He had been trained as a lawyer; he studied at Lincoln's Inn, one of London's four Inns of Court, before taking on military service in the Netherlands and then Ireland. Wingfield would soon become the Jamestown colony's first president but would slink back to England in disgrace less than a year after the landing. With good reason, the venerable *Dictionary of National Biography* would, in the late 1880s, deem him "self-confident, pompous, and puffed up by a sense of his own superior birth and position, unable to co-operate with common men and unfit to rule them." *The British Empire in America*, John Oldmixon's history published in London in 1708, would judge him "a covetous haughty person."

John Smith, like the rest of the passengers, would have slept on a straw mattress on the decks or in a hammock. His companions there were the less exalted gentlemen, as well as the various tradesmen and laborers who had signed on. Among the latter, some are known today only as lines in the passenger list: Henry Tavin, laborer; John Herd and William Garret, bricklayers; Nicholas Scott, drummer. Unlike the Roanoke expedition, this one had no women on board. There were four boys: Samuell Collier, Nathaniell Pecock, James Brumfield, and Richard Mutton.[3]

Well-to-do and poor, young and old, the passengers had one thing in common: they had legal ownership of their own bodies. The ships were not carrying any slaves; the slave trade would take another dozen years to reach Virginia, in the form of twenty or so Africans brought over on a Dutch man-of-war. In another sense, though, all of the passengers were in servitude, having bound themselves—in return for a one-way ocean passage and a share of the company's profits—to obey the company's appointed leaders and to work without wages. The length of that servitude is uncertain, but was probably around seven years.

The passengers may have had something else in common: a sense of disquiet regarding their crew. From the time they boarded, the colonists must have wondered whether they had made a serious mistake in trusting the sailors with their lives and welfare. On November 23, about a month before the departure, the *Susan Constant* had crashed into another ship while sitting at anchor. The *Susan Constant* suffered minor damage; the other ship, the *Philip and Francis*, came out worse and needed extensive repairs. When the case went to the High Court of Admiralty in mid-December, the sailors of the *Philip and Francis* maintained that the men of the *Susan Constant* had failed to adjust their anchor cables to keep the ship clear because they were "tiplinge and singinge." (John Harvey of the *Susan Constant* averred that "none of the company of the *Susan Constant* were drunck or had drunck hard to his knowledge when the said hurte hapned, for as he sayth there was no other beare but four shillinges beere on borde at that tyme.")

Along with the colonists and crew, the three ships held provisions, tools, and the parts for a smaller boat to be assembled in Virginia for inland exploration. The *Susan Constant* was armed with cannon for protection against pirates. The ships also carried another crucial article—namely, a sealed box containing the Virginia Company's instructions to the colonists and the names of the settlement's leaders. For safety's sake, there were three copies, one on board each ship, in case one of the ships was unlucky enough to run into trouble on the way across. The instructions were to be opened "within four and twenty hours" of arrival at Virginia, the company directed, "and not before."

Smith traveled on the *Susan Constant*, which was under the command of Christopher Newport. Newport, a battle-tested veteran of the Atlantic, had Smith's respect—at least for the time being. For fifteen years, off and on, Newport had been a privateer raiding Spanish freighters in the Caribbean. A group of London merchants financed his missions and shared in his spoils, all under the approving eye of the British government. Commanding a series of privateer ships—the *Little John*, the *Margaret*, and the *Golden Dragon*—Newport captured or destroyed some twenty Spanish vessels. Among his exploits was his leadership in the capture of the greatest English plunder of the

century, the *Madre de Dios*, off the Azores in August 1592. In bringing
the *Madre de Dios* to port in England with its treasure of more than
five hundred tons of spices, silks, gemstones, and other valuables, he
became England's preeminent mariner of the American seas. He continued to return to Caribbean waters; in 1605, knowing of King James's
fascination with exotic animals, he brought back two baby crocodiles
and a wild boar as gifts for the king.

The Virginia Company put great store in Newport's reputation.
Besides giving him the helm of the fleet's largest ship, the company put
him in overall command of the fleet "until such time as they shall fortune to land upon the coast of Virginia." Newport led the Jamestown
voyage single-handedly, having lost his right arm during one of his privateering attacks off the coast of Cuba.4

The *Godspeed* was under Bartholomew Gosnold. Educated at the
University of Cambridge and the Inns of Court, Gosnold had entered
privateering in his late twenties, making a successful career change from
law practice. In 1602, Gosnold explored present-day New England,
discovering Cape Cod and Martha's Vineyard in the process and naming Martha's Vineyard for his firstborn daughter, who had died at a
young age. Gosnold and his twenty men attempted to establish a trading post, but abandoned it after realizing they lacked enough food for
the winter—another chapter in the history of failed efforts to create an
English outpost in the New World. He would then spend the years
leading up to 1606 as an organizer of the Virginia Company, setting
the enterprise into motion.

At the time of the Virginia sailing, both Newport and Gosnold
were well into midlife by the standards of the day, with Newport
around forty-six and Gosnold roughly thirty-five. They were among
the few known family men of the voyage: Newport left behind his wife,
Elizabeth Glanfield, and four young children; waiting for Gosnold
were his wife, Mary Golding, and three young children.

John Ratcliffe, captain of the *Discovery*, is a comparatively shadowy
figure, who apparently had left few tracks in the sands of human events
before going to Virginia. He was a gentleman, born John Sicklemore,
later adopting the alias of Ratcliffe—a quirk that would lead to taunting from his antagonists in the colony. ("A poore counterfeited imposture," John Smith tagged him.)5

Of the three captains, only Newport would escape death in
Virginia.

At the opposite end of the pecking order from the captains, officially speaking, the lowest-ranking member of the crew was the swabber, whose duty was to keep the ship clean. Yet unofficially, on English ships of the period, there was one person whose rank was lower still: the liar. Each week, the unfortunate crewman first caught in a lie would loudly be proclaimed the liar by the rest of the crew. At that point, he would be placed under the command of the swabber and given the truly Herculean task of keeping the beakhead clean—the beakhead, a platform of open slats suspended at the bow, being the rudimentary sanitary facility that served the entire ship.

Like all mariners of the era, Newport, Gosnold, and Ratcliffe were, of course, completely dependent on the winds to get them where they wanted to go. If the weather refused to cooperate, they had no choice but to drop their wooden anchors and wait—which they were forced to do almost as soon as they cast off. Starting January 5, about two weeks out, storms and contrary winds kept them pinned in the Channel, just off an area known as "the Downs," on the coast of Kent. Never leaving sight of England, constantly hoping for a break in the weather, the voyagers were anchored there for a month.

Tempers were stoked by the frustration and the close quarters, and so a fateful feud began on the *Susan Constant* during that time of waiting. On one side was the commoner John Smith; on the other, the powerful Edward-Maria Wingfield. Wingfield and some others of high rank had grown impatient with waiting around in bad weather and were ready to head back to the nearby comforts of home; Smith, not one to defer to his betters, argued against them. The expedition's preacher, the Reverend Robert Hunt, successfully intervened on Smith's side, even though Hunt was miserably seasick himself. Characteristically, in his later account of the incident, Smith rated Hunt according to his toughness: "Master Hunt, our preacher, was so weak and sick that few expected his recovery. Yet, although he were but 20 miles from his habitation (the time we were in the Downs), and notwithstanding the stormy weather . . . all this could never force from him so much as a *seeming* desire to leave the business." The example of Hunt's fortitude won the day and kept the fleet from turning around.[6]

With the squabbling over for the moment, and with England finally receding into the distance by early February, the Atlantic journey could get under way. But in which direction? For the uninitiated, the answer would seem obvious: draw a straight line from the Channel to Virginia. On paper, that's the most expeditious route. The route that Newport actually plotted, though, was wildly circuitous. Instead of heading directly for Virginia, the ships would sail south to the Canary Islands off the coast of Africa (near today's Morocco), then southwest to the Caribbean, ending up below Virginia by well over a thousand miles. From there, they would work their way northward to their destination.

Newport, the former Caribbean pirate, knew what he was doing. The success of the voyage hinged on getting the right winds—and as mariners had long known, the aptly named trade winds of the North Atlantic provide a steady, reliable western current from the Canaries to the Caribbean, ideal for the purposes of voyagers sailing to the New World. (Columbus himself had pioneered the trade winds route in his 1492 expedition.) The winds of the Atlantic form an enormous and convenient circle, in effect, between Europe, North Africa, and the Americas: the trade winds, the bottom part of the circle, are complemented by the westerlies, which blow from the northeastern tip of North America back to Europe.

The Canaries route also had something else to recommend it: simplicity of navigation. In 1607, sailors had little means of figuring out where they were at sea. There was no accurate way for them to determine their longitude—that is, their east-west position. In theory, they could judge their latitude from the angle of the sun or a known star over the horizon; in practice, even latitude was hard to come by, because the instruments for measuring the positions of the sun and the stars were still rudimentary. A modern sailing dictionary facetiously defines longitude and latitude as "a series of imaginary lines on the Earth's surface drawn at intervals parallel to the Equator (latitude) or the poles (longitude) as an aid to navigation. Since they are invisible, many mariners find them of limited usefulness." That was all the more true in 1607.

Measures of time and speed were only a little better. On land, clocks of the era were accurate only to within fifteen minutes per day—and no instruments of the era could keep time at sea, with a ship's extremes of rolling motion, temperature, and humidity. Seafarers managed as well as they could using an hourglass and the overhead sun. To reckon their speed, and thus their distance, they threw overboard a "log line," which was a board attached to a rope. As the board receded, the navigator noted the length of rope that unreeled while a thirty-second sandglass emptied. The navigator took the length by counting the evenly spaced knots in the line as they passed (hence the term "knots" as the standard measure of nautical speed). If no sandglass was within reach, the navigator spoke some pattern of words that would reliably take around thirty seconds to say, or so he hoped.

Sailors did have a reasonably good measure of their direction, however. The *Susan Constant*, the *Godspeed*, and the *Discovery*, like other ships of the period, would each have had a compass near the helmsman's tiller. Each compass would have been placed in a square box held together with wooden pegs (because the magnetism from metal nails would throw off the results); inside the box was a circular card rotating on a pin, with a magnetic lodestone attached. Above the apparatus was a glass painted with points for north, northwest, and so on. On lengthy voyages such as this one, the navigator had to adjust periodically for the difference between true north and magnetic north. Still, that compass was virtually all the voyagers needed to follow the Canaries route to the New World. As the old-time mariner's dictum puts it: If you want to go from Europe to the New World, just head south until your butter melts, then turn right.7

Hence, the three ships followed the Canaries current southward for two weeks from Europe toward the Canary Islands. The bitter chill of the open air grew milder at first, and then it disappeared under the tropical sun. As the ships headed south, the men would have spent less time huddled below, and more time above decks regarding the horizon by day, the moon and stars by night, and imagining life in a new place. The men had come to the enterprise with a range of motives, and their hopes and fantasies would have run likewise. A few, like Smith, were after adventure; at the mature age of twenty-seven, Smith would have been delighted by the thought that the adventure of a lifetime was still ahead. For preacher Hunt, who was around ten years older, America meant founding a new church and saving the souls of innocent "savages." Others, less sanguine, were wayward sons who "dailie vexed their fathers hearts at home," one observer in London later wrote, "and were therefore thrust upon the voyage."

Most of the travelers, however, were on board because they—like the Virginia Company itself—expected quick treasure. Indeed, the 1606 "Ode to the Virginian Voyage," a dozen stanzas of celebratory

verse by the poet Michael Drayton, a friend of a Virginia Company
investor, marked the ships' departure with an approving recital of
those expectations:

> And cheerfully at sea
> Success you still entice
> To get the pearl and gold,
> And ours to hold
> Virginia,
> Earth's only paradise!
>
> Where nature hath in store
> Fowl, venison, and fish,
> And the fruitful'st soil
> Without your toil,
> Three harvests more,
> All greater than your wish.[8]

Those cheerful assumptions about life on the frontier were skew-
ered by 1605's *Eastward Ho*, in which a sea captain pulls the legs of two
gullible adventurers with tales of the awaiting riches. Thanks to the
natives' acquaintance with the Roanoke colonists, claims the captain,
the natives are so much "in love" with the English "that all the treasure
they have they lay at their feet." When one of the men asks just how
much treasure that is, the captain enlightens him:

> Gold is more plentiful there than copper is with
> us. . . . Why, man, all their dripping-pans and their
> chamber pots are pure gold; and all the chains with
> which they chain up their streets are massy gold; all the
> prisoners they take are fettered in gold; and, for rubies
> and diamonds, they go forth on holidays and gather
> 'em by the seashore.[9]

Such were the likely thoughts—only slightly exaggerated—of many
of the Virginia voyagers as they made their way toward the tropics.

When they reached the Canaries, the voyagers stopped briefly to
take on fresh water. Smith was in familiar territory there; while on his

way home from the Turkish wars, he had spent some time as a rider on a French buccaneer's vessel en route to Morocco, passing by the Canaries during his travels. Tempers again flared between Wingfield and Smith the day after the three ships left the islands. Tensions may well have been increased not only by Smith's lesser social origins, but also by his geographic roots. The people of his native Lincolnshire, isolated by stretches of impassable marshland, were held by the better classes of England to be backward and uncouth, verging on barbarous. Just what transpired between the men is now unknown, but Smith, with the impatience of one who had been there and felt he knew his way around, may have overstepped his social bounds by sharing his opinions with the worthies: Don't drop anchor on *this* side of the island, do it on the other side. Don't load the casks like *that*, load them like *this*. Pull up anchor by morning, or the Spanish will spot us. Do things *this* way. Do everything *my* way.

In any event, Smith in the end was accused of plotting an insurrection. By his account, he was charged "upon the scandalous suggestion of some of the chief, envying his repute, who feigned he intended to usurp the government, murder the council, and make himself king." The charges were trumped up. (The Reverend Samuel Purchas, a chronicler of the English voyages of the period, wrote that "Captain Smith was suspected for a supposed mutiny, though never no such matter.") Nonetheless, Wingfield prevailed upon Newport to have Smith placed under arrest on the *Susan Constant*, and so Smith remained in confinement for the duration of the history-making journey.

There, Smith no doubt set to work on notes of his observations (and grievances!) for his future writings. "Julius Caesar wrote his owne Commentaries," Smith later noted approvingly, "holding it no lesse honour to write, than fight." It was Smith's philosophy, as well, reflected in his eventual output of nine books covering Virginia, New England, and the ways of seamanship. While he would inevitably have seethed at his restraint, he would also have found it agreeable to his literary pursuits—like so many other jailhouse writers to come.[10]

The voyagers spent the next month sailing westward under the power of the Atlantic trade winds, the closest thing to sailing downhill. Harvard historian Samuel Eliot Morison, writing in 1954, offered a rhapsodic description of the experience of sailing this stretch of ocean, based on his own re-creation of the early Atlantic crossings:

Sailing before the trades in a square-rigger is as
near heaven as any seaman expects to be on the ocean.
You settle down to a pleasant ritual, undisturbed by
shifts of wind and changes of weather. There is the
constant play of light and color on the bellying square
sails (silver in moonlight, black in starlight, cloth-of-
gold at sunset, white as the clouds themselves at noon),
the gorgeous deep blue of the sea, flecked with white-
caps, the fascination of seeing new stars arise, the silver
flash when a school of flying fish springs from the bow
wave, the gold and green of leaping dolphins.[11]

The ships reached the West Indies on March 23, with the sighting
of the island of Martinique. The colonists, still some 1,500 miles from
their destination, sailed past Martinique and landed the next day on
Dominica to replenish their water and food. There, they began eighteen days of island-hopping, working their way northward by sail from
one small, lush landmass to another. Colonist George Percy recalled
Dominica as "a very fair island, the trees full of sweet and good
smells." It was also the site of the voyagers' first encounter with the
natives of the New World.

The English, true to form, were contemptuous of the culture of
the "savage Indians" of the island, known as the Caribs. The Caribs
wore jewelry through their noses, ears, and lips—"very strange to
behold," Percy thought—but were otherwise naked. The men of the
tribe spoke one language, the women another. Beyond these curiosi-
ties, the English had also gleaned an unsettling (and accurate) travelers' advisory from Spanish accounts: namely, that the Caribs sometimes
ate human flesh.

The Caribs, for their part, were suspicious of the English because
they resembled the Spanish, whom the Caribs had repeatedly battled
over the course of the preceding century. Dominica had been visited
by Christopher Columbus, and the Caribs had since repulsed every
Spanish attempt to settle there. Their favored tactic was to raise a contingent of hundreds of warriors assembled from the Carib-controlled
islands, bring them together in a fleet of dugout canoes, and then over-
whelm one of the Spanish settlements with a surprise attack from the
sea. The Caribs thereby preserved their freedom against the slavery
of the *encomienda* system, succeeding through force where the more

trusting Aztecs and Incas had failed. Yet the Caribs did not have entirely clean hands themselves: some time earlier, they had conquered and expelled the Arawaks, the original inhabitants, from Dominica and some of the other small Caribbean islands. Tradition had it that the Caribs had arrived by canoe from parts unknown before sending the less militaristic Arawaks on their way. (The surviving Arawaks resettled in Puerto Rico and other islands in the vicinity.)

The Caribs finally satisfied themselves that the visitors were not Spaniards—and, presumably, that they did not intend to stick around and settle. The Caribs then came to the three ships in canoes, ready to trade food in exchange for European knives and hatchets ("which they esteem much," Percy observed) as well as copper and beads. The colonists acquired various fruits and vegetables, and also a supply of French linen that the Caribs had liberated from a Spanish ship.[12]

After spending some hours on shore, the English reboarded and headed north again, passing the island of Marie Galante, landing briefly on Guadeloupe, then anchoring at the island of Nevis on March 28 in the early afternoon. Newport assembled all the men on shore, and from there they marched a mile inland, hacking their way through the dense vegetation with hatchets and swords. They carried muskets in anticipation of a surprise attack; they knew from Spanish writings that the other side of Nevis was Carib territory. They went unmolested, however, and eventually reached a valley with a comfortable spring, where the men bathed. The long-suffering travelers took a respite on the island for six days. "We . . . spent none of our ships victuall," remembered one, "by reason our men, some went a hunting, some a fouling, and some a fishing: where we got great store of conies [rabbits], sundry kinds of fowles, and great plentie of fish."

One hunting party spotted a few Caribs and beckoned them to come forward. The natives instead ran away through the woods. The hunting party tried to follow them at first, then lost them. The English finally became panicked by the thought that they were being lured into an ambush, and turned tail to run back toward their camp.

As on Dominica, the English never faced any attack from the Caribs of Nevis. Their antagonist on Nevis was neither man nor animal, but vegetation: the manchineel, a tree common to the region. It looks innocuous enough with its leafy branches and apple-like fruit. What the Spanish explorers knew, and the English evidently did not, is that it's best to keep one's distance: the touch of the manchineel's toxic sap is like acid, causing the victim's skin to burn severely and swell. The Caribs poison-tipped their arrows with it. The fruit of the tree is also toxic; the tree's scientific name, *Hippomane mancinella*, means "little apple that makes horses go mad."

Merely brushing against the tree is not harmful, but sap squirts out from the tree if someone chops into it—which is exactly what the Englishmen did while slicing their way through during the march inland. Some of the men, in John Smith's words, "became so tormented with a burning swelling all over their bodies they seemed like scalded men and near mad with pain." They found that bathing in the spring eased their distress, and they were back to normal after two or three unhappy days.

The animosity among the voyagers flared up again at Nevis; again, few details are recorded. Smith, still under arrest, was all too typically at the center of the hostilities. A gallows was actually built on Nevis for Smith's neck, but Smith, as he wryly recalled, "could not be persuaded to use" it. With Smith having faced down his adversaries, the mysterious matter ended; the mutual resentment didn't.[13]

The three ships sailed from Nevis on April 3 and anchored at one of the Virgin Islands. The men spent Easter Sunday there, once more living off the land with their catches of fish, tortoises, and wildfowl. After several days, they sailed again, passing the southern coasts of Vieques and the main island of Puerto Rico. On April 7, they called at Mona, an island lodged between the Spanish strongholds of Puerto Rico and Hispaniola (the latter is today home to Haiti and the Dominican Republic).

By now, the ship's water stank so badly that the men could no longer put up with it, so a group of sailors refilled the casks from the island's fresh water. Meanwhile, a party of soldiers and gentlemen went on a hunting expedition. The expedition seemed sporting at the start; the men killed two boars and some iguanas—"a loathsome beast like a crocodile," a group of colonists later wrote. (The West Indies iguana, *Iguana delicatissima*, is five or six feet long.) But like so much else, the hunt went badly wrong. Misjudging their own ability to hold up in the tropical heat, the men tackled an arduous six-mile march through the rocky and hilly terrain. They weren't carrying water. Many of the marchers fainted, and one of them, a gentleman named Edward Brookes, became the enterprise's first fatality, his "fat melted within him by the great heate and drought of the countrey." The others barely took notice; there was nothing they could do for him, and they had their own hides to worry about in any case. "We were not able to relieve him nor our selves," Percy recalled, "so he died in that great extreamitie."

The hunting party, minus one, eventually made it back to camp. The voyagers left Mona in the afternoon on April 9 for the adjacent island of Monito, followed by another tough climb up that island's hillside. When the men reached higher ground, they encountered a typically fertile Caribbean scene, but this one was already inhabited—by an enormous flock of wildfowl, their squawking so loud that the men couldn't hear one another speak. "Wee were not able to set foot on the ground," Percy reported, "but either on Fowles or Eggs which lay so thicke in the grasse." The men filled two large barrels full of the birds, which they caught from the bushes with their hands, and hauled them to the ships.

Monito was their last stop in the West Indies; the men spent the night and then set sail northward for the presumed utopia of the North American mainland. When ten days went by without sight of land—three days longer than the sailors had reckoned for their arrival—John Ratcliffe of the *Discovery* became agitated and pressed for the fleet to head back to England. He wasn't alone. It was four months since they had left Blackwall, and Ratcliffe and other gentlemen decided they had had enough. The idea of returning home was being seriously considered when fate stepped in: a powerful thunderstorm opened up, lasting through the night—and forcing the mariners to bring down their sails and wait while the colonists cowered below decks. The experience led the men to think twice about recrossing the Atlantic, and so they decided to give the search for land a little more time.

A few days later, on April 26, at around four in the morning, the travelers saw land in the distance. From their latitude of around 37 degrees, they assumed they had reached Virginia, and they were right. The ships entered the Chesapeake Bay and dropped anchor near a spot they called Cape Henry, after one of King James's sons. Newport chose a party of thirty to join him in going ashore, the party being weighted, of course, toward the socially exalted rather than the experienced; John Smith remained on board the *Susan Constant* and had his first sight of North America as an unfree man.

At the same moment in Christopher Columbus's first voyage, eyewitnesses would recount Columbus "kneeling on the ground, embracing it with tears of joy for the immeasurable mercy of having reached it." His officers and crew, meanwhile, hailed him "with as much joy and pleasure as if the victory had been all theirs." There was evidently no such exuberance when the landing party from the *Susan Constant*, the *Godspeed*, and the *Discovery* reached North American soil. Despite the successful conclusion of the four-month voyage, the surviving accounts don't indicate any rejoicing at all over landfall: exhaustion appears to have won out over celebration.

The men landed on a sandy shoreline and hiked to the crest of the sand dunes. From there, they took in the view of Virginia's woodlands and fresh water. They spent the rest of the day exploring the area, most likely in hopes of encountering a taste of the gold and silver they had just traveled thousands of miles to find. In that, they were disappointed. "Wee could find nothing worth the speaking of," Percy wrote, "but faire meddowes and goodly tall Trees."[14]

But there was more to the woods than the men realized; they had not been alone. That night, as the party headed back to the ship, a detachment of five native warriors followed them, unnoticed, toward the shore. With arrows clenched in their mouths, the native men crept down the sand dunes on their hands and feet, expertly keeping themselves invisible in the darkness.

When the natives closed in and began their charge, they probably did not seem to the English like terribly formidable attackers. Granted, they were physically more massive than the English, both taller and stockier. The flashes of war paint on their cheeks and foreheads might have been disconcerting at first. But the English knew that they alone had guns; the natives' arrows, with their heads crafted from sharpened bone or a splinter of stone, were rudimentary in comparison.

What the English did not yet realize is that those arrows, in the hands of an experienced native archer, were deadly accurate at forty yards. The native men could shoot down birds in flight. Not only were the arrows more accurate than English muskets, they could be fired more rapidly. During the short encounter on Cape Henry, Gabriel Archer, gentleman—like Gosnold, a Cambridge graduate—was shot through both hands. Mathew Morton, a sailor, was shot "in two places of the body very dangerous," as Percy later put it. Newport fired at the attackers, who withdrew after expending the last of their arrows. Archer and Morton survived their injuries.

Of the two detailed eyewitness accounts of the attack, only one shows any recognition that the natives with their bows and arrows might be a real match for the English guns. In the account of George Percy, one of the better sort, the skirmish ends "after they had spent their Arrowes, and felt the sharpnesse of our shot." But in another, more discerning version, Newport "made a shot at them, which the Indians little respected, but having spent their arrowes retyred without harme." That account was John Smith's, watching from shipboard, and the subtle difference in his interpretation of events here foreshadowed his coming disagreements with the others over the colony's life-or-death question: What stance to take toward the natives?[15]

3

HAVE GREAT CARE NOT TO OFFEND

⋞⋐⋠⋟

The Virginia Company had commanded that its mysterious sealed orders be opened within twenty-four hours after the expedition arrived on the Virginia coast. Once the men made their way back to the ships after their first foray onto the American mainland, the time had come for the captains of the ships to gather—probably on the flagship *Susan Constant*—and unfasten one of the three boxes containing duplicate copies of the directives.

Inside the box was a list of the seven men who would govern as members of the colony's ruling council. Most of the names were predictable: Edward-Maria Wingfield, the investor; Christopher Newport, who had commanded the *Susan Constant*; Bartholomew Gosnold, who had instigated the creation of the Virginia Company and who was in charge of the *Godspeed*; and John Ratcliffe of the *Discovery*. Also unsurprising were the names of two well-connected colonists: George Kendall was a protégé of secretary of state Sir Robert Cecil, the earl of Salisbury, a Virginia Company leader and major investor; John Martin was the son of Sir Richard Martin, master of the mint and Lord Mayor of London, and a brother-in-law of Sir Julius Caesar, master of the rolls.

The remaining name, however, must have caused some faces to darken, and some Anglo-Saxon expletives to reverberate against the walls, when the captains relayed the list to the other gentlemen of the journey. The name was that of John Smith, the riffraff who addressed these Cambridge and Inns of Court graduates as if he were their equal, if not their superior. He was still a prisoner on the ship for plotting insurrection in the West Indies. For the time being, that is where he would stay; the news of his appointment to the council was not enough to set him free—not yet.[1]

Next came the reading of the company's detailed instructions. Many of the instructions were sensible and well informed, and probably had the benefit of suggestions from participants in earlier English missions. Take your time in selecting a site, the instructions advised; "for if you make many Removes, besides the loss of time, you shall greatly spoil your victuals and your casks, and with great pain transport it in small boats." The site should not be too heavily wooded, the company said, since you do not have enough labor to clear a forest. One of the three ships, the diminutive *Discovery*, would remain with the colonists for use in exploring; when it is idle, keep it tied up close by, and bring its anchors and sails ashore, "least some ill disposed persons slip away with her."

The company urged the colonists to "have great care not to offend the naturals"—that is, the natives. It was eminently good advice for an outnumbered contingent in a distant land, and consistent with the hopeful attitude and kindly intentions that were prevalent at the time. Although you came over with food supplies, the instructions continued, you should still begin trading immediately with the natives for more food, "not being sure how your own seed corn will prosper the first year."

If you hire natives to serve as guides when you explore, be alert in case they try to leave you stranded. For added safety, bring a compass along "and write down how far they go upon every point of the compass; for that country having no way nor path, if that your guides run from you in the great woods or deserts, you shall hardly ever find a passage back." And to keep the natives intimidated by English firearms, never let novices shoot in their presence, "for if they see your learners miss what they aim at, they will think the weapon not so terrible, and thereby will be bould to assault you."

On the dubious premise that the colonists would conduct themselves inoffensively toward the natives and stay vigilant, the company assumed that the natives would not be a significant threat. A different danger was uppermost in the minds of the English: namely, their Old World foes, the Spanish. Do not be surprised, the company exhorted, "as the French were in Florida by Melindus," meaning Don Pedro Menéndez de Avilés, the Spanish commander who wiped out a nascent

French settlement of about three hundred at Fort Caroline, Florida, in 1565. To reduce the chance of a Spanish surprise attack, settle the colony far from the ocean, preferably a hundred miles or so upriver from the Chesapeake Bay. Place an outpost at the mouth of the river with a light boat for the lookouts, "that when any fleet shall be in sight, they may come with speed to give you warning." Finally, do not allow any of the natives to "inhabit between you and the sea coast," or else they may serve as guides to foreign invaders.

Once the colony's leaders chose a site and landed the voyagers there, the instructions continued, the colony was to start seeking a return for the investors right away: Newport should take forty of the men to explore upriver for a route to the "Other Sea" (as the Pacific was called) and to look for minerals. Then, with its final two instructions, the company struck an ominous note: One, that no man would be permitted to return to England except with the permission of the president and the council—but who would want to leave paradise? And two, the public at home was not to hear bad news; no one would be allowed "to write any letter of any thing that may discourage others."[2]

The next morning, the men built a small boat, called a shallop, from pieces that had been carried aboard one of the ships from England. The boat was, in essence, a kit. It had room for two dozen men. For Newport's exploring party, the shallop would be easier to maneuver than the *Discovery*. While the assembly of the shallop was progressing, another group hiked eight miles inland to get an idea of the territory. They did not see any "savages" in the course of their outing, but they stumbled across evidence that they were nearby: a fire with oysters roasting on it.

When preparing to eat, the natives had obviously heard the Englishmen coming and left in a hurry. The colonists looked at the oysters and said to themselves, Why thanks, don't mind if we do, and proceeded to take what they saw. A member of the party remembered the oysters as "very large and delicate in taste."

On the following several days, April 28 to April 30, the colonists explored the coast of the bay and erected a cross near the site of their landing. On the third day, as the men were approaching the opposite shore of the bay in the three ships, they saw five native men there carrying bows and arrows. Newport and a small party went ashore in the shallop. As a witness recalled it, Newport "called to them in signe of friendship, but they were at first very timorsome until they saw the captain lay his hand on his heart." Then the natives put down their weapons and made signs for the English to come to their town. Newport agreed, and the colonists' first visit to the natives was soon under way.

None of the colonists had come face-to-face with a Virginia native before, apart from the brief skirmish four days earlier. The five men they had encountered were from a tribe known as the Kecoughtans, numbering fewer than a hundred. Newport's group landed and followed the men to the town, which was also called Kecoughtan. There, they found the natives making "a dolefull noise, laying their faces to the ground, scratching the earth with their nailes." The English gathered that they had arrived in the middle of a religious ceremony. Once the ceremony ended, the natives went to their homes and retrieved mats to spread on the ground. The highest-ranking of the tribe seated themselves on the mats, while the lesser ones set out a welcoming repast of "such dainties as they had," together with corn bread. The drink of the day was water; the natives had not learned how to make wine and other alcoholic drinks, which the English would introduce to their diet later.

Some of the English, already in the habit of grabbing at the natives' food, apparently reached for a helping of the Kecoughtan meal before even sitting down. This the Kecoughtans refused to allow, insisting that the English could eat only upon sitting with them on the mats. They readily, and hungrily, complied.

The meal had one awkward aspect, which was that neither side could communicate with the other in its native tongue. The Kecoughtans did not yet have reason to know English, and no one in Newport's party appears to have had any knowledge of the Algonquian language of the region. Thomas Hariot, a member of the first Roanoke expedition, had compiled an Algonquian phrase book; if any copies of it came over with the Jamestown colonists, though, they were not on hand that day. Communication took place by "signs"—that is, with gesturing. If the Kecoughtans were unable to ask Newport's men about their long-term intentions, at least it saved the English the trouble of dissimulating.

The native men at the table were naked except for a leather covering, probably deerskin, over their privates. Their coverings were adorned with small dangling bones or animal teeth. Some men had painted their bodies black, and others red, decorated with bright colors—"very beautifull and pleasing to the eye," one colonist thought. Birds' legs hung from their ears. Their black hair was shaven (using shells) on the right, and grown long to three or four feet on the left; at the end of their hair was a knot with feathers.

Amid the eating and polite gesturing, the visitors would have noticed the natives' homes, which were made of reeds covered by tree bark for the walls and thatch for the rounded roofs. Mats, rather than doors, covered the entryways. Most of the homes were built under trees or groups of trees to shelter them from foul weather. The walls had no windows—logically enough, since bare openings would expose the interior to the elements, and the natives did not know how to make glass. Outside some of the homes were scaffolds hung with mats overhead to serve as covered porches. Newport's men perhaps noticed, too, that all of the houses were built alike; some were larger, some smaller, but the design did not vary—even for the chief's. "Who knoweth one of them knoweth them all," an English observer later wrote.

The English ate with the Kecoughtan leadership until their stomachs were "well satisfied." After the meal, the Kecoughtans continued the hospitality by presenting a dance. A group of native men formed a circle; one man in the center kept time by clapping. For a half hour, the visitors watched the men "shouting, howling, and stamping against the ground, with many antic tricks and faces, making noise like so many wolves or devils." With the stomping of their feet, the native men were in perfect unison—but with the movements of their hands, their torsoes, and their distorted faces, each man's dance was distinct. For the English, the performance was at once mesmerizing and thoroughly alien.[3]

The Kecoughtans viewed the performance as entertainment for honored guests. The English evidently saw it as further proof of the "savage" nature of the Virginia natives—primitive, un-Christian, childlike. After the dance concluded, Newport gave the dancers "beades and other trifling jewells." From accounts of the Roanoke expedition, the English knew that the natives were fascinated by European baubles.

The colonists spent roughly the next two weeks scouting up and down the river, the present-day James River, for a settlement site. Newport sought "the most apt and securest place, as well for his company to sit down in as which might give the least cause of offense or distaste" to the locals. Along the way, they called on several other tribes: the Paspahegh, the Rappahannock, and the Appomattoc. The

Paspahegh seemed to welcome them warmly, though one tribal elder "made a long oration, making a foule noise, uttering his speech with a vehement action." The English could not understand what he was saying, and shrugged it off.

At the Rappahannock village, the tribe's chief, or *weroance*, met them on shore himself, with others of the tribe behind him. He left a bemused impression. "The werowance comming before them playing on a flute made of a reed, with a crown of deares haire colloured red . . . with two long feathers in fashion of a pair of hornes placed in the midst of his crowne." He received the English with great pride and majesty, "as though he had beene a prince of civill government." His body was painted red, and his face blue—dotted, the colonists noted hopefully, with what they assumed was silver ore.

The Appomattoc proved less receptive to foreigners, meeting the English at the waterfront with a contingent of warriors bearing bows and arrows and swords. The commander stood with his arrow notched in his bow and spoke angrily; the English took him to be asking why they were there and telling them to go away. The English responded with gestures of peace, which the man eventually accepted, permitting them to land for a brief visit.

On May 12, the ships stopped at a point on the James that the colonists called Archer's Hope, presumably because Gabriel Archer had been the first to notice it. ("Hope" in this context meant "inlet.") The colonists still did not have a place to put down stakes, and Archer's Hope seemed ideal. It would be easy to defend against a Spanish incursion: unlike much of the frontage on the winding James, it afforded an unobstructed view of the river, and thus of any approaching ships, for miles downstream. The soil was rich. Rabbits, a staple of the English table back home, were abundant, as were turkeys and turkey eggs.

While some gentlemen of the expedition favored Archer's Hope, Edward-Maria Wingfield preferred a peninsula that the ships had passed about five miles up the James. That site had the advantage of deep water; any of the colonists' ships could pull up directly alongside to be moored to the trees and offloaded. It was unoccupied by any natives. It was connected to the Virginia mainland only by a narrow land bridge, which could be guarded to defend against Spanish or native attacks coming from that direction on foot. John Smith, who had no say in the matter, thought the peninsula was a good choice.

Newport sided with Wingfield, both because the peninsula was more secure and because he thought settling in that out-of-the-way venue would give the least offense to the natives. Hence, the ships left Archer's Hope the next day for Wingfield's site, which the colonists would name James Town. The men spent that night on the ships. On May 14, 1607, they landed and brought their provisions ashore.4

The company's instructions had mandated that the seven councilors elect a president immediately after Newport, Gosnold, and Ratcliffe opened the orders. For some reason, this had not happened. Perhaps Newport was in no hurry to give up his absolute authority over the expedition, which he had held up to that point as commander of the fleet. In any case, with the fleet's arrival at the settlement place, the colonists were no longer under nautical authority by any stretch. Now, after a delay of three and a half weeks, the councilors would swear their oaths of office and choose a president for a one-year term.

Wingfield, Newport, Gosnold, Ratcliffe, Kendall, and Martin pledged to "be a true and faithful servant unto the Kings majestie" and to "faithfully and truely declare my mind and opinion according to my heart and conscience in all things treated of in that counsel." The presidency went to Wingfield.

Keeping to their word, they then declared their opinions as to why John Smith should not be admitted to his place on the council. Smith recalled an "oration made" as to why he "was not admitted of the Councell as the rest." No one recorded what was said, but the likely flavor of it is captured by a later comment of Wingfield that "if he were in England, I would thinck scorne this man should be my companyon." In short, Smith would not get a seat on the council without divine intervention—and divine intervention was still almost a month away.5

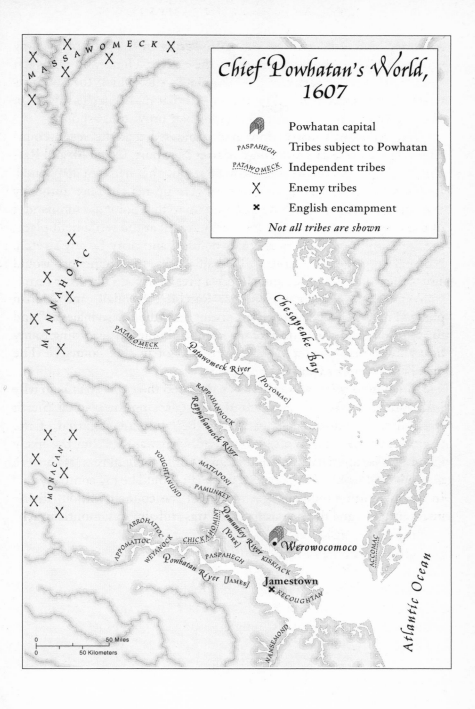

Chief Powhatan's World, 1607

Powhatan capital
PASPAHEGH — Tribes subject to Powhatan
PATAWOMECK — Independent tribes
X — Enemy tribes
✗ — English encampment

Not all tribes are shown

MASSAWOMECK

MANNAHOAC

PATAWOMECK

Patawomeck River [POTOMAC]

RAPPAHANNOCK

Rappahannock River

Chesapeake Bay

MONACAN

YOUGHTANUND

MATTAPONI

PAMUNKEY

Pamunkey River [YORK]

ARROHATTOC

APPOMATTOC

WEYANOCK

CHICKAHOMINY

PASPAHEGH

KISKIACK

Werowocomoco

ACCOMAC

Powhatan River [JAMES]

Jamestown
✗ KECOUGHTAN

NANSEMOND

Atlantic Ocean

0   50 Miles
0   50 Kilometers

4

WINGFIELD

❧

John Smith did not have his place on the council—but every available hand was needed to prepare the site, so the colony's leadership released him from his captivity on the *Susan Constant*. In an initial burst of enthusiasm, even those of the gentlemanly rank joined in the labors. Some men chopped down trees to clear an area for tents; others planted gardens. With the company's profit motive well in mind, still another group cut the fallen trees into clapboard, to be loaded onto the returning ships and sold in England. Natives made friendly visits. Two messengers from the Paspahegh brought news that their chief, whose name was Wowinchopunck, would soon call on the English and bring a deer for feasting.

President Wingfield's policy toward the natives began with a bold stroke. Encouraged by the cordiality of the visitors, and remembering the company's instruction "not to offend the naturals," he decreed that there would be no building of fortifications, or any exercises in the use of arms. The guns would remain in their shipping crates. Councilor George Kendall persuaded Wingfield to allow the building of one small wall or fence out of the limbs of trees. Otherwise, Wingfield had committed the colony to remaining intentionally defenseless.

On May 18, four days after the colonists landed, Wowinchopunck arrived—with an entourage of a hundred men who were armed with bows and arrows, and who were guarding him, as the English saw it, in a warlike fashion. Whether Wowinchopunck's intentions for the visit were peaceful or malign is impossible to say. Although the peninsula had been empty of people when the English came, the Paspahegh considered it part of their territory. Wowinchopunck may well have wanted harm to befall the newcomers; on the other hand, it could have really been just a social call.

Regardless, the colonists did not share their president's trusting attitude. Some of the English had firearms ready. Wowinchopunck motioned for the English to put their weapons down, which they refused to do. A scuffle erupted after one of the colonists saw a Paspahegh pick up an English hatchet, and the *weroance* "went suddenly away with all his company in great anger"—his villainous plans having been foiled, many of the English believed.

Two days later, a second visit from the Paspahegh followed the same pattern. This time, Wowinchopunck stayed home, instead sending forty men with another deer. The men sought to spend the night at Jamestown, a suspicious-sounding idea that the English rejected. Before the natives left, one of the gentlemen decided to have some fun at the Paspaheghs' expense: he set up a target that an arrow would obviously not be able to penetrate—since a pistol shot could not go through it—and motioned to one of the visitors to take aim.

The Paspahegh took a three-foot arrow from the quiver on his back, drew, and proceeded to send the arrow a foot through the target. The gentlemen onlookers, still unable to grasp that the native weapons might be superior to their firearms, found this "strange." Not wanting the natives to have the last laugh, they now set up a steel target. The archer shot again, and saw his arrowhead break apart. The Paspahegh left in anger once more.

Despite the signs that all might not be going smoothly between the English and their Paspahegh neighbors, Wingfield held to his policy of nondefense—a decision that an infuriated John Smith attributed to "the Presidents overweening jealousie" regarding his own authority.[1]

Newport, meanwhile, decided he was ready to make the exploratory trip that the company had ordered in its instructions. His orders were to take councilor Bartholomew Gosnold and forty other men up the river for up to two months; if they saw high lands or hills, Gosnold was to take twenty of the men there to look for minerals, while Newport and the rest continued exploring by boat. But the orders assumed that there were 120 colonists altogether; in fact, there were only around 105, perhaps because only that many could be recruited. Jamestown couldn't spare forty colonists, if the colony was to make any progress on the home front.

So Newport took twenty-three men and left Gosnold behind. With his years as a privateer, he kept his own counsel in picking a team for a risky journey. While the Virginia Company had been short-sighted in weighting its selection of colonists toward "the better sort," Newport was far more pragmatic. He brought only five colonists in all. John Smith was one of the five, along with the gentlemen Gabriel Archer (as chronicler), Thomas Wotton (as physician), George Percy, and John Brookes. Newport filled out the group with eighteen seamen from the *Susan Constant*, the *Godspeed*, and the *Discovery*.

They left on the shallop around noon on Thursday, May 21. They rowed and sailed about eighteen miles that first day, then dropped anchor for the night. The next morning, they encountered a half dozen or so natives in a canoe, and asked them where the river went. After Archer showed one of the men how to draw with pen and paper, the native sketched a map of the river. As Archer recounted, the man had good news: The English would "come to an overfall of water; beyond that, two kingdoms which the river runs by; then, a great distance off, the mountains Quirank, as he named them"—and then the Pacific. Newport's crew immediately headed off in that direction.[2]

On Saturday, the shallop reached the territory of Arrohattoc, *weroance* of the tribe of the same name. The canoeists who met the English two days earlier had been alternately following them and paddling ahead of them; they had alerted the Arrohattocs to Newport's imminent arrival. There, the colonists dined on venison, mulberries, corn, beans, and cakes, and gained a vital piece of information.

For the first time, they learned of the existence of a paramount chief, or chief of chiefs (the *mamanatowick*, in Algonquian). Every *weroance* they had met so far, it turned out, was subservient to a Chief Powhatan. Arrohattoc was merely the first to let this on. The English were not yet able to understand the significance of what they had been told—fortunately for their dinnertime digestion.

What the English did not realize was that they were facing a tightly run, martially adept empire. Only gradually, over some months, would they come to understand the reach of Chief Powhatan's power. The head of the Powhatan Empire had inherited six tribes from his father, and went on to conquer and subjugate at least twenty-two more. He was now in his sixties or seventies (his exact age was indeterminate), and he was still fit in mind and body.

Chief Powhatan, also known among his people as Wahunsenacah, collected steep tributes from the conquered tribes—fully 80 percent of all that they grew, caught, or made, from grain and fish to pelts and pearls. The tributes went directly to his storehouses and temples. His empire in 1607 covered all of present-day eastern Virginia, spreading from the south bank of the Potomac River down to an approximation of the modern Virginia–North Carolina line. Westward, the border corresponded more or less with today's Interstate 95, reaching the present sites of Richmond and Fredericksburg. The Algonquian name for his territory was Tsenacommacah.

There was no mystery to his success as a conqueror. Under Powhatan, males of the empire were trained from early childhood to be hunters and warriors. Boys began training with bows and arrows by the age of six; mothers did not give their young sons food in the morning until the boys succeeded at the morning's target practice. When Powhatan judged the time right for action, his men executed it with precision and without mercy.[3]

One such occasion had come about shortly before the English arrived at Jamestown. One of Powhatan's priests had delivered a Delphic prophecy: A nation would arise from the Chesapeake Bay and overcome his empire. After consulting with his council of advisers, Powhatan duly ordered the extermination of the Chesapeake tribe, which became extinct that day. The English, of course, had themselves come from the Chesapeake Bay; soon Powhatan and his advisers would have to decide whether it was the English who were the objects of the prophecy, and if so, what to do about them.

Although Newport's party knew nothing of this, they understood that it would be wise to attempt to meet with Powhatan and show their friendship. As they sat eating, the Arrohattocs told them that another chief was coming. The language barrier intervened: the English thought they had been told the visitor was Powhatan—an excellent stroke of luck. In fact, though, it was just Powhatan's son Parahunt, who, confusingly, was *weroance* of a town named Powhatan.

Believing that he was in the presence of the natives' maximum leader, Newport greeted Parahunt with "gifts of divers sorts, as penny knyves, shears, bells, glasse toyes, etc.," more than he had given any other native. Parahunt was no doubt delighted by this trove, especially the knives; the Powhatans had no means of making iron tools themselves. The English then departed on amicable terms with the chief of chiefs, or so they assumed.

The colonists made their way to the furthest navigable point on the James, the falls in present-day Richmond. It was as far as they would go. Along the way back downriver, they returned to the Arro-hattoc village on Sunday, and the *weroance* arranged for a man named Nauiraus, his brother-in-law, to serve as their guide. Over the next several days, Newport had the expedition dawdle with the Arrohattocs and other tribes in the vicinity and make another trip to the falls. ("We trifled in looking upon the rockes and river," Smith noted.) In their spare time—actually, they had nothing but spare time—the men learned a bit of Algonquian from Nauiraus.4

On Wednesday, May 27, the colonists were with the Arrohattocs' neighbors, the Weyanock tribe. Here, Smith evidently began to grow doubtful of Newport's judgment regarding the natives. Newport was grieved when Nauiraus, whom the men had come to like, abruptly changed his mind about joining the English on the trip back to James-town; Nauiraus took his leave of the English with a flourish of apologies. Smith thought it peculiar and worrisome. Moreover, while some of Smith's fellow travelers thought the Weyanocks "seemed our good friends," Smith detected animosity on their part.

Between their guide's change of heart and the "churlish condition" of the Weyanocks, Smith sensed trouble at home. "This gave us some occasion to doubt some mischiefe at the Fort," Smith complained, "yet Captaine Newport intended to have visited Paspahegh and Tappa-hanocke." (The "fort" was the grandiose name given to Kendall's fence.) Finally, a favorable change in the winds persuaded Newport to head to Jamestown directly.

They discovered, when they got back, that there had indeed been trouble. The day before, hundreds of native warriors had taken the colony by surprise. The colonists were unarmed, their guns still packed away—in accordance with Wingfield's policy. The attackers' arrows wounded somewhere between eleven and seventeen men, one of whom later died, and killed a boy who had sought refuge aboard the *Discovery*. The English pulled together a hasty defense and killed at least one native, whose comrades they saw carry him off on their backs for burial. Wingfield, to his credit, was at the forefront of the defense; he felt an arrow pass alarmingly, but harmlessly, through his beard.

With the overwhelming size of the natives' force, however, it seemed inevitable that the battle would eradicate Jamestown down to the last man. What finally rescued the colonists was cannon fire from the ships anchored nearby; the booming spectacle—enhanced when one of the cannon hit a large tree branch and brought it down— panicked the natives and prompted them to turn back. "Had it not chanced a crosse bar shot from the ships strooke downe a bough from a tree amongst them, that caused them to retire," Smith wrote, "our men had all beene slaine, being securely all at worke, and their armes in dry fats [crates]."

In the aftermath, the colonists realized that preparations for the attack had likely been under way for the past week. After Newport's shallop departed, native visitors had been coming every now and then to the fort, one or two at a time—"practicing upon opportunity," as Gabriel Archer put it—sizing up the colony's defenses and gauging the right time to strike.5

The colonists also understood something else: the ships' cannon would not be enough to protect them indefinitely. For one thing, Newport was to sail the two larger ships back to England the next month. For another, the efficacy of the cannon during the attack had come from their shock value, and there was no telling how much longer that would last.

"Hereupon the President was contented the Fort should be pallisa- doed, the Ordinance mounted, his men armed and exercized," Smith recounted wryly. By "pallisadoed," he meant that the fence of tree limbs was replaced with palisades—substantial walls made of upright logs. The new fort was in a triangular form, with turretlike semicircu- lar areas for artillery at the corners. If erecting fortifications sounds like an unworthy task for gentlemen, that is probably why, as Archer recorded, Newport's seamen did "the best part thereof."6

As work on the fort was under way, the colonists felt vulnerable in the extreme. The colonists had come prepared to meet a friendly foreign population that required only a civilizing influence, the colo- nists' own example, to become fully English themselves. As reality set in, they instead found themselves in a setting where a dull anxiety of further attack was constantly gnawing—and where a man setting foot outside the fort could only interpret the sound of a snapping twig or rustling grass as an omen of another deadly intrusion. Archer's diary reports the unpredictable, haphazard assaults that came and went, all of them minuscule next to the raid that tore out of the woods on May 26, but doubtless unnerving to those who had just lived through it:

May 28. Thursday we labored, pallozadoing our fort.

May 29. Friday the salvages gave on again, but with more feare, not daring approche scarce within musket shotte: they hurt not any of us, but finding one of our dogges they killed him: they shott above 40 arrowes into, & about the forte.

May 30. Satterday, we were quyet.

Sunday they came lurking in the thickets and long grasse; and a gentleman one Eustace Clovell unarmed straggling without the fort, [they] shott 6 arrowes into him, wherwith he came runinge into the fort, crying Arme Arme, thes stycking still: He lyved 8 dayes, and dyed. The salvages stayed not, but run away.

June 1. Monday some 20 appeared, shott dyvers arrowes at randome which fell short of our forte, and rann away.[7]

The English spent Tuesday and Wednesday in peace, continuing the fortification, cutting clapboard, and planting. Thursday brought an attack by three natives who managed to hide themselves in long grass near the fort; they spotted a colonist "going out to doe naturall necessity"—that is, responding to a call of nature—and shot him in the head.

The violence had vindicated Smith's criticisms in the worst way. It was therefore only natural that Wingfield and unknown others wanted John Smith on the ships with Newport when he left for England. But Smith avoided the return trip; Robert Hunt, the preacher, spoke up for Smith and for unity, as he had when the ships were languishing near the coast of England. Hunt had the respect of both sides; Wingfield had recruited him for the mission in the first place. Added to Hunt's "good doctrine and exhortation" was Newport's own support. The council met on Wednesday, June 10, and Newport "vehemently with ardent affection wonne our hartes by his fervent persuasion to uniformity of consent." Smith was permitted to take his oath of office and assume his seat on the council.[8]

That Sunday, following another incident in which a man was shot outside the fort, two native men came unarmed to the fort's entrance.

Newport and Wingfield met them there, and Newport saw that one of them was the canoeist-mapmaker who had helped his party during their explorations. The men had tried to visit a week earlier, yelling out *"Wingapoh!"*—Algonquian for *"friend"*—but had been driven away by the gunfire of a nervous gentleman who had been standing guard. Now the men laid out for Newport and Wingfield which of the tribes were their enemies and which were willing to help them make peace.

Their enemies, the men explained, were the Paspahegh (who claimed the territory in which the English had built), the Weyanock (whom Newport's party had been visiting on the last day of their journey), the Appomattoc, the Kiskiack, and the Quiyoughcohannock. Their friends—the Arrohattoc, the Pamunkey, the Mattaponi, and the Youghtanund—would try to intercede with them. It was an unsettling picture: the hostile tribes, by and large, were their neighbors; their professed friends were the tribes furthest away. The closer a *weroance* was to the English, the more likely he was to regard them as foes. To know the colonists was not necessarily to love them, contrary to their expectations.

On their way out, the messengers pointed out to Newport and Wingfield that the English would be safer if they cut down the long grass around the fort. No doubt the natives were puzzled that the colony's leadership had not already thought this through on its own, after a week of attacks in which the enemy always used the grass to achieve surprise. That Wingfield needed the suggestion in the first place was ample testimony that he was ill equipped to deal with the near-crisis situation.9

Three or four days before Newport left, he asked Wingfield how he felt settled in his presidency. Wingfield answered that the only two men who could possibly stand in the way were his fellow councilor Bartholomew Gosnold and Gosnold's friend Gabriel Archer. Wingfield was not concerned about Gosnold, who was an ally of his, but Archer was another matter. "For the one [Gosnold] was strong with friends and followers, and could if he would; and the other was troubled with an ambitious spirit, and would if he could."

The presidency had subjected Wingfield to great stresses as he found himself facing critics within the colony and enemies without. Confiding in Newport probably gave Wingfield a modest, but welcome, feeling of relief. It was natural for Wingfield to ventilate a little, and utterly harmless. After all, the only thing that could go wrong was that Newport might pass his comments along, and that was inconceivable.

So matters became awkward when Newport, with all good intentions, promptly relayed Wingfield's words to Gosnold and Archer, urging them to "be mindful of their duties to His Majestie and the colony." Thanks to Newport, Archer knew Wingfield was afraid of him, and Wingfield knew he knew.[10]

With that, Newport and his sailors bid adieu on June 22. He carried with him a report from the council to the Virginia Company, with the optimistic news that "within lesse then seaven weekes, wee are fortified well against the Indians, we have sowen good store of wheate, we have sent yow a taste of clapboord, wee have built some houses, wee have spared some hands to a discoverie [exploration], and still, as god shall enable us with strength, wee will better and better our proceedinges." The council also asked the company to compensate the colony for some tools that Newport's men had lost or broken. (No mention was made of their labors building the fort.)

Newport also brought letters from the colonists. These would have been censored by the council for any negativity, in accord with the company's directions, but it is unlikely that much cutting was needed; the colonists had every interest in painting a hopeful picture so that the Virginia Company would keep the colony funded and the supplies coming. William Brewster, a gentleman, told the earl of Salisbury—as noted, a leader in the Virginia Company council in London—that he estimated Virginia "the most statlye, rich kingdome in the woorld." With the earl's continued support of the venture, Brewster said, "you, yet maye lyve to see Ingland, moore riche, & renowned, then any kingdome, in all Ewroopa."

Gabriel Archer sent home his relation of events, together with descriptions of the local land and people. "The mayne river aboundes with sturgeon very large and excellent good: having also in the mouth of every brook and in every creek both store and exceeding good of divers kindes." The soil, he wrote, is "more fertill than can be wel exprest" and "altogether aromaticall." Not only does it yield corn, nuts, and berries, but also drugs for which the "salvages" claim wondrous properties; in the margin, he remarked on a "Virginia bloud wort which heales poysoned woundes."

Archer found much to like in the natives. Of the men, he wrote,

"They are proper lusty streight men very strong runn exceeding swiftly." He termed their skills in battle "admirable" (though this presumably was a virtue only when turned against other tribes). With apparent approval, he noted that the women accomplish all the labor at home while the men "hunt and goe at their pleasure." They wear their hair long, "save clipt somewhat short afore," and, like the men, they dye themselves decoratively. The men may have multiple wives, "to whome as near as I could perceive they keep constant."

Archer did disapprove of the natives' proclivity toward theft. "The people steale any thing comes neare them, yea are so practiced in this art that, lookeing in our face, they would with their foot betwene their toes convey a chizell, knife, percer or any indifferent light thing: which having once conveyed, they hold it an injury to take the same from them." Overall, though, he judged them ready to be civilized and introduced to the Christian faith, "apt both to understand and speake our language."

As the *Susan Constant* and the *Godspeed* pushed away from their moorings at Jamestown peninsula, Newport was leaving behind a colony with a completed fort, but not much else. The council observed in its report that the men of Jamestown had built some houses; while this was true, as far as it went, it was also true that most of the men had not gotten around to building themselves shelter and were still living in tents. Part of the problem was Wingfield's desire to show quick results by sending back clapboard right away, a distracting project that soaked up labor at a critical stage. Another obstacle was simple lack of motivation: springtime in the vicinity of Jamestown is deceptively mild, and so the men would have failed to anticipate the extremes of temperature that were coming their way.[11]

Still, the colony's prospects seemed to be good. Fish and game really were there for the taking. And there was heartening news: Chief Powhatan sent a messenger from his home at Werowocomoco, about twenty miles distant, informing the English that he desired friendly relations, and that they could "sow and reap in peace."

But then something odd happened. When Newport left, taking with him much of the colony's real labor force, rational men would have recognized it as a signal to step up their own efforts—building homes and gathering food, especially. Instead, it seems that the work all but stopped. No one knows why. George Percy, gentleman, complained that Newport's departure had left the colony "verie bare and scantie of victualls"; what was their excuse for not doing something about it?

True, half the colonists were not the sort to get their hands dirty, but even they must have understood that their bloodlines alone were not going to put food on the plate. If they thought someone else was doing the work, one look around would have dispelled that notion. The men apparently felt content to wait for Newport's return with fresh supplies and more free labor, even though it could easily take him six months or more to make the round trip.

Daily rations for each man were half a pint of barley boiled in water and half a pint of wheat, both teeming with worms. Their drink was water, the same as the natives'. "Had we been as free from all sinnes as gluttony, and drunkenness, we might have been canonized for saints," Smith recalled.[12]

Adding to their difficulties was the site they had chosen. Although the Virginia Company had urged them to not to settle in "a low or moist place," they had done exactly that. Having been won over to the Jamestown site by its security, its presumed inoffensiveness to the natives, and its convenience—the river's depth at that spot enabled them to moor large ships right alongside—they had overlooked the fact that large swathes of the peninsula were marshy. That, in turn, made the area especially humid during the spring and summer, and created an ideal breeding ground for mosquitoes.

Even the drinking water was a problem. No one had dug a well, or looked for springwater on the mainland, so they took water from the river—which had been fresh water in the springtime, but became increasingly brackish from the salt water of the bay as the summer went on. At low tide, it was "full of slime and filth," as George Percy recorded.

Up to then, death had come to Jamestown only sporadically—one man here, another man there. Now that was about to change as disease and malnutrition collected their victims. Percy's journal tells the story:

> The sixt of August there died John Asbie of the bloudie flixe [dysentery]. The ninth day died George Flowre of the swelling. The tenth day died William Bruster Gentleman [William Brewster, one of the optimistic letter writers], of a wound given by the savages, and was buried the eleventh day.

The fourteenth day, Jerome Alikock Ancient, died of a wound, the same day Francis Midwinter, Edward Morris Corporall died suddenly.

The fifteenth day, their died Edward Browne and Stephen Galthrope. The sixteenth day, their died Thomas Gower Gentleman. The seventeenth day, their died Thomas Mounslic. The eighteenth day, there died Robert Pennington, and John Martine Gentleman [the son of councilor John Martin]. The nineteenth day, died Drue Piggase Gentleman.[13]

The dismal chronicle continued for several more weeks. "Our men were destroyed with cruell diseases such as swellings [probably salt poisoning from the brackish water], flixes [dysentery, probably from amoebic parasites], burning fevers [probably from typhoid infection], and by warres, but for the most part they died of meere famine." Men groaned and cried out inside the walls of the fort until they were finally relieved by the blessing of death. The scant number who remained able-bodied—at times as few as five—took turns standing guard and dragging out the dead to be buried.

John Smith became ill and weak during this time, as did councilor John Ratcliffe, but both men recovered. Through all of the misery, however, one man never got sick: Edward-Maria Wingfield. Smith thought he knew the secret of Wingfield's miraculous health; shortly he would disclose it.

Bartholomew Gosnold, the first European explorer of Cape Cod and Martha's Vineyard, joined the ranks of the sick in early August. With Gosnold on his sickbed, Wingfield became truly worried for the first time about his political future. Gosnold was Wingfield's highest-ranking supporter; the Gosnold and Wingfield families were neighbors back home and had intermarried extensively. "In his [Gosnold's] sickness time, the president did easily foretell his own deposing from his command," Wingfield wrote of himself, "so much differed the president and the other councillors on managing the government of the colony."

Gosnold passed away on August 22. As he was buried, the able-bodied colonists shot off cannon in his honor.

As Wingfield feared, when the hourglass ran out on Gosnold's life, it ran out on his own presidency. Smith accused Wingfield of keeping private stores for himself and his friends, with provisions infinitely better than the infested gruel he was rationing out to the colony at large—including beef, eggs, oatmeal, liquor, and white wine. Smith and two other councilors, John Martin and John Ratcliffe, made a compact among themselves to depose the president. They agreed they would vote Ratcliffe into the presidency once the incumbent was out of the way.

Each of the three men had his own motives. Martin was in grief over his son's death and blamed Wingfield for it. Ratcliffe would get power. Smith did not particularly admire Ratcliffe, but had come to believe anyone would be better than Wingfield. On the other hand, while Smith thought Martin "verie honest" and "wishing the best good" for the colony, Smith felt he was ineffectual on account of his weak constitution—Martin was sick and feeble throughout his time in the New World.

Meanwhile, in late August, George Kendall was arrested for "heinous" conduct (the details of which are regrettably left to the modern imagination). Upon his arrest, he was stripped of his place on the council, apparently with the unanimous concurrence of the rest of the councilors. With Newport en route to England, Kendall in captivity, and Gosnold in the ground, the dissidents were now a controlling majority, with three votes against Wingfield's two votes as president.

By this time, nearly half of the colonists were dead. In their time of weakness, the colonists assumed the natives would come to finish them off, and so they waited, "each houre expecting the fury of the salvages." To the colonists' great surprise, however, the natives instead began bringing corn and other provisions from a recent harvest to trade—enough to get the survivors back on their feet.[14]

The move reflected another failure of leadership, this time on the part of Chief Powhatan. The chief of chiefs was no doubt getting reconnaissance reports about the long series of burials at Jamestown. Yet he evidently failed to realize just how weak the foreigners were by this point, and how easily he could have put an end to them. What he apparently focused on instead were the beads, hatchets, and other English goods that his tribesmen could obtain through bargaining, and which they did indeed obtain. It was a small price for the colonists to pay for their lives.

Wingfield had just barely avoided presiding over the extinction of the colony. On September 10, Martin, Ratcliffe, and Smith presented him with a signed order discharging him from the council and from his office. (The "instructions for government" of the colony, issued by King James in November of 1606, provided that "the major part" of the council could remove the president or a councilor "upon any just cause.") Wingfield, who was not surprised, haughtily told them "that they had eased him of a great deale of care, and trouble." He concluded, "I am at your pleasure, dispose of me as you will without further garboile [fuss, ballyhoo]." A sergeant then sent him to join Kendall in captivity on the *Discovery*, the small ship Newport had left behind.

The next day, Wingfield was brought to an assembly at which Ratcliffe, the new president, gave a speech to the colonists about why Wingfield had been overthrown. Smith and Martin also spoke, as did Archer, who had been named the colony's recorder, or secretary. The only account of the assembly is Wingfield's, and its uncertain reliability is suggested by this description of Martin's remarks:

> Master Martyn followed with, he reporteth that I doe slack the service in the collonye, and doe nothing but tend my pott, spitt, and oven, but he hath starved my sonne, and denyed him a spoonfull of beere; I have friends in England shalbe revenged on him, if ever he come in London.[15]

From Martin's point of view, of course, Wingfield had deprived his son of much more than "a spoonfull of beere."

In any event, Wingfield denied any wrongdoing. He later told the Virginia Company that he had kept nothing for himself but some salad dressing: "2 glasses with sallet oyle which I brought with me out of England for my private stoare." His nemesis, Archer, had instigated his overthrow, he said, and had given men bribes of "Indian cakes" to speak against him. But ultimately it was Wingfield who had brought himself down, having lost the colonists' confidence and then some. Near the end of the proceeding, Wingfield recalled, a gentleman named Richard Crofts spoke up and said he wanted to "pull me out of my seate, and out of my skynne too." An unnamed councilor urged Wingfield to take a bodyguard.

Wingfield's misfortunes were not quite over. King James, in his November order, had granted the council the power to hold trials in civil and criminal cases, the long arm of English law being otherwise absent from Virginia. With an action for slander, Smith took the opportunity to clear his name of the accusation of mutiny that Wingfield had leveled against him at the Canary Islands—for which Smith had spent thirteen weeks under restraint. Wingfield argued, on unknown grounds, that the suit was outside the council's jurisdiction. President Ratcliffe overruled the objection and convened a jury. The twelve jurors awarded Smith £200; to satisfy the award, Wingfield was obliged to hand over to Smith his private food stocks and other possessions, which Smith in turn donated to the colony's stores for general use.

Looking back on the summer of 1607, Smith later commented,

> At this time our diet was for most part water and bran, and three ounces of little better stuffe in bread for five men a meale, and thus we lived neere three months: our lodgings under boughs of trees, the salvages being our enemies, whom we neither knew nor understood; occasion I thinke sufficient to make men sicke and die.[16]

Notable was Smith's emphasis on the dearth of practical knowledge of the natives. Survival would not come from drawing the natives to the allegedly superior ways of the English; it would come from the English gleaning much more about the natives—their factions, their methods of warfare, their language, their culture.

Smith would presently have the chance to back up his criticisms with action. One of those who had died in August was Thomas Studley, the colony's cape merchant, or supply officer. President Ratcliffe appointed Smith his replacement. In addition, Ratcliffe put Smith in charge of the building of houses and, more crucially, in charge of relations with the natives. They had stopped coming with gifts, and there was enough food in the stores for only around two and a half weeks.[17] It would fall to Smith to make more of it somehow materialize.

5

THE RESCUE

⟨❧⟩

After waiting impatiently for two weeks, Don Pedro de Zúñiga, Spain's ambassador to London, had finally obtained an audience with King James on Sunday, October 7, 1607, at two o'clock in the afternoon. The subject on the ambassador's mind was the new settlement in Virginia, a region that the Spanish regarded as theirs and theirs alone—an extension of the Indies they had dominated (at least against other Europeans) since 1492.

Zúñiga had been getting updates on the colony from informants whose identities remain unknown. One of them seems to have been involved in the Virginia Company at home: "I have found a trustworthy person through whom I can learn everything that goes on in the [company] council" in London, Zúñiga wrote to his employer, King Philip III.[1] Another was probably former councilor George Kendall, who was executed in Jamestown in November for exactly that offense.[2] While the reports Zúñiga received were not always reliable, they were enough to alert him to the essential truth: namely, that the activities upriver from the Chesapeake Bay, in the region that the Spanish called Ajacán, threatened Spain's supremacy in the New World.

Zúñiga had repeatedly advised his king to move against the interlopers in Virginia before they became too established. "It is wise not to regard it lightly," he wrote, "because very soon they will have many people, and it will be more difficult to get them out." In another letter, two days before his meeting with King James, Zúñiga tried another tack to stir King Philip III to action, arguing (logically, but erroneously) that "it is thoroughly evident that it is not their desire to people [populate] the land, but rather to practice piracy, for they take no women—only men." But Philip preferred to pursue diplomatic means for the time being.

King James received Zúñiga courteously that Sunday afternoon. After Zúñiga had seated himself, he offered the king condolences on the death of his two-and-a-half-year-old daughter, Mary, just a few weeks earlier. The king expressed his appreciation. Then the ambassador got down to business. "I told him how much against good friendship and brotherliness it was for his vassals to dare to people Virginia, since it is a part of the Indies belonging to Castile." The Virginia Company's actions, Zúñiga continued, "could have inconvenient results"—a thinly veiled threat of retaliation.

As Zúñiga expected, James embraced a tactic of plausible deniability. James replied to the ambassador that he was unfamiliar with the details of the Virginia voyages, and that he had been unaware that Spain had a right to that territory. Virginia seemed to him quite distant from where the Spanish had settled. But those who went did so at their own risk. If they were captured and punished, so be it. The king's answer was not entirely disingenuous; apart from granting the company's charter, he had taken little interest in its affairs.

Zúñiga said it would be preferable if England kept them from going in the first place. "There can be no other object in that place other than it seems good for piracy," he added. James said that since Zúñiga had assured him Virginia belonged to Spain, and that piracy could be practiced there, he would look into the matter.

Zúñiga understood perfectly that James had put him off. In his report to Philip on the meeting, written the next day, he concluded with another endorsement of military action. "I think it would be a good idea if the few who are there should be finished outright, because that would cut the root, so that it would not sprout again." Several weeks later, Philip sent Zúñiga his reaction:

> I am quite satisfied with the offices which you performed with that King on the subject of Virginia, and you are to continue to keep an eye on it in order to provide what is proper. In the meantime, manage to find out what ships leave there [England] for there [Virginia], and report to me what you learn.[3]

Philip, in other words, did not view the Virginia Company as a priority. He was unpersuaded by Zúñiga's alarmist arguments and rejected his recommendation. With his brush-off of the Virginia issue, Philip made John Smith's situation infinitely simpler. The notion of war in Virginia would recur from time to time in the councils of Spanish government, but there would be no war. Although they did not know it, Smith and his fellow councilors had just been freed from the burden of defending against a Spanish enemy. From Smith's point of view, the only foreigners he would have to cope with in Jamestown would be the natives.

Christopher Newport had promised the colonists he would be back in twenty weeks—that is, in November—with more supplies. The colonists unwisely placed their hopes on his returning on schedule. They counted on Smith to induce the natives to feed them in the meantime. For reasons that remain enigmatic, most of Smith's fellow colonists were still not working; they were wallowing "in such despaire," Smith recalled, "as they would rather starve and rot with idlenes, then be perswaded to do anything for their owne reliefe without constraint."[4]

There is no clear-cut explanation for this persistent apathy, but some possibilities can be ventured. Apart from the lack of an ingrained work ethic in the majority of the colonists—this much seems clear—the communal nature of the stores made freeloading powerfully attractive. The motivation to freeload could be dealt with through strict discipline. It could also be dealt with through an individualistic, fend-for-yourself approach to provisioning. At this point, the colony had neither.

Additionally, Smith's phraseology suggests that many were simply resigned to dying in Virginia sooner or later, and had stopped caring about it—a state of mind that the twentieth-century psychiatrist Viktor Frankl called "emotional death." Frankl, a concentration camp survivor, observed that those prisoners who forestalled emotional death were the ones who felt a deep-seated purpose in their lives: a desire to see a loved one again, an ambition to carry out some scientific or creative accomplishment.[5] In literal terms, of course, the world of the colonists could not have been more different from that of concentration camp inmates, considering the natural abundance that Virginia offered the colonists for the taking. Yet it takes no great leap to envision certain of the colonists—having come to Virginia for no higher purpose than easy riches, cut off from the English social establishment that defined them, and possibly rejected by their own families—falling into apathy as the gritty reality of Jamestown life hit them.

Lacking enough willing and able hands to gather food, President Ratcliffe directed Smith to go to the town of the Kecoughtans, the first tribe the colonists had visited, and trade for corn. When Smith and his small party reached their settlement at the mouth of the James River, however, the Kecoughtans were dismissive. The English, for all their showy weaponry, had demonstrated that they could not feed themselves—a damning indictment, in the natives' eyes. "The Indians thinking us neare famished, with carelesse kindnes offred us little pieces of bread and small handfulls of beanes or wheat, for a hatchet or a piece of copper."

Smith understood that he would never get anywhere as long as the Kecoughtans (accurately) believed the English to be weak and desperate. "In like scorne" he offered them one-sided bargains. To bolster the image of economic strength that he sought to project, he liberally dispensed small gifts—beads and the like—to the children. Then he retired to his boat for the night.

The next day, the Kecoughtans' attitude had changed, now "no lesse desirous of our commodities than we of their corne." Smith and his men traded with them for fish, oysters, bread, and venison; the natives bartered so eagerly that he wished he had brought more men and a larger vessel. On the side, he sent one of his men, on the pretense of fetching water, to "discover" (explore) the town and its corn supply.

The English left with sixteen bushels of corn and a variety of other food. On the way back to Jamestown, they met with a group of natives in two canoes, who evidently saw the contents of Smith's shallop and assumed he was prosperous. The natives guided Smith to their town of Warraskoyack, about twenty miles up the James from the Kecoughtans; there, Smith's party bargained for another fourteen bushels, and returned triumphantly to the fort.[6]

As those victuals dwindled, Smith was off on further trading missions. He took note of the distinct personalities and approaches of the different tribes. At the town of the Rappahannock, some women and children ran from their houses when he arrived, possibly fearful of plunder or worse. Smith gave signs of peaceful intentions, and in the end they had a friendly parley. He visited the colonists' neighbors, the Paspahegh, "that churlish and trecherous nation." In the darkness, the Paspahegh tried using stealth to spirit away some English guns and swords, and were angry when Smith's men stopped them. He succeeded in trading for ten bushels of corn, but with the grim feeling that the Paspahegh were on the lookout for the chance to make an assault. "Seeing them dog us, from place to place, it being night, and our necessitie not fit for warres, we tooke occasion to returne."

On November 9, Smith departed on the shallop for a mission up the Chickahominy River, a tributary of the James. The colonists were aware that the most distant tribes were the most friendly to them, and the Chickahominy tribe fit the bill; in addition, the Chickahominies were one of the few tribes in the region to maintain their independence from Chief Powhatan's empire. The *Discovery* would follow later and rendezvous with the shallop at a place they called Point Weanock, twenty miles upriver. Under Smith's command were eight men on the shallop and seven on the *Discovery*.

The first day, they visited at a half dozen towns of the Chickahominies, showing them the copper and hatchets Smith was ready to barter for corn. Rather than amassing all the food he needed from one tribe, he bought smaller quantities here and there, then headed further up the river for more, "least they should perceive my too great want." Weakness in appearance, in Smith's mind, was weakness in reality.

With the shallop heavily laden, and the *Discovery* not to be seen at Point Weanock, Smith returned that night to the fort, where he found the ship run aground. The next morning, after unloading the shallop, Smith returned with it to the Chickahominy town of Mamanahunt. "So desirous of trade wer they, that they would follow me with their canowes, and for any thing give it to me"—that is, they were selling at any price. When the townspeople asked to see Smith shoot an English gun, he was happy to oblige with a touch of spectacle; he fired from the river, where the echo made it sound like cannon fire. He returned to the fort again to unload another boatful.

During Smith's years of European military service, acquiring the rudiments of alien tongues had proven to be an essential survival skill; it seems he could speak at least pidgin French, Dutch, and Italian, and probably one or more local Central European languages. Given that background, and given Smith's frequent involvement with the natives, it was inevitable that he would emerge as one of the colony's more effective speakers of Algonquian. That process was already under way, as Smith started to build up his vocabulary in the course of his trading. Among the phrases he left behind in his phrase book are *ka ka torawincs yowo*, meaning "What call you this?" He ascertained that *mockasin*s are shoes, *pokatawer* is fire, *attonce* are arrows, and *suckhanna* is water. *Wingapoh* or *netoppew* meant friends; *marrapough* meant enemies. The natives counted *necut*, *ningh*, *nuss* for one, two, three, onward to *necut-tweunquaough* for one thousand. Among the English goods that the natives wanted were *tomahack*s (axes), *pamesack*s (knives), *mattassin* (copper), and the forbidden *pawcussack*s (guns).

Smith also acquainted himself with the natives' daily lives. The men, he found, did no work other than hunting, fishing, and fighting wars, and were accomplished in each of those arts. Groups of men would hunt deer by seeking out a herd, then building fires in a circle around it; the deer, too fearful of the flames to run out of the circle, were then easy pickings. A man hunting alone might disguise himself as a deer using a deerskin with a stuffed head. "Thus shrowding his body in the skinne by stalking he approacheth the deare." The women and children did everything else, from planting and harvesting corn to making baskets and clay pots, "which is the cause that the women be verie painefull [always taking pains] and the men often idle." The women, Smith recorded, "love children verie dearly."[7]

November came and went, and Newport's resupply ships never turned up. Some of the men, including Wingfield, anxiously agitated for the reduced colony to return to England on the *Discovery*. Smith and Martin stood against the idea. Then the approach of winter brought geese, ducks, and other fowl to the rivers, easily hunted. This, together with the provisions from the natives, and the hunting of some deer and other wild game, was enough to quiet the malcontents for the moment, so that (in Smith's words) "none of our tuftaffaty humorists [fancy-dressed nervous Nellies] desired to go for England."[8]

Smith now came under a different sort of pressure, namely, to make progress on the search for a continental river passage. In previous excursions, the colonists had found the James impassable beyond the falls. Smith's fellow councilors thought that perhaps the route to the Pacific would be found through the Chickahominy River. Smith began hearing "idle exceptions" against his failure to finish exploring the Chickahominy, with an imputation of cowardice. One can only speculate how concerned these voices really were about carrying out the company's instructions, and how much they simply hoped that

Smith would have a fatal encounter with the natives and not come back—thus opening the way for them to return to the old country.9 In any event, his critics had found his sensitive spot; in early December, he left again on the shallop, this time taking nine men.

Thus began the most famous and controversial journey of Smith's career. In more recent times, some have charged that Smith fabricated key parts of it for the sake of romanticism. Smith himself looked on the episode as "a tragedie,"10 not a romance—and with good reason, as will be seen. To grapple with the controversy over Smith's account entails a digression into historiography and ethnology, which is taken up in the Marginalia at the back of this book. For the present, suffice it to say that the evidence points compellingly toward the truthfulness of his description of the events.

Smith's party rowed and sailed the shallop some fifty miles up the Chickahominy. Along the way, he noted plentiful wildfowl and fish, planted fields larger than any he had seen in Virginia, and people in abundance. At around the forty-mile mark, the party passed by Apokant, the last town on the river; beyond was total wilderness. Ten miles or so later, the shallop reached a large tree that was blocking the way, perhaps having been downed in a storm. Smith reckoned hopefully that they were not far from the head of the river, and so the men cut the tree in two to make way.

The river became narrower, shallower (only six or seven feet at low tide), and faster. Smith grew concerned about the danger to the boat, but heading back to Jamestown was out of the question: the "malicious tungs" waiting for him there would seize on any perceived failure to try to discredit him. Smith decided to return to Apokant to see if he could hire native guides and a canoe.11

At the town, on the pretext of wanting to hunt for birds, Smith recruited two men to take them upriver by canoe. The next morning, he set off in the canoe with the two guides. Also accompanying him were carpenter Thomas Emry and a gentleman who is referred to in various accounts as either John or Jehu Robinson. The rest of his party stayed at Apokant on the shallop. Unsure how far he could trust the Chickahominies there, Smith gave an order to the men who were staying behind: namely, to remain on board the shallop at all times until he came back.

The five men on the canoe headed out. They paddled about two miles further than the shallop had gone, and then pulled ashore to rest and eat. Meanwhile, back at the town, the seven Englishmen on the shallop had disregarded Smith's instructions and clambered onto land, having spotted some native women whom they fancied—and who seemed to be returning their admiration. After living for almost a year in isolated, female-free enclaves, the men were primed to make a close study of the subject.

The testosterone-powered move proved to be a miscalculation. The natives, it turned out, were as distrustful of Smith as he was of them, and apparently were not fooled by his cover story: to travel fifty miles for bird hunting did not make sense, even for the English. Determined to find out the real story, the natives had stationed the women near the shore to serve as bait. A contingent of Chickahominy warriors surprised the colonists, who ran back to the boat and shoved off in a hurry. All of them made it except one.

The straggler was George Cassen, a laborer. After seizing Cassen, the natives stripped him of his clothes and tied him to a pair of stakes. The full purpose of what was about to happen to him is unclear. By one account, the natives were using Cassen to placate their god, whom the English took to be "the devill"; by another, the natives were punishing Cassen as an enemy trespasser. Of course, the two possibilities are not mutually exclusive.

Fate had written a most unhappy ending to Cassen's life story. The natives prepared a large fire behind his bound and naked body. Then a man grasped his hands and used mussel shells to cut off joint after joint, making his way through Cassen's fingers, tossing the pieces into the flames. That accomplished, the man used shells and reeds to detach the skin from Cassen's face and the rest of his head. Cassen's belly was next, as the man sliced it open, pulled out his bowels, and cast those onto the fire. Finally the natives burned Cassen at the stake through to his bones.[12]

Smith, Emry, and Robinson, unaware of the events downstream, were cooking their food on a bank of the Chickahominy. As Smith recalled it, he decided to use the break to explore inland a little and to bag some birds for the meal. He took one of the guides with him. Before departing, he told Emry and Robinson to keep their guns at the ready; at the first sign of any intruders, they were to fire a shot to signal for Smith to rush back.

No more than a quarter of an hour after Smith left, he heard "a loud cry, and a hallowing [hollering] of indians" from the direction of his cohorts—but no distress signal.[13] He deduced that the guide with Emry and Robinson had betrayed them. He put a gun to his own guide and felt ready to take revenge, until he noticed that the man "seemed ignorant of what was done."

The man urged Smith to run. Seemingly out of nowhere, an arrow hit Smith on the right thigh; it did not penetrate far enough to do real harm. He turned and saw two natives drawing their bows. He fired a shot and missed, but it was enough to make the attackers hit the ground and then scurry away. As he reloaded, a time-consuming procedure, three or four new attackers appeared, and sent more arrows harmlessly into his heavy winter clothes. These men, too, ran when fired upon.

Smith brought his guide in front of him as a shield. Momentarily, he discovered that he was now surrounded by what looked like an army of hundreds. The guide, naturally anxious to save his skin, called out that the Englishman was a leader—and thus, according to local custom, was to be taken alive rather than killed, if possible. The man then pled with Smith not to shoot. While waving his pistol at the attackers and staying behind his unhappy bodyguard, Smith demanded to be allowed to return to the canoe. As Smith and the guide moved in that direction, the leader of the attacking force shouted back that he must lay down his weapon. The other men were dead, he continued; "only me they would reserve [spare]."

As he continued to work his way toward the river, Smith was watching his adversaries, not his own path. He stepped backward into a marshy "quagmire" and tumbled in; his guide fell in the ooze with him. Both men struggled, and failed, to free themselves and get back on their feet.

Finding himself out of luck, Smith threw his pistol aside in surrender and "resolved to trie their mercies." Several of the warriors pulled him out and presented him to the leader of the attack: a Powhatan chief named Opechancanough, one of three younger brothers of Powhatan himself. Estimated to be around sixty years old at this time, Opechancanough is remembered as "a man of large stature, noble presence, and extraordinary parts."[14] He was third in line of succession to Chief Powhatan; in the meantime, the chief of chiefs had installed him as *weroance* of the Pamunkeys. Now it was up to him to decide what to do with this captive who had confronted an army without flinching.

Smith knew that natives shared his own countrymen's awe of rank and status. If he wanted to live, he would have to convince the chief that he was indeed a person of importance. The question was how. Thinking fast, he produced his compass dial. He had observed that the natives (and not only the natives) tended to regard anything they could not understand as supernatural.[15] So he invited Opechancanough to have a look at the moving needles, which the chief could see, but could not touch through the glass. As Smith turned the compass, the needles kept pointing in the same direction. Opechancanough was intrigued.

To build on the imposing impression he had created, or possibly just as a stalling tactic, Smith then followed with a disquisition on

> the roundnesse of the Earth, and skies, the spheare of the sunne, moone, and starres, and how the sunne did chase the night round the world continually; the greatnesse of the land and sea, the diversitie of nations, varietie of complexions, and how we were to them antipodes [on opposite sides of the Earth], and many other such like matters.[16]

How much, if at all, Smith was able to communicate these grand sentiments within the limits of his workaday Algonquian language skills is unknown. The chief listened with apparent interest. Nonetheless, Smith soon found himself tied to a tree, and surrounded by warriors prepared to shoot in case he managed to work himself free. He was headed, it seemed, for the same fate as Cassen. Then Opechancanough abruptly ordered the warriors to put down their weapons, and raised the compass over Smith's head. Smith was untied, and escorted by the chief to a hunting camp some miles away. "Great [large] salvages" held him by each arm, and another dozen men accompanied them, arrows nocked in their bows.

The on-again, off-again execution makes Opechancanough's thought processes sound illogical, if not utterly random. Looking at the circumstances from his point of view, however, one can surmise what was going through his mind. Doubtless he was initially inclined to torture Smith for information on the puzzling English presence before killing him. If Smith truly was an English leader, there was much he could usefully reveal: Where had the other ships gone? Would they be coming back? Why did the English live without women? How long did the men intend to stay? And above all, why were they there in the first place?

In light of events of later years, it is obvious that Opechancanough was far more skeptical of English intentions, and more eager to be rid of these foreigners, than was his older brother. He held a more coldly realistic view of the long-term threat from the English—much as Don Pedro de Zúñiga saw the future of English America more clearly than King Philip III. The right intelligence extracted from this short, bearded man would help Opechancanough make his case.

But even as the prisoner was fastened to the stake, Opechancanough began to have doubts. He was not the chief of chiefs yet. An ordinary captive like Cassen could be tortured and dispatched on the spot; if Smith was an English commander of some kind, that was a different matter. What was he? The round device crafted of ivory was impressive. His long speech made sense only here and there—but he delivered it like a commander. If Opechancanough had him killed, and Powhatan found the results inconvenient, the personal consequences to Opechancanough could be very unpleasant. Like many a corporate vice president in later years, Opechancanough finally deemed it prudent to bring the question to the man in charge.

Once Smith, Opechancanough, and the Pamunkey soldiers reached the tentlike hunting lodges, the soldiers gathered into a ring and performed a dance similar to the one that the Kecoughtans had performed for the English that spring, "dauncing in such severall postures, and singing and yelling such hellish notes and screeches." The men were painted scarlet on their heads and shoulders ("exceeding handsome," Smith thought), with fox or otter skin on their arms, and birds' wings tied to their hair.

Afterward, a captain brought Smith to a lodge where he was given a supper of venison and bread, and then Smith was shown to the lodge where he would stay for the next several days. In the mornings, three women carried additional platters of bread and venison to him— enough for ten men, Smith recalled. He was pleased at being treated so kindly; at the same time, he half suspected he was being fattened up to be eaten. (The English already understood that their neighbors, the Paspahegh, were "no canyballs,"[17] but the Pamunkeys' dietary preferences in that regard were still an open question. In fact, none of the Virginia tribes were cannibals.)

Opechancanough visited Smith to converse about "the manner of our ships, and sayling the seas, the earth and skies and of our God." The chief likely paid particular attention to any scraps of information about Newport's fleet, whose intimidating cannon had proven to be the colonists' best security. From these conversations, Smith came to believe that Opechancanough was plotting an attack; to forestall it, Smith fed him misinformation about Jamestown's defenses, telling of nonexistent cannon and explosive mines in the fields around the fort. For his part, Opechancanough gave Smith tantalizing news of a place called Ocanahonan, a distant settlement of men who wore English clothing—a possible clue to the destiny of Walter Ralegh's lost colony at Roanoke.

At some point, Smith asked Opechancanough for a messenger to carry a letter to the colony. Smith claimed he merely wanted to assure the English "that I was well, least they should revenge my death." The chief consented to this, and so Smith composed a letter in his note-book telling the colonists of his suspicion of an imminent attack. He instructed the colonists to give the messenger a frightening display of cannon fire, and to send back some items he had promised the Pamunkeys. He also passed along word of Ocanahonan, though the investigation of the lost colony was a low priority by then; Jamestown was all too close to becoming a lost colony itself.

Three messengers went out in the bitter cold with Smith's letter. The colonists did as Smith had told them, scaring the messengers out of their wits with the cannons, then loading the men with the items Smith requested. On their return, the natives were disturbed and fascinated— disturbed by the news of the cannon, and fascinated that the colonists had sent back exactly what Smith said they would. The natives had no written language. Somehow, they concluded, the English could make paper speak.

Next came Smith's turn to face the cold. For a week, the Pamunkeys marched him through the countryside to one village after another. The chiefs at each village received him cordially. At one stop, the vil-lagers wanted to see whether he was the same man as a foreigner who had come previously, murdering their chief and taking away some locals. But the wanted man was tall, and Smith did not fit the descrip-tion, so they treated him well.

At a village called Menapacute, another brother of Powhatan, named Kekataugh, invited Smith to feast at his house. Kekataugh was not long in revealing his agenda, as he asked Smith to shoot his pistol at a target. Forty bowmen looked on to guard against Smith's escaping. It seemed like an innocuous request, on its face, until Smith noticed the target's distance. He judged it to be 120 feet or so away, roughly the accurate range of the natives' bows and arrows. That was the game: Kekataugh wanted to know whether the Englishmen's guns could shoot as far and as well as their own weapons. Smith knew that the answer was negative; the target was too far away for him to hit reliably. He covertly broke the cock of his expensive French-built firearm, and reported in regretful tones that it wasn't working.[18] The limitations of the colonists' guns, as he saw it, had to be kept from the natives at all costs.

By now, Smith had spent Christmas 1607 in captivity. Finally he was brought to the capital of the Pamunkeys, where he would be the subject of a conjuring ceremony. Early in the morning, his guards left him seated in a longhouse with a fire burning in the middle of the floor. "Presently came skipping in a great grim fellow, all painted over with coale, mingled with oyle; and many snakes and weasels stuffed with mosse, and all their tayles tyed together, so as they met on the crown of his head in a tassell."[19] The man began an invocation, and six more like him came in.

Smith understood the first man to be the chief priest. The seven natives painstakingly laid down kernels of corn in two concentric circles around the fire, and an inner circle of ground cornmeal. Between every few grains of corn, they put small sticks. The circle of meal, they explained to Smith, represented their country, the circles of corn represented the sea, and the sticks represented his country. Over the following three days, the priests alternated between conjuring with song and dance and feasting with the prisoner. From the ceremony, they explained, they would learn whether he and his countrymen meant the Powhatans good or ill.[20]

At the end of the three days, the priests kept their conclusions to themselves. From Smith's point of view, though, the signs must have seemed hopeful: he was taken to feast at the home of Opitchapam, the oldest of Powhatan's three brothers, and the first in line of succession. His most august host of all would be next.

No Englishman had yet laid eyes on Chief Powhatan, or even

knew his whereabouts. On December 30, Smith was brought to the emperor's capital town, Werowocomoco. It was on the north side of the present-day York River, downstream from the Pamunkey territory where Smith had been held. Smith waited outside Powhatan's reed-and-thatch assembly lodge, where some two hundred courtiers looked on him as if he were a monster.[21]

As Smith was led in, and his eyes adjusted to the gloom of the windowless interior, he saw a figure seated on a low bed of ten or twelve mats in front of a fire. He was wearing a raccoon-skin robe, the tails still attached. Chains of pearl hung from his neck. Young women sat on either side of him. Ten men lined the walls to the left and right of the fire, and behind them ten more young women. All of them gave a thunderous shout in unison as Smith walked forward.

The emperor, Smith saw, was old and gray-haired, perhaps sixty, perhaps eighty, but with the physique of a younger man—tall, fit, broad-shouldered, and well proportioned. On his chin were a few strands of a thinning beard. Those attending the emperor held him in fearful awe; "at the least frown of his brow, their greatest will tremble." His face, on this occasion, showed "a grave and majesticall countenance."[22]

Also watching the events was a girl, between ten and twelve years of age, a daughter of the emperor by one of the hundred or so wives he had taken over the decades. She was pretty, and no doubt had fully earned the nickname Pocahontas—"little wanton"—with her feisty, mischievous nature. (She was more formally known as Matoaka or Amonute.) Smith later remembered her as "a child of tenne yeares old, which not only for feature, countenance, and proportion much exceedeth any of the rest of his [Powhatan's] people, but for wit and spirit the only nonpareil of his country." As her father's favorite (his "delight and darling," another colonist would observe), she was probably accustomed to bending the chief of chiefs to her whims.[23]

A high-ranking woman named Opossunoquonuske, the "fat, lusty, manly" sister of the *weroance* of the Appomattoc, now came forward with water, and motioned for Smith to wash his hands in it.[24] Another brought him feathers with which to dry his hands. Then attendants brought Smith a meal, potentially his last.

Although Smith had been examined closely by Opechancanough and by the priests, Powhatan evidently intended to arrive at his own judgment regarding the prisoner and his fate. He inquired of Smith why the English had come. Smith realized it would be imprudent just then to explain their plans for a permanent settlement, so he concocted a story about their ships having been in a fight on the high seas with their enemies, the Spanish. The Spanish had overpowered them, Smith explained, so they had to beat a retreat, and then extreme weather sent them to the Chesapeake Bay. Now they had to stay to repair one of the ships, which was leaking, while they waited for Smith's great father, Captain Newport, to return and spirit them away.

Under those circumstances, the emperor thought it peculiar that Smith and his party had been found so very far from their camp. What was Smith looking for with the boat, he asked?

Smith told him he was looking for a sea on the other side of the country (which was true). The reason, he explained, was that the people there had slain one of Newport's men (another concoction). The English were a vengeful people, and they intended to exact justice for the man's death. Powhatan surely got the message: if Smith failed to come back, a boatload of Englishmen with muskets would be looking for Powhatan next.

Powhatan consulted with his advisers. Nearby, awaiting Powhatan's decision, were men with clubs in their hands. If the emperor so resolved, the clubs would be used to smash the prisoner's brains—a charitably swift form of execution that the natives employed. Alternatively, if the emperor believed Smith to be a *weroance*, it would be against custom to put him to death; chiefs of enemy tribes, like women and children, were kept in servitude, not killed.

Yet the decision confronting Powhatan was one of strategy and practicality as much as custom. Could Smith, and perhaps all of the English, be won over as allies against Powhatan's hostile neighbors over the horizon? The colonists' novel firearms and cannon could give him a decisive edge against his native adversaries, with whom the Powhatans uneasily coexisted—the Massawomecks, an Iroquois tribe to the north, and the Monacans and the Mannahoacs, Siouan tribes to the west.[25] On the other hand, were the English not the people who had been prophesied to emerge from the Chesapeake and bury his empire? The unknowns that Powhatan had before him were momentous.

After long deliberation, Powhatan made his choice. A pair of large stones were set in front of him, and Smith was brought forward to accept the inevitable.

What happened in the moments that followed is, in all probability, the most often told tale in American history, inspiring drama, novels, paintings, statuary, and films. The first chief justice of the United States, John Marshall, writing in 1804, narrated it as well as anyone:

> There he was doomed to be put to death, by laying his head upon a stone, and beating out his brains with clubs. He was led to the place of execution, and his head bowed down for the purpose of death, when Pocahontas, the king's darling daughter, then about thirteen years of age, whose entreaties for his life had been ineffectual, rushed between him and his executioner, and folding his head in her arms, and laying hers upon it, arrested the fatal blow. Her father was then prevailed on to spare his life.[26]

Pocahontas's sudden intervention put Powhatan in an awkward spot. He was careful, always, to maintain imperial dignity. To remonstrate with his daughter in front of everyone in the packed hall would undermine his stateliness. He could order his attendants to carry her off—another undignified spectacle. Powhatan instead allowed himself to be won over by his daughter's plea, and declared that he was content for Smith to live. The prisoner will make hatchets for him, he announced, and bells, beads, and copper objects for his daughter. (The latter was perhaps at Pocahontas's whispered suggestion.)

Just why Pocahontas interceded is impossible to know for certain. Smith attributed it to her compassion for a man in distress. Others through the centuries have put a romantic gloss on the scene, holding that Pocahontas was infatuated with him. Still another possibility is that she had some pragmatic purpose in mind for him, as the requirement of the bells, beads, and copper would suggest. Smith's own view of her motives is presumably due some extra weight, since, after all, he was there.

Smith remained a prisoner, and he was still apprehensive of the natives' seeming inconstancy, expecting "every houre to be put to one death or other." After two days, Powhatan appeared (in the company of around two hundred painted men) and informed Smith that they were now friends. Smith, he explained, simply needed to go to Jamestown and send back two "great guns" and a grindstone. With that done, Powhatan would give Smith some land and esteem him as much as his own cherished son, Nantaquoud. Smith was only too happy to pretend to agree. Powhatan sent him home with twelve guides, who would also supply the muscle to bring back the guns and the grindstone that Powhatan thought he would be getting.[27]

Smith now owed Pocahontas his life. Before long, he would owe her his life several times over.

6

GILDED DIRT

❦

John Smith, newly liberated from captivity in Chief Powhatan's capital, arrived at Jamestown within an hour of sunrise on Saturday, January 2, 1608. With him was a contingent of Powhatan's men, led by the chief's most trusted messenger, Rawhunt.

In the course of their journey, Smith found Rawhunt to be "of a subtill wit and crafty understanding"; nonetheless, Powhatan's man was in for a surprise. To keep his part of the bargain—two large guns and a grindstone—Smith puckishly directed Rawhunt to a pair of demiculverins, which were cannons weighing over three thousand pounds apiece. (The men "found them somewhat too heavie," Smith noted.) Then Smith had the cannons, which were loaded with stones, blast away at a tree that was weighed down with icicles. The messengers ran off in fright as the branches and ice came crashing to the ground. Smith beckoned them to come back; they returned after regaining their composure, and Smith gave them gifts to take back for themselves and for Powhatan—but no guns.[1]

Smith had a surprise of his own awaiting. During the month that he had been gone, President Ratcliffe had sworn in a new member of the council, over the ineffectual objections of the still-sickly John Martin. The new councilor, who had not been named to the council in London's instructions, was Gabriel Archer—yet another lawyer and another gentleman antagonist of John Smith. Archer had long been ambitious for a place on the council, which conferred status and also came with a salary attached. With the onset of winter, however, the reasons behind Archer's interest had become more urgent: he, along with some other gentlemen (possibly including the president himself), was ready to go home. Of the original 105 colonists, only some 40 were left alive.

Thus, on the day of his return, Smith found a group of colonists, "some ten or twelve of them who were called the better sort," commandeering the *Discovery* in an attempt to head to England. He ordered cannon and muskets trained on them, with an ultimatum to stay or be sunk. They opted to stay, but Smith had won himself still more enemies.

As word spread that day of the plentiful food that Smith had seen in the Powhatan villages, some colonists took heart that they might survive the winter after all—Jamestown's rations had been dwindling again. Ratcliffe and Archer, however, felt desperate pressure to get Smith out of the way so they could get the *Discovery* moving. The fates of Thomas Emry and Jehu Robinson gave them the excuse they needed. Their tactic was cynical and extreme: they held Smith responsible for the deaths of Emry and Robinson, and determined to have him executed the next day. Ratcliffe's two votes as president plus Archer's one was all they needed.

Smith's accusers did not even try to justify their actions under English common law. Rather, the charges were based on a creative interpretation of Leviticus, probably the passage at chapter 24, verses 17–20: an eye for an eye, a tooth for a tooth, a life for a life. The theory, apparently, was that Smith could be considered culpable because the men had been in his care when the natives ambushed them. Having barely avoided Chief Powhatan's executioners, he was set to hang at the decision of the colony's own leadership.

That evening—quite possibly as he was dining on his last meal, his second one in a week—Smith was blessed with another stroke of luck. Christopher Newport reappeared at Jamestown, in command of the ship *John and Francis*. Newport, finding the colony in chaos, took command of the situation. He quickly saw through Ratcliffe's charges, and Smith walked free.[2] (At the same time, Edward-Maria Wingfield was released from his imprisonment aboard the *Discovery*, but was not reinstated into the council or his former office.)

Newport had brought around sixty new colonists and fresh supplies. Both the passengers and supplies stayed on board the ship for a couple of days, then landed on Monday. Several days later, on January 7, one of the newcomers accidentally set off a fire in his lodgings.

The fire spread through the town in an instant, leveling all of the living quarters and destroying the supplies in the storehouse, and much else besides. Miraculously, no one seems to have been killed or even seriously hurt. But the colonists were nearly destitute again. "Everything my son and I had was burned, except a mattress which had not yet been taken off the ship," wrote the newly arrived Francis Perkins to a friend in England. Perkins pleaded for "ten pounds worth of discarded clothing, be it [outer] apparel, underwear, doublet, breeches . . . for we need everything." Smith took the occasion to laud the fortitude of Robert Hunt, the preacher, who "lost all his library and all he had but the cloathes on his backe; yet none never heard him repine at his losse."[3]

The mariners and the able-bodied among the colonists worked at rebuilding. Some basic rations had not yet been unloaded from the *John and Francis* when the fire broke out, but what kept the English from dire straits was, once again, trade with the natives. There was also other help: every week or so, Powhatan sent gifts of venison and bread, half for Smith and half for Smith's "father"—that is, Christopher Newport, whom Smith had extolled as a fearsome leader during his captivity. Powhatan accurately inferred Newport's presence from the arrival of the large ship.

While pleased by Powhatan's generosity, Smith grew worried about the overgenerous prices that the colonists and the mariners were giving the natives for their food. "In a short time, it followed, that could not be had for a pound of copper, which before was sold for an ounce," wrote John Martin's servant, Anas Todkill. Todkill, like Smith, blamed President Ratcliffe for setting off the inflationary trend. Ratcliffe, with his prideful jealousy of Smith's reputation among the natives, had been granting munificent terms to prove to the natives his own "greatnesse and authority." For the sake of his image, Ratcliffe had "cut the throat of our trade."[4] But there was nothing to be done.

In February, Powhatan sent word that he wanted to meet Smith's "father." Newport and Smith headed to Werowocomoco with thirty or forty armed men on the barge and the *Discovery*. The English were suspicious that Powhatan might be setting a trap for Newport; hence, Smith went ashore without him the first day, taking twenty of the men with him.

As Smith's men stood guard outside Powhatan's house, the chief greeted Smith warmly. With Powhatan were dozens of his wives or concubines—Todkill, who was with Smith, thought there were around forty—as well as a number of his nobles. Smith was again impressed with Powhatan's aura of command, seeing in him "such a majestie as I cannot expresse, nor yet have often seene, either in pagan or Christian."[5]

Smith presented several gifts from Newport: a suit of red cloth, a white greyhound dog, and a hat. Powhatan seemed gratified, and three of his nobles accepted the gifts "with a great oration" and a pledge of friendship between the two peoples. With regard to the greyhound, at least, Powhatan's enthusiasm was genuine; the dog stayed with him and dined as well as his royal owner did.

Powhatan then inquired where Newport was; Smith explained that he remained on board the ship and would come the next day. Thus assured, Powhatan asked "with a merrie countenance" about the guns Smith had promised—having heard from Rawhunt the story of the demiculverins. Smith replied with mock innocence that he had offered the messengers some large guns, just as he had agreed, but for some reason they declined to take them.[6]

At that, Powhatan laughed and requested Smith to give him some that were not quite so heavy. Then he asked about Smith's men. Why were they waiting outside? Powhatan indicated they should come in, too. Smith pretended to concur and stepped out to give orders.

Gifts and words of friendship were all very well, but Smith remained wary of Powhatan's motives. Gathering his men inside, he decided, would make them vulnerable to ambush. He told them that the chief wanted them to enter, and so they would—two at a time. Then those two men would leave to rejoin the others in standing watch, and the next pair would enter. No more than two of the English guards would ever be inside at once.

After Smith returned, his men carried out the plan, presenting themselves in pairs and giving thanks to Powhatan for his hospitality. Powhatan, in turn, gave them each four or five pounds of bread. That concluded, Powhatan told Smith pleasantly that he expected all of the men to lay their weapons down before him, as his subjects would have done. Smith said it was out of the question: this "was a ceremonie our enemies desired, never our friends."

But Smith was not interested in facing down Powhatan just now. Newport would be landing tomorrow; it would not do for him to find Powhatan in a peevish frame of mind. Smith had been touting the respect and admiration he had won from the natives, and he was not about to jeopardize that reputation in front of Newport. He prepared to win Powhatan over, at least for the time being, with another spurious promise.

Powhatan should not doubt the colonists' love, Smith told him. Smith vowed grandly that the English would, in due course, conquer his enemies—the Monacans to the west and the Susquehannocks to the north—and deliver them to him in subjection. Powhatan, although normally subtle and astute, was only too eager to believe what he had heard. Overjoyed, he loudly proclaimed Smith a *weroance*, and that "the corn, women, and country" should be to the English "as to his own people." Smith thanked him graciously and took his leave. Powhatan rose from his mats and conducted Smith to his lodge, where they spent several hours in "pretty discourses."7

The next morning, as Newport came ashore with the rest of the expedition, Smith met Newport at the river's edge. An English trumpeter preceded Newport, Smith, and their men on their way to Powhatan's house. There, with Smith acting as interpreter, Powhatan welcomed Smith's "father" and provided the English visitors with breakfast. Newport presented Powhatan with an English boy of thirteen to live with him and learn his language. No doubt it was an idle sense of humor, as much as anything, that led the English to pick a boy named Thomas Savage for this purpose. Savage, for his part, seems to have gone along with the idea willingly. Powhatan reciprocated by entrusting to the English one of his servant boys, by the name of Namontack.8

Having taken his measure of John Smith, Powhatan now took that of Christopher Newport. Powhatan asked why the party had come bearing weapons: "Seeing hee was our friend, and had neither bowes nor arrowes, what did we doubt?" Smith interpreted for Newport, then answered Powhatan himself, explaining that it was merely an English custom—not any aspersion on his kindness. Newport, however, overruled Smith and sent the rest of the men to the shore, more than a half mile distant. Smith was profoundly irritated; Newport's gesture did not square at all with Smith's own view of Powhatan, which was "to beleeve his friendship, till convenient opportunity suffered [allowed] him to betray us."9

The discussion now turned to trading. The English had brought hatchets and copper cooking pots to exchange for food. As Newport moved to initiate the bargaining on the first item, Powhatan stopped him short: "Captain Newport, it is not agreeable with my greatnes in this peddling manner to trade for trifles, and I esteeme you a great *weroance*. Therefore lay me down all your commodities together. What I like I will take, and in recompense give you that I thinke fitting their value."

Smith, interpreting, urged Newport not to go along. From his trading up and down the river, he believed they would do better by offering and selling one piece at a time, and seeing what price they could get for each. Newport preferred instead to outshine Powhatan in "ostentation of greatnes," as Todkill put it. So he agreed to Powhatan's plan, with the disheartening result that "we had not 4 bushels for that which we expected 20 hogsheads." Now Smith's frustration was evident to the other Englishmen, "Newport seeking to please the humour of the unsatiable salvage; Smith to cause the salvage to please him."[10]

Smith then assumed an outward calmness and began toying with some blue beads. Powhatan inquired about them. Smith put him off. Powhatan pressed him. Smith said he was very sorry, but he could not possibly part with his collection. These beads, he said, were "composed of a most rare substance of the colour of the skyes" and favored "by the greatest kings in the world." The conversation continued in this vein until Powhatan was "half madde" for the alleged valuables. In the end, Smith allowed himself to be prevailed upon to part with the beads for two or three hundred bushels of corn, and the English shoved off from Werowocomoco with their barge well loaded.[11]

If Newport felt outdone by Smith, he did not have time to dwell on it. One thing after another—the factionalism he found when he arrived, the fire, the meeting with Powhatan—had distracted him from the real mission of his return trip. When he made it back to England the previous July, he had sent good news to the earl of Salisbury, a member of the Virginia Company board in London. "The countrie is excellent and verie rich in gold," he reported, adding that he had brought back a sample to be assayed. "I wishe I might have come in person to have brought these gladd tidings."[12]

The company hired experienced assayers, who made four trials of Newport's sample and came up with the same answer each time: "All turned to vapour." Newport had brought back fool's gold. (Don Pedro de Zúñiga, the efficient and all-knowing Spanish ambassador, promptly passed word to Madrid.) The gold-colored flecks in Newport's bucket of soil may have been pyrite, marcasite, or even mica that had been yellowed by sediment. Whatever they were, Newport was in an embarrassing position.

Instead of cutting his losses, Newport insisted he truly had found gold; he had merely brought the wrong sample to England. He was certain of it, he said. Perhaps he believed the company's own propaganda about Virginia's riches too earnestly. Or he may have been taken in by the English folk wisdom of the day, which held that spiders—plentiful in Virginia—are "signs of great store of gold." He was determined to get the credit for discovering those riches on England's behalf. If he were right, it would make the booty from the *Madre de Dios* seem like small change. Through an intermediary, he passed word to the earl that he resolved "never to see your lordshippe before he bring that with him which he confidentlie beleeved he had broughte before."[13]

Thus was born the gold fever of 1608. On his resupply voyage, Newport had brought with him two gold refiners, William Dawson and Abram Ransack, who could test ore for purity on the spot at Jamestown. Also with him were two goldsmiths, Richard Belfield and William Johnson, to craft jewelry and other objects from the gold that the colonists were going to find. In March, after returning with Smith from Werowocomoco, Newport was impatient to put these men, and the rest of the colony, to work locating gold for London.

President Ratcliffe and John Martin shared Newport's enthusiasm for the project. The plan was to send the *John and Francis* back laden with promising soil for further assaying. The colonists and Newport's sailors spent weeks poring over the riverbanks, scooping up dirt in their buckets and pans, and swirling the dirt around in hopes that it would turn out to be studded with little gold flakes.

Smith vehemently disagreed with the turn that events had taken, feeling that the men were chasing after a phantom. He had once hoped, evidently, that the colonists would locate silver and gold in Virginia; he had signed on to the council's report to the Virginia Company the preceding June, in which the council urged London to send another supply quickly "leaste that all devouring Spaniard lay his ravenous hands" upon Virginia's ore. In the months since then, however, he had seen more of the land and its people, and had adjusted his expectations accordingly. If there was so much gold to be found, why did the natives not have any—unlike the natives of the Spanish New

World? "Victuals you must know is all their wealth," Smith wrote of the native Virginians around this time.[14]

England's slice of the New World did offer riches, Smith believed, but they were to be found in more mundane articles, like cedar, fish, and iron, not in the glistening daydreams he saw taking hold of those around him. Meanwhile, important work was being left undone, and the sailors were maintaining themselves with the colony's food supply long after they should have sailed off. "Our gilded refiners with their gilded promises made all men their slaves in hopes of recompenses," Todkill recalled. "There was no talke, no hope, no worke, but dig gold, refine gold, load gold." Todkill overheard Smith arguing with his employer, councilor Martin, over the project. "Never did any thing more torment him [Smith], then to see all necessary business neglected, to fraught such a drunken ship with so much gilded durt."[15]

Amid Smith's aggravations, he found respite from time to time in the visits of a young acquaintance. "Very oft she came to our fort, with what she could get for Captaine Smith," two colonists wrote of Pocahontas. "Her especially he ever much respected." If she had originally pictured him as a captive servant who would spend his days making her bells and jewelry, their relationship had evolved to give her something of greater value: friendship with someone who shared her inquisitive sensibility. She was curious about the English, and she enjoyed being among them; in Smith, she had found an Englishman who could speak her language and requite her curiosity about these foreigners. Although Smith had practical reasons to encourage the visits—honing his Algonquian, maintaining lines of communication with an ally in Powhatan's court—he also formed an admiration for the "nonpareil" and took an avuncular interest in her. *Kekaten pokahontas patiaquagh ningh tanks manotyens neer mowchick rawrenock audowgh*, he wrote in his phrase book: "Bid Pocahontas bring hither two little baskets, and I will give her white beads to make her a chaine."

She was not yet on the cusp of womanhood, and her visits found her playing energetically with the few boys of the fort as well as talking with Smith. She would, a colonist remembered, rally the boys "and make them wheel falling on their hands, turning their heels upwards, whom she would follow and wheel herself so naked as she was all the fort over." (Only when girls reached puberty would they regularly wear the apronlike deerskin dresses of Powhatan women.) Whether she visited furtively or with her father's knowledge is unclear, but it is doubtful that Powhatan would have knowingly let his daughter go to Jamestown alone and make herself vulnerable to capture by the untrustworthy colonists.[16]

On Sunday, April 10, Newport and his men finally set sail, having stayed almost three and a half months. As far as Smith was concerned, two weeks would have been time enough for them to unload and get going. Doubtless Smith continued to feel a measure of respect for Newport, as well as gratitude for Newport's having saved him from the noose with his providential arrival. Nonetheless, the men's widening rift on matters of policy—the gold digging, the amateurish bargaining with Powhatan—left Smith relieved to see Newport go.

The *John and Francis* was loaded with ore samples, not the planks of wood Smith had argued for. But the ship carried off certain other cargo with Smith's wholehearted support: namely, Edward-Maria Wingfield and Gabriel Archer, who were being dispatched home in dishonor. Not having much need for "petitions, admirals, recorders, interpreters, chronologers, courts of plea, nor justices of peace," Todkill said of the two lawyers, the colony "sent Master Wingfield and Captaine Archer with him [Newport] for England to seeke some better place of imploiment."[17]

7

POWHATAN BECOMES AN ENGLISH PRINCE

❧

Shortly before Christopher Newport's second departure in April 1608, Powhatan had sent a band of messengers to him bearing twenty turkeys—and word that Newport was welcome to the birds if he would send back twenty swords. It was an outrageous proposition, but Powhatan had correctly sized up the English captain's eagerness to please: in a parting gesture of magnanimity, Newport sent him the swords.

With Newport on his way to the Chesapeake Bay, and thence to the Atlantic, Powhatan decided to try his luck with John Smith. This time, he sent the turkeys to Jamestown accompanied by a young messenger—his foreign exchange student, Thomas Savage, the English boy placed with Powhatan a month or six weeks before. On arriving at the fort, Savage told Smith of the emperor's renewed offer of turkeys for swords. Smith saw no reason at all to arm a potential enemy; he sent the rest of Powhatan's messengers home with gifts for themselves and a curt no for Powhatan.

Powhatan, displeased at Smith's refusal, began sending small groups of men to try to steal what he had not been able to buy. A series of minor skirmishes followed as the English confronted the intruders. With the council's assent, Smith put one man, who had been caught stealing two swords, in the stocks. Others were chased away, though some managed to run off with spades, shovels, or tools in the process.

On Wednesday, April 20, as Smith and other colonists were cutting down trees, an alarm trumpet or an alarm bell called out. They rushed to pick up their guns, assuming a native attack was under way.

The alarm instead turned out to be signaling the approach of a ship: the *Phoenix*, commanded by Thomas Nelson. The *Phoenix* had left England with Christopher Newport's *John and Francis* in 1607, but it had been missing at sea for almost four months and presumed lost. In fact, Nelson had become separated from Newport by a storm near the mouth of the Chesapeake; the storm and contrary winds forced him to turn back toward the West Indies, where he wintered.

Nelson's safe arrival, with supplies and forty to sixty more colonists, was cause for satisfaction. Since his passengers and crew had been living off the land in the islands, Nelson could be generous in sharing the ship's supplies with the colony. If anyone had doubts about his motives in heading to the Caribbean for the cold months, they kept those doubts to themselves. "Now we thought ourselves as well fitted, as our harts could wish," Smith remembered, "both with a competent number of men, as also for all other needful provisions, till a further supply should come unto us."[1]

Ratcliffe and Martin, who had still not shaken off their gold obsession, argued with Smith over whether the *Phoenix* would be loaded with still more "gilded dirt." Meanwhile, Ratcliffe ordered Smith to explore beyond the falls of the James (perhaps seeing another chance to be rid of his antagonist). Smith was agreeable; he still had his yen for exploring, and he saw an opportunity to do it on a large scale. Not wanting to repeat the failure of the small, undisciplined party that had come to grief on the Chickahominy River, Smith recruited sixty or seventy volunteers from among the colonists and Nelson's sailors. Leading the expedition with him would be twenty-eight-year-old Matthew Scrivener, the newest councilor, who had come over on Newport's ship in January; Smith had found him reliable and sensible.

The volunteers spent a week training under Smith to fight "amongst the trees" against any native attackers. With the training came drilling, drilling, and more drilling. Afterward, they judged themselves ready to take on Powhatan's entire forces, if need be—this, at a time when it was hazardous for an Englishman even to leave the fort. The project ran into unexpected opposition, however: Captain Nelson, unlike Newport, was not inclined to wait around. At the eleventh hour, he declared that his sailors could not join unless the company were to cover the cost of the ship's waiting time and the sailors' extra wages. As the project died on the vine, it nonetheless served the purpose of reminding the colonists who could and could not be trusted to lead. Ratcliffe, by ordering the mission and then declining to take part, had marked himself a coward.[2]

The petty assaults from the Powhatans continued, culminating in the apprehension one afternoon of a dozen natives. These men became prisoners, joining another four or five natives that the English were already holding for one cause or another. When the Powhatans observed the next day that their men had not returned, they twice sent emissaries to speak with Smith. Each time, Smith sent a bellicose message back: the Powhatans must return all the English spades, shovels, swords, and tools they had stolen—or the prisoners would hang tomorrow.

Soon there was another message from the Powhatans. They reported they had captured two Englishmen, who had been foraging in the woods beyond the fort. These two men would be returned, Powhatan's messenger said, in exchange for the sixteen or so men held by the English.

Smith was not an inhumane man, fundamentally. But where Newport wanted to be loved, Smith had read his Machiavelli and felt it was better to be feared. Nor was Smith interested in a drawn-out game of tit-for-tat. He laid a plan to let the natives "know what we durst [dared] to do." That night, with the approval of President Ratcliffe and councilor Martin, Smith set out on his first offensive in Virginia. He and Scrivener led a party of Englishmen on the barge to a series of native towns on the river, where they left a path of destruction—the natives' highly ignitable buildings burned, their canoes wrecked. He may have used the incendiary and explosive arts he had practiced against his enemies in Central Europe. Although no native lives were taken, it was a costly and painful loss for them. Each of the canoes had been laborious to build: the natives had to hollow out a large log by burning it partway, and then form the desired shape by scraping the log inside and out with clamshells. The two English prisoners were returned the next day, with no mention of the prisoners that the English held.

Ratcliffe released one captive. As for the rest, the council directed Smith to "terrifie them with some torture" to find out the Powhatans' intentions. He chose one and had him tied down, with six men aiming muskets at him. Smith advised the prisoner to tell him what his comrades were up to, or else. The victim of this treatment, duly terrified, told Smith that he could not answer his questions, but that another prisoner named Macanoe could. Macanoe, he said, was a counselor to the chief of the Paspahegh.

Smith had the man untied and turned his attention to Macanoe. Once Macanoe was brought to him, Smith directed his gaze to an English rack, an instrument that was unknown to the natives, but whose awful purpose could readily be guessed. Then he put Macanoe before the muskets. Macanoe did not wait. Six tribes, he said, had been hunting together when they took him prisoner near Apokant: the Paspahegh, the Chickahominy, the Youghtanund, the Pamunkey, the Mattaponi, and the Kiskiack. Now the Paspahegh, the colony's neighbors, together with the Chickahominy, planned to surprise the English and make off with their tools and weapons.

Newport had taken the servant boy Namontack with him to England; the English had told Chief Powhatan that Newport would bring him back on his next voyage. Powhatan and all his tribes would "seem friends" until Newport returned with the boy, Macanoe said. Upon the boy's homecoming, the natives would invite Newport and other English leaders to festivities where they would be lulled by good feeling, and then ambushed.

On hearing this, Smith wondered whether Powhatan had sent Thomas Savage back to Jamestown for a reason: namely, that Savage was on the brink of seeing and hearing too much, and in danger of piecing the emperor's plans together. Indeed, Savage had taken note that Powhatan was frequently having secret meetings, and he felt in the air that something was afoot. Smith, testing his theory as to Savage's return, sent him back to Powhatan again. Sure enough, Savage soon turned up at the fort once more, this time with his chest and his English clothes. Powhatan, he said, wanted another boy—presumably a less perspicacious one.[3]

All the while, John Martin was "most confidently" pleading Powhatan's case, in the belief that the emperor was a true friend. Smith, this time acting without the council's approval, took it upon himself to settle the question. Smith and Scrivener separated the remaining captives, and then had volleys of gunshots fired; the captives could hear the shots, but could not see them. Smith and Scrivener led the men to believe that their companions were being executed. Each man was then given the chance, so he thought, to save himself by talking. "First I, then Master Scrivener, upon their severall examinations, found by them all confirmed, that [the] Paspahegh, and Chickahammania [the Chickahominies] did hate us," Smith recorded. The men also revealed that the stolen English tools and swords went to Chief Powhatan, and that the Paspahegh and the Chickahominies were planning further trouble for the colony.

Smith the realist had long understood that the colony's neighbors hated the English. Not only that, they would hate the English no matter what the English did to make themselves lovable—short of packing up and going back home. Where the colonists saw themselves merely as occupying some fallow, unused ground, the natives plainly had come to regard their presence as an unwanted intrusion. The Virginia Company was not ready to assimilate this unpleasant piece of data.

One morning, on the third day of the prisoners' captivity, a pair of emissaries from Powhatan appeared at the fort to appeal for their release. Powhatan had made an adroit choice of representatives. One was Rawhunt, the messenger "of a subtill wit and crafty understanding" who had accompanied Smith on his return from Werowocomoco. The other was his favorite daughter. The symbolism could not be missed: Smith owed his life to Pocahontas, and Rawhunt stood for Smith's own liberation from captivity some five months earlier.

Rawhunt presented Smith with a gift of a deer and bread, with apologies for the wrongdoing of "some rash untoward captaines his subjects." He then entered into a lengthy discourse on Powhatan's love and respect for Smith. Powhatan missed the boy Thomas Savage, Rawhunt added, and desired for him to come back. It is unlikely that Smith believed any of this. Pocahontas said nothing, allowing Rawhunt to speak for her father. Smith observed that Pocahontas had apparently been instructed not to take any notice of the prisoners herself, that being beneath the dignity of a king's daughter.

Later in the morning, the fathers and friends of the prisoners also came to the fort to join Rawhunt and Pocahontas in asking for the men's liberty. In the afternoon, after those visitors went away, the prisoners were taken to the colony's makeshift church for prayer, as they had been from time to time over the previous several days. Then Smith returned the prisoners' bows and arrows and released the men to Rawhunt and Pocahontas. In recognition of his debt to Pocahontas, Smith made a show of claiming he had spared them only at her request, "for whose sake onely he fayned to have saved their lives, and gave them libertie."[4]

The prisoners evidently went on to spread the word of their ordeal to their countrymen: the English, at least in the persons of Smith and Scrivener, were to be feared. The native attacks came to an end for the time being.[5]

Afterward, certain "councel" (who could only have been Ratcliffe and Martin) censured Smith for his cruelty. To modern ears, that charge sounds apt enough. Smith's supporters, such as Anas Todkill, argued in his defense that "none was slaine to any man's knowledge"; his modus operandi had been to instill fear, not to slaughter.[6] Smith's actions in the spring of 1608, especially the ravaging of the villages, were a template to which he would return time and again, and he made no apologies for them. It is clear that he respected the talents and intelligence of the native leaders more than he did the leaders of his own side, but he also meant for the colony to survive. The alternative to intimidation was not love and friendship; it was open war—which the English, in 1608, would have lost to the last man.

On June 2, Thomas Nelson was ready to leave with the *Phoenix*. This time, Smith had won the battle of the cargo: Nelson would carry cedar, not purported gold ore. Accompanying Nelson would be John Martin, an honorable man, but one who had been ill with one ailment or another for most of the preceding year. "Desirous to injoy the credit of his supposed art of finding the golden mine, [he] was most willingly admitted to returne for England."[7] So wrote his servant Todkill. (No man is a hero to his own valet.)

Meanwhile, in London, the Virginia Company was exhibiting Namontack, recently arrived with Newport, through social functions and an appearance at court. It was a publicity stunt aimed at drumming up political support and impressing potential investors. The company decided to enhance the fund-raising appeal of Powhatan's servant boy by having him masquerade as a native prince, a ruse that greatly entertained the Spanish ambassador. "This Newport brought a lad who they say is the son of an emperor of those lands," Zúñiga wrote to Philip III, "and they have coached him that when he sees the King he is not to take off his hat, and other things of this sort, so I have been amused by the way they honor him, for I hold it for surer that he must be a very ordinary person."[8]

Nelson's *Phoenix* followed close behind Newport, returning in early July. "I hear not of any novelties or other commodities she hath brought more than sweet wood," a disappointed investor in the Virginia Company wrote to a friend.9 The letter writer, John Chamberlain, had probably already heard that Newport's second load of gold ore proved as worthless as the first.

Yet Nelson had brought a kind of treasure, in the form of a sketch map of Powhatan's tribes and a bundle of papers, both of which Smith had handed to him just before he headed homeward. The latter was a manuscript of more than 13,000 words that recounted what the colonists had experienced, starting with the foul weather they endured off the English coast and ending with the release of the native prisoners and some minor shenanigans afterward. Smith had obviously started the chronicle during his captivity on the Atlantic crossing, and had somehow found time to continue writing in the midst of his explorations and political wrangling.

Smith's intentions for the document are unknown, as is its intended recipient. It could have been a report to the company, or a private letter to a friend. The style was mostly understated and matter-of-fact; the grammar was often convoluted. But its contents were too sensational to stay private for long. Within weeks after Nelson's landing, the document had made its way, second- or thirdhand, to an editor named John Healey, and from there to the printing press.10 By summer's end, it appeared for sale under the prolix title of *A True Relation of Such Occurrences and Accidents of Note as Hath Hapned in Virginia Since the First Planting of that Colony, which is now resident in the South part thereof, till the last returne from thence.*

The *True Relation* was the first published account of the distant colony to reach the public's hands. The soldier with a grammar school education had, as it turned out, written the earliest history of English America's birth. He had done it unwittingly; the editing and publishing of the book took place entirely without Smith's involvement, or even his knowledge. Healey explained that he had omitted some material "fit to be private." He also tacked on a hopeful concluding sentence in which he had Smith portray the colonists as "being in good health, all our men wel contented, free from mutinies, in love one with another, and as we hope in continuall peace with the Indians."11

The colonists were not all in love with each other. Smith's adversaries on the council, however, were down to one: Ratcliffe. Indeed, with the departure of Martin, and in the absence of Newport, the entire council consisted of Ratcliffe, Smith, and Smith's ally, Matthew Scrivener. The latter two were by now distrustful of the president's self-aggrandizing tendencies, which were becoming ever more pronounced. Smith had already been disturbed by the indulgent trading prices Ratcliffe had given the natives—for the sake of his own image, Smith believed. More recently, Smith and Scrivener had become concerned about his prodigious consumption of the colony's diminishing rations.

At the same time, Smith clearly felt there was no use just sitting around. As Nelson set off for England, Smith took fourteen men with him on the barge to explore the Chesapeake Bay. Scrivener stayed behind to attempt to apply some degree of restraint to Ratcliffe. Joining Smith were newcomer Walter Russell, a "doctor of physicke"; Anas Todkill, who had quit John Martin's employ to stay in Virginia; a half dozen tradesmen and laborers, including a fisherman, a fishmonger, and a carpenter; and another half dozen from the gentlemanly ranks. Among the tradesmen, Smith pointedly included James Read, the blacksmith, who had struck Ratcliffe during an altercation soon after Ratcliffe became president.[12]

Over the next seven weeks, the men explored countless inlets and waterways, eventually making their way beyond Powhatan's domain and reaching as far as present-day Delaware. They sought to determine the "mineralls, rivers, rocks, nations, woods, fishings, fruites, victuall, and what other commodities the land afforded."[13] They stopped to parley with various tribes along the way to make the acquaintance of these more distant nations, and in hopes of hearing something about a route to the "other sea." The threat of villainy was always an issue, and so the English and the natives lubricated some of these encounters by exchanging hostages temporarily to ensure each side's good behavior.

By this time, it was conventional for English explorers to name the places they found after kings, queens, and princes. The Spanish were sometimes in the habit of naming places for saints. As Smith and his men made their way through uncharted territory, they did neither of these things. They made careful note of the natives' place-names, and amused themselves now and then by putting their own names on the map: Keales Hill for Richard Keale, the fishmonger; Russells Isles for their doctor. A group of islands near the southern tip of the Eastern Shore became Smiths Isles (today's Smith Island). Extreme wind, rain, and lightning forced them to spend two days on an island that they unaffectionately dubbed Limbo.

On the Nanticoke River, at a town inland from the Eastern Shore, the party met with the Nantaquake, whom Smith termed "the best merchants of all other salvages." The Nantaquake told the English of Powhatan's mortal enemy, the Massawomeck, a powerful and cruel nation that was feared by the other tribes of the region. Smith seized on the idea of establishing relations with the Massawomecks, and in short order the barge was on its way up the bay to find them.

The party never reached the Massawomecks' dominion, thanks to uncooperative weather and the fearfulness of some of the men. They did, however, accomplish the colonists' first exploration of the Pata-womeck River—the Potomac—reaching as far as the future site of Washington, D.C.[14]

In mid-July, as Smith was about to lead the men back to James-town, he elected to take a brief detour up the Rappahannock en route. With the ebb of the tide, the barge ran aground on a shoal near the river's mouth, and so the men opted to while away some time. There were plentiful fish in the shallow water, and Smith made a game of catching them by skewering them on his sword. The rest of the men followed suit, with satisfying results; "thus we tooke more in one houre than we could eate in a day," several of the voyagers recalled. After hundreds of miles of sailing and rowing, after at least a dozen encoun-ters with unfamiliar native tribes (some of them violently unwelcom-ing), the grounding of the barge had opened up a hard-won occasion for simple fun.

In this unlikely setting, Smith encountered a deadly adversary. He took a stab at a strange-looking creature, flat and undulating, which onlookers found hard to describe: "much in the fashion of a thornback, but with a long tail like a ryding rodde, whereon the middest is a most poysoned sting, of two or three inches long, bearded like a saw on each side." Smith had caught a stingray, almost certainly one of the variety known as *Dasyatis sabina*, which is found in the Chesapeake Bay and sometimes even ranges into fresh water. The stingray defended itself by whipping around its black-tipped tail, which finally connected with Smith's forearm and plunged in almost an inch and a half. Smith screamed. "No bloud nor wound was seene, but a little blue spot, but the torment was instantly so extreame."

The stingray's venom was working. Dr. Russell hastened to apply a "precious oyle" of unknown description, but Smith's hand, arm, and shoulder swelled frighteningly. As his agony continued for some hours, Smith asked his men to dig a grave for him on a nearby island. This they did, and "with much sorrow" prepared for his funeral. But the grave was not to be filled; Russell's ointment, or perhaps Smith's own robust constitution, unexpectedly overcame the effects of the poison. As Smith's pain receded, he addressed the situation with typical pugnacity by eating the stingray for supper.

The party then hurried back toward Jamestown, where Smith could recuperate. As they made a stop at the village of the Kecoughtans the next day, the natives noticed that he had been injured and that another man was bloody (from a minor wound, seemingly incurred by tripping on something). The Kecoughtans also noticed the men's swords, as well as the piles of furs and other loot they had bought during their travels. From that scene, the natives logically concluded that the fifteen Englishmen had just come back from battle, and insisted on knowing whom they had beaten and plundered. Smith, seeing an opportunity to instill awe in the locals, demanded secrecy and then confided that they had taken the spoil from the Massawomecks. The lie had its intended result. "This rumor went faster up the river than our barge," the explorers found.[15]

Arriving back at Jamestown on July 21, Smith found that the state of the colony had taken a turn for the worse. Scrivener, who was now feverish, had been unable to check President Ratcliffe's excesses. Ratcliffe himself had fallen into alarming delusions of grandeur. During the height of Jamestown's humid and malarial summertime, he had commanded the colonists to leave everything else aside in order to build him a stately capitol in the woods—"Ratcliffe's Pallace," some groused—while he continued to fatten himself on their limited food supply. Several members of the party recalled the conditions they discovered when they came back:

> There we found the last supply [that is, the colonists recently brought by Newport and Nelson] were all sicke, the rest some lame, some bruised, all unable to doe any thing but complaine of the pride and unreasonable needlesse crueltie of the silly president, that had riotously consumed the store: and to fulfill his follies about building an unnecessary building for his pleasure in the woods, had brought them all to that misery.[16]

A faction of the colonists was ready to take matters into its own hands and wreak revenge on Ratcliffe personally. With the return of Smith's party, a more level-headed idea took hold: namely, to replace Ratcliffe with Smith, a leader who had shown that his ambitions were for the colony, not just for himself. If there was any vote on the idea, that vote was never recorded, and it is unknown how many colonists supported Smith's taking office. In any event, Ratcliffe either resigned or was illicitly overthrown, although he had less than two months left in his term of office. One colonist would later describe him tersely as "not worthy of remembering, but to his dishonor."

Smith does not appear to have been longing for the promotion, as evidenced by the fact that he immediately named Scrivener as his substitute—and then took off several days later for the Chesapeake again. (He named some "honest officers" to assist Scrivener while he recovered from his illness.) For this voyage, Smith took a dozen men, some who had been with him on the barge the last time and others who were starting fresh. Much like the previous exploration, this trip found Smith and his men engaged in diplomacy, hard bargaining, and fending off both illness and occasional enemy attacks.

The six-week trip had one casualty, of unrecorded cause: Michael Fetherstone, gentleman. For all of Smith's resentment and suspicion of "the better sort," he chose a select few for his missions—those who had redeemed themselves in his eyes through meritorious conduct. Fetherstone was one of these. "All the time he had beene in this country, [he] had behaved himselfe, honestly, valiantly, and industriously," his companions wrote.[17] They fired a volley of gunshot in his honor as they buried him.

Shortly before the barge was to return to Jamestown, Smith decided to investigate some of the less-familiar lands near the settlement. Among these was the village of the Nansemonds, who lived on a river by the same name near the mouth of the bay. From their proximity to Cape Henry, Smith no doubt considered the possibility that they were behind the attack on the English landing party there the year before. On Smith's approach, though, the Nansemonds made a great display of hospitality as they waved the barge further up the narrowing river, "with all shew of love that could be." Smith complied, and invited some in nearby canoes to come on board—to guarantee the Nansemonds' good behavior.

When none of the natives would join him and his men on the barge, Smith sensed that he had been too trusting. The Nansemonds had set their eyes, it seems, on the hoard of weapons, tools, and other treasures on the barge. Smith's men braced themselves behind wooden shields—which, as it happened, they had recently received as gifts from another tribe—and got their muskets ready to shoot. Soon seven or eight canoes of armed men were behind him, and arrows were flying from the canoes and from shore. The English got off twenty or so musket shots, enough to make the attackers on shore back away and to scare the canoeists into jumping overboard and swimming off.

Smith's party took stock and found that none of the company had been hurt; one man had an arrow resting harmlessly in his hat, and another had an arrow dangling from his sleeve. Scores of arrows were embedded in the shields.

If the watching Nansemonds expected the party to retreat gracefully to Jamestown, they were wrong. The colonists commandeered the now empty canoes and moved them out of range of the shore. Smith directed the men to take their hatchets and axes and begin chopping the canoes into pieces. Seeing the slow destruction of their invaluable and painstakingly built watercraft, the Nansemonds put down their bows and arrows and called out that they wanted peace. Fine, Smith told them; they could have their peace if they brought out their chief's bows and arrows, and a chain of pearls. Also, when the English came again at harvesttime, the Nansemonds would have to give them four hundred baskets of corn. "Otherwise we would breake all of their boats, and burne their houses, corne, and all they had." The Nansemonds had little choice but to acquiesce.[18]

From there, the barge headed to Jamestown and arrived the same day, three days before Ratcliffe's official term of office was to expire and Smith was to take over. Scrivener, the interim president, was now healthy. Ratcliffe was in prison for mutiny, having apparently tried to regain his former post in Smith's absence.

On September 10, 1608, Smith took his oath of office as president of Jamestown. His immediate concerns were predictably practical. Scrivener, with Smith's concurrence, had allowed the men a respite from work during August in consideration of "the weaknesse of the company, and the heat of the yeare";[19] indeed, the labors on Ratcliffe's "pallace" had likely brought that weakness about. Now, with summer turning into fall, Smith declared the respite over. Storehouses and living quarters had to be made ready for the provisions and the new colonists that Newport was expected to bring—the "second supply," as it was called. The rotation of the watches, or lookouts, had to be beefed up and the men trained. The whole colony needed regular target practice to keep up their shooting skills. The colony's crops, meager as they were, would have to be harvested.[20]

All of this was getting under way when Newport arrived in late September, sooner than expected. With him were seventy colonists, including two new councilors by the names of Peter Winne and Richard Waldo, two boys known only as Milman and Hilliard, and the colony's first women: a Mistress Forrest and her maid, Anne Burras. Mistress Forrest was with her gentleman husband, Thomas. Anne Burras was thus the only unattached woman in a colony of about two hundred long-deprived men. None of her letters or journals have survived, if there were any, so it can only be imagined how she felt about being at the center of this particular attention. At any rate, she did not care to keep it going; one of the original settlers from 1607, John Laydon, quickly won her over and the two were married before the end of the year.[21]

Newport also brought orders from the Virginia Company directing the colony's leaders to assist and obey him in carrying out his new mission. That mission was twofold. First, he must find something in Virginia of major value: a site for a gold mine, a route to the Pacific Ocean, or the survivors of the lost Roanoke Colony. The company's management and investors had become impatient with "ifs and ands, hopes, and some few proofes." Yet the company continued to have faith in Newport, who had the benefit of being present in London to make his case—a tactical advantage that Smith did not possess.

Second, Newport was to place an English crown on Chief Powhatan's head, thus rendering him (in theory) a loyal tributary prince of King James. This was exceptionally ludicrous, and it can be assumed that Smith's jaw dropped when Newport read it to him. Smith made a futile attempt to rally the rest of the council against the idea. Winne and Waldo were "auncient soldiers, and valiant gentlemen, yet ignorant of the busines (being but newly arrived)." Although Scrivener was usually a Smith ally, he too supported the idea of crowning Powhatan; he was "desirous to see strange [foreign, unfamiliar] countries," and he welcomed the chance to see Powhatan's capital.[22]

So management's orders would be followed without question, as usual, whether they made any sense or not. In Smith's mind, the orders seemed almost like a deliberate effort to make the enterprise fail: "Now there was no way to make us miserable, but to neglect that time to make provision [gather food] whilst it was to be had," he wrote. Newport's "strange coronation" would accomplish nothing, he thought, but to puff up the emperor's self-importance vis-à-vis the English, meanwhile causing the colony to "lose that time [and] spend the victualls we had. . . . God doth know they little knew what they did."[23]

Newport chose 120 men to accompany him as guards at his meeting with Powhatan, perhaps wanting to project a stately image. Smith, having been outvoted, bowed to Newport's authority. As a last-ditch attempt to avoid losing the labors of 60 percent of the colonists for the duration, Smith proposed to take a message to Powhatan inviting the chief to come to Jamestown. That was all right with Newport.

Taking a dig at Newport for the inordinate size of his party, Smith brought just three men with him. He also brought two boys, Powhatan's servant Namontack and Samuel Collier. (Smith was probably indulging the latter's youthful curiosity.) When Smith arrived at Werewocomoco, Powhatan was at another village. The natives sent for the chief, and gave the English visitors a surprise in the meantime.

The natives took Smith and his companions to a field at the rim of a forest, and seated them on mats in front of a fire. It was night, and the setting put the men on edge. Shrieks emerged from the woods nearby. The visitors seized two or three old men nearby as shields, fearing that Powhatan had set an ambush. A young girl rushed to the scene; she turned out to be Pocahontas, who vowed that no harm was meant. Smith saw that spectators had arrived, including women and children, and realized that his men were being treated to royal entertainment.

With that, the English relaxed and watched with Pocahontas as thirty young women emerged from the woods. They were naked except for body paint and a few strategically placed leaves; each wore a pair of buck's horns on her head. More exotic still, the women had assumed the form of warriors; some women carried bows and arrows in their hands, while others held clubs or swords. For an hour, the women danced in a circle around the fire, transfixing the visitors "with most hellish shouts and cryes, rushing from among the trees, casting themselves in a ring about the fire, singing and dauncing with most excellent ill varietie, oft falling into their infernal passions, and solemnly againe to sing and daunce."

The women left and then reappeared, this time inviting Smith to their house; there, they found it amusing to crowd around him, chanting "Love you not me? Love you not me?" Smith and his men afterward enjoyed an evening of banqueting, singing, and dancing with them. The women then conducted each visitor to his sleeping quarters—and here Smith's account of the evening chastely ends. It was customary, however, for native chiefs to provide honored guests with a bedmate, and it can be assumed that the dancers and the Englishmen continued their entertainment into the night.[24]

The next day, Chief Powhatan returned. Smith presented Namontack to him, and extended the invitation on behalf of Newport for Powhatan to come to Jamestown and receive certain "presents" from the English king.

Powhatan balked. For him to come to Jamestown was beneath the dignity of his station. "If your king have sent me presents, I also am a king, and this is my land," Smith translated his answer. "Eight days I will stay [at Werowocomoco] to receive them. Your father [Newport] is to come to me, not I to him, nor yet to your fort, neither will I bite at such a bait."[25]

Smith's fallback measure had failed. After Smith and his party returned to Jamestown with the news, Newport sent Powhatan's presents ahead to Werowocomoco on three barges—including an English bed, a washbasin, a pitcher, a scarlet cloak, a pair of shoes, and some other furniture and clothing. Newport and his party, which did not include Smith, went by foot.

The morning after they arrived was to be the occasion of Powhatan's coronation, whether he wanted it or not. Powhatan had stayed at Werowocomoco, as promised, waiting for his presents. He accepted them with equanimity until the English came to the cloak; he distrusted their intentions in trying to put the cloak on his back until Namontack convinced him that they meant no harm.

Newport now turned to the solemn ceremony, which he had no doubt organized in some detail and rehearsed beforehand. There was just one glitch: Powhatan did not understand (or pretended not to understand) what the crown was for, and could not be persuaded to bend his knee to receive it. Newport tired himself out showing him what to do and trying to persuade him to follow suit. Finally, someone on the English side had the presence of mind to lean hard on Powhatan's shoulders, forcing him to stoop a little. As three men rushed to put the crown on his head, another man fired a pistol into the air as a signal to the *Discovery* to unleash cannon fire marking the moment. Powhatan jumped, startled by the barrage. He quickly regained his self-possession and thanked Newport for his kindness, giving him his old deerskin mantle and moccasins.

Before leaving Werowocomoco, Newport irked the emperor by mentioning that he would be calling on one of Powhatan's enemy tribes, the Monacans. Newport stopped briefly at Jamestown, then took his men up the James River in the *Discovery* to explore beyond the falls. The plan was to carry a disassembled barge (which Newport had brought from England) past the falls, then assemble it and seek a route to the Pacific. The five pieces of the barge proved too heavy to carry, however, so Newport abandoned that idea and the men went to the Monacan settlement on foot. The Monacans treated the English visitors with indifferent courtesy. Newport nonetheless had one of their petty chiefs captured and forced him to serve as a guide while the English searched for a gold mine. On the expedition was one of the gold refiners, who reported at one point that he thought he had found a little silver, and that "better stuffe might be had for the digging." Nothing ever came of the samples; it was another wasted effort, like the rest of Newport's trip.[26]

At Newport's direction, Smith had stayed behind at the fort to lead eighty or so colonists in starting to produce small quantities of glass, pitch, tar, potash, and clapboard to send home as samples. (Newport's second supply had brought eight German and Polish tradesmen; the Germans were glassmakers and the Poles made pitch, tar, and potash.) Once Newport returned to Jamestown, however, Smith made himself scarce. Possibly he wanted to spend as little time as he could in Newport's presence—the disagreement between the two over the crowning of Powhatan had widened into outright hostility. Smith selected thirty men and took them five miles downriver to cut down trees for clapboard, leaving the fort to the council's supervision.

Among the thirty were two proper gentlemen from the second supply, Gabriel Beadle and John Russell. At first, Smith recalled, "the axes so blistered their tender fingers that many times every third blow had a loud oath to drown the echo." Yet they stuck to it. By the end of a week, they were adept lumberjacks, and had come to enjoy the newfound experience of labor, "making it their delight to hear the trees thunder as they fell." Smith was delighted, too. Thirty gentlemen like that, he thought, would accomplish more than a hundred of the lazy-bones who would work only under compulsion—though twenty good workingmen would be better still.[27]

When Smith and his companions returned to the fort, he learned that his fears had been realized: Newport had undermined the colony's position with the crown and the gifts. Powhatan's estimation of his own power and importance had evidently increased, or else he had taken offense once he understood that the coronation was supposed to represent his subjugation to the English king. Consequently, he had forbidden his people to bargain with the English for food; he was inclined to let the foreigners starve, and the sooner, the better. At around this time, Smith composed a letter to the treasurer and governing council of the company in England. It was astonishingly frank in its criticisms of his bosses:

> Expresly to follow your directions by Captaine Newport, though they be performed, I was directly against it; but according to our commission [orders], I was content to be overruled by the major part of the counsell, I feare to the hazard of us all; which is now generally confessed when it is too late.[28]

The plan to carry the barge past the falls was ridiculous, he continued. "For the quartred boat to be borne by the soldiers over the falles, Newport had 120 of the best men he could chuse. If he had burnt her to ashes, one might have carried her in a bag, but as she is, five hundred cannot." (The men were "soldiers" in that they were bearing arms.) For Newport to take the majority of the colony on his exploration was inexcusable in any case, Smith argued; one man could have accomplished as much as Newport's 120. As for Powhatan's bed and the other offerings, "by whose advice you sent him such presents, I know not; but this give me leave to tell you, I feare they will be the confusion [ruin] of us all ere we heare from you againe."

Having burned his bridges with Newport, Smith now made his attack personal. Rumor had it, Smith said, that Newport received £100 a year from the Virginia Company for his services. If so, it was a needless expense: "For every [ship's] master you have yet sent can find the way as well as he, so that an hundred pounds might be spared, which is more than we have all, that helpe to pay him wages."

Finally, Smith made a plea to the company to adjust its expectations of the business. The colony could not supply "present profit"; that would have to wait until the colony had the means to sustain itself. By diverting the colony's labor into get-rich-quick schemes, like the search for nonexistent gold, and by sending men without needed skills, the company was simply pushing the day of real profitability further into the distance. Goldsmiths, gold refiners, and glassmakers (to say nothing of effete layabouts) could do nothing but eat into the supplies. For the present, the key was to put the right people in place to continue laying the groundwork—literally, in some cases. "When you send againe," Smith asked, "I entreat you rather send but thirty carpenters, husbandmen, gardeners, fishermen, blacksmiths, masons, and diggers up of trees, roots, well provided, then a thousand of such as we have."[29]

Smith had only one way to get his letter to England, and that was by way of Newport's return trip. In December, Newport left Virginia carrying the trials of glass, pitch, tar, potash, and clapboard—and Smith's letter, which one assumes was well sealed. The letter did not change the Virginia Company council's mind about Newport, who would continue to serve for several more years. In another way, the letter was a success: despite its caustic commentary on the council's management, it substantially influenced their view of relations with the natives and the type of settlers the colony needed. Smith would not learn of this for a long time to come, however, thanks to the vagaries of weather around an uninhabited island called Bermuda.

8

POCAHONTAS SAVES JOHN SMITH AGAIN

In the wake of Ratcliffe's maladministration, the colonists faced another winter in which they would have to depend on the natives to ward off famine. When Newport arrived in late September, he had reckoned that Chief Powhatan's crowning would fill him with such affection for the English that they would have no more worries in that department. Newport planned, in fact, to fill the *Discovery* twice over with the boatloads of grain he expected to receive from Powhatan and from the Monacans. This assumption had been crucial, because Newport brought little food with him in the second supply. He would, in fact, need to tap into the colony's stores to feed his sailors on the voyage home.

But events had transpired differently: Newport returned from his expedition all but empty-handed. Chief Powhatan gave Newport an almost nominal fourteen bushels, and the Monacans gave him nothing. For the second year in a row, Newport had come in, taken charge for a few months, then left behind a mess for the colonists to cope with.

Now it was December 1608, and Smith once again needed to figure out where the winter's food would come from. Hunting and fishing were possibilities, in theory, but there weren't enough capable hunters and fishermen in Jamestown to feed two hundred hungry mouths. "Though there be fish in the sea, fowls in the air, and beasts in the woods, their bounds [territories] are so large, they so wilde, and we so weake and ignorant, we cannot much trouble them," he had informed the company in his letter.

Smith elected to begin by collecting on the Nansemonds' debt.

Joined by Peter Winne and Matthew Scrivener, he went back to the Nansemond village to demand fulfillment of the harsh surrender terms he had imposed after beating back their ambush—namely, four hundred baskets of corn. The Nansemond *weroance* refused him; their own supplies were low, and Powhatan had ordered his tribes not to give the English any food for love or money. Smith resorted to his now customary tactics, frightening the villagers away with musket shots, and then setting fire to one of their homes. The message was clear: capitulate or the rest of the village would be next. As the thatch roof shot up in flames, the villagers called out for the men to stop and promised to give up half of the food they had. Smith accepted the offer, and by nightfall they had loaded the English barges. "How they collected it I know not," Smith mused. In return for Smith's forbearance, the Nansemonds promised to plant a field especially for the English the next season.[1]

Smith, Winne, and Scrivener camped four miles downriver, returning to Jamestown the following morning. There, Smith and Scrivener split up. Smith and Richard Waldo took two barges to the riverfront villages of various tribes, all of whom fled as they arrived; word of Smith's reprisal against the Nansemonds had traveled quickly. Finally, the Appomattocs gave them a modest amount of food—Smith understood it to be half of all they had left from their harvest—in exchange for "copper and such things as contented them." (Smith may have used strong-arm methods on the Appomattocs, as well, though this is unclear.) Scrivener and George Percy went on another barge and came back with nothing.

Back at the fort, Smith pondered their disappointing results. It was clear that time was working against the colonists. Powhatan had deemed it expedient to cut off the colony's food trade while biding his time and waiting for the English to starve.

A radical plan took shape in Smith's mind: he would lead a raid on the storehouses in Powhatan's own capital. He could draw on his observations of Werowocomoco's defenses from his captivity there a year before. It was the last thing Powhatan would expect. Waldo, who had impressed Smith as "sure in time of need," would be his second in command.

Waldo was in favor of the idea, but the rest of the council was not—not even Scrivener, whom Smith could usually count on for support. In all likelihood, they considered the idea audacious to the point of unreality, and it hardly squared with the company's desire to keep up good relations with the "naturals." Smith, for his part, was confident of success with the element of surprise on his side—and if he ran afoul of the company's preferences (not for the first time), the option of seeking forgiveness later was much more attractive than the alternative of starving now.

Shortly after the rejection of Smith's proposal, a breakthrough came in the form of a communication from Powhatan. If Smith would send him men to build an English-style house, along with a grindstone, fifty swords, some guns, a rooster and a hen (which were new to Virginia), copper, and beads, Powhatan would load his ship with food. In calling for swords and guns as part of the deal, Powhatan showed that he well understood the dire effect of his trade embargo; indeed, it was a vise tightening on the colony. Smith, mindful of the emperor's "devises and subtiltie," thought the offer might be a trap. Left with no palatable choice, however, Smith decided to give Powhatan what he wanted—minus the swords and guns.

Smith sent the German glassmakers and two Englishmen to begin work on Powhatan's house at first; then he sent a dozen more men, nearly all of them tradesmen and laborers. He directed one of the glassmakers to serve as a spy and take note of any clues to Powhatan's war preparations. After giving those men a head start to get the house under way, Smith appointed Scrivener as his substitute at the fort and made ready to travel to Werowocomoco with another two dozen men and Powhatan's goods.

Traveling by river on the *Discovery* and two barges, Smith stopped for the first night at the village of the Warraskoyacks, with whom he had established friendly relations on an earlier trip. The Warraskoyack chief, Tackonekintaco, cautioned Smith against continuing the journey: Powhatan may treat you well at first, he told Smith, but he has sent for you only for the chance to seize your weapons and cut your throats. Smith thanked him for the advice, but he had already decided to take his chances. He left the boy Samuel Collier in Tackonekintaco's care to learn the language as Thomas Savage had, and continued on.[2]

The next night, they stayed at the Kecoughtan village. Before they could shove off the next day, extreme winds and rain hit, and so they were forced to remain for the next week, celebrating Christmas 1608 among the "savages." Despite the blustery weather and the uncertainty as to whether they would come back alive—or perhaps because of that—it was as warm and joyous as any Christmas at home in England. "We were never more merry, nor fed on more plentie of good oysters, fish, flesh, wildfoul, and good bread," several of the voyagers remembered, "nor never had better fires in England, then in the dry smoky houses of Kecoughtan."

Unfavorable weather continued to hamper their travels as they made their way toward Werowocomoco, which they finally reached on January 12. After sitting down with the visitors for a welcoming meal, Powhatan asked when they would be on their way home, pretending ignorance of the message offering food for guns. Smith noticed that the messengers who had brought the offer were right there among them, and said so. "The president shewing him the men there present that brought him the message and conditions, asked Powhatan how it chanced that he became so forgetfull." Powhatan took this jovially and conceded the truth of the matter, but insisted that there was no deal without the guns and swords. To this, Smith replied with some posturing of his own:

> Though I had many courses to have made my provision, yet beleeving your promises to supply my wants, I neglected all to satisfie your desire: and to testifie my love, I send you my men for your building, neglecting mine owne. What your people had, you have engrossed, forbidding them for our trade: and now you thinke by consuming the time, we shall consume [die] for want. . . .3

As for guns and swords, Smith continued, Powhatan already knew that the colony could not spare any. "And you must know those I have can keepe me from want," he added archly. But he would not violate their friendship unless Powhatan forced him to with ill treatment.

Powhatan listened to this impassively, and told Smith he would spare what he could in a couple of days. But he had a grievance of his own. "Some doubt I have of your coming hither," he continued, "that makes me not so kindly seeke to relieve you as I would: for many do inform me, your coming hither is not for trade, but to invade my people, and possesse my country."

Strictly speaking, Powhatan was only half right. While the English did indeed mean to settle themselves in Virginia permanently, their conception at this point was to occupy only "waste ground"—territory the natives were not inhabiting. (When it came to waste ground, the marshy Jamestown peninsula was a prime specimen.) Support for dispossessing the natives outright would not come until later: four years after Powhatan's death, to be precise. In this, the emperor proved prescient.

Powhatan's rebuke was not meant as idle prophecy, though; it was a gambit to persuade Smith to disarm. Leave your weapons on your ships "to free us of this feare," he now admonished Smith. "Here they are needlesse."

Smith stuck to his guns, in both senses. That night, he and his men lodged in Werowocomoco. The Germans who had been working on Powhatan's house took the occasion to agree covertly on a course of action. They had been surprised by the comparative abundance and comfort that the natives enjoyed, and it was looking ever more appealing than the privation they had left behind in Jamestown. There was no real reason to believe their English hosts would even last through the winter. All of the Germans, including the man Smith had sent to spy on the Powhatans, concurred in the plan: to save their skins by turning against the English.

The next day, they made it known to the Powhatans that they wished to enter the emperor's service. Would he care to learn the details of the colony's defenses and its state of affairs? As expected, the Powhatans were very much interested. It was agreed that they would slow the construction of the house; the more the project was stretched out, the longer they would have cover for traveling between Jamestown and Werowocomoco.

Powhatan and Smith, meanwhile, got their negotiations started in Powhatan's bark-and-thatch home. The emperor opened with another try at inducing Smith to disarm. Where Newport's weakness was his eagerness to please, perhaps Smith's would be vainglory. Powhatan's tack this time, then, would be flattery. "Thinke you I am so simple, not to know it is better to eate good meate, lye well, and sleep merrily with my women and children, laugh and be merry with you, have copper, hatchets, or what I want, being your friend?" he asked. The alternative, he said, was to be "so hunted by you that I can neither rest, eate, nor sleep; but my tired men must watch, and if a twig but breake, every one cryeth, 'There commeth Captain Smith.' "

Surely Smith realized that Powhatan had no wish for such a life,

Powhatan observed. "Let this therefore assure you of our loves, and every yeare our friendly trade shall furnish you with corn; and now also, if you would come in friendly manner to see us, and not thus with guns and swords as to invade your foes."

Smith was always both impressed with and wary of Powhatan's "subtill" cunning. He would not be taken in so easily. "Had we intended you any hurt, long ere this we could have effected it," he riposted. "Your people coming to Jamestown are entertained with their bows and arrows without any exceptions; we esteeming it with you as it is with us, to wear our armes as our apparell." As for the corn, Smith put on a mask of indifference. If food was not forthcoming from Powhatan, he asserted, he could find it somewhere else. Powhatan's "friendly care" in that regard was "needlesse."4

As the two men continued in this vein, Smith concluded that Powhatan was merely passing the time while awaiting some preplanned attack. At the time, Smith had only one Englishman in the house with him—the "exceeding heavie" John Russell, one of the gentlemen-turned-lumberjacks from the previous year. (Russell had continued to earn Smith's respect with his hard work.) Smith felt they were vulnerable, and sent word for some of the men who were waiting on the boats to come to the house. Shortly afterward, Powhatan received the news that his own warriors were ready; he had several women distract Smith and Russell with conversation while he excused himself. Powhatan's men quietly ringed the building outside.

Smith became aware of the activity outside, possibly hearing the men's movements through the flimsy bark walls as they made footfalls in the snow. Smith indicated to Russell that they would be making a run for it. Russell followed Smith in pushing through the low-slung door. As Smith fired a warning shot from his pistol, the warriors backed away, and the two Englishmen sprinted flat out, with guns and shields in hand. They ran until they reached the cluster of Smith's men who were still making their way to the house. Now there were twenty of them altogether, with considerable firepower among them.

Seeing this, the natives claimed Smith had misunderstood. "With the uttermost of their excuses they sought to dissemble the matter," several English participants wrote later. An elderly man sent by Powhatan gave Smith a bracelet and a pearl chain, and explained that Powhatan had fled out of fear of their guns. The warriors, he said, were there to protect Powhatan's corn in case one of Smith's men tried to steal it—without Smith's knowledge, of course.

Smith's response is unknown. He was scarcely in a position to take umbrage at the idea, since, after all, he had just tried to sell the council in Jamestown on a plan to do more or less what Powhatan's messenger had just said. Nonetheless, he regarded the explanation as a lie and remained suspicious. When some native men brought heavy baskets of corn in trade for Smith's presents, they solemnly offered to guard the Englishmen's guns and swords while the English loaded their boats. The English cocked their guns and said, in effect, no thanks: *We'll* guard the weapons while *you* load the boats.5

By the time they had finished, the tide was out and the barges were grounded on mud. There was no choice but to spend another night. Both sides were still affecting friendliness, and the Powhatans welcomed Smith and his men back to their quarters from the night before.

After darkness fell, a visitor appeared at their door. Pocahontas, alone and shaken, had something to tell Smith. Her father, she said, would soon be sending dinner—and the men who brought it were going to kill the English with their own swords while they ate. If those men did not succeed in killing them, there would be a much larger attack afterward. "Therefore if we would live shee wished us presently to be gone."

Her forewarning Smith points toward strong feelings of attraction on her part—or, if not that, then some other extraordinarily powerful motive. She had gone far beyond a daughter's headstrong defiance: this time she was taking a reckless chance with her life. She had come through the woods in mortal fear of being detected. She knew that if a sentry spotted her and reported back to Powhatan, it would be the end for her. She had been his favorite daughter for a lifetime, but he would not be inclined toward leniency if she were caught in the act of treason. Worse, she now had to run the same risk going back.

That she had been drawn to Smith was unsurprising. He was a strong leader of his people, as her father was of his, and he was capable in the masculine arts of hunting and fighting, which Powhatan girls were brought up to admire. He did not seek her out, as a besotted boy of her own tribe would have done, yet he was approachable to her, and warm.

Smith, however, was oblivious to any change in Pocahontas from the easy friendliness of their conversations at the fort. He thanked her for her information and, falling upon old habits, offered her some beads and other English trinkets. That was a mistake.

As she saw the beads in Smith's hand, tears streaked down her face. The surprising hurt of his rewarding her like a trusty woodland guide evidently got the better of her, along with the grinding anxiety of her journey. As best she could, she explained that no, she could not accept the beads, because if her father were to find her carrying them, she would be as good as dead. "And so shee ran away by herselfe as she came."[6]

Pocahontas's warning soon came to fruition. Within an hour, eight or ten large, strong men brought platters of venison. Their more sophisticated approach to disarming the English suggests that they may have been tutored that day by the German renegades. Most of Smith's men had matchlock guns, whose firing mechanisms could not operate without a length of fiber cord—the "match"—that needed to be kept aflame. (Only a few officers, such as Smith, had the more modern snaphaunce guns, fired by flint and steel.) So the food bearers complained of the smoke from the match cords, and demanded that they be extinguished. It was a dubious request in a room that was perpetually smoky from the warming fire, but it showed an acute sense of the colonists' vulnerabilities.

Smith disregarded their demands and told them to taste every dish. Satisfied that the food was safe, Smith sent the men back to Powhatan with a sly message: they were expecting him and hoped he would come soon. The party then spent the night vigilantly in watches. The follow-on attack never came. The next morning, the two sides kept up the veneer of amicability, the English striving to appear as friendly to the Powhatans "as they to us." They sailed at high tide, and left behind Edward Brinton to shoot wildfowl for the Powhatans (and to serve as observer and informant for the English). The Germans stayed to continue work on the house, and more that Smith had not yet guessed at.

Practically as soon as the Englishmen left Werowocomoco, Powhatan returned. Two of the Germans, named Adam and Franz, either volunteered or were told to bring some weapons from Jamestown. They showed up at the fort and met with councilor Winne. They told him that their situation in Werowocomoco was fine, but that Smith had needed to take their weapons with him—could they have new ones? They also had a list of tools they required. Winne accepted the story and arranged for them to get what they asked for.

Six or seven colonists with kindred minds had decided that they, too, would be better off casting their lot with the Powhatans. They approached Adam and Franz, who confided that they could "live free of those miseries that would happen [to] the colony" if they brought Powhatan what he wanted: English weapons and metal tools. Adam and Franz then left for Werowocomoco with their prizes. The new coconspirators pilfered swords, guns, shot, and gunpowder from the fort, and sneaked off the next day.

When Adam and Franz reached Werowocomoco, two of the loyal Englishmen there—Richard Savage, one of the tradesmen, and Edward Brinton, the hunter—perceived that the Germans were arming the Powhatans. Savage and Brinton left to take this disturbing news to Jamestown, but Powhatan's men apprehended them on the way. Perhaps because the two were exceptionally useful, they were not put to death on the spot, but instead were merely kept under restraint for the time being.[7]

In the meantime, Smith and his men had taken stock of the outcome of their adventures in Werowocomoco. On the plus side, everybody was still in one piece; on the minus side, what they had bought was still not enough to get the colony through the winter. They would have to run the gauntlet again. Smith thought that Powhatan's brother, the powerful *weroance* Opechancanough, would have plenty, and might be prevailed upon to trade some of it—out of self-interest, to be sure, not love.

Two or three days after leaving Werowocomoco, the boats arrived at Opechancanough's village of Pamunkey. The chief welcomed his former prisoner genially. After some prodding from Smith, he sold the English what he had at a fair price (in Smith's estimation), and promised more to come if they would stay around. He then gave the visitors an oration "with a strained cheerfulness" as to the pains he had taken to help them in their hour of need—an oration that was interrupted by John Russell rushing in and telling Smith that they had all been betrayed. Hundreds of armed men were outside the house and in the fields beyond; Russell guessed there might be as many as seven hundred.

From Opechancanough's uneasy expression, Smith was sure he had deduced the nature of Russell's news. There was no time for discussion, but Smith could not resist venting against those who had condemned him for being too hard on the natives. "I could wish those here, that make these seeme saints, and me an oppressor," he groused to his men. Recovering himself, he assured them they would get out all right; their adversaries would scramble away at the sound of gunfire. Yet if they started killing every native within shooting distance, they would have nothing to show for it but dead natives—and no food. Be ready to "fight like men," he exhorted. "But first, I will deale with them."[8]

Smith challenged Opechancanough to a man-to-man fight with his choice of weapons. Opechancanough hastened to assure Smith that the men outside were there only to bring him a special present. Smith ordered one of his men to look out the door to see what was afoot, but the man was too scared to do it. Although the rest of Smith's men quickly volunteered to go, Smith's fury at the coward had already led him to a more belligerent plan. He surprised Opechancanough by grabbing the long knotted lock of hair hanging from the left side of his head, and put a pistol to his breast. He marched the chief outside, to the astonishment of the assembled crowd. Still grasping the chief's hair, he shouted out an oration of his own.

"I see the great desire you have to kill me," he began. He had made a vow of friendship to them last winter, he said, and his God would protect him as long as he kept it. But if they shed so much as "one drop of bloud of any of my men, or steal the least of these beads or copper . . . I will not cease revenge"—that is, not until he had hunted down every last person who admitted to being a Pamunkey. One way or another, he was going home with food:

> If I be the marke [target] you aim at, here I stand,
> shoot he that dare. You promised to fraught my ship
> ere I departed, and so you shall, or I meane to load her
> with your dead carcasses. Yet if as friends you will come
> and trade, I once more promise not to trouble you,
> except you give me the first occasion.[9]

By this time, the chief had submitted, and his men had put down their weapons. Smith and his party would leave Pamunkey enriched with rations. "Men may thinke it strange there should be such a stirre for a little corne," four of the colonists wrote, "but had it been gold, with more ease we might have got it."[10] He had lost no one and killed no one. His men felt an overwhelming sense of relief when they realized they had gotten out alive—a sense of relief recalled by the second verse of a poem that several of them later wrote in appreciation of their leader:

> Pamaunkees king we saw thee captive make
> Among seaven hundred of his stoutest men,
> To murther thee and us resolved; when
> Fast by the hayre thou ledst this salvage grim,
> Thy pistoll at his breast to governe him:
> Which did infuse such awe in all the rest
> (Sith their dread soveraigne thou had'st so distrest)
> That thou and we (poore sixteene) safe retir'd
> Unto our helplesse ships.[11]

Shortly before the colonists sailed from Pamunkey, another Englishman joined the group. Richard Wiffin, gentleman, had spent three days looking for Smith, relying on "extraordinary bribes" to shake his pursuers and get information on Smith's whereabouts. He came with bad news: there had been an accident with one of the barges, which had overturned on the frigid waters of the James. Two of the councilors, Matthew Scrivener and Peter Waldo, had died along with nine other men. Smith swore Wiffin to secrecy so as not to dispirit the rest of the group; he had more stops to make before returning to the fort to deal with the damage.

At the villages of the Youghtanund and Mattaponi tribes, Smith's party searched for food, and learned from the ordinary people that they simply had none to spare. The "teares from the eyes of women and children" convinced Smith that to try to trade with them would be fruitless, and to roll out his practices of intimidation against these needy tribes would be a cruelty. He moved on.

He had no such compunctions, though, about returning to Werowocomoco to mount a surprise attack on Powhatan's stores. When he had brought up the idea with the council, he had been voted down. Now virtually all of the council was either gone to England or dead. With the drowning of Scrivener and Waldo, only Peter Winne was left. Smith, with his two votes as president, did not need the council's permission any longer; he *was* the council.

Smith sent Wiffin and Thomas Coe ahead to reconnoiter the capital. When they came back, what they had to report was a shock: Powhatan had cleared out with his wives and children to an unknown location with all of his food. Smith still did not know Powhatan had well-informed spies; the Germans had revealed Smith's proposal for raiding Werowocomoco, and Powhatan had taken no chances.

When Smith returned to the fort, he found—predictably, by this point—that little good had happened in his absence. The food in the stores had become infested with rats and worms (the rats, incidentally, had been brought over by the English ships). Most of the tools and a good many of the weapons had disappeared, having been spirited away and turned over to the Powhatans. With the food that Smith and his men had brought back, there was enough to carry the colony through the next harvest. Now that Smith was fully in charge, however, some things were going to change. He called an assembly of all the colonists and told them bluntly that neither his own efforts nor the investors' money could support them forever while they sat on their hands:

> I speake not this to all of you, for divers of you I know deserve both honour and reward, better then is yet here to be had. But the greater part must be more industrious, or starve, how ever you have been heretofore tollerated by the authoritie of the councell. . . . You see now that power resteth wholly in my selfe: you must obey this now for a law, that he that will not worke shall not eate (except by sicknesse he be disabled), for the labours of thirtie or fortie honest and industrious men shall not be consumed to maintaine an hundred and fiftie idle loyterers. . . . There are now no more counsellers to protect you. . . .[12]

He that will not work shall not eat. The new operating principle of the colony was alien to the "loyterers," but it proved effective. Within three months, the men had built twenty houses, dug a well that brought clean, fresh water, and planted thirty or forty acres. In the latter endeavor, they had the help of two native prisoners, by the names of Kemps and Tassore, who had been treated well enough that they took it upon themselves to teach the English native methods of planting. Smith commanded the building of a checkpoint at the neck of the peninsula, guarded at all times by a well-armed garrison that allowed neither Englishmen nor natives to cross without his orders. With that measure, the mysterious pilfering of the colony's weapons and tools came to an end, and the colonists no longer lived in fear of petty raids as they had the year before.

In the springtime, work was under way on a new hillside fort; Spanish attack was still a worry, and the fort was intended as a highly defensible retreat in case that happened. In the midst of the project, Smith received a spot of bad news. Much of his hard-won corn had been put away in casks for later use—and someone had just discovered that those casks were infested by the English rats. The rats had multiplied to such an extent that there was no hope of saving what little corn was left.

The loss was not the dire crisis that it would have been in the cold months, but it was crisis enough. Smith opted to emulate the natives, who, he noticed, took a divide-and-survive approach when their food ran low by dispersing into small groups. The colonists, he decided, would do the same. Around a third of them went downriver to live on oysters; twenty went to a place near the mouth of the bay to fish; another twenty went upriver. They would be exposed and vulnerable to attack there, but it was a necessary gamble. Smith reduced the risks somewhat by sending the men far enough that they would not be within the range of the colony's most hostile neighbors. To hedge his bets further, Smith sent some men away to live temporarily with friendly tribes, who hosted them in exchange for copper.[13]

The gamble paid off: no attacks came, and no one died of starvation. A group of natives—their tribe was not recorded—brought daily presents of squirrels, turkeys, and deer. Some of the Englishmen rose to the occasion of their own accord, gathering "more sturgeon then could be devoured by dog and man," along with herbs and fruits. Others had to be compelled. "Such was the strange condition of some 150," Smith noted, "that had they not been . . . forced to gather and prepare their victuall they would all have starved or eaten one another." These "lubberly gluttons," as he called them, demanded that Smith sell the colony's swords, guns, even its cannon, to enable them to live off the natives' food in idleness. They would have sold their very souls, Smith marveled, for a half basket of corn that would have lasted them less than a week.

A gentleman named William Dyer—"a most craftie knave"—

organized another plot to make off with the *Discovery*. Someone tipped off Smith, and Dyer was "worthily punished" (probably by whipping). Smith called together the rest of the colonists and told them of the collapse of Dyer's scheme. The next time, Smith added, he would not be so forgiving; if anyone else wished to try their luck at commandeering the ship, "let him assuredly look to arrive at the gallows." And if they considered themselves too elevated in their stations to partake of the same fruits and wild animals that the natives ate, it was no one's problem but theirs. "This salvage trash you so scornfully repine at; being put in your mouthes your stomackes can digest. If you would have better, you should have brought it."

While Smith was attacking the colony's troubles in his usual truculent form, ambitious plans had been moving forward in London, unknown to him or anyone else in Jamestown. Those plans were about to bring him new challenges.

From Smith's reports and others, the officers of the company had come to believe that they were taking the wrong approach. First of all, they decided, they had been thinking on too small a scale. Where they had been sending colonists over in little dribs and drabs, only to see most of them die off, they now believed the answer was to plant a comparatively massive group that would be harder to dislodge—whether by famine, disease, native attack, or Spanish invasion. With that group, moreover, would go a greater number of practical men, such as fishermen, bird hunters, and carpenters; the company had assimilated that much of Smith's critique.

Conceiving a large expedition and talking about it was all very easy. To make it happen in the real world, the company needed a new round of funding. This time, the shares would be offered to the public at large; the offering price would be twelve pounds, ten shillings per share. The company hit on an effective promotion strategy: enlisting clergymen—who believed the New World ripe for Christian evangelism—to support the stock offering by spreading the word from their pulpits.

"They have collected in 20 days an amount of money for this voyage that frightens me," the ever watchful Don Pedro de Zúñiga informed King Philip III. The campaign enlisted some 659 individuals as shareholders, including some who had invested in the first round. These ranged from peers and knights to merchants and ordinary citizens. In addition, fifty-six London companies and guilds bought shares, among them the Company of Grocers, the Company of Fish-mongers, and the Company of Brewers. Another six hundred or so people had agreed to venture themselves, so to speak—that is, to go to Virginia as colonists in return for one share of stock. All of these "adventurers" of purse or person were entitled to a payout at the end of seven years: a grant of land, plus, in the hopeful words of the stock certificates, their proportionate share of "such mines, and mineralls of gold, silver, and other metall or treasure . . . or profitts whatsoever which shall be obteyned."[14]

Various promotional tracts emphasized the economic possibilities of the colony, and the commendable civic and religious spirit of those who supported it. One of these tracts, entitled *A Good Speed to Virginia*, gave assurance that the natives, although "savage and incredibly rude [primitive]," are "by nature loving and gentle, and desirous to imbrace a better condition." There would be no repetition of Spanish brutality by the English; "farre be it from the nature of the English, to exercise any bloudie crueltie amongst these people." To allay any qualms that investors might have regarding the rights of the natives (and, tacitly, the risk of interference from them), the author explained:

> There is no intendment to take away from them by force that rightfull inheritance which they have in that countrey, for they are willing to entertaine us, and have offered to yielde into our handes on reasonable conditions, more lande then we shall be able this long time to plant and manure: and out of all question uppon easie composition with them, wee may have as much of their countrey yielded unto us, by lawful grant from them, as wee can or will desire, so that we goe to live peaceably among them, and not to supplant them. . . .[15]

It was a reasonable description of the company's intentions, but a largely fictitious version of the natives' receptivity.

Apart from raising the funds and recruiting the voyagers for a large-scale expedition, the company realized that it needed to change the terms of its royal charter. As things stood, the local management scheme in Virginia gave the president too little power vis-à-vis the council. This diluted authority was standing in the way of effective action. The company asked for and received a new charter, made final on May 23, 1609, which replaced the current Virginia president and council with a single governor.

In many ways, Smith was the obvious person for this new position. Through observation of the natives' culture, plus sheer force of will, he had battled the Grim Reaper and his scythe to a standstill. But he would not be the leader under the new charter. Indeed, it is improbable that he was ever seriously considered. He had ended up in charge through the twists and turns of events in Virginia, not by the choice of the company. Now the company was undoubtedly eager to install someone who would inspire the confidence of investors. Edward-Maria Wingfield had fit the bill; the lowborn young soldier from Lincolnshire did not.

Beyond that, Smith had another deficiency: he lacked the patience and the diplomacy to hide his disgust with the foolishness of influential people. Smith valued effectiveness over internal politics, but could not understand that playing internal politics was sometimes part and parcel of effectiveness. Hence, one leader after another had gone back to England as his antagonist—Wingfield, Newport, Archer, and Ratcliffe, among others. Smith's conspicuous lack of collegiality kept him from rising far in the clubby reaches of the Virginia Company. He had proven himself in handling the natives (although a touch harshly for the company's tastes), and the company would be eager to keep him in that capacity, but that was all.

Instead, the company's choice for governor was Sir Thomas Gates, another veteran of the Dutch war of independence. He had commanded English troops in Ireland, and earlier served as a lieutenant in the fleet of Sir Francis Drake that rescued the first Roanoke expedition in 1586. He was well known to the company, having been a charter investor, with Wingfield, in 1606.[16] The following year, as the company had planned it, Gates would become second in command, superseded by Thomas West, Lord De La Warr, whose title would be Lord Governor and Captain General.

Smith received an inkling of the changes on July 13, when a ship under the command of Samuel Argall pulled in. Argall would prove, in time, to be one of the more odious characters of the period. For now, he was just finishing an innocuous mission to test a new, more direct route across the Atlantic—heading west from the Canaries to North America without a stopover in the Caribbean. Although the revamped charter had not been in final form by the time Argall left England in early May, he was able to give Smith some generalities about the new regime and the huge resupply expedition that would come later in the year. Argall found the colonists in good health, though he was surprised to find that many of them were dispersed from Jamestown, either billeted among the natives or living off the oyster beds as they awaited their fall corn harvest.

Before sailing up the river, Argall had evidently loitered in the bay to do some fishing. By chance, he encountered a Spanish ship under Captain Francisco Fernández de Écija, on a mission to gather intelligence about the English presence. (Zúñiga had finally persuaded Philip III to order that much.) Argall shadowed the Spaniards in the bay until they broke off and fled. Assuming Argall related the incident to the company, it would have added to the general jumpiness in London about Spain's intentions. "Those who have embarked their capital . . . are afraid that the Spanish will end by making the same slaughter of these as they did of the French in the same Indies," the Venetian ambassador had reported to his government, "nor are they confident that, if the necessity arose, the king would show himself openly in their defense."

Smith, for his part, could only have been surprised and disappointed by the news of the forthcoming change in command. Possibly with an eye toward snaring the leadership job—or, rather, keeping it— he drafted another letter to the company. He knew from Argall that his replacement had already been chosen, but he may well have assumed there was time to change that. He wrote again of the causes of the colony's problems and the need for more "men and meanes."[17]

On August 11, before Argall could return with Smith's letter, the first four ships of the resupply (or the "third supply," as it became known) entered the mouth of the James River. They had come much sooner than either Argall or Smith expected. Informed by sentries that ships had been sighted, Smith assumed they were Spanish and ordered the colony to stand armed and ready for an attack. They turned out to be the *Blessing*, the *Falcon*, the *Unity*, and the *Lion*, bearing several hundred men, women, and children, plus provisions.

Instead of waiting for temperate weather, the company had sent the ships off in early June, as soon as the money was collected and the ink dried on the charter. As a result, the voyagers crossed the Atlantic on their tropical route with the summertime sun straight overhead. Heatstroke was widespread, and thirty-two bodies had to be thrown overboard. Two baby boys were born at sea, and died there.

Soon Smith would wish the ships had been Spanish attackers after all. Four more ships were coming, he learned. The fleet had become caught in a hurricane in the West Indies, and so the eight ships were temporarily separated. (A ninth ship had also sailed from England, but turned back about six days out.) Soon John Sicklemore, alias Ratcliffe, would be back in Jamestown, along with George Percy. Christopher Newport would be arriving on the flagship, the *Sea Venture*. Gabriel Archer was already there, having sailed on the *Blessing*. Excepting Edward-Maria Wingfield, it would be a reunion of practically all of the leaders that Smith had quarreled with or offended over the past two years. Also on the flagship would be Smith's replacement, Thomas Gates.

The *Diamond* arrived in a few days with Ratcliffe (he of the "pallace" in the woods), and the *Swallow* landed three or four days after that. Archer recorded that Smith "gave not any due respect to many worthy gentlemen that came in our ships."[18] That was an understatement of Smith's feelings on the matter.

While the colonists waited for Gates's ship, the senior men among the new arrivals delivered their demand to Smith: step down. Under the new charter, he was relieved of his duties. Reading between the lines of the surviving accounts, Smith seems to have said, fine, show me the charter. As it happened, the sealed box with the charter and company's orders to Gates was also on the flagship. Smith then appears, in essence, to have shrugged; as far as he was concerned, they were still operating under the first charter until the alleged second charter turned up. Although he had long criticized the sailors of the various expeditions for undermining the colonists' trade with the natives, he found it expedient this time to form an alliance with the sailors to protect his authority. In any case, his one-year term of office was due to run out shortly, on September 10.

He would have been more dismayed by the changes if he could have seen the company's orders. On the plus side, the company showed that it had been persuaded by his cautions regarding the natives. "If you hope to winne them and to provide for your selves by trade," the orders instructed, "you will be deceived for already your copper is embased by your abundance and neglect of prizing it, and they will never feed you but for feare." But Smith's own role was to shrink dramatically, far beyond his loss of his presidency. The company wanted to keep him on, but on its own terms. To be exact, the rescuer of English America and dominator of the Powhatans was to have command of a small lookout garrison near the mouth of the James, some thirty miles away.

In a ham-handed effort to soothe Smith's ruffled pride, the company claimed that this was actually what he wanted—and was by no means to be mistaken for a demotion: "To this commaunde wee desire Captain Smythe may be allotted as well for his earnest desire as the greate confidence & trust that we have in his care & diligence." Smith was also named as a member of the colony's new nine-member council, which was now strictly advisory, not having any "bindinge or negative" power on the governor.[19]

Gradually, the colonists realized that the *Sea Venture* was not going to appear, ever. None of the other ships had seen it after the hurricane. The notion that it was going to be spotted the next morning, or the morning after that, was recognized as wishful thinking. Smith's antagonists gave grudging acceptance to his opinion that the first charter still controlled for the time being, and he would be permitted to finish out what little was left of his term.

Fed up with infighting, Smith then turned his office over to John Martin, the former councilor, who had come back on the *Falcon*. Notwithstanding Martin's record of gold lust, sickliness, and general inadequacy, Smith regarded him as the least objectionable of the newcomers. After a few hours of dealing with the demands of the colony's "unruly gallants," however, Martin reconsidered whether he really wanted to be president—and turned that hot potato back over to Smith.

The leaders from the third supply then agreed that after Smith's term elapsed, Francis West would serve as provisional president in Gates's absence while they figured out what to do. (West's only apparent qualification was that he happened to be the twenty-three-year-old younger brother of Thomas West, the future Lord Governor and Captain General.) Smith, meanwhile, ruminated on his "ill chance to end when he had but only learned how to begin."[20]

9

THE STARVING TIME

❧

At some point in early 1609, Smith was alerted to the role of the German traitors in bringing English weapons to the Powhatans. After an abortive attempt to secure their return to Jamestown for punishment, Smith sent word to the Germans that they would be pardoned if they came back of their own accord. Although the offer was an unusual one for him, he may have looked around at the talent he had on hand and decided it was a necessity: better to forgive and forget if that was the price of bringing more practical men onto the scene. Or he may have felt pressure from the company not to stand in the way of its experiment with Virginia glassmaking. Whatever the reasons for his offer, two of the men, Adam and Franz, took him up on it in July, around the time Samuel Argall arrived.

Within a month, however, Adam and Franz shifted their loyalties again. They absconded to the new capital that Powhatan had established at Orapakes (which was farther from the English, and therefore safer for the chief of chiefs). There, they told Powhatan of the expected coming of a new supply, and of a new leader who was rumored to be a lord. They proposed to collect intelligence about the vulnerabilities of the strengthened colony. Powhatan considered this and then answered them curtly through an interpreter: "You that would have betrayed Captaine Smith to mee, will certainely betray me to this great lord for your peace." With that, he ordered Adam and Franz's execution, and his men beat out their brains with clubs.[1]

In Jamestown, during the waning weeks of Smith's presidency, Smith faced a knotty question regarding the several hundred newcomers: should he continue his policy of dispersing the colonists, or keep as many of them as possible in Jamestown? Dispersing the colonists put more food within reach while consolidating them near the fort kept them safer from attack. (He could have embraced a third alternative—to defer making a decision, so that the issue became someone else's problem—but it is doubtful that he seriously considered it.)

Smith opted for dispersal, a choice probably favored by the senior men of the latest supply; with new outposts beyond Jamestown, there would be additional leadership positions for them. Whether Smith knew it or not, the plan also fit with the company's desire to build up new outposts.

Thus, Smith sent John Martin and George Percy with roughly sixty colonists to settle in Nansemond territory downriver, and sent Francis West upriver with somewhere between 120 and 140 colonists of West's choosing to settle near the town called Powhatan, ruled by the emperor's son Parahunt. The town was located by the falls in present-day Richmond, on the perimeter of the Powhatan Empire. With ten weeks' worth of rations in the storehouse and a newly gathered harvest, and with plenty more wild game, fish, and berries there for the foraging, a little prudence was all it would take for the colony to muddle through another winter.

Dispersing the colonists had been a necessary risk in the spring when food supplies were down to nothing. It was still risky now. The English were technically at peace with local tribes, but the peace was more a result of intimidation than any feelings of friendship on the part of the natives. Neither of the settlements would be close enough to receive timely help from Jamestown in case of an attack. For the policy to work, the leaders of the outposts would have to be capable survivalists and able to deal on a practical level with the natives. The risks were magnified by the fact that, as a political matter, Smith was stuck with choosing the leaders from among the worthies sent by London, rather than his own trusted and proven men.

The combination of people and policy was problematic from the outset. Shortly after Martin and Percy landed in Nansemond country, they led an attack on the natives. A group of Smith's supporters claimed that the Nansemonds had treated the interlopers amicably, and that Martin and Percy had attacked out of nothing more than fear. Percy claimed that the *casus belli* was the disappearance of two messengers who had been sent to negotiate with the Nansemonds for the purchase of a populated island near their settlement. When the messengers did not return, Percy said, he and Martin assumed the worst and decided to take the island by force. In either case, in Percy's words, they "beat the savages out of the island, burned their houses, ransacked their temples, took down the corpses of their dead kings from off their tombs, and carried away their pearls, copper, and bracelets wherewith they do decorate their kings' funerals." The Nansemonds, who had formerly submitted to Smith's terms of surrender, no longer saw much benefit to peaceable coexistence.

Colonists under Martin's command captured a son of Parahunt and held him as a prisoner on the island. While the man was tied down, a young sailor picked up a pistol and accidentally shot him in the chest—at least, Percy said it was an accident. The wound was not fatal; the agitated prisoner managed to break loose from the cords with which he had been tied, dive into the river, and swim across to the mainland with blood streaming behind him.[2]

It is tempting to conclude that Smith had Machiavellian purposes in sending Martin, Percy, and West out as commanders—calculating that their ineptitude would ensure their failure, thereby strengthening Smith's own power. Yet the reality is that Smith took an interest in the welfare of the new settlements. After receiving no reports from West's company, he headed to the falls to see how those men were faring. On his way, he was puzzled to notice West himself sailing back to Jamestown.

When Smith arrived, he found out why West had fled: attacks from Parahunt's men had been constant. Smith found an inspired solution, sending word to Parahunt that he wanted to buy the town. Parahunt was agreeable to relocating himself and his villagers for a suitable quantity of copper, plus English protection from the Monacans beyond the falls. It was an attractive deal for the colonists, inasmuch as the town was on higher ground than the area West had chosen (which was periodically inundated by the river) and was bordered by hundreds of acres of good farming fields. A fourteen-year-old Englishman named Henry Spelman would stay with Parahunt to learn the Algonquian language. Parahunt's people would be obliged to leave behind their lodgings for the colonists to move into, and to pay an annual tribute to the English for their defense.

The new arrivals would have none of it, however. Like earlier colonists, they were obsessed with "great guilded hopes" of gold mines, and they had little interest in moving into native dwellings to tend crops. "Both this excellent place and those good conditions did those furies refuse, contemning both him, his kind care and authoritie," wrote two of Smith's supporters. He stayed for nine days to attempt to defuse the situation. With only five men under his command, he found it a challenge to save his own skin, let alone to impose government on West's 120 settlers. "That disorderlie company so tormented those poore naked soules [the natives], by stealing their corne, robbing their gardens, beating them, breaking their houses, and keeping some prisoners, that they daillie complained to Captaine Smithe he had brought them protectors worse inimies then the Monacans themselves."

Smith was sympathetic, but felt there was nothing he could do. Percy would claim that Smith had "incensed and animated the savages against Captain West and his company." It is safe to assume that the colonists successfully incensed the natives without the need of Smith's help. Smith finally gave up on West's men and sailed toward Jamestown.

Now events in the colony became more convoluted than usual. Before getting far, Smith's boat ran aground. The delay led him to think better of abandoning the situation, and he went back with his five men. In the meantime, a dozen of Parahunt's men had raided the settlement almost as soon as Smith left. Making quick work of the colonists' ineffectual defense, the raiders had liberated the prisoners held in West's makeshift fort and killed some men they found in the woods.

On his return, Smith found the colonists terrified by the "poore sillie assault"—so much so that the greater part of them were ready to accept Smith's rule. He ordered the arrest of six or seven of the chief mutineers and directed the rest to settle in Parahunt's empty, "readie built" town, which he named Non-such. He made peace again with Parahunt.

As Smith prepared to leave, Francis West—bravely absent until then—came ashore and soon took umbrage at what had been done without his involvement. West and the arrested mutineers incited the other colonists back into factionalism, and into dreams of finding El Dorado on the James. As they abandoned Non-such and filed back to the open-air homes of West's low-lying settlement (probably tents), Smith realized his aid had been an exercise in futility. West and his company were beyond help.3

Smith started downriver a second time with his men, and stretched out for a doze during the seventy-four-mile trip. At some point, a spark or a cinder from someone's pipe or musket matchcord went astray and landed badly: Smith had lain down still wearing his powder bag, which was ignited into a flash of searing heat. The flame, wrote several colonists, "tore the flesh from his body and thighes, nine or ten inches square in a most pitifull manner; but to quench the tormenting fire he leaped over-boord into the deepe river." He was nearly drowned before his men could pull him out.4

This time, there was no doctor on board to treat him. His men rushed him back to the fort, where he was carried to his quarters. There was no doctor at the fort, either. Dr. Walter Russell, credited with saving him from the stingray's poison a little more than a year earlier, was no longer on the scene, nor was the colony's other doctor, Anthony Bagnall. (They may have been part of the group dispersed to Nansemond.) Smith was unable to stand, and was helpless against his excruciating pain, which had rendered him "neere bereft of his senses." In that state, he either saw or imagined he saw a man with a pistol who had been sent to finish him off. The assassin (or phantasm of Smith's mind) took pity on his intended victim, however, and stopped short of firing on him.

Although still in agony, Smith recovered sufficiently to be able to assess his circumstances. In the new charter, London had taken his presidency away from him—based on what shortcoming in his loyal service, he did not know. The leaders of the third supply were openly planning to usurp his authority, or what was left of it. In early September, shortly before the end of his term of office, he sent for the masters of the six ships that were to leave for England the next day, and secured a place for himself on board.5

Smith's antagonists, unenthusiastic about the idea of him speaking freely in London and pointing fingers, ordered the ships not to leave yet. For the next several weeks, when the council ought to have focused on building up the food stocks, it instead spent its time collecting denunciations of Smith from everyone he had ever punished or contended with. One or more of the survivors among the German turncoats testified that Smith had tried to do them in with rat poison.

Others accused him of trying to starve them by sending them to the oyster banks, rather than letting them live off the (nonexistent) rations at the fort. "Some that knewe not anything to say, the councel instructed, and advised what to swear."

The most intriguing accusation came from an unnamed "propheticall spirit" (as two of Smith's supporters sarcastically put it), who accused him of scheming to inherit Powhatan's kingdom by marrying his daughter. Smith's attitude toward Pocahontas was platonic from all appearances, and there was no reason to suspect otherwise. In any case, he knew he would not have stood to inherit the role of *mamanatowick*, or emperor, by marrying Pocahontas. Neither she nor her husband would be in the line of succession, which—radically different from the European model—went from Powhatan to his brothers, to his sisters, and then to his sisters' children.

Pocahontas herself had saddening news in store. After Smith's departure, the colonists told any natives who inquired that he was dead. Pocahontas heard this and accepted it as true.[6] She turned her back on the colony, and would not return to it for another four years.

Shortly before the ships cast off, John Ratcliffe gave one of the captains a letter for Robert Cecil, earl of Salisbury, a member of the Virginia Company council in London. Ratcliffe reported that the *Sea Venture* with Sir Thomas Gates and Christopher Newport was feared lost—a harsh blow from the company's point of view. Smith, he noted, had refused at first to give up authority to the new arrivals. "This man," he added snidely, "is sent home to answere some misdemeanors whereof I perswade me he can scarcely clear him selfe from great imputation of blame." Ratcliffe closed by mentioning that it was rather a lot of trouble to clear the wooded ground for planting, and so could the company send a year's food supply?[7]

Smith's thoughts on the occasion are unrecorded. One imagines him waiting for the ship to be untied from its mooring—a tree or two perched on the edge of the Jamestown peninsula—and then asking a crewman to prop him up for a view of the fort as it receded into the distance. His emotions were likely still raw and confused, a brew of outrage, betrayal, and bewilderment that kept his bile close to the surface. No doubt his plans for the future, while still inchoate, centered on an intention to get to the bottom of why he had been passed over. Then it would surely be a simple matter to straighten things out with the company, and ultimately return to Jamestown with responsibility befitting his talents. Gates, after all, was lost at sea. As for men like Ratcliffe and Archer who had crossed him, well, they would be sorry soon enough—or so Smith must have mused.

Then there were the thoughts of those Smith had left behind. A total of roughly five hundred colonists were in Jamestown now, the majority of whom were newcomers who neither knew nor cared about his monumental contributions. Like most new arrivals before them over the past two and a half years, they were looking forward to lives of idle leisure supported by supplies from London, food from the natives, and gold from the ground. Smith's supporters, who had lived through Virginia winters and summers, knew better. There was no free emigration from Virginia, and unlike Smith, they had not been blessed with a passport home. For them, his departure could only presage worse times to come. William Fettiplace, a colonist who served under Smith's command in the death-defying expedition to Werowocomoco in January, marked the occasion with an account that reads like a manual of leadership:

> What shall I say? But thus we lost him, that in all his proceedings, made justice his first guide, and experience his second; ever hating baseness, sloth, pride, and indignitie, more then any dangers; that never allowed more for himselfe, then his souldiers with him; that upon no danger would send them where he would not lead them himselfe; that would never see us want [in want of] what either he had, or could by any meanes get us . . . whose adventures were our lives, and whose losse our deathes.[8]

The council consisted of George Percy, John Martin, Francis West, and Ratcliffe, with "some few of the best and worthyest" of the rest acting as advisers. The majority of the councilors thought better of putting West in charge, as they had intended to do, and instead elected Percy to take the helm. Percy, twenty-nine, was from the nobility—he was the eighth son of an earl—and had studied at Oxford and the Middle Temple, one of London's Inns of Court. Because he was not the eldest son, he had not inherited the estate that would have enabled him to continue living in high style and free of monetary worries. That was very likely the reason he had turned up, for the second time, on the shores of the New World, where gold always seemed to be just around the corner.

Like Smith, Percy had put in a stint fighting in the Netherlands, but otherwise the two men could not have been more different. Percy derided his predecessor as "an ambitious, unworthy and vainglorious fellow"; ambition being a character flaw in the mind of the seventeenth-century English gentleman, it is unsurprising that it took first place in Percy's list of epithets. Where Smith thought it necessary for Englishmen to adapt to the realities of a different land, Percy, like so many others, preferred to bring the ways of London society to Virginia. He felt obliged to maintain, as he put it, "a continual and daily [dining] table" in Jamestown "for gentlemen of fashion"—and then had to ask his eldest brother to pay the bills. He also sent home for, and received, a new wardrobe comporting with the august nature of his position: five suits, adorned in front with taffeta and stiffened with canvas; a dozen pairs of shoes, stockings, and socks, plus ribbon for shoestrings; six pairs of boots; nine pairs of gloves; a dozen shirts from Holland; three hats ("2 with silke and goulde bands"); a dozen handkerchiefs; six nightcaps; a sword "hatched with goulde"; and six pairs of garters.9

Yet Percy was by no means an unintelligent man. His writings are those of an articulate person with reasonably acute powers of observation. He may well have been a competent mediocrity within his natural element, that is, noble English society. In the autumn of 1609, however, he was far from his natural element, and he was soon to be plunged into a situation for which neither his education nor his social background had prepared him.

Once the natives comprehended that Smith was out of the picture, Powhatan saw an opportunity to wage war on the colony, and he took it. An anonymous witness wrote that the natives "all revolted, and did murder and spoile [make spoil of, plunder] all they could incounter." John Martin left the settlement at Nansemond to join Percy in Jamestown, ostensibly to deal with the colony's business. Percy suspected the real reason was that Martin had been spooked by the surprise attacks that the natives had started to mount against the settlement. Jamestown, with its fortification and its narrow point of access at the neck of the peninsula, was by far the safer place to be.

If Percy's hunch was right (and there is no reason to doubt it), then Martin, with his cowardice, showed a good instinct for self-preservation. Martin had deputized Lieutenant Michael Sicklemore—no apparent relation to John Sicklemore, alias Ratcliffe—to take charge at Nansemond in his absence. As the attacks continued there, seventeen of the men decided to follow Martin's example; they made off with a boat and fled from the settlement. They did not prove as fortunate as their erstwhile leader. None of the seventeen deserters were heard from again, and it is likely they were captured and killed.

Sicklemore and an unknown number of his men then went on an expedition from the settlement, apparently to attempt to trade for food. Within a few days, someone from the settlement came across them: all dead, their mouths stuffed full of bread. *Here* was their food. It was the natives' suitably mordant expression of scorn for the self-superior foreigners who came to them in weakness, and a warning to any who might follow in search of relief. The scene was reminiscent of the treatment given almost a century earlier, in 1514, to Spanish colonists under the command of Pedro Arias de Ávila in present-day Panama. The natives there, weary of the Spaniards' gold-seeking, took to capturing them alive and pouring molten gold down their throats.[10]

The rest of the colonists at Nansemond withdrew to Jamestown for safety. Around the same time, Francis West and the rest of the colonists at the falls came back to Jamestown after a series of fatal attacks there. Percy had earlier sent Ratcliffe to Point Comfort, near the bay, with a detachment to build a fort (the command that the company's instructions had given as a sop to Smith); Ratcliffe and his men were safe there, and so there they stayed. But as for the rest, Percy now had a problem: how to keep everyone fed through the winter?

The council had spent most of September on its hearings against Smith, and nobody had shown much industriousness in the meantime. With the collapse of the settlements at the falls and Nansemond, no one would be foraging from there. All fourteen of the colony's fishing nets had been allowed to rot in the water and were useless. The harvest had been eaten. The storehouse had been drawn down to support the sailors from six ships for the extra time they had been kept waiting. Daniel Tucker, the cape merchant, or supply officer, informed Percy that there was no more than three months' rations left—and that was assuming a meager allowance for each man of half a can of meal a day.

The solution seemed to come in the form of a communiqué from Chief Powhatan. Powhatan had sent Thomas Savage, escorted by four or five native men, as a bearer of a gift of venison to Percy. A few weeks later, probably in November, Powhatan followed up by sending Henry Spelman either to Percy at Jamestown or to Ratcliffe at Point Comfort (the accounts are unclear) with a message of friendship and an invitation to visit and trade for part of their harvest. It was a godsend. With Percy's approval, Ratcliffe took fifty men by ship to call on Powhatan at Orapakes.

Powhatan received Ratcliffe with all the courtesies of local protocol. Ratcliffe reciprocated. In doing so, however, he made a mistake right at the start, by failing to insist on the usual trading of hostages as a guarantee of good behavior. It was seemingly a repetition of the habit he had developed during his presidency the previous year: trying to build up an image of lordliness for himself among the natives by giving away the store. Perhaps he also felt that he was essentially a supplicant, and thus in no position to insist on anything. Smith, with his philosophy of projecting overwhelming strength (regardless of the facts), would not have fallen into the same error.

An unknown number of the Englishmen stayed behind on the ship. Powhatan directed Ratcliffe and the others to a house about a half mile from the river, where they were to spend the night. The next morning, Powhatan and a group of his guards escorted the visitors to his storehouse. There, Ratcliffe bartered copper and beads for corn; as the baskets of corn accumulated, he surely savored the idea of the enthusiastic reception he would get from hundreds of grateful settlers when he made a hero's return to Jamestown.

Accounts differ as to what happened next. By one report, the natives began cheating the English by pushing up the bottoms of the baskets, so that less corn would appear to make a full basket. The English and the natives quarreled over this, with the result that Powhatan left the scene with his wives, his young guest Henry Spelman, and a German named Samuel who was still living with him. As the English were carrying their baskets the half mile back to the ship, native men who were hidden in the cornfields along the way attacked and killed them. By another report, Ratcliffe carelessly let his men straggle away in ones and twos into the natives' homes, lured there by who knows what—promises of food? women?—and the men were then ambushed and killed. Given the dual accounts, it is thus unclear whether the conflict between Powhatan and the English flared up on the spot, or whether Powhatan's invitation had been a trap for the English all along.

The outcome was the same from the perspective of the expedition's leader. In failing to exchange hostages, and in letting his men drop their guard, Ratcliffe had ignored the realities of life on the Virginia frontier. He paid for his insouciance in much the same way George Cassen had. Captured alive, Ratcliffe was tied to a stake in front of a large fire. This time it was women, rather than men, who carried out the procedure, removing his skin from his flesh with mussel shells, and then tossing it into the flames as he watched. Finally he was burned at the stake. "And so for want of circumspection [he] miserably perished," Percy recorded, sparing scant sympathy for a fallen comrade.[11]

The natives rarely attacked any English vessel larger than the twenty-four-man shallops, or barges, since the English ships possessed intimidating firepower. Giving further proof of their new boldness, however, the natives carried out an assault on Ratcliffe's ship, now under the command of William Fettiplace, as it made its hurried getaway from Orapakes. Fettiplace lost an unrecorded number of men, and barely escaped being completely overwhelmed by the attackers. The ship was expected to return to Jamestown fully laden with corn, thus saving the day for the English. Instead, it appeared at the colony bearing no food at all, and it carried only sixteen of the fifty men who had gone out.

After Percy saw the remnants of Ratcliffe's failed mission, he sent Captain James Davis to replace Ratcliffe as the commander of the fort at Point Comfort, and he directed Francis West to attempt to trade with the Patawomecks. Percy intended a peaceful bartering session, doubtless assuming that the distant Patawomeck tribe would be less hostile to the English. When cooperation was not forthcoming, West "used some harsh and cruel dealings," Percy explained, "by cutting off two of the savages' heads and other extremities."

West's mission succeeded—up to a point. His bloody tactics caused the Patawomecks to load his ship with as much grain as he wanted. But when he emerged from the mouth of the Potomac River, instead of turning into the James to bring relief to Jamestown, he and his men headed for the open ocean and, from there, to the comforts of home in England. Captain Davis watched in dismay from Point Comfort as West sailed away with the food that had been Jamestown's last hope.[12]

"Now wee all found the want of Captaine Smith," wrote the anonymous witness, "yea his greatest maligners could then curse his losse." The thirty-six men who had left with West were fortunate indeed. The thirty-four or so who perished with Ratcliffe were only slightly less so. For the rest, the winter of 1609–1610 became known as "the Starving Time." With the stores running low, the English now felt what Percy called "that sharp prick of hunger, which no man truly describe but he which hath tasted the bitterness thereof."

It was a perfect confluence of bad fortune, brought about by the fact that Percy was in over his head. On top of his improvidence in failing to set aside food for the winter and in letting the nets fall into disrepair, his administration had given Powhatan confidence that the English could be beaten. If Powhatan had once merely suspected it with the departure of Smith, the only Englishman who had seemed a serious adversary, the chief no longer needed to rest on gut feelings and suspicions. The ease with which Powhatan had driven the English from Nansemond and the falls, the ease with which he had defeated Ratcliffe: all this made it clear that he could starve the English out with no fear of repercussions.

Powhatan's men released some of the English boats at Jamestown from their moorings, hampering the ability of the colonists to mount their own raids or to reach out to his enemies for help. Powhatan attacked Hog Isle, an island that had been stocked with sixty or so free-roaming hogs as a backup food source the previous spring, during Smith's administration. The hogs by then numbered in the hundreds, until the natives slaughtered them all. It was a moot point, in a sense, since the colonists had evidently not been drawing on Hog Isle for sustenance in the first place; they were too fearful of straying from the fort. Although Powhatan did not conduct any full-scale attacks on Jamestown—unnecessary under his strategy of starvation—his men did make opportunistic raids on any small groups that they found.

Some hungry colonists robbed the storehouse, for which Percy had them put to death. As the stores dwindled, the colonists looked to any source of food that was at hand. First they consumed the colony's horses, cats, and dogs. Next were the rats and mice. Then came the leather of their shoes and boots. A few hardy souls left the fort to tromp through the snowy woods in search of snakes; if they did not make it back, it was that many fewer mouths to be fed.

A quirk of Elizabethan and Jacobean fashion among English gentlemen provided a source of nourishment for some. Around their necks they wore a ruff, a pleated circular collar usually nine inches wide or more. To keep the ruffs in properly stiff form, the gentlemen (or their servants) washed them in starch, brought over from the old country. The starch turned out to be edible, and so down the hatch it went, in the form of a "gluey porridge."

While en route to the New World, the founding colonists of 1607 had been apprehensive of the cannibalistic Caribs who resided on the islands of Dominica and Nevis in the West Indies. When cannibalism did come to Jamestown, though, it was not brought by indigenous "savages"; it was practiced by the colonists' own desperate countrymen. "Now famine beginning [began] to look pale and ghastly in every face [so] that nothing was spared to maintain life and to do those things which seem incredible," Percy recalled. Under the right conditions, it was a short step from eyeing rats and mice to eyeing the freshly fallen corpses. An untold number of the English fed on the meat of their dead fellows. After one native was killed during an attack and buried, a group of colonists dug him up several days later and ate him.

A man by the name of Collins—probably Henry Collins, gentleman—cast a hungry stare at his pregnant wife and murdered her in her sleep. He then chopped apart her remains, salted them, and feasted on them. He stopped short of consuming his own child, whose body he had first removed from its mother's womb and dropped into the river under the cover of night. It is pleasing to note that when Collins's depravity was discovered, Percy had him hung by his thumbs with weights on his feet until he confessed, and then had him executed. Virginia Company propaganda would later seek to minimize the incident, claiming that Collins had killed his wife because he hated her, not because he was hungry; that he had dismembered her only to conceal the evidence; and that a search of his house had refuted his excuse of hunger by uncovering "a good quantity of meal, oatmeal, beans, and peas."13

For those with the moral compass to keep them from eating other humans, the reward was usually slow death. Some dug their own graves, lay in them, and waited for the end to come. Others ran away to the natives, expecting succor from the colony's enemies—but those days were over. They found instead that death awaited them at the natives' hands. Percy saw a colonist named Hugh Pryse, at the end of his tether, come to the fort's public square, "crying out that there was no God, alleging that if there were a God He would not suffer His creatures, whom He made and framed, to endure those miseries, and to perish for want of food and sustenance." Pryse went into the woods later that day to root around for something to eat; when his body was discovered, it was still shot through with the arrows that the natives had used to kill him, and had been torn apart by wolves or other roving animals.[14]

By March 1610, six months after Smith had gone, sixty colonists out of five hundred in Jamestown were left alive—plus, of course, Francis West and the lucky thirty-six in his party who had absconded. The mortality rate for the winter, in other words, had been around 80 percent. What made the Starving Time doubly tragic was that it could have been avoided with astute leadership: when Percy worked up the gumption that month to visit James Davis at Point Comfort, he was dumbfounded to discover that the men there were hale and hearty. They had been living well on Chesapeake Bay crabs and their own hogs.

Percy berated Davis for "not regarding our wants and miseries at all," but the real lesson was that the Starving Time never had to happen. Even with all the colonists' improvidence, Smith's policy of dispersal would have gotten them through the winter if it had been sustained. That would have required an effective defense of the outposts at Nansemond and the falls, which the new leaders had been too timid to undertake. Instead, Percy, Martin, and West had pursued an incoherent response to the natives' hostility, a course that alternated between craven retreat and random atrocity—with disastrous results. Added to that was Ratcliffe's tactical incompetence.

"It were too vile to say what we endured," wrote the anonymous reporter, "but the occasion was only our owne, for want of providence, industrie, and government, and not the barrennesse and defect of the countrie, as is generally supposed. . . . Had we been in Paradice it selfe (with those governours) it would not have been much better with us."[15]

10

RESTORATION

⚜

For the voyage of the 1609 resupply, a council of the ships' captains and pilots had decided not to follow the usual route. Rather than heading south for the Canaries, and then across to the West Indies before heading north again to the mainland, the ships would veer north of the West Indies on their way to Virginia. By shunning the tried-and-true West Indies route, they hoped to elude detection by the Spanish, and perhaps gain a shorter crossing in the bargain. Their plotted course was similar to the one taken by Samuel Argall a month earlier. Under the overall command of Sir George Somers, the fleet's admiral, the nine ships sailed from England on June 2.

The route worked out fine for Argall, but not so well for the Somers fleet. On Monday, July 24, just seven or eight days' distance from Virginia, the voyagers found "the clouds gathering thick upon us, and the winds singing and whistling most unusually." As the sky turned black, a storm came from the northeast and tossed the ships for the next four days. All but one of the ships made it through and carried their star-crossed passengers to Jamestown, where the Starving Time winter of 1609–1610 awaited them. The fate of the ship that did not reemerge from the storm—the *Sea Venture*, the 300-ton flagship of the fleet—would prove crucial to Jamestown's future.

On the *Sea Venture*, recalled passenger William Strachey, the "hell of darkness" in the sky left even the most experienced and hardened mariners unable to keep their anxiety from their faces. They unfastened the towline to the *Virginia*, a smaller ship that the *Sea Venture* had been towing, for fear that the two boats would be smashed into each other. As the *Virginia* bobbed away through the rising waves, the men braced themselves.

For a full twenty-four hours, the wind and the rain were so loud and punishing that it seemed as if they could not possibly get worse. Many on board held out hope that the storm would soon exhaust itself. "Yet we did still find it not only more terrible but more constant," Strachey remembered, "fury added to fury, and one storm urging a second more outrageous than the former." A wall of ocean water periodically hit the decks and washed down below, terrifying the passengers—men, women, and children—who shouted out prayers for deliverance.

The sailors expected the ship to break apart at any time. On Tuesday morning, they became aware of another danger: while they had been expecting destruction from above, hidden leaks were bringing in a flood from below in the ship's lowest reaches. The caulking material used to seal the ship's joints had been torn open in multiple places. By the time the water was discovered, it was five feet deep above the ship's ballast. Given time, and not that much of it, the leaks would take the *Sea Venture* down. Word of them spread quickly among the crew and passengers, who were struck with redoubled panic.

Members of the crew crawled along the ribs of the ship in the dark with candles, searching frantically for the openings and listening for the sound of flowing water. A number of leaks were found this way and plugged; one, discovered in the gunner's quarters, was so large there seemed no way to handle it, until someone thought to stop it up with slabs of beef from the stores. Yet as the crewmen continued to plug holes, the water kept rising.

The men on board, both crew and passengers, were ordered to divide into three groups, stationed in the front, middle, and rear of the ship, to take shifts on a bucket or a pump. Each man bailed furiously for an hour with water up to his waist, rested for an hour, then went to work again. Thus they continued for the next several days, without eating, drinking, or sleeping. The water had completely taken over the hold, so the colonists could not get at the rations. The sky remained as black during the day as it was at night. There was an interruption in the darkness on Thursday past midnight, when a ball of flame appeared to float in the air among the masts for three or four hours; this appearance of Saint Elmo's fire (actually an electrical phenomenon, and not fire at all) further terrified the superstitious crew.

By Friday morning, the fourth morning of their ordeal, the crew and passengers were completely spent in body and spirit. They were ready, as Strachey put it, to leave their "sinful souls" to the Almighty, and to entrust the *Sea Venture* to "the mercy of the sea."

Shortly before noon, however, the skies cleared ever so slightly— enough for a stunned Admiral Somers to call out a one-word announcement: *"Land!"* He had, in fact, spotted the Bermuda Isles. Trees could be seen in the distance, swaying with the wind.[1]

The Bermudas were also known at the time as the "Devil's Islands" for the foul weather and perilous rock and coral shoals surrounding them. Those shoals, which had been the ruin of French, Dutch, and Spanish ships over the previous century, had made the islands impregnable up to this time, leading "every navigator and mariner to avoid them . . . as they would shun the Devil himself." Still, Somers had no real choice but to try.

Fortunately for the voyagers, Somers was that rarity among Virginia leaders, a man who combined elevated social position with John Smith's practical effectiveness. During the days and nights of frantic bailing out the *Sea Venture*, the admiral had set the tone by taking his shifts the same as everyone else, though he could have pulled rank without a moment's question from anyone. It was a characteristic move for Somers, whom Smith would laud in later years for his "extraordinary care, paines, and industry" and for "the ever memorable courage of his minde."

The former naval commander, a veteran of sea and land battles with the Spanish, had first gone to sea as a young man, rose to become a naval commander, and finally retired to a life of ease at the ripe age of forty-nine, in 1603. That year, he accepted a knighthood for his service and soon settled down to a parliamentary seat representing his native Lyme Regis, Dorset. Six years later, perhaps feeling a mixture of patriotism and cabin fever, he gave it all up to lead the largest Virginia fleet up to that time.[2]

As Somers approached Bermuda with around 140 men on board, as well as ten women and an unknown number of children, his experience and his battle-hardened nerves would be put to the ultimate test. The boatswain dropped the sounding line and reported that the bottom was at thirteen fathom, or around seventy-eight feet deep. With the next reading, it quickly fell to forty-two feet, then only twenty-four—and they were still more than a mile offshore. It was clear that the *Sea Venture* would wreck a good distance from land, and quite possibly shatter beneath them.

Thinking quickly, Somers found a way out. He made the wreck a controlled wreck, running the *Sea Venture* into, and partway through, a V-shaped formation of coral sitting a half mile or three-quarters of a mile from shore. The coral wedge held the ship fast. By nightfall, every one of the men, women, and children on board—plus the ship's dog—had been carried to land on small boats taken from the ship.

Thanks to the islands' frightening reputation, they were uninhabited. The crew and passengers of the *Sea Venture* soon discovered that they had landed in paradise—a real paradise, unlike the "paradise" that the Virginia Company touted in its propaganda. Thousands of wild hogs roamed free, probably the offspring of hogs from an earlier shipwreck, and were easy to hunt with the dog's help. There were large tortoises for the taking, large enough that one of them yielded more meat than several hogs. Fruits and berries were plentiful, as were a dozen kinds of fish. Broad-leaved palm trees gave shelter from rainstorms. Clear ocean water—turquoise near the shoreline, darker blue in the distance—lapped against pink sand. "Whereas it hath been and is still accounted the most dangerous, unfortunate, and forlorn place of the world," recorded Silvester Jourdain, a passenger, "it is in truth the richest, healthfullest, and [most] pleasing land . . . as man ever set foot upon."[3]

The decision about what to do next fell to Somers and to Sir Thomas Gates, the appointed governor of the colony. For them, there was no question: the voyagers must keep to the company's instructions by leaving paradise for Jamestown. One of the boats was outfitted for ocean travel, and one of Somers's senior men, Henry Ravens, was sent with a crew of six on the seven-hundred-mile journey to Virginia; his instructions were to bring back a ship to pick up the stranded colonists.

Ravens and his crew successfully sailed to the mainland, but were killed by natives before they could reach Jamestown. As weeks went by in Bermuda with no sight of them, Somers conceived another plan, a strategy of self-help. He put Richard Frubbisher, an experienced shipbuilder, in charge of building a new ship there on the island. Frubbisher was to build it with Bermudan cedar and with oak beams and planks salvaged from the *Sea Venture*. Somers took responsibility for the building of a second, smaller ship himself.

The men of the *Sea Venture* had their roles in working on the ships, some cutting timber, some hewing it, others shaping and fastening the planks and beams. Most of the ships' seams would have to be caulked with wax, carried away from the hold of another shipwreck, since the colonists had recovered only one barrel of pitch and tar from the *Sea Venture* to use for sealant. Their lowermost holds would have to be layered with ballast of rocks or lead. Few of the men were experienced in shipbuilding; there were only four carpenters on the island. For the small company, it was a monumental project that would require months to complete.

In the meantime, the cycles of life went on. The day was taken up by the tasks of shipbuilding, and also by morning and evening prayers led by the Reverend Richard Buck. George Somers's cook, Thomas Powell, found that Bermuda was just the place to woo and win Elizabeth Persons, a gentlewoman's maidservant, and so the two were married in November. Two women gave birth on the island, one to a baby girl and the other to a baby boy. Their parents declared their spiritual attachment to Bermuda in the most emphatic way anyone could, naming the children for their island home.

The girl was born to Mr. and Mrs. John Rolfe in February 1610. Bermuda Rolfe did not survive long—the cause of her death is unknown—and she was buried on the island whose name she bore. John Rolfe had already been touched by death once: his own twin brother, Eustacius, had not lived through infancy.4

Despite the manifest attractions of life on the island, the great majority of the colonists were resolved to follow Gates and Somers to Jamestown. Despite the Virginia Company's rosy tracts, the travelers must have realized that Jamestown would be no Bermuda; that much was obvious from Smith's *True Relation* of the previous year, with its portrayals of natives who were mercurial and sometimes dangerous. That the *Sea Venture* survivors remained committed to continuing to Jamestown was a testament to the leadership of Gates and Somers, and also to the colonists' own sense of the importance of their mission. Then, too, some of them were still hoping to find gold mines.

A handful of dissenters saw things differently, anticipating "nothing but wretchedness" in Jamestown compared to their tranquil new home, and they wanted nothing to do with it. A half dozen men—John Want, Christopher Carter, Francis Pearepont, William Brian, William Martin, and Richard Knowles—secretly pledged among themselves to do nothing to further the building of the ships. Then they went a step further, planning to leave the main island for another that they would inhabit on their own while the others attempted to continue to Jamestown.

The plot came to light in early September 1609, and the men were sentenced to the same fate they had intended for themselves: they were taken to a distant island and left there. In their isolation, they soon found their separate existence to be a prison without walls. No doubt they found it irksome to have to feed themselves, even in paradise. In due course, they lost their bravado and sent Gates entreaties for forgiveness. The governor, soft of heart, ordered them readmitted.

The lesson of the plotters was forgotten by January, when another man was found guilty of mutiny—though it is unclear how much of it was simply wishfulness and idle talk. Stephen Hopkins imagined staying in Bermuda with his wife and children, it seems, as a sort of seventeenth-century Swiss Family Robinson. He gave himself away, however, by confiding his plans to colonists Samuel Sharpe and Humphrey Reede. Hopkins explained to them that the authority of Gates and Somers had disappeared with the shipwreck; Gates was the governor of Virginia, not Bermuda, and Somers could no longer claim authority as admiral of the ship if he didn't have a ship. It was a plausible line of reasoning, but alas, it did not get him far when Sharpe and Reede turned him in. After he was sentenced to death, he begged Gates to spare him for the sake of his family. Gates, moved by his pleas, forgave Hopkins as he had the others.

A gentleman named Henry Paine was not so fortunate. His trouble began when he got into an argument with his watch commander on the night of March 13, as he was about to begin his guard duty. There had been rumors in the air that someone was plotting to empty the storehouse and abscond—though how anyone could abscond without a boat is unclear. For the first time, Gates had ordered a round-the-clock guard, and ordered all of the men to carry weapons (which they had not needed on Bermuda up to then). Paine's commander told him to keep an extra-careful watch; Paine, fed up with the burdens of guard duty, told his commander off and gave him a shove or some such blow. The exchange escalated into a scuffle as others on duty watched in surprise. Paine was warned that if the governor learned of his insolence, it would mean his life. Paine answered, in Strachey's prim words, "that the governor had no authority of that quality to justify upon anyone, [no matter] how mean [low-ranking] soever in the colony, an action of that nature, and therefore let the governor (said he) kiss, etc."

Paine's words spread around the settlement, and the next morning, he was brought before Governor Gates with the entire company watching the proceedings. With the testimony of the commander and the witnesses to the fight, Paine was convicted of insubordination and condemned to be hanged on the spot. This time Gates was not inclined to be merciful. Paine's noose was soon ready. As his last act, before he was to ascend the ladder, he requested the privilege of a condemned gentleman: death by firing squad. "Towards the evening he had his desire, the sun and his life setting together."[5]

At the end of April, Somers's bold plan had come to fruition: two new vessels had been built to carry all the Bermudans onward. It had taken nine months. Frubbisher's 40-foot ship was named the *Deliverance*; Somers's 29-foot ship was called the *Patience*. Somers had labored on the *Patience*, Jourdain observed, "from morning until night, as duly as any workman doth labor for wages." On top of all the other challenges he had faced in building the *Patience*—salvaged parts, no shipyard, mostly amateur workmen—there was a paucity of iron that could be recovered from the *Sea Venture*. Somers had surmounted that problem by building the *Patience* with exactly one bolt, which he used in attaching the keel.

For their departure, the colonists awaited a westerly wind, which finally came on May 10, 1610. They had reason to feel blessed: all told, they had lost only six of the company (including Henry Paine and Bermuda Rolfe) to various causes during their sojourn. Before setting off, they put up a cross made from timbers of the *Sea Venture* in memory of their survival of the storm—and, implicitly, in memory of the months they had spent as castaways. Accounts of the colonists' island adventure would later provide the inspiration for Shakespeare's romantic comedy *The Tempest*.[6]

When they arrived in Virginia twelve days later, what they found was neither romantic nor a comedy. They stopped at the new fort at Point Comfort, where George Percy had taken up residence. Percy gave Gates and Somers the general idea that Jamestown had been in misery. Yet nothing could have prepared them for what they would see when they continued upriver. On May 24, they moored at the

Jamestown peninsula, walked into the fort, and witnessed a scene that beggared belief. At first, the settlement appeared to be a ghost town. The gates of the fort were off their hinges. Some of the houses had been torn apart, by men who were desperate for winter firewood, and too scared to get it from the forest beyond the fort's walls. There were no signs of life.

Gates ordered someone to ring the church bell. With that, men staggered out from their homes, their bodies shrunk down almost to skeletons, resembling corpses held upright by unseen marionette strings. Some could greet their rescuers only with repetitive cries of "We are starved! We are starved!" They were the sixty-odd survivors of the Starving Time. Richard Buck, the preacher, overcome with grief, said a "zealous and sorrowful" prayer for the living and the dead.

Expecting to arrive at a functioning colony, even a thriving one, Gates and Somers had brought only enough rations for the journey from Bermuda. There was some to spare because Somers had estimated conservatively, but it still amounted to no more than two weeks' supply. After taking stock of the situation over several days, and organizing two unsuccessful attempts at gathering food, Gates made his inevitable decision: the colony would be abandoned as soon as the ships could be made ready. The settlers would head north to the fishing grounds off Newfoundland and attempt to disperse themselves among English fishing boats there. Everyone, it was hoped, would thereby make his or her way back to England.

Most of the ships from the 1609 resupply had long since sailed away, but the colonists had four small vessels at hand: the *Discovery*, the *Virginia* (which had held together after the *Sea Venture* cut it loose), the *Deliverance*, and the *Patience*. On the morning of June 7, these were loaded with the colonists' guns and anything else worth bringing home. The cannon from the fort had been buried outside the gate. The beating of a drum was the signal for the colonists finally to line up and board the ships. That drumbeat, solemn as it may have been, no doubt evoked joyful whoops and hollering. (Gates had met the same response when, shortly after his arrival, he announced gravely that he was *thinking* about sending the men home.)

Their departure was distinctly lacking in wistful sentimentality. Among the colony's rank and file, there was much enthusiasm for the idea of setting all of Jamestown on fire just before they left, and watching it burn as it faded from view—a satisfying panorama for those who had endured so much there. Gates opposed the idea, holding that "we know not but that as honest men as ourselves may come and inhabit here." To make sure Jamestown did not go up in flames, he had to assign a company of his trusted men to stand guard and then board the ships after the rest.

Gates, Somers, Percy, and James Davis (who had been in charge of the fort at Point Comfort) were the last to board—Gates on the *Deliverance*, Somers on the *Patience*, Percy on the *Discovery*, and Davis on the *Virginia*. Around noon, with a ceremonial firing of pistols, they set sail.7

That day, the ships made it as far as Hog Isle, where the colonists spent the night. The following afternoon, they noticed an unidentified boat approaching with just one man on it. Edward Brewster, the man on the boat, pulled up and presented a letter addressed to Thomas Gates. The letter was about to hit the course of American history with the force of a meteor.

It was from Thomas West, Lord De La Warr. West had sailed from England on April 1, 1610, ten months after Gates and Somers— unknown to anyone in Jamestown. With him were three ships carrying 150 new settlers, an ample store of provisions, and a commission naming him governor and captain-general of Virginia for life. He had arrived at Point Comfort on June 6, his letter explained. There he found a small detachment of men who were waiting to be picked up by Gates's departing fleet on its way to the Atlantic. They had given him the news of what had taken place in Jamestown since autumn. (West undoubtedly asked after his younger brother, Francis, and learned— after an awkward silence—that Francis had sailed out in late 1609, when the getting was good.) Help was on the way, West told Gates in so many words, and he ordered him back to Jamestown.

Gates complied, "to the great grief of all his company," as some of them later wrote. With favorable winds, the four ships made it back to Jamestown by that night. When West's fleet pulled up two days later, on the afternoon of Sunday, June 10, West found it "a very noisome [smelly] and unwholesome place occasioned much by the mortality and idleness of our own people." That, he decided, was going to change. After Richard Buck delivered a sermon marking West's arrival, Gates formally turned his office over to him. As West took his turn in greeting the colonists, any of them who expected a pep talk were in for a disappointment:

> Then I delivered some few words unto the company [he remembered], laying some blames upon them for many vanities and their idleness, earnestly wishing that I might no more find it so lest I should be compel'd to draw the sword in justice to cut off delinquents which I had much rather draw in their defense to protect from enemies.

Not being able to find a suitable house for himself in Jamestown, and likely put off by the smell, West spent the night on his ship. The next day, he dealt with the "noisome" conditions by ordering a general cleanup of the town's garbage and trash, which the colonists threw into an open pit and then covered with dirt—winning the gratitude of future generations of archaeologists.[8]

Despite the grumbling of those who thought they were on their way home, the colony's situation had, in fact, improved markedly. West's cargo amounted to enough food for a year. The English in Virginia would never experience another Starving Time. The role of sheer coincidence, or Providence, in restoring English settlement to Virginia was aptly summed up by the Virginia Company in a tract published in London later that year:

> For if God had not sent Sir Thomas Gates from the Bermudas within four days, they had been [would have been] all famished. If God had not directed the heart of that worthy knight to save the fort from fire at their shipping, they had been destitute of a present harbor and succor. If they had abandoned the fort any longer time and had not so returned, questionless the Indians would have destroyed the fort, which had been the means of our safety among them, and a terror unto them. If they had set sail sooner and had launched into the vast ocean, who could have promised that they should have encountered the fleet of Lord La-ware?— especially when they made for Newfoundland, a course

contrary to our navy's approaching. If the Lord La-
ware had not brought with him a year's provision, what
comfort could those souls have received to have been
relanded to a second destruction?[9]

On Wednesday, June 13, West met with his newly appointed advisory council, which consisted of Gates, Somers, Percy, and several others, to discuss the immediate issues in front of them. Foremost among
these was how to find fresh meat. Since Jamestown had plenty of other
rations, such luxuries could now be considered matters of priority. The
problem was that the colonists had killed and eaten all their own
horses and other animals, down to the very smallest, during the previous winter. Powhatan's men had killed the hogs, and driven away most
of the deer, all as part of the chief's starvation plan. West could have
brought salted meat with him from England, but no one there had
conceived of a scenario in which the colony's own hogs would be gone.

As the council pondered, Somers surprised everyone with a suggestion: he would make a return trip to Bermuda, capture some of
the wild hogs there, and bring them back. West took him up on it.
As attractive as Bermuda was, the voyage would be dangerous, and
Somers's offer was a potentially deadly gamble. As word of the plan
spread around the settlement, those who knew Somers were again
impressed with (as Jourdain put it) his "being willing to do service to
his prince and country without any respect of private gain." Somers
and his crew left on June 19 on the *Patience*, accompanied by Samuel
Argall on the *Discovery*.

While the colonists waited for Somers to return, West and his
advisers turned their attention to the problem of relations with the
natives. The company in London still believed in winning the natives
over to English ways, with the ultimate result of an integrated society
in Virginia, one rooted in Protestant Christianity and English culture.
Yet the reports of Smith and others had led to a modicum of realism:
the natives would never accept the English presence, the company
believed, as long as they were under the influence of their present
chiefs and the priests. Accordingly, the company (still unaware of Powhatan's war of starvation) had recommended that if the natives gave
resistance, the colonists should capture "their weroances and all other
their knowne successors at once, whom if you intreate well and educate
those which are younge and to succeede in the government in your

manners and religion, their people will easily obey you and become in time civil and Christian." The priests, too, should be seized—and, if necessary, put to death:

> for they are so wrapped up in the fogge and miserie of their iniquity, and so terrified with their continuall iniquity tirrany chayned under the bond of the devil, that while they live amonge them to poyson and infect them their mindes, you shall never . . . have any civill peace or concurre with them.[10]

That was the theory. The course that the colonists actually pursued, however, tended to be made up on the spur of the moment in reaction to the latest events. John Smith had been reprimanded by the company for his hard dealings with the natives, but it was only now, with Smith absent from the scene, that English massacres of native civilians would begin.

The tenderhearted Gates, whom West had made his lieutenant general, started with a belief in nonviolence toward the natives— "thinking it possible by a more tractable course to win them to a better condition," Strachey recorded. But on July 6, on a sailing expedition downriver to Point Comfort, Gates witnessed one of his men, Humphrey Blunt, captured and killed by a party of Kecoughtans. Shaken by what he had seen, Gates wanted vengeance.

Several days later, most likely with West's approval, Gates led an attack on the Kecoughtan town. Reflecting the English view of the natives as childlike in their ignorance, Gates had settled on the tactic of drawing the Kecoughtans out with the entertainment of a taborer—a musical jester who played a drum and fife. Arriving by boat in the early morning, Gates directed the taborer to play and dance in a clearing. When the natives emerged to watch the spectacle, Gates's men ambushed them and killed five of them by the sword and wounded a large number of others. The rest of the townspeople fled into the woods. No one on the English side was hurt. Gates ordered his company to occupy the town and its adjacent fields. About two weeks later, Gates left for England to provide an update to the council in London.

West himself began more cautiously. Sometime after Gates's assault, West sent two gentlemen as messengers to Chief Powhatan with a demand that he return the tools and weapons the natives had stolen, which evidently numbered in the hundreds. West also demanded that Powhatan return the prisoners that the English believed he was keeping, and turn over the perpetrators of a recent murder at Point Comfort (apparently the killers of Humphrey Blunt). West diplomatically suggested that the misdeeds were done without the chief's knowledge. If Powhatan met West's demands, the gentlemen told him, then West, "their great weroance," would extend his friendship on behalf of King James.

At this point, Powhatan no longer took the English seriously as a threat; he found West's message laughable. He sent the gentlemen back with, in the words of George Percy, "proud and disdainful answers." Either stay on the Jamestown peninsula or leave the country, Powhatan told West. Otherwise, he would kill the English at his pleasure. The messengers should not come back, he added with a final dash of scorn, "unless they brought him a coach and three horses, for he had understood by the Indians which were in England [presumably Namontack] how such was the state of great weroances and lords in England to ride and visit other great men."[11]

Now West, too, was violently angry. He put Percy in command of seventy men to strike at a nearby Powhatan tribe, the Paspahegh. The strategic value, if any, of the target was immaterial; West had been insulted. Percy had his own reasons to spoil for a fight, having been duped by Powhatan into sending Ratcliffe and fifty others into a fatal ambush the previous year. This puffed-up nonentity also despised Powhatan because he blamed the chief of chiefs (rather than his own failure of leadership) for the Starving Time. Percy saw no need to bring a taborer for comic relief. On the night of August 9, his troops killed fifteen or sixteen men in the village of the Paspahegh, burned down the village, and captured the Paspahegh queen and her children.

When Percy's lieutenant brought him the queen and children and another native man, Percy was irked that the lieutenant had spared their lives. The lieutenant told him indifferently that the prisoners were his to deal with as he pleased. "Upon the same I caused the Indian's head to be cut off," Percy wrote.

As the queen and her children were marched three miles back to the boats, Percy's men grumbled because they had not been executed. When the party reached the boats, Percy called a council, in which the men prevailed on him to allow the killing of the children. This they accomplished by throwing them overboard and firing at them in the water, riddling their heads with musket shot. "I had much to do to save the queen's life," Percy noted.

But he had not saved her life for long. When he and his men returned to Jamestown, they rowed directly to the ship where West was still keeping his quarters. For some reason, Percy did not speak directly with West, instead sending Captain James Davis in his place. Davis reported back to Percy that the governor did not understand why the queen had been taken alive, and he wanted her "dispatched"— preferably burned to death. Percy was unsure that West had actually said this, but unaccountably, he did not take the trouble to confirm the orders himself. His own preening account tells the rest:

> To the first I replied that having seen so much bloodshed that day, now in my cold blood I desired to see no more; and for to burn her I did not hold it fitting, but either by shot or sword to give her a quicker dispatch. So turning myself from Captain Davis, he did take the queen with two soldiers ashore, and in the woods put her to the sword. And although Captain Davis told me it was my lord's direction, I am persuaded to the contrary.[12]

Even the natives' own narrow conception of rules of warfare, of humane considerations in combat, forbade the killing of an enemy ruler's wife and children. They were to be enslaved, at most, not executed.[13] As much as Percy attempted to distance himself from the atrocity, it was a damning indictment of his inadequacy as a commander, unable to govern the men under him and lacking the judgment to make sure he understood the orders of the man over him.

Despite the uneven quality of Jamestown's leaders in 1610, the colony was no longer the fragile, vulnerable endeavor it had been in its first years. Warfare against Powhatan would continue, with occasional brutality on both sides, for several more years. There would be waves of illness and other setbacks. But as Don Pedro de Zúñiga had predicted, the sheer scale of the colony now made it difficult to dislodge. The formidable challenges still confronting the colony—achieving peace with Powhatan or victory over him, for one, and keeping the investors happy, for another—would not have to be dealt with under the shadow of imminent extinction.

John Smith, the man who had done the most to keep the colony functioning in the years leading up to 1610, received scant credit from Governor West and his council. In their report to the Virginia Company in London that July, they tacitly criticized his disregard for social rank, and promised that they would allow no repetition of it. Wrote West:

> Nor would I have it conceived that we would exclude altogether gentlemen and such whose breeding never knew what a day's labor meant, for even to such this country, I doubt not, but will give likewise excellent satisfaction, especially to the better and staid spirits. For he amongst us that cannot dig, use the [carpenter's] square, nor practice the ax and chisel, yet he shall find how to employ the force of his knowledge, the exercise of council, and the operation and power of his best breeding and quality.[14]

George Somers, who played perhaps the most crucial role after John Smith and Pocahontas in the colony's survival, would not return from his errand to the Bermuda Isles. After leaving Virginia in June, Somers and Argall became separated in another storm; both men fell back to the coast of today's Sagadahoc, Maine, to look for each other, in accord with their prearranged plan for such an eventuality. When they failed to make contact, Argall made his way back to Virginia, while Somers, undeterred, attempted again to carry out the mission. This time, he did reach Bermuda, and died there on November 9 of "overtoiling himselfe." Before his crewmen took his body back to England, they respected his last wishes by burying his heart on the island where he died.[15] It is now called St. George's Island, Bermuda, named for the patron saint of England—not so fittingly for the island that wrecked the *Sea Venture*, but fittingly enough for the island that sustained the men and women on it, and thus saved English America from vanishing.

11

THE MARRIAGE

ᴂ⁊ᴥ

By 1612, English investors had lost all patience with the Virginia Company. Only the most delusional could still believe that gold bricks from Virginia would eventually make their way from Jamestown to the docks of the Thames. The company was now holding out hopes of revenues from "masts, deals [lumber], pitch, tar, flax, hemp, and cordage," to say nothing of "sweet wines, oranges, lemons, anise seeds, etc."—but those revenues were still just a vision. The colony had delivered none of these things in any substantial quantity. As a get-rich-quick scheme, the colony was, so far, a disaster. "Only the name of God," it was said, "was more frequently profaned in the streets and market places of London than was the name of Virginia."

There was no longer any question of going back to London's capital markets. A stock offering the previous year had raised only 60 percent of its goal—£18,000 of an intended £30,000. The company would not even see all of that. The subscribers had been allowed to pay in three yearly increments; as the enterprise took on the odor of a looming financial failure, some of them simply stopped paying after the first installment.

Yet money was needed. It occurred to someone—perhaps Sir Thomas Smythe, the company's treasurer—that if selling stock would not work, lottery tickets might be the next best thing. On March 12, the company received royal permission to run lotteries, and the first Virginia lottery was soon under way. The grand prize, a handsome one thousand pounds, went to a London tailor named Thomas Sharplisse and was taken to his house, as company records put it, "in a very stately manner." The clergy tolerated the gambling contest, and fortune smiled upon them in return: the two runner-up winners of the first lottery were churches.

The lottery device proved successful, and the company came back to it again and again for nearly a decade. Among all the means for "gettinge in monneys," the company found, "the first & most certaine is by the lotteries." Their operation was simplicity itself: The tickets went into a locked container. The winning tickets were pulled by hand from the container. To counter suspicions of a fixed contest, the task of pulling the tickets at random from the container was sometimes assigned to children, who were presumed (then as now) to be less corruptible then their elders.[1]

Meanwhile, Thomas West, Lord De La Warr, had left Virginia in March 1611, after suffering from one ailment after another, including dysentery and scurvy. The governor and captain-general for life had lasted in the colony less than ten months. It was not exactly a rousing recommendation for life in the New World, and the news of his return to England was a further embarrassment to the company. After his departure, the colony was led at various times by George Percy, by Sir Thomas Gates (who returned in August 1611), and by a newcomer named Sir Thomas Dale.

During much of Dale's time in Virginia, he was theoretically second in command to Gates—as "marshal and deputy governor"—but as a practical matter, Dale was in charge and molded the government of Virginia in his image. Dale had been a fighter in the Netherlands, like so many of the colonial leaders; he and Gates, as it happened, were comrades in arms there. Gates, for some reason, emerged from the experience as a bit of a soft touch. Dale did not.

As a ruler, Dale is sometimes described as a martinet. It would be more accurate to say he was a martinet's ideal of a martinet. He enlarged and toughened the colony's "Lawes Divine, Morall and Martiall" to the point that execution was the penalty for adultery, for stealing anything in the least amount from the stores, for unauthorized trading with the natives, or for removing so much as a flower or an ear of corn from another man's garden. In battle, any man under arms who would "runne away cowardly" was to be executed "with the armes which he carrieth."

The laws called for the workday to begin promptly with the beating of a drum in the morning, and to end the same way in the evening; those who started late or quit early were to be whipped for the second offense, and sentenced to a year in the galleys for the third. To "do the necessities of nature" within a quarter mile of the fort was also punishable by whipping, "since by these unmanly, slothfull, and loathsome immodesties, the whole fort may bee choaked and poisoned with ill aires." (No doubt many went ahead and risked the punishment, considering that the colony was still at war with the natives, who might be ranging beyond the fort's walls.) Furthermore, any colonist who failed to keep his home "sweete and cleane" was liable to face a court-martial.

Anyone who disagreed with Dale's policies was best advised to keep quiet: to "detract, slaunder, calumniate, [or] murmur" against an order of any official was itself an offense punishable by three lashes of the whip. Those who wished to vote with their feet—by leaving—were in even worse luck. Emigration had been forbidden since the colony's first days, but it had not been punished by death; now it was. Apart from some rare grants of permission in individual cases, the company would not allow colonists the liberty to return to England until 1617.

Justice in the home country was severe to begin with, so it is all the more notable that the English in Virginia saw Dale's justice there as a horror. Upon the recapture of some colonists who had run away to the natives, Percy recalled, Dale seized the chance to show he meant business. "Some he appointed to be hanged, some burned, some to be broken upon the wheel, others to be staked [burned at the stake], and some to be shot to death," Percy recorded. "All these extreme and cruel tortures he used and inflicted upon them to terrify the rest. . . ." Dale ordered another group of men, convicted of stealing from the communal stores, to be tied to trees and starved to death. A group of colonists later remembered "continual whippings, extraordinary punishments, working as slaves in irons for terms of years—and that for petty offenses!"[2]

In the continuing Anglo-Powhatan war, Dale and Gates had more than martial discipline on their side. Beginning in late 1612, they enjoyed another advantage: a friendship with the Patawomecks, who lived on the south bank of today's Potomac River. The Patawomecks were nominally part of Powhatan's empire, yet distant enough that they were independent in fact. The word *Patawomeck* is thought to mean "trading place," and the tribe was true to its name, selling the colonists as much grain as they could carry away (1,400 bushels, on one occasion). As far as the English were concerned, Powhatan's food embargo against them had become a nullity.

For this, the colonists could thank the mariner Samuel Argall. The company had retained Argall merely to serve as the hired transportation between Virginia and England—it was Argall who hauled Lord De La Warr back to his life of comfort in London—but his role as a pilot to the distant shores of the Potomac evolved into the broader role of intermediary there. He was evidently charming, and projected an image of trustworthiness in the eyes of native leaders. "Yea, to this pass he hath brought them, that they assuredly trust upon what he promiseth. . . . ," wrote Ralph Hamor, Jr., who had recently become the colony's recording secretary. "They have even been pensive and discontented with themselves because they knew not how to do him some acceptable good turn. . . ."

Argall was not so trustworthy as he seemed, however. In March 1613, after delivering some lumber to carpenters at Point Comfort, he and his men took a side journey up the Potomac to explore the countryside inland from the river. Along the way, he hired several Patawomeck men to serve as guides. In the course of his sightseeing, Argall obtained a most interesting piece of intelligence:

> Whilst I was in this business, I was told by certain Indians my friends that the Great Powhatan's daughter Pokahuntis was with the Great King Patawomeck, whither I presently repaired, resolving to possess myself of her by any stratagem that I could for the ransoming of so many Englishmen as were prisoners with Powhatan, as also to get such arms and tools as he and other Indians had got by murther and stealing from others of our nation, with some quantity of corn for the colony's relief.[3]

Pocahontas had not shown herself at Jamestown since John Smith's death (as she thought) three and a half years earlier. By this time, she was known to the colonists only through Smith's writings and through stories told by a few of the colony's old hands. Even so, Argall must have understood that the plot simmering in his brain was aimed at a singularly undeserving victim: the girl who was the best friend the

English in Virginia ever had. She was about to learn that the colonists had a peculiar idea of gratitude.

In a state of excitement, Argall sailed directly to the small Patawomeck village of Passapatanzy. On his arrival, he sent for the local *weroance*, Japazeus, and also for James Swift, whom he had left with Japazeus as a hostage the preceding December. (Exchanging hostages as a pledge of good behavior—or, as Argall put it, "a pledge of our love and truce"—remained a customary part of trading on the Virginia frontier.) Japazeus was one of the Patawomecks with whom Argall had struck up a friendship of convenience, and Argall felt no need to be deferential. Almost as soon as Japazeus greeted him, Argall delivered an ultimatum: he must prove his affection by betraying Pocahontas into his hands that day. If he did, there would be a reward for him. If he did not, Argall said, "we would be no longer brothers nor friends."

Japazeus, understandably, blanched at the idea. It was absurd. Pocahontas, now around sixteen years old, was well known to be the great chief's "delight and darling." Selling the English corn was one thing; *this* would make him Powhatan's mortal enemy. No doubt Japazeus pondered visions of being tied up, his joints sliced with mussel shells, and then . . .

Argall listened to Japazeus's objections, and assured him there was nothing to fret about. He would treat Pocahontas with the greatest courtesy, he said. If Powhatan were rash enough to wage war against Passapatanzy, the English would intervene and beat him back.

On the latter point, Argall was talking through his hat. Japazeus took him at his word, though, and took the proposition to his brother, the *weroance* of all the Patawomecks. Surprisingly, after a few hours of deliberation, they agreed.

Once Japazeus gave his word, he was a model accomplice. He and his wife quickly conceived a plan to bring Pocahontas to the riverbank, whereupon his wife would act as if she were overcome with curiosity about Argall's ship. Accordingly, Japazeus and his wife brought Pocahontas on a stroll past the ship late that afternoon. There, his wife (whose name, unfortunately, is unrecorded) asked if they could go aboard and look around. Japazeus turned her down with a show of irritation. His wife, pretending her feelings were hurt, started to sob—"as who knows not that women can command tears!" remarked Hamor in his account of the incident.

Japazeus, feigning pity for his wife, soothed her by backtracking and agreeing that she could go on board, on one condition. It would not do to leave Pocahontas, he told her. If Pocahontas were willing to join them, that would be fine. Now his wife turned to their young companion. Pocahontas declined at first to go along—possibly she sensed that something was amiss—but finally acceded to her friend's "earnest persuasions."

Argall entertained the party with supper on board his ship, the *Treasurer*. Japazeus and his wife kept their countenances merry to set Pocahontas at ease. They gave Argall a good-natured kick under the table every so often, which Argall took to be a reminder of their eagerness for their reward.

He obliged them after supper. The visitors decided to spend the night, with Pocahontas in agreement, so he escorted Pocahontas to her quarters. Once out of Pocahontas's earshot, Japazeus and his wife told Argall proudly of the subterfuge with which they had conned Powhatan's daughter. For their pains, Argall gave them a small copper kettle and some even more trifling presents. The reward was not trifling in the eyes of its recipients, however; Japazeus could offer them to the Patawomeck god of rain, Quioquascacke, to placate him when the rainfall was too heavy or too little. The couple retired to their room on the ship with a feeling of satisfaction, the reward "so highly by him [Japazeus] esteemed that doubtless he would have betrayed his own father for them."

The next morning, Pocahontas woke up fearful and apprehensive. The murmurs of doubt that she felt the afternoon before had become full-throated voices of alarm. She hurried to the quarters of Japazeus and his wife and woke them up, urging them to leave for their safety's sake. Argall now presented himself and explained that Japazeus and his wife were free to go. Pocahontas, he said, would have to stay as his honored guest—at which, Hamor wrote, "she began to be exceeding pensive and discontented." Argall explained that her father had seven English prisoners and many stolen swords, guns, and tools, for which he would shortly redeem her.

To remove himself from suspicion, Japazeus expressed shock and outrage at Argall. He and his wife then went shoreside with their loot. Pocahontas remained as a prisoner, still unaware that Japazeus had been the engineer of her capture.4

Argall sent a native man, presumably one of his Patawomeck guides, to inform Powhatan "that I had taken his daughter, and if he would send home the Englishmen whom he detained in slavery, with such arms and tools as the Indians had gotten and stol'n, and also a great quantity of corn, that then he should have his daughter restored, otherwise not." The chief of chiefs immediately sent the messenger back with a plea for Argall to treat his daughter well. Argall needed only bring his ship to his royal residence at Matchcot on the Pamunkey River, Powhatan said, and he would have all that he demanded. Argall then sailed from Patawomeck country on April 13 to bring the news, and his prisoner, to Sir Thomas Gates in Jamestown.

Powhatan tired of waiting for Argall to appear. In a few days, he took the initiative and sent his seven English captives home, along with a handful of tools and broken guns and a canoe filled with corn. The men were overjoyed to be free, having lived from hour to hour in fear of an agonizing execution at the natives' hands. The men passed along a message from Powhatan to the effect that the rest of the English guns he had taken were either broken or missing, but that he would provide another five hundred bushels of corn in compensation when the English returned his daughter.

Not good enough, Gates replied. "We could not believe that the rest of our arms were either lost or stol'n from him," Hamor wrote, "and therefore till he returned them all we would not by any meanes deliver his daughter."

Gates then sailed to England and delivered the good news, arriving around August 1. For once, after a half dozen years of airy promises, the company had a tangible cause for hopefulness. At the least, the investors probably assumed, Argall's exploit would let the colonists conclude a peace with the natives. It might bring much more: either from sly insinuations in the company's reports, or as a result of their own wishful thinking, some investors saw the capture of the Virginia princess as cause for renewed optimism about the quest for gold. John Chamberlain, an investor who had fretted to a friend a year earlier that the company "would fall to the ground of itself, by the extreme beastly idleness of our nation," now felt more buoyant about the company's prospects:

> There is a ship come from Virginia with news of
> their well-doing, which puts some life into that action,
> that before was almost at the last cast. They have taken
> a daughter of a king that was their greatest enemy, as

she was going afeasting upon a river to visit certain
friends, for whose ransom the father offers whatever is
in his power, and to become their friend, and to bring
them where they shall meet with gold mines. They
propound unto him three conditions: to deliver all
the English fugitives, to render all manner of arms or
weapons of theirs that are come to his hands, and to
give them 300 quarters of corn. The first two he performed readily, and promiseth the other at their harvest, if his daughter may be well used [treated] in the
meantime.5

Meanwhile, in Virginia, the English waited for word from Powhatan. And waited. Powhatan was ignoring the rest of their demands
and showed no more signs of wanting his daughter back. He had called
the colonists' bluff.

Frustratingly little is recorded about the day-to-day conditions
of Pocahontas's captivity, or about her reactions to them, beyond
Hamor's generalities that the English made "much ado" to calm her
wrath "with extraordinary courteous usage." Neither did anyone in
Jamestown or London seem to have qualms about the kidnapping—
with the predictable exception of John Smith. In Smith's secondhand
relation of the episode, after he described the manner in which she had
been tricked, he sternly editorialized, "thus they betrayed the poore
innocent Pocahontas aboord." It was the only disapproval expressed in
any of the surviving accounts.

What is known is that Pocahontas was taken, at some point, to
Henricus, a newer settlement located at Dutch Gap in present-day
Chesterfield County. Thomas Dale had founded Henricus in 1611
with either 200 settlers (according to George Percy) or 350 settlers
(according to Hamor), and named it for Henry Stuart, prince of Wales.
Alexander Whitaker, a thirty-eight-year-old minister from Cambridge, was assigned the task of polishing Pocahontas's English and
teaching her the ways of a Christian lady.

In the minds of the colony's leaders, evangelism was fine as long as
it did not interfere with anything else. Although Dale reportedly
treated Pocahontas with kindness, he saw no percentage in maintaining her out of the colony's stores merely so she could memorize the

Ten Commandments, the Lord's Prayer, and the Apostles' Creed. When the winter came and went without word from Powhatan, and thus no prospect of ransoming the young captive, Dale took matters into his own hands.

In March 1614, Dale sailed with Pocahontas and 150 men to a Powhatan town on the Pamunkey River where he believed her father was staying. The natives regarded his unexpected appearance with suspicion. "It was a day or two before we heard of them," Dale recalled.

> At length they demanded why we came; I gave for answer that I came to bring him his daughter, conditionally he would—as agreed upon for her ransom—render all the arms, tools, swords, and men (that had run away), and give me a ship full of corn for the wrong he had done unto us. If they would do this, we would be friends; if not, burn all.[6]

Chief Powhatan was actually several days' distance away. As Dale waited for Powhatan's men to send for him, the combination of his impatience and their distrust incubated a brief skirmish with shooting on both sides. Dale's party retaliated by marching through the town, where they burned down some forty houses and killed five or six of Powhatan's warriors. The English then made their way further upriver to Matchcot, where they were met by a force of around four hundred men with bows and arrows. The landing was peaceful but tense, with each side hanging back and waiting for the other to make the first hostile move.

The English brought Pocahontas ashore, where a crowd of well-wishers and the merely curious came to see her. Among the visitors were two of Pocahontas's many half brothers, who rejoiced to find that she had been treated well. They swiftly discovered that Pocahontas was not so enthusiastic about the reunion. She still had her strong-willed spirit, and her capacity for surprise.

Apart from her half brothers and a few of the most senior members of the tribe, Pocahontas would speak to no one. Her message to those few was as astonishing to them as it was to the English. "The king's daughter went ashore," Dale wrote, "but would not talk to any of them, scarce to them of the best sort, and to them only that if her father had loved her, he would not value her less than old swords, pieces [guns], or axes; wherefore she would still dwell with the Englishmen, who loved her."

However unexpected her decision, it was true to form: Pocahontas had found a way, against the odds, to remain master of her fate. In electing to stay with the English, she had several evident motives. One was her longtime affinity for the English, going back to December 1607 when she first laid eyes on John Smith, and her subsequent girl-hood visits to converse with Smith and to play with the boys of the fort. Another was her attraction to Christianity, which had struck a resonant chord in her; she proved an eager student of the English faith.

In considering the attractiveness of English culture, flawed as it was, she had to look only as far as the case of her own mother: having attained the status of royalty as one of Powhatan's wives, she had been cast aside as soon as Pocahontas had been born. It was nothing personal; it was simply the way of Powhatan society. The chief of chiefs sent each of his wives away—divorced her, in effect—after she bore her first child. Once Pocahontas's mother raised her through her earliest years, Pocahontas had been taken away from her (again, in accord with local custom) and raised in Powhatan's household. Her mother, now completely on her own, became a commoner again. She remains nameless to this day.

Lastly, and most importantly, Pocahontas had a secret of the heart, one that was soon to come into the open on Dale's ship. For some time, the air at Henricus had been warming up between Pocahontas and a certain twenty-eight-year-old colonist. That colonist was John Rolfe, one of the *Sea Venture* survivors. He had been hit twice by tragedy since coming to the New World: once with the death of his infant daughter Bermuda several years earlier, and again with the death of his wife in Virginia (of causes now unknown). He had since chan-neled his energies into his ambitions for the colony's prosperity and his own. In that regard, he saw tobacco as a possible export crop for the colony, and had been tinkering with the planting of varieties from the Caribbean and South America. He is said to have been a handsome man; Pocahontas was perhaps attracted, also, by his gentle and devout nature.

Within the Powhatan culture of the time, a woman's favor was to be won through the manly virtue of superior hunting ability. It made sense, given that hunting was the man's only responsibility within the marriage. In this, Rolfe (like all of the colonists) was noticeably deficient in comparison to the men of Pocahontas's tribe. That Pocahontas was attracted to Rolfe anyway was a reflection of her nonconformist spirit, but it might also have been the product of something more. There was an unconfirmed rumor that she had already been married to and divorced from a man of her own people, a Powhatan captain named Kocoum. In that case, it likely would have been Kocoum who divorced her; Powhatan men were free to divorce their wives at their pleasure, but nothing is recorded of the women being able to divorce their husbands. If the rumor of Pocahontas's marriage and divorce was true, the unhappy experience could well have given her a heightened appreciation for the softer virtues that Rolfe presented.7

Rolfe struggled against his infatuation with Pocahontas at first. He was concerned that a romantic attachment to the native girl would render him a laughingstock. Moreover, while a relationship with Pocahontas would not violate the letter of Dale's "Lawes Divine, Morall and Martiall," Rolfe was apprehensive as to how Dale would react—with good reason, since Dale's punishments could be as cruel as Chief Powhatan's. Still, Rolfe visited her discreetly at the Reverend Alexander Whitaker's home, "Rocke Hall," under Whitaker's approving eye.

Rolfe's doubts and fears never had much chance of prevailing. Stationed at the end of the earth, he had happened upon a young woman of exceptional vitality, intelligence, and good looks. Pocahontas's looks were altogether exotic from the perspective of an Englishman in 1614, with her light brown skin, her dark eyes, and the long hair running down her back. As time went on, Rolfe found himself distracted by day with thoughts of her, and sleepless by night. Finally he surrendered to the inevitable and sat down to compose a letter to Sir Thomas Dale explaining that he wished to marry the captive princess.

Rolfe clearly felt that gaining Dale's approval would be a delicate matter. He framed the issue in terms of the good of the colony, a strategy that he probably calculated would win favor from the tough-minded marshal and deputy governor faster than a declaration of undying love. Yet Rolfe's feelings managed to surface despite himself. He was, he claimed,

> [in] no way led—so far forth as man's weakness may permit—with the unbridled desire of carnal affection, but for the good of this plantation, for the honor of

our country, for the glory of God, for my own salvation, and for the converting to the true knowledge of
God and Jesus Christ an unbelieving creature, namely
Pocahontas, to whom my hearty and best thoughts are
and have a long time been so entangled and enthralled
in so intricate a labyrinth, that I was even a-wearied to
unwind myself thereout.[8]

Rolfe wrote that he had attempted to scrutinize the peculiar emotions he had been experiencing, in hopes of understanding where they
had come from—the better, he said, to help him make them go away.
Pocahontas's education, after all, had been primitive, her English
social graces were still ill-formed, and her upbringing had been totally
different from his own. He had pondered the Book of Ezra's warning
against marriage to foreign wives. "Oftentimes with fear and trembling," he recalled, "I have ended my private controversy with this:
'Surely these are *wicked* instigations, hatched by him who seeketh and
delighteth in man's destruction!'" But in the end, he had failed utterly
to put Pocahontas out of his thoughts.

On that day in Matchcot, Rolfe was in Dale's party, but he either
would not or could not talk face-to-face with Dale about his intentions. He would not even hand Dale the letter in person. Instead, he
gave it to Ralph Hamor, to be given to Dale at some suitable moment.
Dale, unaware that anything was up, sent Rolfe and another man on an
expedition to try to find Powhatan and deliver Dale's demands. One
suspects that Rolfe was happy to be off the scene.

After Pocahontas announced to the Powhatans that she wished to
stay with the English, "who loved her," she returned with her half
brothers to the ship. There, the full import of her decision was
unveiled. Hamor pressed the note into Dale's hand, while Pocahontas
broke the news to her brethren: she and John Rolfe wished to become
wife and husband.

After recovering from his surprise, Dale must have smirked at
Rolfe's claim that he wanted to marry Pocahontas for the sake of her
religious conversion. Not only was the contention dubious on its face,
Dale was well aware that Whitaker was already succeeding in that
department; no marriage vows were necessary. That was all beside the
point in any case, from Dale's perspective. He was attracted to the

pragmatic possibilities in the union—possibilities for better relations with the natives—and gave his assent on the spot.

The English returned with Pocahontas to the Henricus settlement, where she asked for and received the rite of baptism. With that done, she became the first native in English America to convert to Christianity. In baptizing her, Whitaker gave her the name of Rebecca, after the Old Testament story of the beautiful and pure foreign girl whose arrival was a sign of God's blessing of Abraham.9

Powhatan learned about the intended marriage from his sons, and found it acceptable. He sent one of Pocahontas's old uncles by the name of Opachisco, apparently a brother of Pocahontas's mother, to stand in for him at the wedding ceremony. (The fact that he did not also send her mother suggests that she had died by this time.) Powhatan also sent two of his sons as observers, though not, it seems, the same ones who had met with Pocahontas at Dale's ship—not surprisingly, since he had twenty sons or more.

The wedding took place in April 1614, in the church at either Jamestown or Henricus. Hard details of the occasion are lacking, but under English customs of the time, a springtime wedding would normally have taken place on a Sunday morning at dawn. A woman of the colony must have been drafted to help Pocahontas dress at first light, draping her in the fanciest clothes that could be made or borrowed on short notice—a "tunic of dacca muslin, a flowing veil and long robe of rich material . . . [and] a chain of fresh-water pearls," it has been conjectured—along with a colorful pair of gloves. Pocahontas's hair may have been braided for the special occasion, and in her hand she probably carried a circle of garland made of flowers or fragrant rosemary.

When ready to emerge, Pocahontas would have led a procession of their guests to the church, where Rolfe awaited the symbolic "delivery" of his bride. Keeping pace just ahead of her would have been a bearer of rosemary (for good luck) and a serenading minstrel, possibly the taborer Thomas Dowse.

Friends of the bride and groom would have decorated the church the night before, knitting flowers together by their stems into lengthy chains and hanging them on the church walls. When the procession reached the altar, Opachisco would have given Pocahontas to the groom, a concept familiar to him from Powhatan custom. Pocahontas would have then stood to Rolfe's left while the others took their seats in the pews. The minister in front of them could equally well have been Richard Buck, Rolfe's compatriot on Bermuda, or Alexander Whitaker, Pocahontas's teacher. The clergyman began the service with the words of the English Book of Common Prayer: "Dearly beloved friends, we are gathered together here in the sight of God, and in the face of his congregation, to join together this man and this woman in holy matrimony. . . ."

In 1614, as in the present, the emphasis after a wedding ceremony was on merrymaking—only more so. With the conclusion of the service, Pocahontas would have arranged her garland on her hair, where it would now serve as her crown. The guests, after sharing cake and ale at the church, would have made a procession to the couple's home, formerly Rolfe's home. The notion of the newlyweds whisking themselves off that night, or the next morning, to the solitude of a honeymoon was altogether alien to the English of this time. Solitude could wait. The celebrants would stay for two or three days of feasting, dancing, and outdoor games.

Yet there was one interval of privacy to allow the couple to complete their union. Pocahontas's attendants would have undressed her in her new bedroom and escorted her to bed. By tradition, Rolfe would have been undressed elsewhere and then brought to bed in the midst of much snickering. Rolfe, being a man of an exceedingly serious cast of mind, might not have submitted to this. Nor is it probable that he tolerated the customary wedding-night antics in which the guests, suitably unhinged by alcohol, sewed the couple in between their sheets. Regardless, the guests would have gathered in the bedroom and waited for Pocahontas—coached by the crowd—to toss her stockings from beneath the covers. This was the signal that she was ready for her husband to make love to her, and the signal for the guests to leave the room.[10]

Dale had expected the union to bring about peace with Pocahontas's father, and in this, he was proved right. "Ever since [the wedding] we have had friendly commerce and trade not only with Powhatan but also with his subjects round about us," Hamor recorded. The ensuing years have been called the "golden age" of relations between the two peoples. From the standpoint of the colonists, at least, the phrase is accurate.

There was more. The Chickahominy tribe, which made its home

on the river of the same name, learned of the Anglo-Powhatan peace with some alarm. The Chickahominies were among the region's last holdouts against Powhatan domination. Now that the English were no counterweight to the Powhatans, the Chickahominies realized the days of their independence were numbered. They decided to cast their fate with the English, and sent two men to Jamestown with a pair of deer as gifts for Dale. They proposed to become subjects of King James, answerable to Dale as the king's representative. They would give up the very name of Chickahominy and instead call themselves *tassantasses*—their word for "Englishmen." After some further negotiation with the Chickahominy elders, Dale agreed to bring them under the protection of King James, while allowing them to continue to live under their own freedoms and laws.[11]

In the aftermath of Rolfe's marriage to Pocahontas, Dale saw another angle. There were plenty of examples of European monarchs, including King James, who schemed to alter the balance of power in their favor by seeking to wed their heirs to foreign princes or princesses. As the absolute ruler of the colony (as he then was), perhaps Dale had thought of carrying a variant of that practice over to Virginia. Or, more likely, he may have taken notice of Rolfe enjoying a woman's affections and decided he was overdue for the same. Whichever his motive, he sent Ralph Hamor on May 15 to visit Chief Powhatan with a most sensitive diplomatic assignment.

Hamor's interpreter was Thomas Savage, the young man whom Christopher Newport had left with Powhatan in 1608. Savage had stayed with the chief of chiefs for several years. When Hamor and Savage arrived at Matchcot, Powhatan greeted his former ward with some affection, and then turned to Hamor and put his hands around Hamor's neck. Hamor, mystified, wondered whether Powhatan was about to kill him.

Where is the chain of pearl? Powhatan demanded. *What* chain? Hamor stammered out. "That which I sent my brother Sir Thomas Dale for a present at his arrival," Powhatan said through Thomas Savage. "Which chain, since the peace concluded, he sent me word [that] if he sent any Englishman upon occasion of business to me, he should wear about his neck; otherwise I had order from him to bind him and send him home again."

Powhatan was right: Dale had advised him that any bona fide emissary from the English would wear the chain as proof of his identity.

Dale had been so giddy over Hamor's mission, it would seem, that he had forgotten about it. Hamor's mission was to bring back one of Powhatan's daughters, a younger half sister of Pocahontas, for Dale to marry. Dale had heard that the lady in question would soon be marriageable: she was fast approaching the age of twelve.

Only the most churlish and nitpicking observer would point out that Dale was already married. His wife Elizabeth, Lady Dale, was at home in England; they had wed on the eve of his departure for Virginia. Moreover, the pursuit of a girl not yet twelve years old by a middle-aged man was abnormal even by the standards of Dale's era. Although it was permissible under English law for a girl to consent to marriage as young as age seven, and to consummate the marriage as young as age twelve, such marriages were a rarity in practice; both males and females normally married in their twenties.

For the moment, any moral discomfort that Hamor may have had with his orders was secondary to the physical discomfort of having Powhatan's hands around his neck. Hamor and Savage persuaded the chief to release his grip, and to disregard the missing chain as an innocent oversight. Powhatan brought the men to his house near the waterside. Inside, he seated himself and his visitors on a mat, joined by his wives and male councilors.

> Then he began to inquire [Hamor recalled] how his brother Sir Thomas Dale fared; after that of his daughter's welfare, her marriage, her unknown son [his son-in-law, whom he had apparently never met], and how they liked, lived, and loved together. I resolved him that his brother was very well, and his daughter so well content that she would not change her life to return and live with him, whereat he laughed heartily, and said he was very glad of it.[12]

Social pleasantries completed, Powhatan invited Hamor to proceed with the business that had brought him there. Hamor explained that his message was to be delivered only in private. Powhatan ordered everyone away, except for two "comely and personable" young women seated on either side of him; these, Savage explained, were his queens and could not be sequestered for any reason.

Hamor told Powhatan of Dale's greetings of love and peace, and handed some presents to him: "two large pieces of copper, five strings of white and blue beads, five wooden combs, ten fishhooks, and a pair of knives." Powhatan examined each of the gifts and indicated his satisfaction. Hamor now came to the point: "The bruit [news] of the exquisite perfection of your youngest daughter, being famous throughout your territories, hath come to the hearing of your brother Sir Thomas Dale . . ." Powhatan interrupted Hamor repeatedly as he spoke, wanting to hear no more. Hamor implored Powhatan to hear him out, and continued:

> . . . who for this purpose hath addressed me hither to entreat you by that brotherly friendship you make profession of to permit her to return with me unto him, partly for the desire which himself hath, and partly for the desire her sister hath to see her [an inspired touch], of whom, if fame hath not been prodigal, as likely enough it hath not, your brother by your favor would gladly make his nearest companion, wife, and bedfellow . . .[13]

When Hamor finished, he could anticipate Powhatan's reply. It was not possible, Powhatan said. The girl that Dale wanted had already been sold to another *weroance* for two bushels of oyster-shell beads. She was already three days' travel away.

Perhaps Powhatan could undo the transaction and bring his daughter home, Hamor suggested. Powhatan could return the beads, and the English would compensate him with three times their value, to be paid in copper, hatchets, and the like.

Predictably, Powhatan was unmoved, and showed signs of exhausted patience. He loved his daughter, he said, and could not go on living if he were unable to look upon her often. He would see her rarely, if ever, if she were to live with the English, for he had long ago resolved never to make himself vulnerable by visiting English territory. "I hold it not a brotherly part of your king to desire to bereave me of two of my children at once."

Powhatan either misunderstood Dale's motives or pretended to misunderstand them, treating the request for his daughter as though Dale were seeking her as a pledge of peace. It is likely that Dale, already confident of the peace, was primarily interested in landing a

"bedfellow." Powhatan, however, opted for the more charitable interpretation, and assured Hamor that Dale needed no further pledge than
he already had. For Powhatan was capitulating to the English, then
and there.

> Further give him to understand [Powhatan told Hamor]
> that if he had no pledge at all, he should not need to
> distrust any injury from me or any under my subjec-
> tion. There have been too many of his men and mine
> killed, and by my occasion there shall never be more. I,
> which have the power to perform it, have said it: no,
> not though I should have just occasion offered, for I
> am old now and would gladly end my days in peace. So
> as if the English offer me injury, my country is large
> enough; I will remove myself farther from you. Thus
> much I hope will satisfy my brother. Now, because
> yourselves are weary and I sleepy, we will thus end the
> discourse of this business.[14]

It is tempting not to take Powhatan's speech at face value—to read
it, rather, as a rhetorical device to divert Hamor from importuning him
for another daughter. Yet the reality was that Powhatan had told
Hamor the truth. The English never learned his age, but they had seen
he was an elderly man in the colony's early days. Now Powhatan felt
his energies in decline. After seven years of persistence, the colonists
had simply outlasted his strength of will. Powhatan stayed faithful to
his word, never again waging war on the English.

12

POCAHONTAS IN LONDON

ᐧᕯᕦᐧ

Within a few months of Pocahontas's marriage in April 1614, Dale began to think of bringing her to England for the company's benefit. It was such a compelling proposition from the company's standpoint that the only mystery is why the company took another two years to bring it about. The company's broadsides, or printed flyers, for the Virginia lottery had been adorned by illustrations of exotic-looking native figures; now the company could bring those drawings to reality. A character in *The Tempest* remarks that although the English "will not give a doit [half a farthing, a trivial amount] to relieve a lame beggar, they will lay out ten to see a dead Indian." As a publicity device for the lottery—the Virginia Company's lifeblood since the collapse of the investors' confidence—nothing could compare to a living, breathing native princess.

There were other benefits. The ministers of London who had done so much to rally public interest in the company's stock offering in 1609 would be able to see their reward: a convert to Christianity. And possibly, just possibly, King James could be roused to take an interest in the enterprise, and to lend it royal support. After granting the charter of 1606, he had become either bored or impatient with Virginia, and lost all enthusiasm for it. The only evident attraction the colony had held for him in recent years was as a source of flying squirrels for his exotic-animal collection.[1]

Pocahontas and John Rolfe (or, more properly, Rebecca and John Rolfe) landed at Plymouth on or shortly before June 3, 1616. They were now the parents of a one-year-old son, Thomas, who was said to resemble his mother. Samuel Argall was captain of the ship—an awk-ward circumstance, no doubt, considering the manner of her capture two years before. The Rolfes were joined by an entourage of ten or twelve Powhatans, including a priest named Tomocomo, from whom Chief Powhatan had ordered a firsthand report on the English home-land; Tomocomo's wife Matachanna, who was also Pocahontas's half sister; and a group of male and female servants. In the hold were bar-rels of John Rolfe's tobacco, along with modest amounts of sassafras (believed to be effective against a range of diseases), sturgeon, pitch, and clapboard.

Dale was also there to bask in reflected glory and, presumably, to become reacquainted with his wife. He was "safely returned from the hardest task I ever undertook," he wrote to King James's principal sec-retary upon his arrival, "and by the blessing of God have with poor means left the colony in great prosperity and peace, contrary to many men's expectation." In truth, the peace could be credited to his fellow passengers, Pocahontas and her husband. Dale did bring discipline and a degree of prosperity to the colony, but it is debatable whether a mer-ciful God would have blessed his methods.

The first task of reconnaissance that Chief Powhatan had assigned Tomocomo was to count the number of Englishmen he saw by making notches in a long stick. About as soon as the party set foot in Plymouth, a busy port town, Tomocomo realized the futility of the assignment and threw the stick away.

The Rolfes and their entourage were carried to London by coach. This was evidently a calculated move on the company's part. The last native visitor, Namontack, had been brought directly to London via the Thames, and had thus seen little of England outside the city. He logically concluded that the English were suffering from a dearth of fields and trees, and brought back word to the Powhatans that this was the real reason the English had come to Virginia. This time, with an overland trip of nearly 180 miles from southwest England to Lon-don, the company would set the natives straight: England was not all buildings.[2]

The journey, which would have taken around a week, was a dusty passage on dirt roads—except when the coach passed through more populous areas, at which point it became a tooth-chattering ride over round cobblestones. What the natives saw, to their surprise, was mostly cropland and meadow, the meadow enlivened here and there by grazing cattle. (There was no country, a French visitor remarked in 1606, "which uses so much land for pasture as this.")

As the coach came nearer to London, the scene began to look less idyllic. Pocahontas's disconcerting first view would have been of a slum, the borough of Southwark, across the Thames from the city proper. Out of Pocahontas's sight, past the tenements of the borough, was Shakespeare's Globe Theater. After passing through Southwark, the coach crossed London Bridge into the city. At the entryway to the bridge they would have seen the severed heads of convicts, mounted on pikes for public exhibition. Just beyond that didactic display, the visitors would have had a hard time telling they were even on a bridge; with the houses and shops that had been built on London Bridge, lining it on both sides, one could get barely a glimpse of the river.

To the natives who had lived all their lives in the small, well-ordered riverside villages of the Chesapeake, London could only have made them doubt their own senses. The streets resounded with the rumbling of coaches and carts, the hubbub of the crowds jostling their way along, the barking of stray dogs, and the cries of the hawkers and peddlers—the fishwife's "Mussels, lily white!" or the costermonger's "Ripe cherry, ripe!" The city had grown from just 70,000 people a century earlier to more than 200,000, and commerce had multiplied with the population: grocers and vintners, haberdashers and apothecaries, in fancy stores or (more often) open stalls. The houses of London tended to be narrow, with fronts of timber and plaster, but many of them reached five or six stories into the sky.[3]

The smells of the city were as hard-hitting as its sights and sounds. The wood smoke from London fireplaces would have been inoffensive to the natives, whose houses in Virginia were kept warm—and smoky—with a log fire. The black, sooty smoke and pungent odor of the burning coal was something else. On the subject of England's trees, Namontack had been more correct than he knew. With the nation's population growth, it had been steadily depleting its forests and clearing them for agriculture. That, in turn, was forcing businesses in growing numbers to convert to the only alternative at hand. A Londoner by the name of John Evelyn later made note of the "hellish and dismall cloud of sea-coale" from the chimneys. The city's inhabitants, he wrote, "breathe nothing but an impure and thick mist, accompanied by a fuliginous and filthy vapour, which renders them obnoxious to a thousand inconveniences, corrupting the lungs and disordering the entire habit of their bodies, so that . . . coughs and consumption rage more in that one city, than the whole Earth besides."

Another smell was the by-product of travel by horse and carriage, namely, dung on the streets. The natives did not have domesticated horses in Virginia, so they had not experienced this odor in full force until now. Lastly, and perhaps most strangely from the perspective of the visitors, there was the abundant human waste: the public latrines in the streets, the sewage in the ditches, and the cesspools behind the houses. The natives must have thought the English a notably unclean people.

As the coach passed the churchyard of St. Paul's Cathedral (the predecessor to the Christopher Wren structure now on the same site), the natives would have seen men in stalls selling the mysterious English talking papers—that is, books. A few blocks later, the coach pulled up to their accommodations on Ludgate Hill. Someone with an overactive sense of humor had booked them at an establishment known variously as the Belle Savage, the Bell Savage, or the Belle Sauvage. It was a none-too-elevated combination of inn and tavern, with one wall adjoining Fleet Prison.4

While the Virginia Company had received Pocahontas with less than royal consideration, another party was working on her behalf behind the scenes.

When John Smith returned to England seven years earlier, he was twenty-nine years old—a man in early middle age, but still well within his prime. It is unknown whether he had recuperated from his powder burn by the time he landed, or whether he sought medical help once he reached London (as he had planned to do). Details of his activities immediately after his return in late 1609 are sparse, but with his obvious and lifelong passion for Virginia, he surely tried to get himself another tour of duty there. With his lack of political acumen and his long list of accumulated adversaries, it was equally inevitable that he failed. When Thomas West, Lord De La Warr, sailed for Virginia on April 1, 1610, with his fleet of three ships—the *De La Warr*, the *Blessing*, and the *Hercules*—Smith was not on any of them.

The publication of his *True Relation* showed him another path. The *True Relation* had been edited and published while Smith was in Jamestown, and he had learned of it only after the fact. He had become a published author without even trying. His first book had brought him notoriety and influence; might another book bring more of both—and money, to boot? And with more of those tangible and intangible assets, might he be able to engineer a return, somehow, to the American frontier? Could he, in effect, publish his way out of the box he was in? Such are the thoughts that must have turned over in his mind. In any case, as his London friend Samuel Purchas put it, "Seeing he cannot there be employed to performe Virginian exploits worthy the writing, here he employeth himselfe to write Virginian affairs worthy the reading."

Smith thus took the notes he made while in Virginia and began assembling them into a description of the country. It is clear that the pistol was still a more natural instrument for him than the pen. He started with a list of Algonquian words and phrases, and then launched into a matter-of-fact—even mundane—account of Virginia's geography and climate:

> Virginia is a country in America that lyeth betweene the degrees of 34 and 44 [actually 45] of the north latitude. The bounds thereof on the east side are the great ocean. On the south lyeth Florida: on the north Nova Francia. As for the west thereof, the limits are unknowne. . . .
>
> The sommer is hot as in Spaine; the winter colde as in Fraunce or England. The heat of sommer is in June, Julie, and August, but commonly the coole breeses asswage the vehemencie of the heat. The chiefe of winter is halfe December, January, February, and halfe March. The colde is extreame sharpe, but here the proverb is true that no extreame long continueth.5

In subsequent chapters, Smith detailed the plants and animals of Virginia, the agriculture of the natives, the goods that England could bring from Virginia, and, finally, the natives' culture. Reflecting his own interests and, perhaps, a canny calculation of his readers' appetites, he devoted over half of his book to his copious observations of the natives—among other things, their attire, their religion, their means of making war, and their government under Powhatan. He showed relatively little overt bias against his erstwhile adversaries; neither did he spend any ink assessing them as potential converts to the English way of life. Rather, his voice is mostly that of a neutral observer saying, in effect, This is who they are and this is what they are like—take them or leave them:

> Their buildings and habitations are for the most part by the rivers or not farre distant from some fresh spring. The houses are built like our arbors of small young springs [saplings] bowed and tyed, and so close covered with mats, or barkes of trees very handsomely, that notwithstanding either winde, raine, or weather, they are as warm as stoves, but very smoaky, yet at the toppe of the house there is a hole made for the smoake to goe into right over the fire. . . .
>
> In their hunting and fishing they take extreame paines; yet it being their ordinary exercise from infancy, they esteeme it a pleasure and are very proud to be expert therein. And by their continuall ranging, and travel, they know all the advantages and places most frequented with deare, beasts, fish, foule, rootes, and berries. . . .
>
> Against all these enemies [the Monacans, the Mannahoacs, and the Massawomecks] the Powhatans are sometimes constrained to fight. Their chiefe attempts are by stratagems, trecheries, or surprisals. . . .
>
> Although the countrie people be very barbarous, yet have they amongst them such government, as that their magistrats for good commanding, and their people for due subjection, excell many places that would be counted very civill. The form of their commonwealth is a monarchicall governement, one as emperor ruleth over many kings or governours. . . .[6]

Along with the notes and recollections that went into his manuscript, Smith had sketched some maps showing the rivers of the Chesapeake and the locations of the native villages. He worked with an artist and engraver named William Hole to turn these into a polished and detailed diagram of the region. The map and the manuscript together went to Joseph Barnes at Oxford, who published them in 1612 under the title *A Map of Virginia with a Description of the Countrey, the Commodities, People, Government and Religion.*

While Smith was assembling his *Map of Virginia*, a group of Smith's friends and supporters were working on a series of eyewitness accounts of the colony's early history. Richard Pots, a colonist who was newly returned from Virginia, collected the chronicles of a half dozen other colonists and contributed some of his own. The other contributors were Anas Todkill (John Martin's former servant), Dr. Walter Russell (who had saved Smith from the venomous stingray), Thomas Abbay, William Fettiplace, Nathaniel Powell, Richard Wiffin, and Smith himself. Pots also obtained notes made by Thomas Studley, the colony's first supply officer, prior to his death in August 1607. William Symonds, a preacher in Southwark, then edited the collection, at which point it too went to Joseph Barnes, and was published as *The Proceedings of the English Colonie in Virginia since their first beginning from England in the yeare of our Lord 1606, till this present 1612, with all their accidents that befell them in their Journeys and Discoveries.*

"If you finde false orthography or broken English," Thomas Abbay wrote in his introduction to the *Proceedings*, "they are small faultes in souldiers, that not being able to write learnedly, onlie strive to speake truely, and be understood without an interpreter." The authors made themselves understood only too clearly: from the first chapter to the last, they rallied around Smith and excoriated the company's appointed leaders. It was likely for this reason that the two books were published in Oxford, rather than London; the guild of publishers in London, the Stationers' Company, had invested substantially in the Virginia Company in 1609, and would have been loath to drive its reputation down any further.[7]

In his book published the same year, *The History of Travel into Virginia Britannia*, William Strachey paid Smith the compliment of reprinting around four-fifths of the text of *A Map of Virginia* without attribution. Smith's work, in fact, makes up around a third of Strachey's book. Although this would be considered a kind of theft by today's standards (and justly so), the standards of attribution in 1612 fell somewhere between lax and nonexistent. It would have been unusual for Smith to have complained. Smith's book has received due credit in the centuries since, though; thanks to his observant eye, the *Map* remains today a major source for ethnographers of the Chesapeake natives.

What was key from Smith's point of view, however, was that his books, his notoriety, and his circle of connections brought him another Virginia voyage—two of them, in fact, in 1614 and 1615. These voyages would not bring him back to Jamestown, or anywhere near it; "Virginia" was the term in his day for the entire East Coast of North America between Spanish Florida and French Nova Scotia. Smith's travels would now take him to Virginia's northeastern shore, and he would give the region its name: New England.

So on March 3, 1614, Smith was in command of two ships with forty-five men and boys bound for the waters of New England. One Thomas Hunt served under Smith as captain of the smaller ship, though he had evidently signed on to the project before Smith. The sponsors of the voyage, and Smith's employers, were a group of investors led by Marmaduke Rawdon, a London merchant and wine trader.

Just how Smith made the connection with Rawdon is unknown. What is clear is that his perseverance had paid off—almost. He was still not involved with a colony. The aim of the enterprise was instead to look for gold and copper, and, if that failed, to fish and to hunt for whales. In Smith's estimation, the talk of gold had merely been Hunt's gimmick to draw in the investors. "For our gold," Smith commented later, "it was rather the masters device to get a voyage that projected it, then any knowledge he had at all of any such matter."

The trip yielded neither gold nor copper nor whales, but from Smith's perspective, those were of secondary interest to begin with. While most of the men fished off the coast of Maine, Smith took eight or nine men in a boat to survey the coastline. He drew a map based on his explorations as he went along:

> I have had six or seven severall plots of those northerne parts [Smith recalled], so unlike each to other, or resemblance of the country, as they did me no more good then so much waste paper . . . but lest others be deceived as I was, or through dangerous ignorance hazard themselves as I did, I have drawne a map from point to point, ile to ile, and harbour to harbour, with the soundings, sands, rocks, and land-markes, as I passed close aboord the shore in a little boat. . . .[8]

Among the landmarks Smith recorded were Cape Cod ("Cape James"), the Charles River, and Plymouth ("Accomack"); he landed at the latter some seven years before the Pilgrims. He deemed it "an excellent good harbour, good land, and no want of any thing but industrious people."

Smith's next voyage, in March 1615, was actually intended to colonize New England. If it succeeded, it would be the first permanent English settlement in New England. An earlier attempt had been made in August of 1607 to establish a settlement on the Kennebec River in coastal Maine; that settlement, known as the Popham Colony—so named for its main financier, Sir John Popham, Lord Chief Justice—was abandoned after only thirteen months. The colony's president, George Popham, nephew of the Lord Chief Justice, died of unknown causes. His successor, Raleigh Gilbert, soon received word that he had inherited an estate in England. After enduring a New England winter, Gilbert decided to go home, and the other hundred or so colonists went back to England with him.

Smith was not burdened by any such lack of commitment. He had a false start when the larger of his two ships suffered mechanical problems at sea and had to return to port. On June 24, 1615, he sailed again. In August, as he came near the Azores, two French pirate ships approached and commanded the English to give themselves up. A group of Smith's men pleaded with him to surrender, fearing that the pirates "were Turks, and would make them all slaves; or Frenchmen, and would throw them overboard if they shot but a peece [gun]." They had not been hired to fight, they told Smith. Smith replied simply that he would blow up his ship with the ship's own powder before he would surrender.

Thus chastened, Smith's men put up a fight and escaped the pirate attack. A day later, though, four more French pirate ships closed in on Smith's vessel. Smith, perhaps on a hunch, decided to meet with the attackers on board one of their vessels. Using his French, acquired on the battlefield in years gone by, he determined that they were privateers whom the French government had licensed to capture only Spanish, Portuguese, and pirate vessels—not English ones. Despite this, the French captain, François Perret, sieur du Poiron, did briefly take Smith's crew and their provisions and weapons before restoring them.

By Smith's account, the majority of his men supported his plan to continue onward to New England. When he returned to du Poiron's flagship to collect the last of their arms, however, a mutinous officer named Chambers refused to send a boat over to pick Smith up, claiming, falsely, that it was split. Chambers and his faction sailed the ship away from du Poiron's fleet and returned to Plymouth. Many of those on board attested later that they were "land-men," not sailors, and hence did not initially understand what the mutineers were up to. Possibly they understood more than they let on, and had simply lost their nerve after this second encounter with pirates on the high seas. Smith, meanwhile, was stuck on du Poiron's ship, the *Don de Dieu*, with nothing but the clothes on his back.

Du Poiron promised to let Smith off at the Azores, but broke that promise. The French captain may have had ransom in mind, or, more prosaically, he may have been worried that Smith would report his unauthorized harassment of an English vessel. As Smith's captivity stretched into September and then October, he began to while away his time by compiling his observations of "north Virginia" into a book called *A Description of New England*—an exercise he undertook "to keepe my perplexed thoughts from too much meditation of my miserable estate [state of affairs]," as he put it.

Around October 23, with the fleet near the coast of France, Smith was transferred to a smaller Portuguese caravel that du Poiron had captured. The caravel was now under the command of du Poiron's lieutenant, who held him captive for about a week before confronting him one night with a choice: sign a paper relieving the Frenchmen from any responsibility before the Judge of the Admiralty, or else "lie in prison, or a worse mischiefe." Smith found neither of these agreeable. A storm blew up that drove everyone below decks, and Smith saw his chance. He made a run for the ship's boat and lowered himself and his manuscript into the Atlantic. Under cold gusts and heavy rain, he rowed and frenetically bailed out seawater until he lost consciousness.

The next morning, some hunters found Smith run aground on the shore of the Charente River, "neere drowned, and halfe dead, with water, cold, and hunger." The night had gone worse for his former shipmates. The *Don de Dieu* had wrecked on a reef some twenty miles down the coast, and du Poiron had drowned along with fifteen others.[9]

Smith made his way back to England by the end of the year. The first six months of 1616 found him preparing his *Description of New*

England for the press, checking proofs at the printer's, and working with the engraver—a Dutch immigrant named Simon van de Passe—on the accompanying map of the region, taken from the survey he made in 1614. The book was an account of Smith's voyages, a report of the land along the New England coast, and propaganda for the concept of a New England colony. Soon it would come to the attention of a group of English Puritans, then in self-imposed exile in Leiden, Holland, who were beginning to cast about for a new place of settlement.

A Description of New England was emerging from the printing press in mid-June, shortly after Pocahontas and John Rolfe landed. Smith received word of their arrival through some unnamed channel, perhaps the Reverend Samuel Purchas, who was collecting and editing various accounts of English colonization, and who was in touch with many of those involved in the Virginia Company. Seeing the chance to do a good turn for his young friend, Smith penned a letter of introduction to Queen Anne before Pocahontas arrived in London.

"The love I beare my God, my King and countrie," Smith began, "hath so oft emboldened mee in the worst of extreme dangers, that now honestie doth constrain me to presume thus farre beyond myselfe, to present your Majestie this short discourse: if ingratitude be a deadly poyson to all honest vertues, I must be guilty of that crime if I should omit any means to be thankful."

Smith then recited his debts to Pocahontas for saving his life at Powhatan's capital in December of 1607, and again when she saved him from ambush there in January of 1609. "At the minute of my execution, she hazarded the beating out of her owne braines to save mine; and not onely that, but so prevailed with her father, that I was safely conducted to James towne, where I found about eight and thirty miserable poore and sicke creatures, to keep possession of all those large territories of Virginia."

Smith gave the queen an abbreviated history of the colony's travails, Pocahontas's friendship to the colony, and her capture. "At last rejecting her barbarous condition," Smith explained, she "was married to an English Gentleman, with whom at this present she is in England; the first Christian ever of that Nation, the first Virginian ever spake English, or had a childe in marriage by an Englishman."

Smith now came to his point. He had evidently discerned—correctly—that the Virginia Company would deal with her as cheaply as it could. From his own experience with the company, he could

readily guess that the Rolfes' accommodations would be undistinguished, their allowance for expenses piddling. For England's own
sake, he urged Queen Anne, it was crucial that Pocahontas be received
as a royal visitor, not as a sideshow attraction:

> However this might bee presented you from a
> more worthy pen, it cannot from a more honest heart,
> as yet I never begged any thing of the state, or [from]
> any: and it is my want of abilitie and her exceeding
> desert, your birth, means, and authoritie, her birth,
> virtue, want and simplicitie, doth make mee thus bold,
> humbly to beseech your Majestie to take this knowl-
> edge of her, though it be from one so unworthy to be
> the reporter, as my selfe, her husbands estate not being
> able to make her fit to attend your Majesty.
>
> The most and least I can doe, is to tell you this,
> because none so oft hath tried it as my selfe, and the
> rather being of so great a spirit, however her stature: if
> she should not be well received, seeing this Kingdome
> may rightly have a Kingdome by her means; her pres-
> ent love to us and Christianitie, might turn to such
> scorne and furie, as to divert all this good to the worst
> of evill, where [whereas] finding so great a Queene
> should doe her some honor more than she can imag-
> ine, for being so kind to your servants and subjects,
> would so ravish her with content, as endear her dearest
> bloud to effect that, your Majestie and all the Kings
> honest subjects most earnestly desire.[10]

Pocahontas apparently never had a formal audience with King
James and Queen Anne. Yet Smith's letter had its desired effect. The
colonial-era historian Robert Beverly, writing in 1705, recounted that
"Pocahontas had many honours done her by the Queen upon account
of Capt. Smith's story; and being introduced by the Lady Delawarr,
she was frequently admitted to wait on her Majesty, and was publicly
treated as a prince's daughter; she was carried to many plays, balls, and
other publicke entertainments, and very respectfully receiv'd by all the
ladies about the Court." Purchas remembered that the bishop of London, John King, "entertained her with festivall state and pomp beyond

what I have seen in his greate hospitalitie afforded to other ladies." She won the respect of those who met her, Purchas wrote, because she "still carried her selfe as the daughter of a king"—the class consciousness of England in 1616 operated in her favor.

Notwithstanding Pocahontas's royal status, Purchas took a greater interest in another member of her retinue. Purchas, a round-faced cleric in his late thirties, was the rector of St. Martin's Ludgate, a church near the Belle Savage Inn. Although he never set foot in the New World, he was acutely fascinated by it. He had already produced two editions of his book *Purchas His Pilgrimage or Relations of the World and the Religions observed in all Ages and Places discovered from the Creation unto this Present.* (The modern equivalent of the phrase "Purchas His Pilgrimage" would be "Purchas's Pilgrimage.") When he learned that a group of Virginia natives were staying in town, it was inevitable that he would attempt to interview one of them. Intending to learn about the religion of the Powhatans, he sought out the priest Tomocomo at the Ludgate Hill home of Theodore Goulston, a physician with connections to the Virginia Company.

"With this savage I have often conversed at my good friends Master Doctor Goldstone [*sic*], where he was a frequent guest," Purchas recorded, "and where I have both seen him sing and dance his diabolicall measures, and heard him discourse of his countrey and religion." The sight of the native dances had unsettled the colonists who witnessed them in Virginia; they would have seemed even more occultlike and "diabolicall" to observers in the wainscoted formal parlor of a well-to-do Londoner, where Purchas no doubt watched in amazement as Tomocomo stomped the floor, and undulated his body, in time with a beat supplied by his howling voice.

For their conversations, a man brought over from Virginia by Sir Thomas Dale served as interpreter; whether this man was an Englishman or a native is unclear. Through him, Tomocomo explained to Purchas that their god was called Okeus, and that it was Okeus who "made heaven and earth." He comes to Powhatan's temples, Tomocomo said, and renders instructions and prophecies. "Being asked what became of the souls of dead men, he [Tomocomo] pointed up to heaven," Purchas reported, "but of wicked men they hung between heaven and earth."

Purchas inferred that Okeus was the Christian devil, and concluded sadly that the natives were devil worshippers. Tomocomo was "a blasphemer of what he knew not," and unlike Pocahontas, he would listen to no encouragement to accept Christianity. Tomocomo waved the subject aside by advising Purchas to try teaching the younger men and women who had come over with Pocahontas; as for himself, he said, he was too old to learn. Purchas, in keeping with the well-intentioned mind-set of many of his countrymen, asked readers of his account to look upon the natives' heathen practices "with pity and compassion," and to "endeavor to bring these silly souls out of the snare of the devil by our prayers, our purses, and all our best endeavors."[11]

Among the festivities that Pocahontas attended, the highlight, in terms of opulence and social cachet, was the royal Twelfth Night masque. Masques were a form of courtly entertainment in King James's day that bore a passing resemblance to musical theater. Their players included selected members of the audience, mostly men and women of the court, who sprang from their seats on cue to join the dancing. Staged in the Banqueting House of Whitehall Palace on January 5, 1617, the masque that Pocahontas attended, "The Vision of Delight," was written for the evening's merriment by Ben Jonson. The extravagant scenery and costumes were designed by the architect Inigo Jones.

Some idea of the event's prestige can be gleaned from the wrangling between the French and Spanish ambassadors over the privilege of attending; both men eagerly sought an invitation, but each one insisted on the exclusion of the other. Because the French ambassador had been invited for the past two years running, that year's invitation went to his Spanish counterpart. On learning of this, the disgruntled Gaul sent "passionat reports into France of the prejudice."

Pocahontas's invitation was a sign of her own social success. She was "well placed" at the masque, having a place of some prominence in the gallery, according to the gossipy John Chamberlain. She was accompanied by Lord and Lady De La Warr and Tomocomo. She met a stream of notables in the course of the evening, one of whom was the none-too-majestic King James himself.

Earlier in his reign, the king had been described by a foreign visitor as "handsome, noble and jovial." But by this time, he was fifty-one years old, and a lifetime of gluttony and immoderate drinking had much reshaped his head and body. (His physician noted that the king's drinking "errs as to quality, quantity, frequency, time and order.") His teeth were gradually falling out, and so he tended to gulp down his food, dispensing with the step of chewing. One Anthony Weldon, knighted by James that year, thought it peculiar that the king "would never change his clothes until worn out to very rags." He was prone to excessive sweat, but his dislike for water was such that he would not bathe on any account.

The picture that the king presented was not enhanced by his uncouth manners and his particular disdain for the female sex. "He piques himself," wrote the French ambassador, "on great contempt for women. They are obliged to kneel before him [rather than curtsy] when they are presented, he exhorts them openly to virtue, and scoffs with great levity at men who pay them honour." Englishwomen, the ambassador found, "hold him in abhorrence." So undistinguished was King James—in form, in attire, in comportment—that when Pocahontas and Tomocomo were brought before him and instructed to kneel, they had no idea that the man in front of them was the British monarch.[12]

Pocahontas had to rely on Lord and Lady De La Warr to help her navigate her way through the names and faces of court society. She evidently did not have her husband with her at the masque that evening, and it is easy enough to see why. If John Rolfe had been presented to James, the king would have received him with brusque indifference, if not hostility. Rolfe, as the father of Virginia's growing tobacco trade, personified one of the king's vexations: the pipe smoking indulged in by more and more of his subjects. For all of the king's shambling appearance and doubtful hygiene, he was repulsed by the tobacco habit. In a commentary entitled *A Counterblaste to Tobacco*, he had argued that smoking pollutes men's "inward parts . . . with an unctuous and oily kinde of soote, as hath been found in some great [heavy] tobacco takers, that after their deaths were opened." He considered it "a custome lothsome to the eye, hatefull to the nose, harmefull to the braine, dangerous to the lungs. . . ." It was perhaps the better part of discretion for the company to keep Rolfe out of sight.

Once the crowd settled down for the performance, Pocahontas would have observed a street scene and elegant buildings onstage, constructed and painted in perspective so the street appeared to recede into the distance. From "afar off" entered a bare-breasted woman representing Delight, joined by Grace, Love, Harmony, Revel, Sport, and Laughter. Delight gave a rhythmic exhortation to the players to "play and dance and sing."

What followed was an hour or so of singing and dancing scenes that became increasingly surreal. Delight's song was interrupted by the appearance of a "she-monster"; from beneath the monster's costume tumbled a series of grotesque clowns, to whom she was giving birth. The half dozen young clowns proceeded to dance with a half dozen old clowns until the clowns and monster both vanished. The daytime turned to a moonlit evening, and the figure of Night beckoned Fantasy "from thy cave of cloud" to "create of airy forms a stream." Fantasy, emerging from a cloud, answered that she was happy to oblige:

> Bright Night, I obey thee, and am come at thy call,
> But it is no one dream that can please these all;
> Wherefore I would know what dreams would delight 'em,
> For never was Fant'sy more loath to affright 'em.
> And Fant'sy, I tell you, has dreams that have wings,
> And dreams that have honey, and dreams that have stings. . . .[13]

Stings indeed. Pocahontas must have become utterly lost as Fantasy's speech descended into a mad gibberish embedded with double entendres and interrupted by a dance of otherworldly "phantasms." The anarchy of the masque progressed until an unseen god banished the chaos and created an idyllic springtime setting for the masque's conclusion. In due course, the players informed the audience that this god was none other than King James. Jonson had not forgotten who was paying the bills:

> Behold a king
> Whose presence maketh this perpetual spring,
> The glories of which spring grow in that bower
> And are the marks and beauties of his power.[14]

Even though Pocahontas likely would not have been able to follow a good part of Jonson's text, the spirit of the masque—dreamlike, mischievous, opulent—would have shone through. In it, she must have seen echoes of the royal entertainment she had staged for John Smith and his company at Werowocomoco years earlier (minus the opulence). Smith certainly saw the parallel between those dances on a Virginia field and the masques of Whitehall, and even called the performance "a Virginia maske." There was a vein of pathos in that grand description; he surely realized that Pocahontas's spectacle was the only royal festivity *he* would be invited to see.[15]

During Pocahontas's stay in London, Smith had been busily making plans for a third voyage to New England. Business brought him to the city from time to time to try to raise investment money from the large guilds and their members. It was probably during one of these visits that he chanced to encounter Tomocomo. After the two men hailed each other and chatted briefly, Tomocomo asked Smith to show him the English god and the English king that he had spoken so much about. Powhatan had ordered Tomocomo to attempt to find them both, he said. "Concerning God, I told him the best I could," Smith recalled. Smith had heard that Tomocomo already met the king at the Twelfth Night masque, and told him so. Tomocomo refused to believe it, until Smith supplied enough detail—a description of James, perhaps—for Tomocomo to realize he had.

Tomocomo was stunned when he understood that Smith was right. Not only did James lack the impressive gravity of Tomocomo's own emperor, James had failed to offer gifts to him as a representative of another sovereign. Tomocomo thought of the white greyhound that Smith had given to Chief Powhatan on behalf of Christopher Newport in the colony's first year, and the regal care that Powhatan had accorded the animal. "Then he replyed very sadly," Smith remembered, " 'You gave Powhatan a white dog, which Powhatan fed as himself, but your king gave me nothing, and I am better than your white dog.' "

King James was not the only one lacking in sensitivity. Smith well knew that by any standard of courtesy, to say nothing of gratitude, he should visit Pocahontas and pay his respects. He had spared the time to write a letter to the queen on Pocahontas's behalf, but he had let six months or more go by without calling on her. In his recollections of the period, he sought to excuse his behavior on the ground that he was preoccupied with his latest project; "being about this time preparing to set saile for New-England," he explained, "I could not stay to doe her that service I desired, and she well deserved."

Doubtless there was some truth in that excuse, yet there was almost certainly another factor behind his reluctance—one that he would have been hard pressed to admit, even to himself. Pocahontas had known him in Virginia as a leader of men: capable, confident, respected by some, feared by others. Now, more than seven years after their last meeting, Smith was no longer what he once was. To be sure, he had achieved a kind of success as an explorer of New England and an author. But the middle-aged Smith, unlike his younger counterpart, had predominantly seen disappointment and frustration, from the loss of his presidency in Virginia to the failure of his two New England voyages. While struggling to make another go of it, he was in charge of no one and nothing. He would have been less than human if he had not wondered whether he was still someone Pocahontas would look up to—and whether he ought to leave her old memories of him undisturbed by his new reality.

Finally Smith found the impetus to do what he needed to. Sometime in early 1617, he learned that Pocahontas had moved to Brentford, an eastern suburb of London, while awaiting a return voyage to Virginia. Evidently the news of her imminent departure jolted him into seeing reason, and he went to call on her.

Pocahontas had been told in England that Smith was alive; the tale of his death, she learned, had been an English deception. Still, she found herself unready to see him in the flesh. "After a modest salutation," Smith recounted, "without any words, she turned about, obscured her face, as not seeming well contented." Smith and John Rolfe left her to herself for some time—two or three hours, by Smith's reckoning.

When they returned, she had regained her composure and had some tough-minded words for her visitor. She "remembered mee well what courtesies she had done," as Smith put it.

Smith stopped her at one point when she referred to him by the title of "father." He had been accused in Virginia of plotting to set himself up as the heir to Powhatan's empire by marrying Pocahontas. The charge had been groundless, but Smith could not accept any suggestion of a family relationship, however colloquial and innocent, that might cause renewed suspicions as to his intent. To establish an alliance with foreign nobility, after all, could be construed as treason. "I durst [dared] not allow of that title, because she was a king's daughter," he recalled.

Pocahontas's reaction to that correction showed she was as spirited as ever. She also made clear that he had nothing to fear about her seeing him as a diminished man:

> With a well set countenance she said, Were you not afraid to come into my father's countrie, and caused feare in him and all his people (but mee) and feare you here I should call you father? I tell you then I

will, and you shall call me childe, and so I will bee for
ever and ever your countrieman.[16]

Toward the colonists in general, Pocahontas was not so warmly
disposed. "They did tell us always you were dead," she told Smith,
"and I knew no other till I came to Plymouth; yet Powhatan did command Uttamatomakin [Tomocomo] to seeke you, and know the truth,
because your countriemen will lie much."

Smith recorded only those fragments of their conversation. It was
an awkward reunion, with neither Smith nor Pocahontas sure of how
to pick up the thread of their friendship. They had crossed into one
another's cultures more than any other Englishman or native woman
had done—John Rolfe, it seems, had not even bothered to learn her
language—but they could not cross the chasm of years and circumstances. Beyond the fragments of Smith's notes, one can surmise what
else their conversation touched on. He would have inquired solici-
tously as to her father's health and fortunes (Smith's fights with Powhatan were all in the past now). When she asked Smith whether he was
going to come to Virginia again, he would have declaimed with excitement about his third hoped-for trip to New England. He must have
asked whether life in England was to her liking; at this, her stomach
would have tightened, and stayed that way long after Smith had said
his farewells.

It was a difficult subject precisely because Pocahontas did like
England and preferred to stay there. The fact had become notorious
within the company. Her husband's advancement, however, demanded
that he resume his work in the colony. London offered much for the
lively woman of twenty or twenty-one to like: the company of other
women of her adopted society (who were still comparatively sparse in
the colony), the attention she received at the stylish festivities, the
energy of the city's hustle and bustle. Above all, there was the chance to
explore a new world—for England was the New World from her point
of view, no less than Virginia was the New World to John Smith.

Pocahontas's dream of staying in London was gratified for a while,
as unfavorable winds delayed the Rolfes' sailing. They finally left from
London with Tomocomo in March, once again traveling on a ship
commanded by her former kidnapper, Samuel Argall.

Some dreams have stings, Fantasy said, and Pocahontas's London
dream proved to be among them. The coal smoke of the city had long

disagreed with her—hence the Rolfes' move to Brentford—and she had begun to struggle with illness as she and her husband waited for a change in the weather. Neither Smith nor Purchas had made note of any visible problems in her health before then. In view of her sensitivity to the foul air, it is generally believed her condition was a pulmonary infection such as pneumonia or tuberculosis.[17]

Rolfe apparently assumed his wife's affliction was nothing more serious than the sputtering that came and went among so many residents of the polluted city. By the time the ship was approaching the town of Gravesend, he could see how wrong he had been. Pocahontas was dying.

Argall anchored his ship, the *George*, at the town and Pocahontas was taken ashore. The details of her final hours are lost, but one can imagine the party having taken her to an inn, where John Rolfe sat by her bedside during her last few hours in a state of shock; two-year-old Thomas Rolfe, who was also ill, sitting in his father's lap, understanding little of what was happening; Tomocomo, looking on with growing bile toward the English; and Argall calculating how his employers in the Virginia Company would react to the news.

One thing is known. In Pocahontas's last moments, it was she who had to soothe her husband, not the other way around. "All must die," she reminded him as her life slipped away. "Tis enough that the child liveth."

Her funeral took place the same day, on March 21, 1617, at Gravesend's medieval church, St. George's Parish. The bells of the church marked her passing. She had been ushered into Christianity and then into marriage by the Book of Common Prayer. Now it would be read for her one more time: "I am the resurrection and the life, saith the Lord. He that believeth in me, yea, though he were dead, yet shall he live. . . ."

Argall, Rolfe, and Tomocomo returned to Argall's ship and continued downriver. Thomas Rolfe, too, was becoming sicker, and his father realized that the boy probably could not survive a crossing to Virginia. John Rolfe found himself forced to choose between one shore, where he could attend his son, and the other shore, where his tobacco and his fortunes awaited.

Rolfe made his decision: when the *George* reached Plymouth, he left his son in the care of an official of the local shire, Sir Lewis Stukely. The *George* then left Plymouth on April 10, with John Rolfe on board, for the crossing to Virginia. Stukely looked after the boy until Rolfe's brother Henry could pick him up. Rolfe's son would survive into adulthood, but he would never see his father again.

Knowing he would be criticized for abandoning his son, John Rolfe defended himself in a letter to the company soon after he arrived in Jamestown. In explaining one of the most momentous decisions of his life, Rolfe clumsily attempted to shift the responsibility to Argall and nameless others:

> At my departure from Gravesend (notwithstanding I was importuned) I hadde no such intent. But in our short passage to Plymouth, in smothe water, I found such feare and hazard of his health (being not fully recovered of his sicknes) and lack of attendance (for they who looked to him hadd need of nurses themselves, and indeed in all our passage proved no better) that by the advise of Captain Argall, and divers who foresaw the danger and knew the inconvenience hereof persuaded me to what I did.[18]

In Rolfe's case, it seems, gentility and piousness of speech were not accompanied by strength of character.

While Pocahontas's death was "much lamented" by her husband and her English friends, the fact remained that she served the same practical purposes in death as she had in life. In Virginia, peace with the Powhatans held: Argall, now promoted to deputy governor, reported a year later that Powhatan "goes from place to place visiting his country taking his pleasure in good friendship with us laments his daughters death but glad her child is living so doth opachank [Opechancanough]. . . ."

In England, Pocahontas remained the embodiment of the tractable native, the presumed forerunner of the many who would eventually be won over by the colonists' culture and good intentions—opening the way for unhindered English settlement and commerce. "At her returne towards Virginia," wrote the Reverend Samuel Purchas, "she came at Gravesend to her end and grave, having given great demonstration of her Christian sinceritie, as the first fruits of Virginian conversion. . . ."

The native who returned to Virginia with John Rolfe had not been won over, however. Tomocomo found little to like about English society and told Opechancanough as much when he returned. (Chief Pow-hatan was away visiting another tribe when Rolfe and Tomocomo landed.) In a letter written on June 9, 1617, soon after their arrival, Argall reported to the company that "Tomakin [Tomocomo] rails against England, English people and particularly his best friend Thomas Dale." Argall got wind of Tomocomo's claims and, he said, "all his reports are disproved before opechanko and his great men whereupon (to the great satisfaction of the great men) Tomakin is disgraced."[19]

Opechancanough and his counselors may have pretended with utter solemnity to have been swayed by the colonists' rebuttal. The English, however, could only have been deceiving themselves if they believed they had discredited Powhatan's hand-picked observer of English life. It would be another five years before they would learn the extent of their naïveté, but they would learn.

13

THE FIRST AFRICAN AMERICANS

⟨₰⟩

Chief Powhatan had lived long and, judged by the values of his people, he had lived well. He was esteemed as a hunter and warrior, respected and feared as a leader. He had been husband to more than a hundred women over the course of his life, and father to dozens of children. "The greatness and bounds of [his] empire," as William Strachey wrote, "by reason of his powerfulness and ambition in his youth hath larger limits than ever had any of his predecessors in former times." He could feel satisfaction in his accomplishments, as well as sadness for the loss of his favorite daughter, when he died in the woods of Virginia in April 1618—eleven months after he learned of Pocahontas's death.

In hindsight, it is clear that he could have eliminated the English threat in its early years with more aggressive methods. Yet it is also true that he faced an unusually formidable diplomatic and martial opponent in John Smith. Much of the time, Powhatan could not be certain of the colonists' true strength or weakness. He also needed to consider the potential value of the English as pawns in his struggle with his neighboring tribes. He had to be mindful, as well, that the English might have a proclivity for sending reinforcements to take bloody revenge, as the Spanish were known to do. Powhatan's caution is understandable in light of those ambiguities, which Smith skillfully capitalized on.

When Powhatan finally did decide to root the English out, following Smith's departure, his starvation strategy in 1609 and 1610 came within a hair's breadth of succeeding. It was a tribute to his cautious and canny leadership—and to the liberal outlook of the English, weighed against that of their Spanish rivals—that Powhatan ultimately achieved a state of peaceful coexistence with the settlers.

The Reverend Alexander Whitaker, the minister who had labored for Pocahontas's conversion, had drowned in a boating accident in Virginia the same month that she died in Gravesend. Pocahontas's former husband, meanwhile, was in good health and seemingly in good spirits. By 1619, John Rolfe had married, or was about to marry, his third wife; his bride, Jane Pierce, was the daughter of one of Rolfe's fellow colonists. Rolfe's financial health was on the upswing, as well. His tobacco experiments, which introduced more palatable West Indian varieties to Virginia soil, had yielded him an increasingly lucrative export—one that could displace Spanish tobacco in the English market.

Other colonists were now emulating Rolfe's path to success. One man, with his own hands, had raised £200 worth of tobacco in one year; another, with the help of six servants, had raised £1,000 worth— mouthwatering sums that led to a local gold rush. Indeed, a newcomer to the colony in 1619 would have found little else growing. "All our riches for the present doe consist in tobacco," a colonist reported. From the first four barrels of tobacco leaf that Rolfe sent to England in March 1614, the Virginia tobacco trade had grown (according to customs records) to 2,300 pounds in 1616, 18,839 pounds in 1617, and 49,528 pounds in 1618.[1]

The tobacco mania led to worries in London. It was easy to see the risks in the one-crop economy, not the least of which was a renewed dependence on the natives for corn. King James's opposition to tobacco prompted him to take a rare personal interest in the colony during this time: he could not afford to ban the trade outright—he needed the revenues from the customs duties—but he encouraged the colonists to plant vineyards and to raise silkworms instead. Neither of these alternatives to tobacco farming took hold; they do not appear to have been seriously tried.

A new governor, Sir George Yeardley, came to Virginia in April 1619 and was alarmed by the situation he found. (Samuel Argall's tenure as deputy governor had ended with recriminations and accusations against him of financial self-dealing; he had sailed away shortly before Yeardley's arrival.) Yeardley sent word back to the company that he intended to curb the ubiquitous tobacco planting, and the company's governing council applauded that intention:

> We have with great joy understood of your arrival in Virginia [the council wrote to him], and of your firm resolution to reforme those errors which have formerly been committed. One chiefe whereof hath been the excessive applying of tobacco, and the neglect to plant corne which of all other things is most necessarie for the increase of that plantation. Wee therefore . . . earnestly pray you that nothing whatsoever may divert you from that worthy course.[2]

It was no use fighting greed, however. Tobacco farming continued to grow despite Yeardley's efforts; by 1628, exports had increased tenfold to a half million pounds. John Smith, watching the colony's progress from afar in England, concluded that the company had been on the wrong track all along. It was trying to overcome human nature when it should have been harnessing it. The former bead trader and Lincolnshire farm boy identified the real culprit as price controls that depressed the profitability of corn crops:

> Because corne was stinted at [had a price ceiling of] two shillings six pence the bushell, and tobacco at three shillings the pound, and they value a mans labour a year worth fifty or threescore pound, but in corne not worth ten pound, presuming tobacco will furnish them all things; now make a mans labour in corne worth threescore pound, and in tobacco but ten pound a man, then shall they have corne sufficient to entertaine all commers, and keepe their people in health to doe any thing, but till then, there will be little or nothing to any purpose [accomplished].[3]

Although the company did not succeed in reducing the colony's dependence on tobacco, Yeardley's administration brought two other innovations that would take hold for the ages. At the company's direction, he carried out the first broad-based assignment of private land ownership in English America. Colonists who had arrived before the spring of 1616 (that is, during Sir Thomas Dale's administration or earlier) would receive one hundred acres apiece, "to be held by them and their heirs and assigns forever." Those who arrived later would receive fifty acres. Tradesmen who chose to practice their trade rather than farm would receive four acres and a house.

Some colonists were still working off an obligation of indentured servitude, the *quid pro quo* for their ocean passage; they would receive their allotments when their service was completed. In the meantime, they could opt to live as tenants on company property and keep half of the profits from their farming.

There were ways for the new landowners to build up their allotments. Colonists who had bought shares of the Virginia Company received an additional allotment of fifty acres or one hundred acres per share, depending on how long the colonist had been in Virginia. To promote immigration, the company also promised that anyone who paid the cost of passage to Virginia for new colonists would receive fifty acres for each person transported.

The company's orders defined four "cities or burroughs," namely, Jamestown (the capital), Henrico (formerly Henricus), Kiccowtan (meaning Kecoughtan), and Charles City (formerly Bermuda City). In addition, the company invited groups of investors in England to band together and create their own companies to operate separate farm communities, known as "particular plantations," which would consist of large landholdings outside the four population centers. These companies would receive acreage in return for investing in the Virginia Company and sponsoring voyagers to settle on their plantations.

At the time of the general land distribution of 1619, a handful of these plantations already existed through special charters; two of the earliest were Smythe's Hundred—owned by a venture known as the Society of Smythe's Hundred, and named for the Virginia Company's treasurer at the time, Sir Thomas Smythe—and Martin's Hundred, owned by the Society of Martin's Hundred, and named for Virginia Company attorney Richard Martin. Both men were leading investors in the respective companies. Whether it was on account of the insider status of Smythe and Martin, or some other reason, these plantations enjoyed huge land grants of around 80,000 acres each; other plantations tended to encompass between a few hundred and a few thousand acres—far smaller, though still substantial.

The introduction of private property for the common citizen had a salubrious effect on the owners' sense of initiative, as John Rolfe would observe. By the end of 1619, he reported, the "ancient" (or longtime) colonists had chosen their allotments, "which giveth all great content, for now knowing their owne lande, they strive and are prepared to build houses and to cleare their grounds ready to plant, which giveth . . . greate incouragement, and the greatest hope to make the colony florrish that ever yet happened to them."4

The other major liberalization of 1619 sprang from the company's desire for "a forme of government there as may bee to the greatest benifitt and comfort of the people, and wherby all injustice grevance and oppression may be prevented." That form of government would be English America's first representative legislature. Sir Thomas Dale's authoritarian "Lawes Divine, Morall and Martiall" would be superseded by enactments of a locally elected body, to be known as the General Assembly.

The plan to introduce self-government reflected the growing influence of one Sir Edwin Sandys within the company's governing council in London. His ascent had culminated in his election as treasurer in April 1619. ("Treasurer" was the equivalent, confusingly, of today's "chief executive officer.") Although the plan was adopted by the council in late 1618, before Sandys's elevation, it bore the unmistakable stamp of his maverick philosophy.

Sandys, the son of an archbishop, had entered Oxford at age fifteen, received his BA two years later, and emerged with a fluent command of Latin and Greek. He began serving as a member of Parliament at twenty-eight, and became involved in the Virginia Company in his mid-forties. He wore the trim, pointed beard of an aristocrat, but his notions of government were antiroyalist—as far as they could be without causing the separation of his head from his neck. In Parliament, he had dared to advocate the abolition of all vestiges of the king's feudal rights; he claimed that a monarch's legitimacy rested on the consent of the governed. Even more remarkably for the era, he framed his arguments within a doctrine of natural rights, that is, rights that individuals possess innately, independent of any grant by a sovereign.

On the face of it, the creation of the General Assembly simply gave the colonists a measure of the rights enjoyed by their counterparts in England. In Sandys's own time, however, the new body was seen by some as the kernel of something more radical. A contemporary of his wrote that "there was not any man in the world that carried a more malitious hart to the government of a monarchie than Sir Edwin Sandys did: for Capt. Bargrave [John Bargrave, an acquaintance of Sandys] had heard him say that if ever God from Heaven did constitute and direct a form of government, it was that of Geneva"—the city-state of Geneva being conspicuously without a monarch.

No account of the rules of suffrage in 1619 Virginia has survived, but it is safe to assume they followed the practice of the mother country in excluding male indentured servants (because they were not property owners) as well as all women. The voters of each city, borough, and plantation elected two "burgesses" to represent them. There were seven plantations by mid-1619, so the burgesses included eight men from the cities and boroughs and fourteen from the plantations, or twenty-two men all together.

The assembly resembled the modern U.S. Senate in that its burgesses represented a wildly variable number of constituents. The 34 adult residents of Charles City (from the census taken in March 1620) had the same number of representatives in the General Assembly as the 83 adults of Smythe's Hundred, the 86 of Henrico, or the 108 of the capital. (Different reports of the census showed 921 or 928 residents in total.)5

The new body was not a pure representative democracy by any means. Apart from the qualifications on suffrage, the democratic character of the assembly was slightly diluted by the fact that it included not only the burgesses, but also the governor's "Council of State," a half dozen men appointed by the company to serve as the governor's advisers. These men were themselves colonists, and were charged with representing the colonists' interests, but they had not been elected by anyone. The governor held a power of veto (a "negative voice"), as did the company's council in London. Conversely, the company promised to submit its own orders for approval by the assembly. In all matters, the assembly was obliged to "imitate and followe the policy of the forme of government, lawes, custome, manners of loyall and other administration of justice used in the Realme of England as neere as may bee."

The first session of the General Assembly opened on Friday, July 30, 1619, in the choir of the small timber church at Jamestown. Sitting with Governor Yeardley as speaker of the assembly was John

Pory, the colony's secretary, who had come over with Yeardley in April. Pory was a witty and intelligent man, yet his appointment as speaker is puzzling; he had been a notorious drunk for years. In 1613, when Pory visited Padua as a guest of his friend Sir Dudley Carlton, the British ambassador to Italy, the ambassador was moved to write that "the poor man cannot stand, being (even while this letter was writing) brought home reeling." When John Chamberlain met Pory in Venice in October 1618, Chamberlain found him "in such a pickle that I perceive the pot and he are so fast friends they cannot easily be parted." After Chamberlain learned a few months later that Pory was to become secretary to the colony, he remarked, "No question but he will become there a sufficient sober man, seeing there is no wine in all that climate."[6] Perhaps that is what happened.

The Reverend Richard Buck opened the meeting with a prayer, after which the burgesses took an oath of loyalty. The assembly debated and resolved questions as to the admittance of some of the burgesses. Then Pory presented the first substantive item on the agenda: How to deal with a complaint against John Martin, the 1607 colonist and former council member, that one of his men had seized corn from a group of natives in a canoe?

A colonist by the name of Thomas Davis testified that Martin had sent a shallop under the command of an Ensign Harrison into the bay to trade for corn. Harrison's men encountered natives carrying corn in their canoe, but the natives refused to trade with them. Harrison's men, according to Davis, "entered the canoa with their armes and took it by force, measuring out of the corne with a baskett they had into the shallop and (and the said Ensigne Harrison saith) giving them satisfaction in copper, beades, and other trucking stuffe."

It is unclear whether Davis was an eyewitness to the incident, or had heard about it later. In either case, the representatives took the matter seriously, agreeing—according to Pory's minutes—that "suche outrages as this might breede danger and loss of life to others in the colony which should have leave to trade in the baye hereafter." There was a question as to the assembly's jurisdiction over Martin and his colonists, arising from the unique patent granted to him in 1617 for his plantation, Martin's Brandon: it gave him the right of "any Lord of the Mannor here in England," and exempted him from any obligation of service to the colony other than military service against foreign or domestic enemies.

After deliberating, the assembly handed down an order against Martin "for prevention of like violences against the Indians in time to come." If Martin did not present himself and rebut the accusation, the assembly ruled, he must no longer trade with the natives unless he first obtained leave from the governor (as other colonists were obliged to do) and must put down some unspecified security "that his people shall comitte no such outrage any more." Martin appeared several days later, on Monday, and agreed to the requirement of security, though he would not submit to requesting the governor's permission.[7]

The assembly's response to the complaint highlighted the colonists' continued hopefulness in their attitude toward the natives, as well as their apprehensions about the frailty of the peace. Yet the episode also underscored their obliviousness to another, more problematic possibility: that they might be giving offense to the natives just by being there, occupying ever-larger swaths of the riverfront. The colonists could define an isolated incident of banditry as a problem in need of a solution, but they obviously could not perceive their own presence in the same terms.

Indeed, if a native man had been allowed to witness the proceedings on Ensign Harrison's offense, he would have found them a strange juxtaposition. The assemblymen were intent on suppressing any "outrage" against the natives, but they were doing so as representatives of cities, boroughs, and plantations on territory the natives had once considered their own. The English, for their part, believed their occupation of those lands was consistent with the natives' rights. The English had viewed Jamestown and Henrico as "waste ground," open to habitation by anyone. Kiccowtan and Charles City, as they saw things, had been legitimately captured. Sir Thomas Gates had driven the Kecoughtans from their territory in 1610 in retaliation for the killing of Humphrey Blunt; Charles City was taken from the Appomattocs by Sir Thomas Dale in 1612 "to revenge the treacherous injury of those people done unto us," as Ralph Hamor wrote—the treachery being an ambush of a boatload of explorers whom the Appomatocs had invited ashore to dine. If the Powhatans had any grievances on the subject, the English probably reasoned, those had been resolved by the peace of 1614—the peace of Pocahontas's marriage. The English had acquired other territory from the natives by purchasing it, "and they very willingly selling it," John Rolfe informed London.[8]

It was after John Martin's appearance that the assembly enacted its first general legislation. At Pory's suggestion, Governor Yeardley had named a committee on its opening day to decide which of the Virginia Company's earlier instructions to the various governors ought to be adapted to the colony's present circumstances and made into law. The eighteen provisions that the assembly enacted on Monday dealt mainly with conduct toward the natives, the suppression of vices such as gambling and drunkenness, and the encouragement of crops other than tobacco. The provisions concerning the natives highlighted the colonists' desire to keep the peace, though not to extend social equality:

> By this present General Assembly be it enacted that no injury or oppression be wrought by the English against the Indians whereby the present peace might be disturbed and antient quarrels might be revived. And farther be it ordained that the Chicohomini are not to be excepted out of this lawe; until either that suche order come out of Englande or that they doe provoke us by some newe injury. [The reference was to an event of the previous year, when a group of Chickahominies killed five Englishmen on a trading mission and looted their belongings.]
>
> As touching the instruction of drawing some of the better disposed of the Indians to converse with our people and to live and labour amongst them, the Assembly who know well their dispositions think it fitte to enjoin, least to counsel those of the colony, neither utterly to reject them nor yet to drawe them to come in. But in case they will of themselves come voluntarily to places well peopled, there to doe service in killing of deere, fishing, beatting of corne and other workes, that then five or six may be admitted into every such place, and no more, and that with the consente of the Governour. Provided that good guard in the night may be kept upon them for generally (though some amongst them may proove good) they are a most trecherous people and quickly gone when they have

done a villainy. And it were fitt a house were built for them to lodge in aparte by themselves, and lone inhabitants by no means to entertain them.9

The assembly members worked all day on Friday and Saturday, and resumed on the following Monday through Wednesday. After the five days of study, debate, and voting, the assembly's first session closed prematurely on August 4 on account of the "extream heat" (typical of the region in August) and the illnesses of a number of the members. One burgess, Walter Shelley of Smythe's Hundred, had died on Sunday of unrecorded causes. The health problems were not unusual; around three hundred people had reportedly died in the colony the previous year, most of them of typhoid, dysentery, or salt poisoning (from the salt water of the lower James). The problems may well have been worse for the assembly than for the population at large, however, given the crowded quarters of the fifty-foot-by-twenty-foot church in the summer humidity.

The establishment of the General Assembly in 1619 and the introduction of broad-based property ownership the same year were critical milestones on the path to American liberty and self-government. It is hard to overstate their lasting effect on American political culture, as the bases for the eventual spread of private property and representative government in the English colonies. Once the company had granted those prerogatives, they could not easily be pulled back; moreover, as new commercially oriented colonies were organized in the mid-Atlantic region and the south in later years, their organizers would have no choice but to offer similar prerogatives if they hoped to compete for new colonists.10

More was planted during the summer of 1619 than the seeds of American democracy, however. By a strange coincidence, no sooner did the first session of the General Assembly close than another American institution had its beginning—one that would prove powerfully malignant. It is too unbelievable to credit, but nonetheless true, that American democracy and American slavery put down their roots within weeks of each other.

At the end of August, a 160-ton ship named the *White Lion* arrived at Point Comfort bearing a cargo of "20 and odd Negroes." The ship, a Dutch man-of-war commanded by a Captain Jope, had met in the

West Indies with a ship out of Jamestown, the *Treasurer,* commanded by Daniel Elfrith or Elfirth. Jope and Elfrith were of like mind and made an informal pact of consortship, that is, they agreed to join together in an attack on foreign shipping and to divide the spoils afterward. The target they then encountered was the *São João Bautista,* a Portuguese slave ship under Manuel Mendes de Acunha that was en route to Vera Cruz, Mexico. Mendes de Acunha had cast off from the Portuguese colonial capital of Luanda, Angola, earlier in the year with 350 Africans on board. The sponsor of that voyage, Antonio Fernandes Delvas of Lisbon, had contracted to pay 115,000 ducats a year to Spain's King Philip III in return for a license to import between 3,500 and 5,000 Africans a year to the Spanish New World.

Jope and Elfrith confronted the *São João Bautista* off the Mexican coast. They took control of the Portuguese ship without firing a shot. A passenger on the *Treasurer* later recalled that they "mett with an Angola shippe which had noe goods whatsoever in her and commaunded her to strike saile," taking Africans and, he added ruefully, "noethinge ells." Jope arrived in Virginia with a little more than twenty slaves, and Elfrith followed a few days later with just over thirty. Mendes de Acunha reached Vera Cruz with 147 slaves of the 350 he started with.

Lurking in these numbers is the first of many questions: what happened to the 140 or so slaves who are not accounted for? The grisly answer is that they were probably already dead by the time the *São João Bautista* reached the West Indies, having starved or fallen ill while crossing the Atlantic from Africa. Indeed, a death rate of around 50 percent would have matched the estimated overall death rate of Africans making that "middle passage" over the centuries. An Englishman who traveled on numerous slave ships in the eighteenth century recounted the circumstances of the chained humans in the holds below:

> Some wet and blowing weather having occasioned the port-holes to be shut and the grating to be covered, fluxes [dysentery] and fevers among the negroes ensued. While they were in this situation, I went down among them till at length their rooms became so extremely hot as to be only bearable for a very short time. . . . The

floor of their rooms, was so covered with the blood and mucus which had proceeded from them in consequence of the flux, that it resembled a slaughter-house. . . .[11]

Governor Yeardley bought the "20 and odd" Africans of the *White Lion* in exchange for the food that Jope sought for his return voyage. When the *Treasurer* arrived, Elfrith sought to buy rations from the residents of the borough of Kiccowtan, and then quickly set out again for the Atlantic after they turned him down. Elfrith was likely fearful of lingering in Virginia because, as the captain of an English-flag vessel, he was at risk of arrest for his unlicensed piracy. (The crewmen of the *Treasurer* would later contend, implausibly and self-servingly, that they had taken part in the raid only because the *White Lion* had threatened to shoot at their ship if they refused.) During Elfrith's short stay, at least one of the African women on board either escaped or was sold, and remained in Virginia. That woman was known only as "Angelo." As it happened, the ship that brought her to America in captivity was the same *Treasurer* that had brought Pocahontas to Jamestown in captivity.

Most or all of the men, women, and children of the *São João Bautista* are believed to have been captured and enslaved in the course of a Portuguese war of expansion against the kingdom of Ndongo, around 125 miles inland from Luanda. The Portuguese forces alone were not sufficient to achieve the conquests desired by the colonial governor, Luís Mendes de Vasconcelos. The Portuguese found willing native allies, however, in the sinister organization known as the Imbangala, who have been described as "a quasi-religious cult dedicated to evil in the central African sense of violent greed and selfishness." They practiced human sacrifice of adults and children. Numbering in the thousands, they lived by marauding through one region of the countryside after another, seizing food, livestock, and people as they went. In their symbiotic relationship with the Portuguese, the Imbangala fought the Ndongo kingdom alongside the colonial forces and sold their captives to Portuguese slave traders.

The Portuguese and Imbangala attacks on Ndongo in 1618 and 1619 resulted in the ensnarement of thousands; they were held in Luanda—now overcrowded by the penned-up humanity—until Portuguese or Spanish ships could haul them away. A total of thirty-six slave ships took captives from Luanda to sell in Brazil, Mexico, and the

Caribbean in 1619. Only those of the *São João Bautista* ended up in Virginia.

When the Africans disembarked from the Dutch man-of-war and the *Treasurer*, they would have noticed a number of contrasts between their new environment and their homeland. The intense heat and humidity of Jamestown in August would have seemed particularly harsh to a people such as those of Ndongo, who had formerly made their homes in a cool, elevated territory. The majority of them probably came from Ndongo's relatively urbanized royal district, populated by twenty or thirty thousand residents living in five thousand or more thatched homes—making it twenty or thirty times as populous as the Virginia colony in 1619. The Africans coming from the two ships were more or less evenly divided between men and women, while the colony itself was lopsidedly male by a ratio of around seven to one.

The Africans had arrived in the midst of the colony's tobacco harvest season, and they were undoubtably set to work in the tobacco fields alongside white servants. Although lucrative, the plant was exceptionally labor-intensive compared to corn or wheat. Thousands of acres of plants would need to be cut down, left in the field for the night to "sweat," and then hung the next day from the rafters of a tobacco house to cure. When the cured plants were brought back down, workers stripped each leaf from its stalk, pulled the largest veins from each leaf, and loaded the leaves into barrels. The harvest was the easiest part of the tobacco cycle, at that—the really backbreaking labor would come during planting and weeding season the following year. "It is a culture productive of infinite wretchedness," Thomas Jefferson would write 168 years later. "Those employed in it are in a continual state of exertion beyond the powers of nature to support."

But what was the Africans' status? Although it is tempting to assume that these first recorded Africans in English America were also the first slaves, there is evidence to suggest they were not. They may instead have had the legal position of indentured servants, like many of the white newcomers, eligible for freedom after completing a period of service. Clear evidence of hereditary slavery does not appear in the records until the 1640s; the question remains whether this reflects a lack of slavery in the years preceding, or a lack of records. The sparse historical evidence on the status of African Americans in those years has vexed historians for generations.

John Smith, as already noted, denounced Englishman Thomas

Hunt for capturing twenty-seven natives in present-day Massachusetts in 1614 and selling their "poore innocent soules" into Spanish slavery. Of course, Smith would have regarded slavery that way, having worn its iron yoke himself for a time. Yet he was not alone. John Pory wrote of the natives of that territory as "mortal enemies to all other English, ever since Hunt most wickedly stole away their people to sell them for slaves."

Virginia law at the time made no provision for hereditary slavery, and the institution had disappeared from England over a century earlier. The Africans from the Dutch man-of-war were recorded in the census of 1620, together with four natives, under the ambiguous title of "others not Christians in the service of the English." What is known is that *some* African arrivals of the early years eventually won their freedom—or won it back, to be more precise. One of them, a man who later took the name John Gowen or Geaween, was free by 1641, when he was working as a servant to farmer William Evans. Gowen had a child with a slave woman owned by Lieutenant Robert Sheppard; although Gowen was free, their child became Sheppard's property.

Gowen was able to get his family partway out of slavery's shadow. At some point, Evans was inspired to give Gowen some hogs to breed, with the proviso that Evans would get "half the increase." This Gowen did with great success, to the delight and profit of his employer. Gowen used his share to buy his child's freedom from Lieutenant Sheppard, and so the child was freed by order of the local court. But Sheppard evidently would not part with the child's mother, who remained in bondage.

Another member of this early group, who arrived in 1621 and was called "Antonio a Negro," went on to become not only a free man under the name Anthony Johnson, but a farmer of substantial means. He had 250 acres of holdings by 1651. With Johnson's prosperity, he evidently came to identify with the white landowning class: he became a slaveowner himself around this time, and in 1654 successfully sued for the return of his slave, John Casor, when Casor escaped and took refuge on a neighbor's land.[12]

If the Virginia Africans of 1619 were not held as slaves themselves, the pathway to American slavery was already clear. "Mislike me not for my complexion [color]," Shakespeare's Prince of Morocco feels it necessary to tell Portia in *The Merchant of Venice*. Unlike their view of the natives of Virginia, the English harbored no belief that the Africans would be white if they merely stopped painting their skin. In contrast with Alexander Whitaker's proud news of his instruction of Pocahontas, there would be no recorded effort to convert and baptize the black "others not Christians" (who may have already been exposed to Christianity by way of the Portuguese missions in Angola). Notions of black racial inferiority seem to have been firmly in place in the colony from the start.

A roster made five years later of the colony's living residents put the matter in stark relief. It showed twenty-two blacks—but where the white residents were generally listed by first and last name, the blacks were listed either by first name only or by no name at all. Ten of the twenty-three blacks were given anonymous listings such as "negors," "one negar," or "a negors woman." A roster made a year later showed much the same pattern. Of the twenty-three blacks in that listing, only four were graced with a first name and a last name, while white servants were almost invariably named in full. Within Jamestown itself, twenty-three of the twenty-four white servants had complete records in the 1625 roster of their names, ages, and arrival dates. For the eight blacks in the capital, the full listing reads "negro men 3 negro woemen 5." In that single line, the colonists conveyed the Africans' bitter social position, if not their legal status: colonial officials were already describing the Africans the same way they cataloged commodities.[13]

14

MARCH 22, 1622: SKYFALL

O n May 17, 1620, as the shareholders of the Virginia Company were about to hold their annual election of the company's chief executive, King James sent a messenger to the meeting with his directions. Out of His Majesty's great care for the colony, the messenger related, the king wished the company to choose from his own list of four names, "Sir Thomas Smith [Smythe, the former treasurer], Sir Thomas Roe, Mr. Alderman [Robert] Johnson, and Mr. Maurice Abbott, and noe other." The hundreds of assembled officers and shareholders, taken by surprise, decided to postpone the vote until they could figure out what to do.

The king could not have made it clearer that he did not want his parliamentary adversary, Sir Edwin Sandys, retained as the company's leader. Soon after the aborted meeting, however, the company sent two members of its council to Whitehall Palace to ask him to give way. Those emissaries—William Herbert, earl of Pembroke, and Henry Wriothesley, earl of Southampton—cautiously reminded the king that he had granted the company freedom of election in his charter. His loving subjects would be grateful, they said, to elect the treasurer of their choice. Possibly His Majesty had received misinformation about Sir Edwin Sandys and the company.

His annoyance growing by the minute, King James retorted that Sandys was his worst enemy. He could scarcely hold a good opinion of anyone who was Sandys's friend, he told Herbert and Wriothesley. "In a furious passion," the two men later recalled, the king broke off the conversation by thundering, " 'Choose the devil, if you will, *but not Sir*

Edwin Sandys.' " The company proceeded on June 28 to elect Wrio-thesley himself, who operated as a front for Sandys in practice.[1]

The Powhatans in Virginia had also seen an unorthodox change in leadership. Upon his death in 1618, Chief Powhatan had been succeeded by his brother Opitchapam in the usual manner. But Opitchapam—now "decrepit and lame," in the words of an English observer—lacked the physical vigor expected of a Powhatan chief of chiefs. Whether by amicable agreement or otherwise, Opitchapam was soon displaced from power by his brother Opechancanough, the next in the line of succession. Opitchapam remained leader in name, while Opechancanough became leader in fact.

Opechancanough was a large man, and dignified, as Powhatan had been. In the eyes of the colony's leaders, he seemed to value his friendship with the English. Even though English plantations were taking up ever larger sections of the waterfront on the James, Opechancanough assured them that he and Opitchapam desired nothing more than to continue the state of peace they had enjoyed since 1614. His avowals of peace brought great comfort to the colonists and the company alike: the cultivation of tobacco, and the acculturation of savages, could proceed apace. The company directed hopefully in 1621 "that the best meanes bee used to draw the better disposed of the natives to converse with our people and labor amongst them with convenient reward, that thereby they may growe to a likeing and love of civility, and finally bee brought to the knowledge and love of god and true religion. . . ."[2]

The company had already set aside 10,000 acres of land at Henricus, the site of Pocahontas's conversion, for a college to carry out the instruction of native youths "in true religion, moral virtue, and civility." An anonymous donor in England, signing himself with the melodramatic name "Dust and Ashes," had donated £550 toward the creation of a free school for younger native children, and promised another £450 if the company would bring eight or ten native children to be educated in London. A new arrival in May 1620 would lead the colony's first serious efforts to win large numbers of the natives to the English way of life.

George Thorpe was officially "deputy for the college lands," reporting to Governor Yeardley, but he conceived his role far more broadly than founding a new college. Thorpe came to believe that the veterans of the colony wrongly viewed the natives as antagonistic and untrustworthy. Christian kindness was needed, Thorpe argued, to gain their esteem. Virtually all of the colonists, Thorpe wrote, held "a violent mispersuasion . . . that these poore people have done unto us all the wronge and injurie that the malice of the Devill or man cann affoord." It was time, he said, to put these preconceptions aside, and to make the natives feel loved.

> In my poore understandinge if there bee wronge on any side it is on ours who are not soe charitable to them as Christians ought to bee, they beinge (espetiallye the better sort of them) of a peaceable and vertuous disposition. . . . They begin more and more to affect English fashions and wilbe much alured to affect us by gifte if the company would be pleased to send something in matter of apparell and househouldestufe to bee bestowed upon them. . . . I thinke likewise the company shall doe well to make some publicke declaration of theire intente and desier of the conversion of this people and there withall a testification of their love and hartie affection towards them. . . .[3]

Thorpe had not developed his sympathy for the natives in a vacuum. For two or three years, a native youth, one of Pocahontas's retinue, had lived as a manservant in Thorpe's London household. With Pocahontas's death and Tomocomo's return to Virginia in 1617, the youth had evidently elected to remain in London with Thorpe. Thorpe had him tutored in reading and writing. That Thorpe and the native developed a close relationship on some level is suggested by the fact that the boy converted to Christianity and was baptized on September 10, 1619, as Georgius Thorp in the church of St. Martin in the Fields. Like Pocahontas, Georgius Thorp was not destined to survive the elements and unfamiliar diseases of England for long; he was near his end at the time of his baptism. Two weeks and three days later, he was buried at the same church, listed as "Georgius Thorp, *Homo Virginiae*."

As Yeardley's deputy, and with his backing, Thorpe was in a position to put his ideas into practice. In contrast with earlier days, the natives were now free to enter and roam the colony at will. Having the memory of his namesake in mind, Thorpe was zealous in disciplining any subordinates who caused the natives the slightest offense. After some natives complained to Thorpe of being frightened by English dogs, Thorpe had the offending dogs killed through hanging—a public hanging, so the natives could see for themselves that the animals would trouble them no more. "He thought nothing too deare [costly] for them," a chronicler wrote a year or two later, "and as being desirous to binde them unto him by many courtesies, hee never denied them any thing that they asked him. . . ."

Thorpe's policies brought him critics among the colonists, and not just the owners of the deceased dogs. A minister named Jonas Stockham, who arrived in Virginia shortly after Thorpe, declared sardonically in 1621 that "as for the gifts bestowed on them they devour them, and so they would the givers if they could." Stockham found little to admire in the conversion efforts of Thorpe, a layman—or perhaps Stockham was merely jealous. "Though many have endeavored by all the meanes they could to convert them," he continued, "they find nothing from them but derision and ridiculous answers."

Yet most of the colony eventually became content to embrace Thorpe's policy, and the company's policy, of drawing the natives closer. The colonists' sentiment probably came less from their hearts than from their purses: smooth relations with the natives meant unhindered profits and an extra source of labor. The longtime colonists could look forward to enlarging their plantations or clearing new ones. In accord with the spirit of openness, they commonly welcomed the natives in their homes and hosted them at their dining tables.

The Powhatans' leader was a particular object of Thorpe's interest and generosity. Thorpe ordered the construction of an English-style house and then gave it to Opechancanough. (Opechancanough was said to have locked and unlocked the front door a hundred times a day at first, so intrigued was he with the lock and key mechanism.) By the summer of 1621, Thorpe was periodically meeting with him to discuss the idea of the Powhatans sending boys to live in the colony and to receive an English education. In aiming to separate the boys from their families, Thorpe was clearly calculating that an immersion in English culture would lead the boys to become promoters of "civility" when they returned home to their villages. Although Opechancanough would not agree to Thorpe's plan, he left open the possibility of sending some entire families to live among the English.[4]

In the course of Thorpe's conversations with Opechancanough, the Powhatan leader dropped hints that he might be won over to

Christianity himself. As the local council of state reported to London with enthusiasm, Thorpe had learned "that he [Opechancanough] had more motiones of religion in him, then coulde be ymmagined in soe greate blindnes, for hee willinglye acknowledged that theirs was nott the right waye, desiringe to bee instructed in ours and confessed that God loved us better than them. . . ." It was just what Thorpe hoped to hear.

Opechancanough also told Thorpe something else. He and his brother had taken on new names: Opechancanough was now known as Mangopeesomon, and Opitchapam had become Sasawpen. The English took note of the information for purposes of protocol, but gave it no other significance. Had the colonists of 1621 been more alert students of native culture, they would have found the change of names worth pondering. In the Powhatan tradition, men received additional names to mark great military exploits—or, in the case of chiefs, their leadership of a great military operation still to come.5

Opechancanough had just such an operation in mind. He revealed his intentions to the chief of the Accomacs, a tribe of the Powhatan Empire residing on the eastern shore of the Chesapeake. Opechancanough would need the Accomacs' help with a key element of his plan. During the era of Sir Thomas Dale's retaliatory raids a decade earlier, Chief Powhatan had experimented with deploying a nonlethal drug against the English. It was a hallucinogen, of unknown origin. On two occasions, a small party of Englishmen was somehow exposed to it, and the men began fighting one another in a delirium. In both instances, however, the men's senses were so addled that they never inflicted any harm on each other, and they recovered their faculties before any injury could be done. After the second failure, the Powhatans abandoned their trial of drug warfare. Opechancanough, not yet holding the reins of power, must have regarded the whole episode as another of his brother's frustrating half measures.

Now in command, Opechancanough was ready to move past drugs of the nonlethal variety. For all his affirmations of friendship with the English, he was inwardly set on the colony's destruction—seething, no doubt, from a hundred slights by the English toward his people over the years. He was well able to foresee, also, that the rapid expansion of the plantation lands would inevitably lead the English and the Powhatans to become enemies sooner or later. The plantations already dotted both sides of the James for 140 miles; there were still miles of open spaces between the plantations, but those spaces would only become smaller with time.

While Opechancanough undoubtably knew that disease was still taking a toll of scores, if not hundreds, of colonists every summer, he also knew there were always more ships bringing newcomers: forty-two shiploads in the three years from 1619 to 1621. There were over twelve hundred colonists alive in 1621, vastly more than the hundred or so who landed in 1607. Opechancanough had decided to take action at a time when he could do so on his terms. Having lulled the English into perfect complacency, he contemplated a blow that would kill enough of them to drive any survivors away for good.

Thus, Opechancanough requested from the Accomac chief a supply of deadly poison from a plant that grew in Accomac territory. The plant was most likely *Cicuta maculata*, which occurs naturally on the Eastern Shore; it is also known as water hemlock. Although the Accomacs were subjects of the Powhatans, they, like the Patawomecks, were distant enough that they could exercise their own will as a matter of practice. The Accomac chief, who was on good terms with the English, balked at Opechancanough's request. Opechancanough sent him presents to soften his attitude. The chief steadfastly refused, and in turn gave the English the most valuable gift he could have given them: a warning of Opechancanough's intentions.

Word of the plot caused a momentary panic in the colony. Governor Yeardley himself went to each of the boroughs and all of the forty or so plantations, ordering them to keep a continual watch for trouble. Opechancanough, however, denied having ever plotted against the English. With no other evidence coming to light, the colonists finally accepted Opechancanough's denial. It was more appealing, from the colonists' point of view, to assume the best than to assume the worst, since the lookout duty was an unwelcome diversion of energy from more lucrative pursuits. "Our people by degrees fell againe to theire ordinary watch," the council in Jamestown later wrote, "not beeinge able to follow their severall labors and keepe so strict a guarde."

In October 1621, nine ships brought another load of settlers; among them was Sir Francis Wyatt, the company's choice to succeed Yeardley as governor when his term ended on November 18. In a report to the company in January, Wyatt's council of state described one of his first official acts upon taking his post: "Findinge the coun-trey at his arrivall in very greate amytie and confidence with the natives, and beinge desirous by all good meanes to continue and enlarge the same," Wyatt sent Thorpe with presents and a message of friendship to both Opechancanough and Opitchapam. The real and nominal heads of the Powhatan Empire responded that they were gratified to learn of the new governor's desire for concord.[6]

Opechancanough bided his time through the first months of 1622. A possible setback occurred in the second week of March—a violent incident involving a Powhatan captain named Nemattanew. Nemat-tanew was a familiar figure to the colonists, who had nicknamed him "Jack of the Feather" for his habit of dressing himself flamboyantly in plumage, and fastening swan's wings to his shoulders as though he might fly. During the earlier era of conflict with the English, he had inspired his troops by claiming to possess special powers that rendered him immune to the effects of English gunshot.

The incident in March began when Nemattanew invited an Englishman named Morgan to join him for a trading journey to the Pamunkeys. After Nemattanew returned alone a few days later, two of Morgan's young servants asked him where their master was. Nemat-tanew told them he was dead, and did not elaborate further. Noticing that Nemattanew had Morgan's cap on his head, the servants con-cluded that Nemattanew had robbed and killed their master. As they told the story later, they intended to bring Nemattanew to George Thorpe, but he resisted. Whatever the truth of the matter, the scene ended with Nemattanew dead, of gunshot wounds.

Fortunately for Opechancanough, the matter did not rouse the colonists' bygone fears. The governor and council in Virginia offered "to doe him [Opechancanough] justice" if Nemattanew were shown to be innocent. Opechancanough suppressed any anger he might have felt and assured the English by messenger that Nemattanew "being but one man should be no occasion of the breach of the peace." He avowed that he wanted no part in disrupting the peace. "The sky," he told them, "should sooner fall."[7]

The sky was about to fall.

For the colonists, Friday, March 22, 1622, started as a day like any other. Morning found native men visiting the plantations in their usual manner, bringing deer, turkeys, fish, and fur to trade in return for beads, glass, and metal. Some of the men joined the English at their tables for breakfast. Others mingled among the English in their workplaces—in the fields, at their brick-firing kilns and their forges, at their building sites and workbenches. The visitors carried no weapons.

A colonist named Richard Pace landed at Jamestown that morning in a state of anguish, demanding to see the governor. He had rowed from his plantation three miles across the river, where a native working as a servant had broken ranks and told him what was going to happen. On account of Pace's warning, Jamestown itself was prepared for March 22—militarily, at least. Governor Wyatt was able to get warnings out by boat to a number of other communities, but the English plantations were too widely scattered for word to reach all of them in time. Some sixteen plantations and numerous smaller settlements were left totally exposed.

At those sites, the colonists and the natives interacted in their everyday manner until the natives abruptly began their assault. They slaughtered men, women, and children with the colonists' own swords and work tools—axes, knives, saws, and hammers. In an instant, hundreds of English were lying lifeless. "Not being content with taking away life alone," noted a report after the attack, "they fell after againe upon the dead, making as well as they could, a fresh murder, defacing, dragging, and mangling the dead carkasses into so many pieces, and carrying some parts away in derision, with base and bruitish triumph."

To achieve surprise, Opechancanough had sent the men without bows and arrows or shields; wherever they encountered resistance, they withdrew. Thus Jamestown suffered no loss of life, while the plantation of Martin's Hundred just seven miles downriver lost nearly its entire population, more than seventy in all. The long list of the dead at Martin's Hundred opened with these entries, which suggest the frenzied and indiscriminate character of the killing:

Lieutenant Richard Kean
Master Thomas Boise, & Mistris Boise his wife, & a sucking childe
4 of his men [servants]
A maide
2 children
Nathaniel Jeffries wife
Margaret Davies

Richard Staples, his wife, and childe
2 maides
6 men and boyes[8]

On the college lands at Henricus, the site of George Thorpe's project, seventeen workmen died in the attack. At a location nearby, where the company had been attempting to establish an ironworks, everyone present was killed except for a boy and girl who found a hiding place.

Thorpe was at his home at Berkeley Hundred plantation that morning. There, too, residents had no foreknowledge of Opechancanough's plan. Thorpe himself did have a kind of warning, however: as the time approached, his servant became suspicious of the natives' behavior and urged him to leave for a safe place. Thorpe dismissed the man's fears. The servant then took his own advice and ran off, thereby ensuring he would live to see another day. Berkeley Hundred evidently managed to put up a defense once the attack started, but still lost nine men along with a woman and her child.

Thorpe's servant had counseled him wisely, and Thorpe paid a high price for his disbelief. The natives took special care of their would-be benefactor that morning. First, the attackers stabbed him or bludgeoned him to death. Then, it was reported, they "cruelly and felly [fiercely], out of devilish malice, did so many barbarous despights and foule scornes after to his dead corpse, as are unbefitting to be heard by any civill eare." The circumspect phrasing was out of consideration, perhaps, for the wife, eight-year-old daughter, and three young sons he had left in England.

At the morning's end, at least 347 English were dead, and possibly as many as 400. The colony's population beforehand had been roughly 1,240, so the mortality amounted to somewhere between a quarter and a third of the colonists. Of equal significance, the membrane of normality that had recently surrounded the English in Virginia—or which they had assumed to be surrounding them—was now punctured. "I thinke the last massacre killed all our countrie," wrote colonist William Capps in a letter to a friend. "Beside them they killed, they burst the heart of all the rest."[9]

Even news as shocking as this could not reach England any faster than the winds over the Atlantic. So it was that when the Reverend Patrick Copland delivered a sermon to the investors of the company in

London on April 18, his subject was "Thanksgiving for the Happie Successe of the Affayres in Virginia This Last Yeare." Copland, who had raised money for the planned free school for the natives, gave the sermon at the company's invitation at St. Mary-Le-Bow Church. Neither he nor anyone in his audience had a hint of knowledge about the massacre that had taken place nearly a month before. "Blessed be God," Copland told the company, "there hath been a long time, and still is a happie league of peace and amity soundly concluded, and faithfully kept, between the English and the natives, that the feare of killing each other is now vanished away."

Not until mid-July did a ship called the *Sea-flower* arrive from Virginia with letters recounting the attack. The news prompted John Donne, the poet and dean of St. Paul's Cathedral, to preach in favor of keeping the colony on the same course Thorpe had set. The colonists, Donne argued, must continue to attempt to win the natives' esteem— and forswear revenge:

> Enamore them with your justice, and (as farre as may consist with your security) your civilitie; but inflame them with your godliness, and your religion. Bring them to love and reverence the name of that King, that sends men to teach them the wayes of civilitie in this world, but to feare and adore the name of that King of Kings, that sends men to teach them the waies of religion, for the next world.[10]

Donne, however, was distinctly in the minority. Although Opechancanough had achieved an impressive tactical victory, his attack would prove to be a strategic error. Indeed, it was a blunder of seismic proportions. The news of the massacre forced the English— gentleman investors, members of Parliament, and divines alike—to reconsider the entire ideology of coexistence and cultural assimilation in the New World. If Opechancanough had been offended by the manifestations of that ideology, he would find its replacement still less congenial. Where English commentators had formerly expressed disgust at the murderous practices of the Spanish colonials, the English view of the conquistadors would now be tempered with some admiration. For those involved in the Virginia Company, the events of March 22 demanded not only revenge, but total and thorough revenge. In his hour of victory, Opechancanough had set in motion nothing less than the inexorable destruction of his own people.

The first written work to be published on the massacre appeared in July, shortly after the news had reached London. No copies of that work, entitled *Morninge [Mourning] Virginia*, are known to have survived. The next to appear, in August, was the company's *Declaration of the State of the Colony and Affaires in Virginia: With a Relation of the Barbarous Massacre in the time of peace and League, treacherously executed by the Native Infidels upon the English, the 22 of March last.* The company had commissioned Edward Waterhouse, its former secretary, to assemble an authoritative account from the various letters and from the eyewitnesses who came back on the *Sea-flower.* His book foreshadowed the angry tone of much commentary to come, casting aside the earlier hopeful depictions of the natives.

For the first time in Virginia Company literature, Waterhouse characterized the natives as "these beasts," or as worse than beasts. Even lions and dragons, he wrote, were known to show gratitude to those who helped them. "But these miscreants [the natives], contrariwise in this kinde, put not off onely [not only put off] all humanity, but put on a worse and more then unnaturall bruitishnesse." Yet there was a positive side to the situation. In light of the natives' perfidy, the English could now justly exercise free rein over the Virginia countryside:

> Because our hands which before were tied with gentlenesse and faire usage, are now set at liberty by the treacherous violence of the savages, not untying the knot, but cutting it: So that we, who hitherto have had possession of no more ground then their waste, and our purchase at a valuable consideration to their owne contentement, gained; may now by right of warre, and law of nations, invade the country, and destroy them who sought to destroy us: whereby wee shall enjoy their cultivated places, turning the laborious mattocke [hoe] into the victorious sword. . . .[11]

For the achievement of that conquest, Waterhouse found convenient models at hand. He praised the mastery of Hernando Cortés over the Aztecs in Mexico, and that of Francisco Pizarro over the Incas in

Peru. Their victories had been achieved through strategies of divide and conquer—methods that he felt the English could emulate in Virginia. The English could also emulate the Spaniards' enslavement of the natives. "The Indians, who before were used as friends, may now most justly be compelled to servitude and drudgery. . . ." All in all, Waterhouse held, the natives had wounded themselves more than the colony.

Of the same frame of mind was Christopher Brooke, a Virginia Company lawyer and published poet, whose "Poem on the Late Massacre in Virginia" appeared in September. When Brooke heard the news of the massacre, his poem recalled, the horror of it seized his power of speech, "and for certaine howres I seem'd a breathing statue." He then struggled to find God's purpose in allowing "those bestiall soules" to kill innocent men, women, and children. That purpose, Brooke concluded, was to impart to the English a warning against trust and complacency:

> Securitie, the Heaven that holds a Hell,
> The bane of all that in this slaughter fell;
> For ever be thou ban'd and banish't quite
> From wisdomes confines, and preventions light.
> Let this example (in the text of blood)
> Be printed in your hearts, and understood
> How deare 'twas bought; for to the price it pulls
> A field of Golgotha [sites of suffering] or dead mens skulls.[12]

After eulogizing some of the prominent men among the dead, Brooke ended with an assurance of a bright future for the colony, along with a call to bring earthly justice upon the natives:

> Take heart, and fill your veynes; the next that bleed
> Shall be those fiends: and for each drop of ours,
> I strongly hope, we shall shed theirs in showers.
> Then keepe your seates, and fearlesly go on,
> For greater gaine to the plantation
> From the late losse, may probably be found.[13]

The Reverend Samuel Purchas joined the fray a few years later with his essay "Virginias Verger," a verger being the person who carries a ceremonial rod or staff in a procession. The procession he had in mind was seemingly a funeral—for the native dead to come. In the aftermath of March 22, Purchas had come far from his days of disputing cordially with Tomocomo and delighting in Pocahontas's conversion. He conceded at the outset of "Virginias Verger" that it is sinful for Christians to steal land away from heathens; normally, only "vacant places" in a country are rightfully possessed by colonizers. The natives' violation of natural law, however, opened the way for just conquest of "these barbarians, borderers, and out-lawes of humanity." The very earth, he argued, "seems distempered with such bloudy potions and cries that she is ready to spue out her inhabitants [the buried dead]: Justice cryeth to God for vengeance, and in his name adjureth prudence and fortitude to the execution."

For John Smith, word of the attack came less as a surprise than as an affirmation of old beliefs. It was obvious that the natives did not like seeing the English plant themselves nearby. Gifts of English copper crowns and English houses, Smith recognized, would not cause the native leaders to lose sight of the fact that the English were a rival power. If the colonists kept up their strength and their caution, they could do business with the natives, to be sure. As for the colonists' dropping the most elementary security to show the natives their good faith and kindness, as for the colonists wanting to be loved—well, that was simply foolish. On the frontier of Virginia, as on the battlefields of Hungary, commanders who substituted wishful thinking for facts were a mortal danger to their men.

Hearing and reading the stories from Virginia over the years, Smith had been "amazed," he wrote, that the natives had been "imploied in hunting and fowling with our fowling peeces [guns], and our men rooting in the ground about tobacco like swine; besides that, the salvages that doe little but continually exercise their bow and arrowes, should dwell and lie so familiarly amongst our men that practiced little but the spade." Smith had read the 1621 letter from the skeptical minister Jonas Stockham to the Virginia Company council; Stockham, Smith said, had been right all along.

Nonetheless, the March 22 tragedy drew Smith into the same "labyrinth of melancholy" (in his words) as his countrymen. Part of the reason was personal: among the dead was Nathaniel Powell, a 1607 settler who had been part of Smith's small band of adventurers and supporters in the early years. Powell had contributed favorable accounts of Smith's leadership to William Symonds's *Proceedings*. After devoting twelve years of his life and labor to the betterment of the colony, Powell had been rewarded in 1619 with a six-hundred-acre plantation, which he proudly named Powell-brooke. He had settled down and married. As Smith remembered him, he was "one of the first planters, a valiant souldier, and not any in the countrey better knowne than him." But Powell, like so many others, was the victim of the colony's "over-conceited power and prosperitie," with the result that the natives killed him and his wife, Joyce, and "butcher-like hagled [hacked] their bodies."

The proper course of action, Smith thought, was obvious. In past years, "soldiers" had been ordinary working colonists on temporary military duty. Now, as Smith saw it, the necessity to drive the natives away and protect against future attacks made it imperative to establish a professional, full-time fighting force. Smith set pen to paper to make an offer to the Virginia Company:

> If you please I may be transported with a hundred souldiers and thirty sailers by the next Michaelmas, with victuall, munition, and such necessary provision, by Gods assistance, we would endeavor to inforce the salvages to leave their country, or bring them in that feare and subjection that every man should follow their businesse securely. . . .[14]

The company did not have the funds to hire a hundred soldiers, however. The council suggested that Smith take on the project himself, at his own expense, in return for half of whatever he could plunder from the natives. Smith walked away from the insulting and ill-informed proposition. "Except it be a little corne at some time of the yeare is to be had, I would not give twenty pounds for all the pillage is to be got amongst the salvages in twenty years," he noted.

Although the colonists would have to take action against the natives on their own, the news of the massacre did bring forth an enormous supply of armaments from the mother country. The company immediately sent forty-two barrels of gunpowder, and King James made a gift of weapons from his supply: a thousand halberds (spears with axlike blades), a thousand light muskets, three hundred pistols, a hundred brigandines (armored vests), four hundred chain-mail shirts and coats, four hundred bows, eight hundred sheaves of arrows, and two thousand iron helmets. A private donor gave another sixty chain-mail coats.

The company sent all of the materiel to Virginia except for the bows and arrows, the donation of which had put the company in a quandary. While the bows and arrows were obsolete for warfare in Europe, they could serve effectively against the enemy in Virginia. The difficulty was that the natives were better-trained archers than the colonists, and it would be potentially disastrous to put hundreds of metal arrows within their reach. Yet to turn the gift away, offending the king in his moment of generosity, was scarcely any more attractive. The company's council arrived at the solution of ordering the bows and arrows to be deposited on Bermuda en route to the mainland—"in a readiness against there should be occasion to use them in Virginia," as the councilors tactfully expressed it. There the cache stayed.

Governor Wyatt, after recovering from the shock of the massacre, ordered the majority of the plantations to be abandoned. It was clear that the colonists had heightened their vulnerability to attack by spreading the settlements so far distant; they could neither warn nor aid their neighbors in case of trouble. To make the colony defensible, Wyatt relocated all of the nine hundred or so survivors either to Jamestown or to one of the five plantations that he had decided to keep in English hands. The college lands were left behind, along with the notion of founding a college for the natives. The first retaliatory raids got under way in June with two expeditions against the Rappa-hannocks. Wyatt subsequently ordered his predecessor, Sir George Yeardley, to "make warr, kill, spoile, and take by force or otherwise whatsoever boote of corne, or any thing else he can attain unto, from any the salvadges our enemies."

The company sent a letter to Wyatt and his council in August, patently written with an eye to diverting blame from the the company's own policies in setting the stage for the massacre:

> We have to our extreame grief understood of the great massacre executed on our people in Virginia, and that in such a manner as is more miserable then the death it self; to fall by the hands of men so con-temptible; to be surprised by treacherie in a time of known danger . . . and almost guiltie of the destruction

by a blindfold and stupid entertaining of it; which the least wisdome or courage suffised to prevent even on the point of execution: are circumstances, that do add much to our sorrow. . . .[15]

After that starkly unsympathetic preamble, the company urged the colonists to undertake "perpetual warre without peace or truce."

King James's weapons arrived late in the year, together with another letter from the company. In this missive, the council scolded Wyatt for ordering the withdrawal from most of the plantations. "We conceave it a sinne against the dead, to abandon the enterprize, till we have fully settled the possession, for which so many of our brethren have lost theire lives." The council then repeated its admonition to pursue unstinting warfare: "a sharp revenge upon the bloody miscreants," it directed, "even to the measure that they intended against us, the rooting them out for being longer a people uppon the face of the Earth."[16]

The leadership in Virginia fully agreed with the goal of exterminating the natives. "Wee have much anticipated your desires by setting uppon the Indyans in all places," Wyatt responded on January 20, 1623.

We have slaine divers [diverse, many], burnte their townes, destroyed their wears [fishing weirs] and corne. . . . It is most aparant that they are an enemy nott suddenly to be destroyde with the sworde by reasone of theire swyftnes of foote, and advantages of the woode . . . but by the way of starvinge and all other means that we can possiblely devise we will constantlie pursue their extirpatione. By computation and confessione of the Indyans themselves we have slayne more of them this yeere, then hath been slayne before since the begininge of the colonie.[17]

London's feigned ignorance of its own culpability, however, was too much for Wyatt and his council to stomach.

Wheras in the begininge of your letters by the [ship] *Trewlove* you pass soe heavie a censure uppon us

as if we alone were guiltie, you may be pleased to consider what instructions you have formerly given us, to
wynn the Indyans to us by a kind entertayninge them
in our houses, and if it were possible to cohabitt with
us, and how ympossible it is for any watch and warde to
secure us against secrett enemies that live promiscous-
lie amongst us, and are harbored in our bosomes, all
histories [accounts of the massacre] and your owne discourse may sufficyently informe you.[18]

Notwithstanding the colonists' aggressive tactics, they still had
much to fear from the natives, who continued to make periodic smaller
raids. In addition, a series of circumstances brought about near-famine
conditions: the loss of many men just before planting season, the danger of fresh attacks on laborers in the fields, and the need to divert men
from field work to guard duty meant that there was little to harvest
in the autumn of 1622. Inadequate diet, disease, and renewed attacks
from the natives would kill more colonists over the year than the massacre itself had—more than five hundred, by one account.

Letters sent home in March and April of 1623 told of despair. "To
write of all crosses and miseries which have befallen us at this time we
are not able: The Lord hath crossed us by stricking most of us with
sicknes and death," wrote Samuel Sharpe. "Thorp he hath brought
such misery upon us by letting the Indians have their head and none
must controll them," William Capps complained to John Ferrar, the
company's former deputy treasurer. "Instead of a plantation itt [Vir-
ginia] will shortly get the name of a slaughter house," opined a visitor,
Nathaniel Butler. Colonist Edward Hill wrote to his brother Joseph,
"We lyve in the fearfullest age that ever Christians lyved in."

An enduring mystery is the number of African deaths in the massacre. Waterhouse's roster of the dead did not include any Africans; if
any had appeared in the list, he or she would certainly have been identified as "a negro" or in some similar form, in keeping with the custom
of the day. (A few white, non-English victims did appear on the list,
such as "Francis, an Irishman" and "Mathew, a Polander.") This raises
the possibility that all of the Africans were spared, whether on account
of good luck, their greater caution around the natives, or a feeling of
solidarity on the part of the natives themselves. Because the list was
explicitly intended for the benefit of the victims' heirs at home, how-

ever, it is not clear that Waterhouse would have included any African dead in the first place. A high proportion of the Africans in Virginia did die around this period—their numbers fell from thirty-two in 1620 to twenty-three in 1624, or by nearly a third—but they could have died from the same malnutrition and illnesses that were killing the whites.

The company continued to recruit new settlers with promises of ready wealth to be had thanks to the labors of those now dead. What time could be more opportune, many of the newcomers must have reckoned. No doubt some were moved by a desire to aid an important national enterprise. Others, as in years past, were recalcitrant or otherwise unemployable youths sent abroad by their parents. One of these was Richard Frethorne of Martin's Hundred, who arrived around Christmas of 1622, and soon wished he had not:

> Loveing and kind father and mother, my most humble duty remembered to you hopeing in God of your good health, as I my selfe am at the making [writing] hereof, this is to let you understand that I your child am in a most heavie case by reason of the nature of the country is such that it causeth much sicknes . . . and when we are sicke there is nothing to comfort us; for since I came out of the ship, I never ate anie thing but peas, and loblollie (that is water gruell) as for deare or venison I never saw anie since I came into this land, ther is indeed some fowl, but wee are not allowed to goe, and get yt, but must worke hard both earlie, and late for a messe of water gruell, and a mouthful of bread, and beife. . . .
>
> People crie out day, and night, Oh that they were in England without their lymbes and would not care to loose anie lymbe to bee in England againe, yea though they [would have to] beg from doore to doore, for wee live in feare of the enimy everie hour. . . .
>
> If you love me you will redeeme me suddenlie [pay off my indenture immediately], for which I doe intreate and begg. . . .[19]

Throughout 1622 and early 1623, raiding parties from the colony continued to strike at the native towns, stealing their corn, destroying what the raiders could not carry away, and setting their homes to the torch. The natives, too, were feeling the effects of a diminished food supply. In late March, Opechancanough sent a messenger to Martin's Hundred proposing a truce. The gist of the message, as Wyatt and his council summarized it for London, was "that blud inough had already been shed on both sides, that many of his people were starved by our takinge away their corne and burninge theire howses," and so Opechancanough asked for his people to be able to plant freely in some of their territories. If so, he said, he would release twenty English who had been taken prisoner on March 22, and would also allow the English to plant in peace.

The English had been frustrated by their inability to achieve a truly decisive blow against the natives, with their capacity to vanish into the woods. Opechancanough's offer opened up an appealing alternative: not peace, but the appearance of peace. If the natives came to feel safe, Wyatt and the council decided, it would be all the easier to surprise them. Two could play at the game of treachery. In the words of George Sandys, the colony's treasurer in Virginia (and brother of Sir Edwin), the English would "trie if wee can make them as secure as wee *were, that we may follow their example in destroying them.*" (Emphasis in original.) The colonists readily assented to Opechancanough's proposal.

The opportunity to betray Opechancanough came on the very day the peace was ratified. On May 22, 1623, William Tucker sailed with a dozen colonists to the Pamunkey River to meet with the Powhatan leader and to receive the English captives. Opechancanough was accompanied by the chief of the Kiskiack tribe and a large contingent of his own men. After many speeches were made on both sides, Tucker offered to share the contents of a large wooden cask of white wine that he had brought for the occasion—wine that had been laced with poison by the colony's physician, John Pott. Tucker and his English interpreter made a show of drinking first; their drinks had been drawn from a separate container out of the natives' sight. Opechancanough somehow survived, but a large number of the natives fell from poisoning in the countermassacre (around two hundred, by an estimate at the time). Tucker's men encountered more native men afterward and shot some fifty of them. They released Opechancanough's English prisoners and brought home a collection of native scalps.[20]

Governor Wyatt recognized the lasting significance of the

March 22 attack with a decree shortly before the first anniversary of the event. To ensure it would not be forgotten, Wyatt ordered that March 22 would now be an annual occasion for the colonists to abstain from work and give prayers of thanksgiving, in observance of "God's most mercifull deliverance of so many" from the natives on that date. The General Assembly enacted the holiday into law the next year.

Opechancanough had expected the event to have an epochal effect on English attitudes, but an effect of a very different kind. Shortly after the attack—shortly after he brought the sky down on the English—he had boasted to the chief of the Patawomecks that "before the end of two moons" there would not be a single Englishman left in their lands. He was convinced, clearly, that the blow would force the English to recognize his superior strength and to evacuate the colony while they could.

Many of the survivors had fervently wished to do just that. Yet the overall reaction of the English defied Opechancanough's expectations. Following the difficult first year after the massacre, the colonists adapted to the new conditions and harvested a substantial food supply. Not only did the colonists quickly take the military offensive, the influx from England increased their numbers: by the end of 1624, the colony's population was up to its pre-attack level of a little over 1,200, and the colonists had spread out again into eighteen settlements beyond Jamestown. Governor Wyatt could truthfully advise the company that "the colonye hath worne owt the skarrs of the massacre"—apart from the psychological scars borne by the survivors. The population continued to increase rapidly to around 2,600 in 1629, to 3,200 in 1632, and to 5,200 in 1634.

The March 22 attack took one last English casualty, however. Complaints from Virginia Company investors and reports of the continuing death toll after the massacre led King James to appoint a commission in April 1623, to investigate the condition of the company. The commission heard testimony in London and examined the company's records. As the company had been under the control of Sir Edwin Sandys or his supporters since 1619, King James needed little impetus to strike a blow against it. When the commission reported on the extent to which the company had been sending English men and women to their doom in recent years, quite apart from the massacre, King James had ample justification to withdraw his charter. Of course, he had had much the same cause in the colony's early years, but he had not harbored the same personal or philosophical animosity toward Sir Thomas Smythe, Sandys's predecessor.

In the fall of 1623, the king's advisers, the Privy Council, offered to accept the company's charter in return for one that would give the king greater oversight, while maintaining the investors' ownership. The company's council rejected the proposal—a fatal miscalculation. On May 24, 1624, two years, two months, and two days after the massacre, King James ordered the company dissolved. A staggering £200,000, the total of the private investment in the company since 1606, was wiped out. Virginia became a royal colony, meaning that it was now an arm of the king's government. It would retain this status until the American War of Independence. For the moment, it was the first foundation stone of the British Empire.[21]

The change in control of the colony did not lead to any change in policy toward the natives. The summer of 1624 saw a battle between eight hundred native archers and sixty armed colonists; the latter emerged victorious without the loss of one man. The war continued, to the advantage of the colonists, until a 1632 peace treaty brought the decade-long war to a close.

Twenty years after the March 22 attack, the colonists in Virginia were still observing the date as a holiday of commemoration. Inevitably, however, memories of the event had faded. The colonists, of whom there were now around eight thousand, had settled on tobacco plantations along all the rivers of the region. They had again achieved security and prosperity. Like the gambler who has lost his fortune, but believes the next draw of the cards will make all the difference, Opechancanough decided to try his luck one more time.

Skyfall came again to the English on April 18, 1644. With simultaneous attacks on numerous settlements, Opechancanough's men killed even more than they had in 1622, somewhere between four and five hundred. Still, the impact was far smaller, given that the English population in Virginia had grown more than sixfold in the intervening years. The English quickly got back on a war footing and captured Opechancanough two years later. They understood him to be about a hundred years old: unable to walk, his muscles slack, and "his eye-lids became so heavy," it was said, "that he could not see, but as they were lifted up by his servants." The then-governor of the colony, Sir William Berkeley, intended to bring glory to himself by taking the infamous captive from Jamestown to London to show him off.

An English soldier on duty in Jamestown, his name unrecorded, had other ideas. Within two weeks of Opechancanough's imprisonment, the soldier found the opportunity to shoot the prisoner fatally in the back.

Although Opechancanough's war-making abilities were exceptional, his faulty understanding of English culture cost him dearly. In particular, he failed to grasp their tendency toward a cycle in which naïveté or indifference would be followed by an event of disillusionment and then extreme anger. The General Assembly boasted in 1646 that the natives were "so routed and dispersed that they are no longer a nation, and we now suffer only from robbery by a few starved outlaws." About sixty years later, at the dawn of the eighteenth century, the historian Robert Beverly could write regretfully, "The Indians of Virginia are almost wasted"—their numbers dwindled to perhaps six hundred and their lands down to a few small reservations. The colonists' faulty understanding of their neighbors' culture had also cost *them* over the years, but it was the natives, in the end, who suffered the worst.[22]

15

SMITH'S VISION FOR AMERICA

✦

John Smith's visit to Pocahontas in early 1617 was a brief detour
from his preparations for a third New England voyage. After Smith
had said his goodbyes to her in Brentford, he made his way to Plymouth harbor to join the fleet of three small ships sponsored by a
syndicate of investors in the southwest of England. Those investors,
known as the Plymouth Company (or, more formally, the Virginia
Company of Plymouth), had undertaken to finance a mission made up
of a total of sixteen colonists, with Smith as their leader. It was a paltry
effort. It was, nonetheless, the best that Smith could elicit after he had
spent the previous summer evangelizing for New England among
prospective investors in Cornwall and Devonshire.

Whether the voyage had sixteen colonists or sixteen hundred
turned out not to matter. Smith's ships, like a hundred others in the
harbor, were immobile while adverse winds kept them from the open
ocean. For one week after another, Smith could only watch the skies
with hope and fretfulness. A similar misfortune had befallen his first
voyage to the New World in 1606–1607, when storms kept the *Susan
Constant*, the *Godspeed*, and the *Discovery* stuck off the coast of England
for a month. This time, however, the uncooperative weather persisted
for three times as long. By the time it cleared, the chance for the
voyage was over. "The season being past, the ships went for New-
found-land [to fish], whereby my designe was frustrate," Smith recalled.

Smith had an income from his books, as well as a modest inheri-
tance from his parents; he may still have had some of his reward money
from his youthful service in Hungary. Living frugally, he continued to

plot a return to New England for the planting of a colony. In 1618, he unsuccessfully approached Sir Francis Bacon, the king's former attorney general and now his lord chancellor. He sent Bacon a proposal that was essentially a business plan, describing the value of the commodities to be reaped by a New England colony—fish, wood, and beaver skins, among others—and summarizing his own experience in the region. He detailed the financial success of the Dutch fishing fleet, a record that Smith said England could exceed with a permanent presence near the fishing grounds of New England and Newfoundland.

Despite his extreme desire to win support for his dream, Smith refrained from dangling any specious claims of gold.

> And though I can promise noe mynes of gold [he wrote in closing], the Hollanders are an example of my projects, whose endevoures by fishing cannot be suppressed by all the kinge of Spaynes golden powers. Truth is more than wealth and industrious subjects are more availeable to a king then gold. And this is so certaine a course to gett both, as I thinke was never propounded to any State for so small a charge, seeing I can prove it, both by examples, reason and experience. . . .
>
> In the interim I humbly desyre your Honor would be pleased to grace me with the title of your Lordshipps servant: Not that I desyre to shutt up the rest of my dayes in the chamber of ease and idlenes, but that I may be the better countenanced for the prosecution of this my most desyred voyage. . . .[1]

Smith received no reply from Bacon.

Another opportunity for Smith would soon arise thanks to King James's dislike for a faction of militant Protestants known as the Puritans. The king held that religious nonconformity had been the seed of long-lasting civil strife in the Netherlands and Scotland, and he wished none of it. What the Puritans sought went beyond freedom of conscience in the modern sense; a number of their disagreements with Anglicanism reached into the civic sphere of English life, including their opposition to theater and to the custom of playing sports on Sundays. In 1618, King James overruled local Puritan magistrates who attempted to ban Sabbath day sports. "When shall the common people have leave to exercise," he demanded, "if not upon Sundays and holi-days, seeing they must apply their labour, and win their living, in all working days?"

On the scale of European religious repression, King James's treat-ment of the Puritans was relatively mild. At his behest, the bishops of the Church of England fired around ninety of the most conspicuous Puritan ministers from Anglican churches. He banned the worship services of a breakaway group, dissenters within the dissenters, known as the Separatists. On the other hand, his sponsorship of a new Bible translation, now known as the King James Bible, came at the sugges-tion of a prominent Puritan clergyman; several Puritans were also on the team of translators.

In any event, a group of 125 Separatists left England for Amster-dam in 1608. They became troubled by their inability to support themselves in Amsterdam with the trades they knew, and left after a year for Leiden, Holland. They also found it difficult to make a living in Leiden. In 1620, working through connections in England, they obtained a patent from the Virginia Company of London to establish a private plantation on the Hudson River, in the vicinity of what is now New York City, at the northern edge of the company's territory.

Smith heard about the Separatists' plans through his own connec-tions in Virginia Company circles, and hastened to write to them offer-ing his services. Smith's qualifications would have made him the ideal adviser, guide, and military commander for the Separatists in their projected colony. He knew the Atlantic coast of North America and its native peoples better than any Englishman alive. In terms of person-ality, however, Smith and the Separatists would have been a horren-dous combination—both of them sure of their correctness in all things, both of them resistant to any direction or compromise.

Perhaps having sensed this fundamental incompatibility, the Sepa-ratists opted to take Smith's books and maps with them in lieu of Smith himself. They engaged a man with no North American experience, Miles Standish, as their military leader. Smith's absence cost them even before they reached shore: bad navigation sent their ship, the now famous *Mayflower*, to Cape Cod instead of the Hudson. Smith, mean-while, had once again seen his dream of involvement in a new colony pulled away from his grasp. It would be his last real chance—that is, assuming he had had a chance with the Separatists to begin with.[2]

Smith was forty years old. He had spent eleven years since his return from Virginia, more than a quarter of his life, largely in frustration and disappointment. A man of weaker spirit, looking back on those times, might have withdrawn from the field altogether. Yet the ensuing years of Smith's life would prove in some respects to be his most fertile. Channeling his energies once again into his writing, he would turn out a series of books promoting New England, instructing novice mariners in seamanship, and laying out an authoritative history of English colonization. His object, and his passion, remained the settlement and growth of an English New World.

Sometime after the Separatist Pilgrims sailed for Virginia in August 1620, Smith edited and expanded his letter to Bacon into a small book, and saw it published in December under the title *New Englands Trials* (with "trials" meant in the sense of "attempts"). He followed it with a kind of author's tour, addressing thirty or so of the major London guilds and encouraging them to invest in New England exploration. Two years later, he published an enlarged edition of *New Englands Trials* with a report on the first year of the Plymouth colony; "for want of experience," Smith noted pointedly, they wandered "to and again, six weeks [actually five weeks] before they found a place they liked to dwell on."

In reaction to news of the March 22, 1622, massacre in Virginia, Smith added a digression on that event. While angry and heartsick over the results of the attack, he found it unnecessary to account for the attack by projecting a vile, subhuman nature onto the natives—unlike those formerly optimistic toward Anglo-Native relations, such as Samuel Purchas. When the natives attacked the Jamestown colony in its initial years, Smith said, they did so in pursuit of the colonists' "weapons and commodities, that were rare novelties." The March 22 attack had origins that were different, but equally grounded in the natives' basic self-interest: "Now they feare we may beate them out of their dens, which lions and tygers would not admit [allow] but by force."

Needless to say, Smith's recognition of Opechancanough's motives did not translate into tenderness toward his cause. Smith emphasized that the attack should not deter Englishmen from occupying Virginia and New England. Pointing to his own record of success in keeping the Powhatans at bay, he argued that all the English needed to deal with the native threat was martial readiness—which, incidentally, he could provide. "For Virginia, I kept that country with 38 [around this number of colonists were left alive in early 1608], and had not to eate but what we had from the savages." While accurate, it was a less-than-subtle pitch for his services.

The year before, a new edition of Richard Knolles's *Generall Historie of the Turkes* appeared in London. Its title mirrored those of other ambitious works of history during that era, works that traced the entire history of a nation from its beginnings to the present day. (Others of the genre included the *Generall Historie of France* by Jean de Serres, published in England in 1611, and the *Generall Historie of the Magnificent State of Venice* by a Frenchman named Thomas de Fougasses, which reached England in 1612.) Whether or not Smith actually bought a copy of Knolles's book, it can be surmised that the tale of Smith's former adversaries caught his attention.

Hence, after completing the enlarged edition of his *New Englands Trials*, Smith tackled his most audacious work yet: a comprehensive history of English America, which he titled *The Generall Historie of Virginia, New-England, and the Summer Isles* [Bermuda]. The officers of the Virginia Company had considered the idea of commissioning a history of Virginia, but with a significant difference. The project they had in mind was a tribute to "the memory and fame of many of her worthies," living and dead. Smith, however, meant to tell the unvarnished truth as he had seen it and heard it—letting the chips, and the daggers, fall where they may. There was also another difference: the Virginia Company's proposed history never went beyond the discussion stage. Smith had his history fully outlined sometime in 1623 and on the streets of London in July of 1624.

Smith pieced much of the *Generall Historie* together from earlier works by himself and others. The resulting work was as comprehensive as its title promised. The first of its six parts set out the early years of English exploration in North America, from the fateful spurning of Christopher Columbus by King Henry VII (which drove Columbus into the service of the Spanish) to the failed Roanoke colony and other efforts up to 1605. For these accounts, Smith drew on material compiled by the Reverend Richard Hakluyt in his 1589 *Principall Navigations, Voiages and Discoveries of the English Nation* and by Samuel Purchas. The second part gave a detailed description of Virginia, essentially reprinting the text of his *Map of Virginia*. The third was an enlarged version of the *Proceedings*, setting out a history of the Jamestown colony up to his departure in 1609. Part four picked up the story and continued it to the royal investigation of the Virginia Company in 1623–1624. The fifth gave an account of English activities on Bermuda, most notably the castaways of Sir George Somers's fleet. In the final part, he turned to New England, incorporating his *Description of New England, New Englands Trials*, and other accounts.

Characteristic of the period, the *Generall Historie* was accompanied by commendatory verses—poetical words of praise for the author and his book. Fifteen such verses appeared in the *Generall Historie*, one of them contributed by Samuel Purchas and another four written by current or former colonists. Colonist David Wiffin recalled that while Smith governed, neither "force of theirs [the natives'], nor guile / Lessened a man of thine; but since (I rue) / In Brittish blood they did deeply imbrue." (Two years after the March 22 massacre, it was still not far from Wiffin's mind; in all likelihood, it was not far from the mind of anyone involved with Virginia.) John Codrington, signing himself "your sometime souldier," urged Smith to disregard the "spight of envie" from naysayers. Raleigh Crashaw lauded him for handling the natives "with due discretion, and undanted heart . . . In deepest plunge of hard extreamitie." Michael Fettiplace, William Fettiplace, and Richard Wiffin, identifying themselves as "souldiers under Captaine Smiths command," offered one of the lengthiest of the verses, a thirty-eight-line accolade to his skill in extricating them from hopeless situations.

During the time Smith was preparing the *Generall Historie*, the royal commission on the Virginia Company sought Smith's insights for its investigation. The commissioners posed Smith a set of written questions, and Smith printed his responses in the book. His answers returned to a theme he had been sounding from the start: the key to a successful colony was to have the right kinds of colonists in place—hardworking laborers, a small number of capable leaders on the scene (instead of armchair experts setting policy in London), and soldiers for security against outside threats. "To rectifie a common-wealth with debauched people is impossible . . . for there is no country to pillage as the Romans found: all you must expect from thence must be by labour."[3]

Other additions that Smith made to the *Generall Historie* highlighted the bravery and accomplishments of those who had aided him, and whom he admired: among these were Anas Todkill, the former manservant to John Martin; John Russell, the "exceeding heavie" gentleman who had helped Smith fight his way out of the 1609 ambush at Werowocomoco; and Pocahontas, who had died at Gravesend soon after Smith last spoke with her. Smith reprinted his letter recommending Pocahontas to Queen Anne, and told the stories of his conversations in England with Pocahontas and Tomocomo. Although Smith was a firm nationalist, his account was forthright enough to give the English the worst of both conversations, with her rebuke that "your countriemen will lie much" and Tomocomo's lamentation of King James's incivility.

Smith subsequently wrote four more books, beginning with *An Accidence* [Primer], *or the Path-Way to Experience*, his 1626 guide to oceanic sailing and fighting. He enlarged the *Accidence* the next year and published the new edition as *A Sea Grammar*, with the sponsorship of his friend Sir Samuel Saltonstall. His next book, in 1630, was *The True Travels and Observations of Captaine John Smith*, in which he recounted his experiences prior to his involvement with Virginia, mostly his military adventures in Western and Central Europe. Although his books on Virginia and New England had strong elements of autobiography, given that they often recorded events in which he was involved, the *True Travels* was his first and only book with an explicitly autobiographical focus. He capped the *True Travels* with a tag-along "continuation" of his *Generall Historie*, in which he set out the developments in Virginia, New England, and Bermuda since 1624; the addition was not a particularly logical fit, but it reflected his enduring interest in the latest news from the colonies.

Lastly, in his 1631 *Advertisements* [Information] *for the Unexperienced Planters of New England, or Any Where*, Smith returned to his favored subject of urging the English to populate the New World. He was pleased by the prospects for the Massachusetts Bay Company, which had established a large Puritan settlement to the north of Plymouth two years earlier. His conversations with leaders of the Massachusetts Bay Company convinced him, he said, that they understood what the Virginia Company never had: the critical importance of selecting people who were suited for the enterprise, rather than simply sending large numbers of recruits and hoping for the best. The Massachusetts Bay Company was taking care, he commented with approval, to send "men of good credit and well-beloved in their country, not such as flye for debt, or any scandall at home . . . men of good meanes, or arts, occupations, and qualities. . . ."

At the same time, when Smith came to his critics and his former employers, his prose was as combustible as it had ever been. "So doating [was the company] of mines of gold, and the South Sea, that all the world could not have devised better courses to bringe us to ruine then they did themselves, with many more such like strange conceits." He facetiously claimed to have been won over at long last by those who had censured him during his Jamestown years for mistreating and mistrusting the natives:

> Onely spending my time to revenge my imprisonment upon the harmlesse innocent salvages, who by my cruelty I forced to feed me with their contribution, and to send any [who] offended my idle humour to James towne to punish at mine owne discretion; or keepe their kings and subjects in chaines, and make them worke. Things cleanly contrary to my commission [orders]; whilest I and my company took our needlesse pleasures in discovering the countries about us, building of forts, and such unnecessary fooleries, where an egge-shell (as they writ) had been sufficient against such enemies. . . .4

Smith's criticisms in the *Advertisements* were mainly couched in terms of counsel to the new wave of Massachusetts settlers, and admiration for what they were doing differently from their predecessors. Here are the mistakes the Virginia Company made, Smith was saying, and here is how the Massachusetts Bay Company was avoiding them. "Now they [the Massachusetts Bay Company] take not that course the Virginia Company did for the planters there, their purses and lives were subject to some few here in London who were never there, that consumed all in arguments, projects, and their owne conceits. . . ."

Indeed, in all of Smith's later writings about Virginia and New England—the *Description, New Englands Trials,* the *Advertisements,* and his magnum opus, the *Generall Historie*—he was looking to the future of the New World as well as its past and present. In adopting the very title of *Generall Historie,* he was implicitly staking out a new view of English settlement, one in which the American colonists could be viewed as a distinct nation and a distinct people, much as the French,

the Venetians, and the Turks were. The colonies would still be subject
to the English crown, to be sure, but they would not be mere outposts,
and they would not merely replicate the society of the mother country.

The English New World would be a different kind of nation, but
different how? What should it be in order to succeed? During Smith's
years in Virginia, his answer to that question was half-formed and half-
articulable, no more than a set of utilitarian biases—in favor of the
hardworking and the accomplished; against the many around him who
harbored a feeling of entitlement by bloodline; in favor of sustaining
the colony with activities of proven economic value, such as fishing
and farming; against the wishful dictates of leaders with gold fever.

After his return to England in 1609, it became evident that the
opportunity to return to the New World was not awaiting him for the
taking. He would have to create his opportunity. Circumstances thus
led him to transform himself into a promoter of colonization. One way
out of his bind (as he noted in the *Advertisements*) would have been to
make easy promises of gold, a passage to the South Sea, or a base for
piracy "to rob some poore merchant or honest fisher men." Having
decided against that course, Smith instead offered a more honest, but
still positive, view of America's economic opportunities, leavened with
a striking vision of what America could become as a society.

Smith's years in Virginia, combined with his individualistic tem-
perament, led him to see two potential attributes of the New World
that could be as enticing as gold. The first, not surprisingly, was social
mobility. Smith had escaped yeomanry through service on the battlefield; in America, he suggested, poor men with ambition could likewise
make new destinies for themselves. The vestiges of feudal institutions
and feudal ideas could be left behind. "Here [in New England] every
man may be master and owner of his owne labour and land; or the
greatest part in a small time," he proclaimed in the *Description*. "If hee
have nothing but his hands, he may set up this [his?] trade; and by
industrie quickly grow rich; spending but halfe that time wel, which in
England we abuse in idleness, worse or as ill."

This process of self-advancement, Smith contended, would be
more than a route to a fortune; it would be elevating and fulfilling in its
own right:

> Who can desire more content, that hath small
> meanes; or but only his merit to advance his fortune,

then to tread, and plant that ground hee hath purchased by hazard of his life? If he have but the taste of
virtue, and magnanimitie [ambition], what to such a
minde can be more pleasant, then planting and building a foundation for his posteritie, gotte from the rude
earth, by Gods blessing and his owne industrie, without prejudice to any?[5]

The second attraction that Smith saw in America was liberty. The
concept was meaningful to his intended audience, for Englishmen of
the early seventeenth century highly prized their "English liberty"; it
was, in fact, one of the benefits that the supporters of the Virginia
Company imagined the colony would eventually bestow on the Virginia natives. Smith's insight was to harness the ideal of liberty to
earthly practicality: the liberty to pursue one's own interest was not
only mankind's proper condition, but an engine that could power a
society to greatness. (He was writing a century and a half before the
Scotsman Adam Smith set out his famous union of self-interest and
societal well-being in *The Wealth of Nations*.) "And who is he hath
judgement, courage, and any industrie or qualitie with understanding," Smith asked in the *Description*, "[who] will leave his countrie, his
hopes at home, his certaine estate, his friends, pleasures, libertie, and
the preferment sweete England doth afford to all degrees, were it not
to advance his fortunes by injoying his deserts?" He echoed the
thought in *New Englands Trials*, noting that "no man will go from
hence, to have lesse freedome there then here."

The implication, Smith held, was that the proprietors of a colony
should look to the energizing properties of freedom, and rely as little
as possible on indentured servitude, martial law, and the like. There
was an element of irony in the advice, for his own policies in Virginia
had been markedly authoritarian—a by-product of the company policy
requiring that the colonists be fed from a common store. Later experience had shown that the combination of a common store and authoritarian rule was fundamentally flawed. "The benefit of libertie in the
planters," Smith wrote in the *Generall Historie*, had been proven by the
introduction of private plots of land. When the Virginia Company
required that all be fed from the common store, "glad was he [who]
could slip from his labour, or slumber over his taske he cared not how,
nay, the most honest among them would hardly take so much true

paines in a weeke, as now for themselves they will do in a day. . . ." For Smith, the lesson was clear: "Therefore let all men have as much free-dome in reason as may be, and true dealing, for it is the greatest com-fort you can give them, where the very name of servitude will breed much ill bloud, and become odious to God and man. . . ."[6]

Smith made a sharp distinction, however, between self-interest as an instrument of social good and selfishness as a personal creed. He held that the founders of history's great empires, such as the early Greeks and Romans, were "no silvered idle golden Pharises, but indus-trious iron-steeled Publicans: They regarded more provisions, and necessaries for their people, then jewels, riches, ease, or delight for themselves. Riches were their servants, not their maisters." Smith con-cluded his *Description of New England* by calling on his countrymen to build an English New World, not only for the sake of present riches, but also to continue the accomplishments of their ancestors and to leave a legacy for their posterity:

> Was it vertue in them [our ancestors], to provide that doth maintaine us? and basenesse for us to doe the like for others? Surely no. Then seeing we are not borne for our selves, but to helpe each other, and our abilities are much alike at the houre of our birth, and the minute of our death: Seeing our good deedes, or our badde, by faith in Christs merits, is all we have to carrie our soules to heaven, or hell: Seeing honour is our lives ambition; and our ambition after death, to have an honorable memorie of our life: and seeing by noe meanes wee would be abated of the dignities and glories of our predecessors; let us imitate their vertues to be worthily their successors.[7]

By the time Smith reached the last year of his own life in 1631, he was one of only a half dozen or so of the original colonists of 1607 still left alive. Although he had expressed much optimism for the future of the colonies, his efforts to return to the New World were frustrated to the end. A poem that he wrote as a preface to the *Advertisements* inti-mated that he had given in to melancholy. Entitled "The Sea Marke" (in reference to a warning buoy at sea), the verses ended:

The winters cold, the summers heat,
    alternatively beat
Upon my bruised sides, that rue
    Because too true
That no releefe can ever come.
    But why should I despair
    being promised so faire
That there shall be a day of Dome [Doom].[8]

In June, within a few months after the printing of the *Advertisements*, Smith was stricken ill—the specifics are now unknown—and became weak and bedridden in the home of Sir Samuel Saltonstall, where he had been staying. He was fifty-one.

Smith dictated his will on June 21. Afterward, he attempted to muster the energy to sign his name at the bottom. He started to write the first letter of his first name, but he could not finish the stroke. He made another attempt, and again ran out of strength, leaving only a blotch of ink. The scribe to whom he had dictated the will then stepped in and inserted the explanatory words "the marke of the sayd John Smithe." Smith died that day.

Smith had never married and left no offspring. The only hint that he may have ever had a significant romantic relationship lies in a map of "Ould Virginia" that accompanied his *Generall Historie*. There, a pair of dot-size islands, each one appearing barely larger than a smudge, bears the name "Abigails Isles." The identity of "Abigail" remains a nearly four-hundred-year-old enigma, resolved neither by Smith's writings, nor by his will, nor by any other known surviving records. With equal probability, she could have been a hoped-for patroness or a woman close to Smith's heart.[9]

While he lacked mortal posterity, Smith left a legacy of a different kind. Had he been able to return to see America during the Founding Era, he would have observed a society that had developed along just the lines he had described, and whose virtues he had personified. The heart of the new nation—the values and hopes that were everywhere in the air—shared Smith's individualism, practicality, disdain for class rank, and esteem for those who worked hard to get ahead. An emigrant of the era, a French aristocrat turned New York farmer named J. Hector St. John de Crèvecoeur, was awestruck by the unique breed of humanity that America was creating: "Here the rewards of his industry follow, with equal steps, the progress of his labour," de Crèvecoeur wrote in 1782. The American was consequently "a new man, who acts upon new principles," and who had left behind the "involuntary idleness, servile dependence, penury, and useless labour" of the Old World.

It would be an exaggeration to say that the social vision Smith expressed in his writings had directly molded the new society. Thomas Jefferson owned a copy of the *Generall Historie,* and recommended it as a historical reference, but there are no clear signs that either Jefferson or any of the other Founders drew their views of liberty from Smith's writings. Smith's achievement as a social thinker was one of foresight rather than guidance.

As pure foresight, though, it was remarkable. Smith's prescience came not from his expert knowledge of the American land, but from his shrewd assessment of human nature—looking at human beings as they were, rather than as projections of what the observer thought they should be. While not everyone was motivated by materialism for its own sake (Smith himself was not), he understood that it was quintessentially human to have one's own purposes and passions. Smith, like the Founders, imagined America as a place of "libertie" to pursue those things as far as one's merits and industriousness would allow.

The founding generation remembered Smith well, as he loomed large in the popular historical writing of the era. Modern Americans look back two centuries and see a small pantheon of heroic figures; Americans of the late eighteenth century and early nineteenth century looked back to America's earliest years and saw one standing alone. Nations define themselves in large part through their heroes, and historians found in Smith the opportunity to define the qualities of a distinctively American hero: resourceful, of humble origins and high achievement, inclined toward action rather than reflection, peaceable when possible, warlike when necessary. Jeremy Belknap, in his 1794 *American Biography,* included a seventy-nine-page entry on Smith that held him up as "an enterprizing spirit," "an ardent and active genius," and "the life and soul of the colony." Typical of the narrative was Belknap's egalitarian-minded censure of the company leaders who ordered the colony to court the natives with gifts instead of deferring to Smith's superior knowledge:

Though savages, they were men and not children. Though destitute of science, they were possessed of reason, and a sufficient degree of art. To know how to manage them, it was necessary to be personally acquainted with them; and it must be obvious, that a person who had resided several years among them, and was a prisoner with them, was a much better judge of the proper methods of treating them, than a company of gentlemen at several thousand miles distance, and who could know them only by report.[10]

Chief Justice John Marshall, in his 1804 *Life of George Washington*, began with a brief history of the nation that emphasized Smith's importance at Jamestown: "his spirits unbroken, and his judgment unclouded, amidst this general misery and dejection." His river explorations showed "fortitude, courage and patience" that were exceeded by "few voyages of discovery, undertaken at any time." His stand against the "fatal delusion" of gold fever showed his common sense. With a nod to his biographical subject, Marshall praised Smith's presidential administration as "disinterested, judicious, and vigorous."

George Bancroft's highly successful *History of the United States* in 1834 held Smith to be "the father of Virginia," contrasting "the selfish Wingfield" and "the imbecile Ratcliffe" with Smith's "deliberate enterprise and cheerful courage." Smith "united the highest spirit of adventure with the consummate powers of action. . . . He had nothing counterfeit in his nature; but was open, honest, and sincere." Upon his capture by Opechancanough's men in late 1607, Bancroft noted approvingly, Smith "did not beg for his life, but preserved it by the calmness of self-possession"—until his relief by Pocahontas at the last possible moment. If Smith represented the proto-American man for Bancroft, Pocahontas in the moment of the rescue seemed to stand for the proto-American woman, possessed of both "gentle feelings of humanity" and "fearlessness."

Noah Webster's pocket-size book for "young beginners in reading," his *Little Reader's Assistant* of 1791, included a biography that held up Smith's "prudence, fortitude, and resolution" as a worthy model for youth. "How often was he on the brink of death, and how bravely did he encounter every danger!" Webster concluded. "Such a man affords a noble example for all to follow, when they resolve to be *good* and *brave*."

It is unsurprising that historians and other writers of the founding generation found a resonance in the story of Smith's trials in Virginia. In their war for independence and their struggle to create a constitution, the Founders themselves had shown the same pragmatic qualities of mind that rendered Smith a hero. The actions of Smith, like the actions of the Founders, also point to a shared outlook on life: one in which a person does not look inward and wait for life to reveal its answers, for life itself is the one carrying out the interrogation. More than most people, Smith and the Founders attempted to answer the questions that life was constantly asking them—or, rather, the single question it asked them, and asks us, over and over. Life presented them with a series of astonishing possibilities and all-engulfing obstacles, all the while whispering to them:

What are you going to do?
What are you going to do?
What are you going to do?[11]

Marginalia

In the commentaries below, I address some questions that do not quite fit anywhere else. They seem too laden with methodological issues for the body of the book, and yet too important to leave for the notes. Some of the commentaries address matters of current controversy, on which I venture an opinion about the state of the evidence.

CONVERTING MONEY FIGURES

It is obvious that money figures from the early 1600s—such as the cost of a Virginia Company share in 1609, at £12 10s.—must be multiplied by some large factor to yield an equivalent value in today's currency. Four centuries of inflation (with interspersed periods of deflation) have taken their toll on the purchasing power of a pound sterling. But by how much?

Any attempt to translate monetary values across the centuries will necessarily rest on a shaky foundation. The consumer's market basket of goods has changed drastically between the early 1600s and modern times. The English family of the 1600s bought wood or coal to keep its home heated and spent substantially on candles to keep it lit. The purchasing power of a pound in terms of wood, coal, and candles in that day must somehow be translated into modern purchasing power in terms of gas, oil, or electric heat and electric lighting. Four centuries' worth of inventions did not exist at the start of the period, from cars, computers, and refrigerators to the packaged foods inside those refrigerators. English men and women of the early 1600s did not care to drink water if they had a choice; the idea of actually paying money for a bottle of it would have inspired much hilarity.

With that caveat in mind, one can assemble a comparison of English price levels over the period using published economic history data. The standard work remains the 1956 *Economica* article by E. H. Phelps Brown and Sheila Hopkins, "Seven Centuries of the Prices of Consumables, compared with Builders' Wage-Rates." Brown and Hopkins compiled price levels spanning 1264 to 1954, drawing on the purchasing records of schools, colleges, manors, and churches for the years through the seventeenth century. They set out an annual consumer price index, in effect, based on the prices of the items in a representative collection of consumer goods (which varied over the period of their study).

Useful as they are, these findings take us only as far as 1954. A research paper from the Economic Policy and Statistics Section of the House of Commons Library, however, has joined the Brown and Hopkins data with four other price studies covering more recent periods. The result is a set of data covering the years 1750 through 2001. (The House of Commons Library paper ignored earlier years.) On the scale used in that paper, the price level for 1974 has an index value of 100, and years with higher or lower price levels get higher or lower price index figures accordingly.

I have adjusted some of the pre-1750 figures from Brown and Hopkins so they can be tacked on to the data in the House of Commons Library series with the same index scale. A few price levels from the Jamestown colonial period, derived in this way, are listed in the following table along with some more recent data:

YEAR	PRICE LEVEL (*1974=100.0*)
1609	4.7
1614	4.8
1624	4.6
1750	5.0
1850	8.2
1900	9.0
1950	32.9
1990	458.5
2000	619.2
2001	630.1

With these very approximate figures, one can convert the £12 10s. price of a Virginia Company share to a modern counterpart. The overall inflation factor in England from 1609 to 2001 is 630.1/4.7, or roughly 134—that is, 13,400 percent. A pound sterling at this time was made up of twenty shillings; thus, twelve pounds, ten shillings was twelve and a half pounds. Multiplying 12.5 by 134 gives a value of £1,675 per share. Assuming modern exchange rates in the range of $1.50 to $1.70 to the pound, the dollar figure is between roughly $2,500 and $2,850.[1]

THE FIRST RESCUE AND ITS CRITICS

The story of the first rescue of John Smith by Pocahontas fell into disrepute among historians during the Reconstruction era and stayed there until roughly a century later. Modern scholars have reappraised Smith's account in light of ethnographic evidence, and most accept it as true. (These scholars tend to believe Smith misunderstood what he had experienced—that what he saw as a thwarted execution was actually part of an adoption ceremony. For reasons I explain in the next note, I disagree with this interpretation.)

The first direct challenge to the rescue story came in an 1867 article written by Henry Adams for a popular national magazine, the *North American Review*. The impetus for the article was Adams's belief during the war that discrediting John Smith would represent a major propaganda victory against the South. Adams told a family friend that he viewed the piece as "some sort of flank, or rather a rear attack, on the Virginia aristocracy, who will be utterly gravelled by it if it is successful."

From a historical perspective, the identification of Smith with the Confederate cause was a *non sequitur*. Smith spent the last seventeen years of his life advocating settlement of New England. "No man rejoiced more than himself in the establishment of the colonies of Plymouth and Massachusetts [Bay]," Jeremy Belknap wrote in 1794. Smith's image had changed during the nineteenth century, however, in ways he could not have anticipated. Claimed by Virginia and its leading families, some of whom descended from Pocahontas, Smith was now more or less a regional hero, not a national one. Equally misleading was the view of Pocahontas's rescue as the central incident of his life. Although Smith expressed gratitude for it, his writings recounted it almost in passing, en route to other adventures.

In any case, Adams was right about the sentiment of his times. If he could cast Smith as a liar regarding the rescue, he would be pulling down a venerated icon of the enemy. In the process, he could diminish the legend of Pocahontas herself, the ancestral mother of Virginia's elite. Among the Virginia aristocrats with Pocahontas in their family tree, Adams confided in a letter that he specifically had in mind the late John Randolph, a political adversary of both his grandfather, President John Quincy Adams, and his great-grandfather, President John Adams.[2]

The thesis of Henry Adams and later critics was simple: Smith omitted the rescue story from the *True Relation* and his contribution to the *Proceedings* because it never happened, and then he fabricated the story in later works to build up his reputation. But Smith would have been puzzled by the idea that the story cast him in a heroic light. From his standpoint, and from the perspective of his era, the story was not inordinately flattering. To be taken prisoner (after stumbling into a mire!) and then to be saved by a young native girl was hardly an admirable achievement; no Englishman of the early seventeenth century would have viewed it as a point of pride.

Smith's attitude is indicated by his first published reference to the rescue, in the revised 1622 edition of his book *New Englands Trials*. After two long paragraphs reciting his success in fighting and intimidating the Virginia natives, he added, "It is true in our greatest extremitie they shot me, slew three of my men, and by the folly of them that fled took me prisoner; yet God made Pocahontas the King's daughter the means to deliver me." This terse statement is his entire reference to the rescue in the book. It is palpable both from the context and from Smith's reticent phraseology ("it is true . . .") that he preferred not to bring up the subject at all. The statement is, as the lawyers say, an admission against interest. He is mentioning his captivity and rescue because he anticipates that they will be brought up by his *opponents*. The reference in the *Generall Historie* is almost as terse.

Although Smith's account is the only source for the rescue, there are a number of reasons for accepting it. The story of the rescue was believed and reprinted by the Reverend Samuel Purchas, who had numerous connections in and around the Virginia Company, including both friends and adversaries of Smith. It is unlikely that the cleric would have willingly opened himself up to ridicule by including the story (or Smith's other writings) in his chronicles if the story had an

odor of fraud or if Smith had a reputation as a liar. Henry Wharton's
1685 biography, *The Life of John Smith, English Soldier,* also accepted
the rescue story. Pocahontas's *second* rescue of Smith had multiple
English eyewitnesses, and has never been seriously questioned, so far
as I can determine.

The fact that Smith's books carried commendatory verses from
Purchas and from his fellow colonists is further indicative of his gen-
eral reputation for veracity. Colonist William Strachey recommended
Smith's writings, as did William Crashaw, another London cleric with
Virginia Company connections. John Stow's *Annales or a General
Chronicle of England* noted in 1631 that Smith "wrote a book of every
particular place [in the Virginia colony] and of all that hapned there."
The entry for Smith in Thomas Fuller's 1662 comical biography collection, *The Worthies of England,* held it "much to the dimunition of his
deeds, that he alone is the herald to publish and proclaim them," but
this ignored the accounts of Smith's adventures originating in the 1612
Proceedings, most of which came from the nine other colonists who
contributed to that book. Twentieth-century scholarship confirmed
obscure details of Smith's accounts of his Central European military
adventures wherever they could be checked.3

The best and most detailed treatment of the historical controversy
over the rescue is J. A. Leo Lemay's *Did Pocahontas Save Captain John
Smith?* (1992). I am indebted to Professor Lemay for many of the
points above. In my view, he makes an overwhelming case for believing
Smith's report.

RESCUE OR ADOPTION CEREMONY?

Some researchers have argued that Smith misunderstood what he had
experienced during the December 30, 1607, assembly at Werowocomoco. According to these theories, the Powhatans never actually
meant to execute him at all. Rather, Smith was undergoing an adoption-
like ceremony, one that brought him into the tribe, or one that made
the entire English colony a vassal nation of the Powhatans. Pocahontas's role, in this view, was prearranged and scripted.

An immediate problem with such theories is that nothing is known
about seventeenth-century Powhatan adoption ceremonies (assuming
they existed), nor is any other tribe in North America known to have
had an adoption procedure comparable to what was undergone by

Smith. It has been suggested that the ceremony follows the "structure" of "the classic pattern of rites of passage." Yet the Powhatans' own rite of passage for young males does not bear this argument out. The ritual, known to the English as the "black boys" ceremony, did include mock deaths—and, it was said, some real deaths—but otherwise it had little in common with Smith's experience.4

Most notably, the black boys ceremony was not based on a near execution followed by a rescue. Rather, it involved the boys running a gauntlet under the protection of a priest, then playing dead. In other words, it climaxed in a symbolic killing, not in a symbolic rescue and commutation. In addition to this fundamental distinction between the actual Powhatan rite of passage and the one Smith allegedly experienced, there are an array of lesser ones. For example, the participants in the black boys ceremony (aside from the boys themselves) were male guards and priests—not princesses. There was no execution stone. A sacrificial fire was built, though the English witnesses were not permitted to stay to see how it was used.5

Apart from the paucity of empirical support, the theories have another problem: Smith's involvement with the Powhatans did not end on December 30, 1607. Why, then, did Smith never learn of his supposed mistake? How did he stay so clueless about the true nature of what he believed had been his near execution? These questions seem hard to surmount. Smith remained in Virginia, in frequent contact with the natives, including Powhatan and Pocahontas, for some time to come. Indeed, on account of Smith's detailed study of native life and culture in Virginia, his writings are among the principal sources for Powhatan ethnologists today. For that matter, Smith later witnessed the black boys ceremony himself; if his experience had been comparable, he was in a position to put two and two together.6

The one piece of hard evidence relied upon by proponents of the adoption theory is the later conversation between Smith and Pocahontas in England, in which she refers to him as "father" and "countryman." It is more reasonable to assume that the "father" reference was figurative, just as Smith and Powhatan had referred to Christopher Newport figuratively as Smith's "father."7 (Also inconvenient for the adoption argument is that an adoption would have rendered Smith her brother, not her father.) In calling Smith her countryman, she is not calling him a Powhatan; she is referring to her own status by that time as an Englishwoman, and his as an Englishman. This becomes plain toward the end of the exchange, when she says discontentedly, "Your countrymen will lie much"—certainly meaning the English. (That she said "your countrymen" instead of "our countrymen" is a revealing slip.)

Overall, there is no compelling reason to believe that the events in Powhatan's assembly hall were anything other than what Smith perceived them to be. There is even less reason to doubt that Pocahontas was just who she appeared to be that day: a girl acting compassionately toward the pitiable stranger in front of her.

OF TREE RINGS AND SECRET AGENTS

The heavy death toll in the English colony from 1607 to 1610 continues to pique the interest of researchers. Was a hidden cause at work? Were the colonists doomed to die in large numbers no matter how well prepared, no matter how hardworking?

Proponents of two recent theories have argued that the answer to both questions is yes. One of these theories gives an intriguing view of new data, though some important questions remain to be answered. The other theory has had the salutary effect of bringing Jamestown history to greater public attention, but otherwise has little to recommend it.

The first theory holds that both the Jamestown colony and the failed Roanoke colony were established during periods of extreme drought. A team led by David W. Stahle of the University of Arkansas came to this conclusion based on an analysis of tree rings in the regions around Jamestown and Roanoke. In Jamestown, they wrote in a 1998 article in *Science*, the years 1606 to 1612 were "the driest 7-year episode in 770 years."

The researchers obtained core samples from ancient bald cypress trees in those areas (without destroying the trees), and correlated the spacing of the tree rings from 1941 to 1984 with local moisture records. They created a simple mathematical model based on those data and confirmed that their model also worked reasonably well on moisture records for the period 1896 to 1940. They then applied the model to centuries of earlier rings to identify the dry spells. In addition to the 1606–1612 period at Jamestown, they found a severe three-year drought in Roanoke from 1587 to 1589, as well as an earlier drought from 1562 to 1571.

The challenge lies in validating the findings by checking them against the observations of the people who were alive at the time. The researchers were able to corroborate the Roanoke findings for 1562–1571 by pointing to observations of a Spanish missionary of that period. The Jamestown findings, however, are a different story. While the narratives from the theorized "drought" years indicate occasional episodes of dry weather (naturally enough), in no way do they point to a period of either drought or bad harvests spanning multiple years.

The colonists' writings of the period make numerous incidental references to stormy weather, rain, and snow. John Smith's 1612 *Map of Virginia* noted brief extremes of weather, both wet and dry, but specifically stated that the climate was congenial for good crops if men would take the trouble to raise them. "Some times there are great droughts other times much raine, yet great necessity of neither, by reason we see not but that all the variety of needfull fruits of Europe may be there in great plenty by the industry of men, as appeareth by those we planted." Elsewhere in the same book, he described the native planting cycle in some detail, depicting the natives as successful planters. Gabriel Archer in 1607 found the soil moist ("somewhat slymy in touch"); based on the colony's limited attempts at agriculture that year, he judged it to be "more fertill then can be wel exprest."[8]

Further research and analysis may lead to a reconciliation of the tree-ring data with the human record. Continued work in this area could lead to new insights into the application of tree-ring data to climate issues across periods of many centuries—dendroclimatology, as this subdiscipline of tree-ring analysis is called—with potential benefits far beyond the boundaries of Jamestown.

Not so promising, at least for the present, is the theory that the waves of Jamestown deaths from 1607 to 1610, including the Starving Time of 1609, represent a case of mass murder. Dr. Frank Hancock, a pathologist by training, has argued in the news media that the deaths probably came about through deliberate poisoning. He believes the symptoms reported, such as dysentery and weakness, point to arsenic. Dr. Hancock suspects a Spanish plot, carried out on their behalf by an English Catholic, Baron Thomas Arundell.

It is a fact that Arundell offered his services to Don Pedro de Zúñiga, the Spanish ambassador, to aid in defeating the English settlers. He told Zúñiga he would bring a Spanish agent of King Philip's choosing to Virginia, and advise that person as to how the settlers could be forced out "without recourse to arms." By that, Zúñiga understood Arundell to mean that the settlers would be threatened and ordered to leave.[9] Anything is possible, however, and it is conceivable Arundell was talking about poisoning.

Unfortunately for the theory, the discussion between Zúñiga and Arundell came in March of 1609, well after the colony had already suffered its first waves of mortality. Equally significant, the intrigue went no further: the Spanish did not accept Arundell's offer. King Philip's *junta de guerra*, or war council, reported on the situation in Virginia in May of 1611, and recommended that the king take action to drive the English away—with no indication that any prior attempt had been made, by Baron Arundell or anyone else. Lists of colonists show no record of Arundell ever having traveled to Jamestown.

At any rate, one does not have to resort to international power politics to explain the mass deaths at Jamestown. Sixteen years after the first settlement, Sir Francis Wyatt would write as governor that the colony was *still* losing waves of men to summer illness. He found "great multitudes of new comers" lost each year to "a burning fever, which thorough intemperate drinking of water often drawes after it the flixe [dysentery] or dropsy. . . ." Impractical policy choices—which brought about mortality from disease, starvation, bad water, and native attacks—were deadlier than any conspiracy.[10]

Notes

Editorial Method

Dialogue. Dialogue that appears within quotation marks (or in block quotes) is quoted from sources of the period. Unless otherwise indicated, dialogue appearing *without* quotation marks is a paraphrase of accounts in period sources.

Period text. Seventeenth-century English material is challenging to read in its raw form, with its unfamiliar (and internally inconsistent) orthography and capitalization. My approach to this problem has been eclectic. I have modernized the capitalization throughout; I have interchanged *u*'s and *v*'s where appropriate (as in *liue* or *natiue*); I have interchanged *i*'s and *j*'s likewise (as in *ioy* or *Iones*); I have expanded some archaic contractions; and I have inserted paragraph breaks in some long passages for readability. Beyond that, I have normally kept to the spelling and punctuation of the original texts. Yet where it seemed essential to modernize the Jacobean spelling of a word here or there to make a quotation clearer, or to add a comma for that purpose, I have done so. In no case have I exchanged an archaic word for a different modern one. I have sometimes inserted a modern equivalent in square brackets to illuminate a word or phrase.

Colonial place-names. The locale of the 1607 Virginia settlement was variously referred to during the course of the period as "James Fort,"

"James Towne," or "James Cittie." For consistency, I have referred to it throughout by the modern name of Jamestown. Where the fort structure specifically is indicated, I have referred to "the fort." Also, the satellite settlement established in 1611 was called "Henricus" and "Henrico." To avoid confusion with present-day Henrico County, I have used the former name.

Dates. The English used the old-style Julian calendar during the period covered by this book. I have retained the use of old-style English dates, except that I have adjusted the years to correspond with the modern new year: January 1, rather than the old-style new year of March 25. For example, the old-style date February 15, 1617—which would appear in some modern sources as February 15, 1617/18—is rendered in this book as February 15, 1618.

Authorship of collaborative works. The *Proceedings* of 1612, edited by William Symonds, and the *Generall Historie* of 1624, edited by John Smith, include contributions from numerous colonists. In the notes to this book, the first citation to a given chapter of the *Proceedings* or the *Generall Historie* is accompanied by the names of the authors of that chapter.

ABBREVIATIONS

The following abbreviations in the chapter notes refer to collections of primary documents:

J.V. Philip L. Barbour, ed. *The Jamestown Voyages Under the First Charter: 1606–1609.* 2 vols. London: Cambridge University Press, 1969.

Narratives Edward Wright Haile, ed. *Jamestown Narratives: Eyewitness Accounts of the Virginia Colony: The First Decade: 1607–1617.* Champlain, Va.: Round-House, 1998.

N.A.W. Volume 5 of David Beers Quinn, ed. *New American World: A Documentary History of North America to 1612.* New York: Arno Press, 1979.

Va. Co. Recs.   Susan Myra Kingsbury, ed. *The Records of the Virginia Company of London.* 4 vols. Washington: U.S. Government Printing Office, 1906–1935.

Also, *DNB* and *OED* refer to the *Dictionary of National Biography* and the *Oxford English Dictionary* respectively.

CHAPTER NOTES

I: PROLOGUE

1. Gold, silver, and other riches: Charter of April 10, 1606, reprinted in Bemiss (1957), p. 6. trade route by river: Craven (1957), pp. 10–11; Purchas (1625), vol. 19, p. 152. Joint-stock company: Craven (1957), p. 3. Public stock offering: Ibid., p. 17. Half were "gentlemen": In John Smith's list of the first Jamestown colonists, fifty-four are listed as gentlemen or councilors. Smith (1624), pp. 140–42. "Do nothing; be like a gentleman": George Chapman, Ben Jonson, and John Marston, *Eastward Ho*, act 1, scene 1, reprinted in Spencer (1933), p. 479. Peggy Lee: John Davenport and Eddie Cooley, "Fever," score, 1956.

2. "Compassionate pitiful heart": Smith (1624), pp. 258–59.

3. John Smith's early background: Smith (1630), pp. 153–54; Smith (1986), vol. 1, pp. lv, lvii. Height: Barbour (1964a), p. 470 n. 1. A portrait made later in his life: The portrait accompanies his 1616 *Description of New England*. It is reproduced in various places, including at Smith (1616), p. 320. "He was honest, sensible, and well informed": Jefferson (1787), p. 177.

The grammar school that Smith attended, the Royal Free Grammar School of King Edward VI, is still in operation (see *www.kevigs.lincs.sch.uk*).

4. Fighting in Netherlands, woody pasture, fighting in Hungary, slavery and escape: Smith (1630), pp. 155–56, 163–79, 182–89, 200; Barbour (1964a), pp. 9–15, 26–63.

5. Outnumbered the English: Recent estimates of the population of the Powhatan Empire at this time range from approximately 13,000 to as many as 34,000. See Gleach (1997), pp. 26, 169; Horn (1994), p. 132. Of course, the Powhatans' numerical advantage on the battlefield would have been less pronounced, since only the Powhatan males were soldiers, but the imbalance would still have been extreme. "Thou Virginia foild'st": From a verse accompanying Smith's *Description of New England*, signed by colonists Michael Fettiplace, William Fettiplace, and Richard Wiffin. Smith (1616), p. 317. "Exclaim of *all* things": Smith (1612), pp. 175–76.

6. Sebastian Cabot: Bancroft (1834), vol. 1, pp. 10–11. Sir Humphrey Gilbert's: Foss (1974), pp. 128–29. Roanoke colony: Quinn (1985). Ralegh, Raleigh, or Rawleyghe: Jones (1987).

The story of Ralegh and the mud puddle appears to have originated in the mid–seventeenth century with the Reverend Thomas Fuller's entertaining but unreliable biographical reference, *The Worthies of England.* See Fuller (1662), p. 133.

7. Record of Spain: For a précis of Spanish exploration and conquest after Columbus, see Wright (1971), pp. 2–10. Two rich contemporaneous accounts are Benzoni (1565) and Las Casas (1542). On the *encomienda* system, see Haring (1947), chapter 3.

8. "No Spanish intention": Strachey (1612), p. 85. "Others not pleasing": Smith (1624), p. 206. This section of the *Generall Historie* was written by colonists Richard Wiffin, William Fettiplace, Jeffrey Abbot, and Anas Todkill. "Not by stormes of raging cruelties": Robert Johnson, *Nova Britannia* (1609), reprinted in *N.A.W.*, p. 240. To preach the Gospel: Council of Virginia [in London], *A True Declaration* (1610), reprinted in *Narratives*, p. 469.

9. Don Luis: Lewis and Loomie (1953), pp. 15–55; Axtell (1995), p. 5; Rountree (1990), pp. 15–18; Gleach (1997), pp. 90–94.

10. "We are taught to acknowledge": Strachey (1612) p. 12. John Smith later denounced: Smith (1616), p. 352. Civilizing influence: See, for example, the argument of the Reverend Alexander Whitaker, a minister in Virginia in 1613. "Oh remember, I beseech you, what was the state of England before the Gospel was preached in our country. How much better were we then and concerning our souls' health than these [natives] are now?" Whitaker, *Good News from Virginia* (1613), reprinted in *Narratives*, p. 731.

To the same effect, the Reverend Samuel Purchas, an energetic promoter of colonization, and an editor and compiler of many of the surviving accounts, added an editorial comment in the margin of William Strachey's story. "Were not we ourselves made and not born civil in our progenitors' days?" Purchas asked. "And were not Caesar's Britons as brutish as Virginians [natives]? The Roman swords were the best teachers of civility to this and other countries near us." William Strachey, *A True Reportory* (1625), reprinted in *Narratives*, p. 435 n. 1. John Smith argued, "Had the seede of Abraham, our Savior Christ, and his Apostles, exposed themselves to no more daungers to teach the Gospell, and the will of God then wee; [then] even wee our selves, had at this present been as salvage, and as miserable as the most barbarous salvage yet uncivilized." Smith (1616), p. 360.

11. "Their skynn is tawny": From an account tentatively attributed to colonist Gabriel Archer. Archer, *Description of the People* (1607), reprinted in *J.V.*, vol. 1, p. 103. "They would be of good complexion": Edward-Maria Wingfield, no title (n.d.), reprinted in *Narratives*, p. 202. William Parker: Ralph Hamor, *A True Discourse* (1615), reprinted in *Narratives*, p. 836. John Smith reported that the natives are "of a colour browne when they are of age, but they are borne white." Smith (1612), p. 160. See also Strachey (1612), p. 63.

12. "Had not this violence": Strachey (1612), pp. 17–18. "There is no other moderate and mix'd course": Council of Virginia [in London], *A True Declaration* (1610), reprinted in *Narratives*, pp. 469–70. "Their children": Robert Johnson, *Nova Britannia* (1609), reprinted in *N.A.W.*, p. 247.

2: THE CROSSING

1. Blackwall, tonnages: Smith (1624), p. 137. Testimony in a case before the High Court of Admiralty involving the *Susan Constant* indicates its capacity at 120 tons. See *N.A.W.*, pp. 171, 178, 180. Dimensions: In planning the replica ships that are now harbored at Jamestown Settlement, historians there derived the estimates of the origi-

nal ships' dimensions from their tonnages using other ships of the period as bench-marks, and from treatises of the period on ship design. Fee and Faucett (1958), pp. 6–9; Nancy Egloff, personal communication. Those approximate dimensions are as follows:

> *Susan Constant*
> Overall length, 116 feet
> Deck length, 82 feet
> Width (beam), 24 feet, 10 inches
>
> *Godspeed*
> Overall length, 68 feet
> Deck length, 52 feet
> Width (beam), 14 feet, 8 inches
>
> *Discovery*
> Overall length, 49 feet, 6 inches
> Deck length, 38 feet, 10 inches
> Width (beam), 11 feet, 4 inches

Nautical historian Brian Lavery estimates the width of the *Susan Constant* at a narrower 22 feet, 9 inches. Lavery (1988), p. 10.

2. Distribution of passengers and crew: Barbour (1964a), p. 113. 1985 reenactment: Interview with Neil Tanner.

The *Susan Constant* was chartered from Colthurst, Dapper, Wheatley and Company. *N.A.W.*, p. 171. The Virginia Company purchased the *Discovery* from the Muscovy Company. Fee and Faucett (1958), p. 5.

3. Shipboard accommodations: Lavery (1988), pp. 24–26. Wingfield background: *DNB*. At least two servants: Wingfield, *Discourse* (1608), reprinted in *J.V.*, vol. 1, p. 230 (referring to "my servauntes" in Virginia). "A covetous haughty person": Oldmixon (1741), vol. 1, p. 357. The reference is to Oldmixon's second edition. Passenger list: Smith (1624), pp. 140–42.

4. Slaves: See chapter 13. Servitude: A. E. Smith (1947), pp. 8–10. Seven years: This was the term of obligation for the 1609 voyagers. Ibid. *Susan Constant* had crashed: Depositions in *N.A.W.*, pp. 171, 176, 180. Cannon: Lavery (1988), pp. 38–39. Sealed box, command of Christopher Newport: *Orders for the Council of Virginia* (Nov. 20, 1606), reprinted in *J.V.*, vol. 1, p. 46. Smith traveled on the *Susan Constant*: Barbour (1964a), p. 114. Newport background: Andrews (1954). King James's fascination: Willson (1956), p. 182.

5. Gosnold background: Gookin (1949); Wilson (2000). Midlife by the standards of the day: One writer of the period defined "youth" as lasting through age twenty-five, "middle age" from twenty-five to fifty, and "old age" from fifty onward. Cuffe (1607), pp. 118–19. "A poore counterfeited imposture": Smith (1624), p. 189.

6. The liar: Smith (1627), p. 84. Wooden anchors: Lavery (1988), p. 21. A fateful feud began: Smith (1624), p. 137; Barbour (1964a), pp. 109–11. "Master Hunt, our preacher": Smith (1624), p. 137. See also Smith (1631), p. 296, in which Smith describes Hunt as "an honest, religious, and couragious divine."

7. Trade winds: Waters (1958), p. 261. Columbus himself had pioneered: Morison

(1955), p. 38. Navigation and timekeeping methods: Waters (1958), pp. 57–59, 427, 580, 592; Morison (1955), pp. 39–40. Modern sailing dictionary: Henry Beard and Roy McKie, *Sailing: A Sailor's Dictionary* (New York: Workman, 1981), p. 57. Compass: Waters (1958), p. 59; Smith (1627), pp. 65–66.

8. Wayward sons: Johnson, *The New Life of Virginea* (1612), p. 10, reprinted in Force (1836), vol. 1. Celebratory verse: Michael Drayton, "Ode to the Virginian Voyage" (1606), reprinted in *Narratives*, p. xxi. Friend of a Virginia Company investor: Rowse (1959), p. 194 n. 2.

9. "Gold is more plentiful": George Chapman, Ben Jonson, and John Marston, *Eastward Ho*, act 3, scene 3, reprinted in Spencer (1933), p. 496.

10. Reached the Canaries: Smith (1624), pp. 137, 139; Barbour (1964a), pp. 113–15. in familiar territory: Smith (1630), p. 212. People of his native Lincolnshire: Hill (1956), pp. 6–7, 11. In 1536, Henry VIII called the shire of Lincoln "one of the most brute and beastly of the whole realm." Ibid., p. 45 n. 1. Educated opinion of Lincolnshire at the time is further suggested by the Reverend Fuller's humorous reference to Lincolnshire men as "country clowns, overgrown with hair and rudeness." Fuller (1662), p. 327.

Purchas: A marginal comment to his publication of Percy's *Discourse*. See Percy, *Observations Gathered Out of a Discourse* (1608?), reprinted in *J.V.*, vol. 1, p. 129. "Julius Caesar wrote": Smith (1627), p. 47.

11. Sailing before the trades: Morison (1955), p. 93.

12. Martinique, Dominica: Percy, *Observations Gathered Out of a Discourse* (1608?), reprinted in *J.V.*, vol. 1, pp. 129–30; Smith (1624), p. 137. Background on Caribs: Boucher (1992); Bell (1902).

13. Nevis: Percy, *Observations Gathered Out of a Discourse* (1608?), reprinted in *J.V.*, vol. 1, pp. 130–32; Smith (1630), pp. 235–36. Manchineel: On the identification of the toxic trees as the manchineel (or "manchioneel"), see Barbour (1964a), p. 429 n. 3. On the effects of the manchineel's sap, see Lampe et al. (1985), pp. 91–92; Oakes and Butcher (1962), pp. 50–51.

14. Mona, Monito, thunderstorm, landing: Percy, *Observations Gathered Out of a Discourse* (1608?), reprinted in *J.V.*, vol. 1, pp. 132–33; Smith (1624), pp. 137–38. Columbus "kneeling on the ground": Morison (1942), pp. 228–29.

15. Attack: Smith (1608), p. 27; Percy, *Observations Gathered Out of a Discourse* (1608?), reprinted in *J.V.*, vol. 1, pp. 133–34. Deadly accurate: Strachey (1612), p. 106. Superiority of bows and arrows: Peterson (1956), p. 19.

Through the sixteenth century, English armies had themselves relied on bows and arrows, and English soldiers were the preeminent archers of Europe. By the time of the Jamestown expedition, however, those skills had fallen into desuetude thanks to the adoption of firearms. See Gleach (1997), pp. 80, 83.

3: HAVE GREAT CARE NOT TO OFFEND

1. Virginia Company had commanded: *Orders for the Council of Virginia* (Nov. 20, 1606), reprinted in *J.V.*, vol. 1, p. 46. unfasten one of the three boxes: Smith (1608), p. 27; Symonds (1612), p. 205. This chapter of Symonds's *Proceedings* is uncredited, but was most likely written by John Smith. See Smith (1986), vol. 1, p. 195.

2. Instructions: *Instructions Given By Way of Advice* (1606), reprinted in *J.V.*, vol. 1, pp. 49–54.

3. Exploration, Kecoughtans: Percy, *Observations Gathered Out of a Discourse* (1608?), reprinted in *J.V.*, vol. 1, pp. 134–36. The natives' homes: Rountree and Turner (2002), pp. 64–65, 70; Rountree (1989), pp. 60–61. How to make glass: Strachey (1612), p. 71. "Who knoweth one of them": Ibid., p. 70.

4. "The most apt and securest place": Strachey, *A True Reportory* (1625), reprinted in *Narratives*, p. 428. Called on several other tribes, Archer's Hope: Percy, *Observations Gathered Out of a Discourse* (1608?), reprinted in *J.V.*, vol. 1, pp. 136–38.

5. The company's instructions: *Orders for the Council of Virginia* (Nov. 20, 1606), reprinted in *J.V.*, vol. 1, p. 47. Oaths of office: Ibid., pp. 47–48. "Oration made": Symonds (1612), p. 205. Comment of Wingfield: Wingfield, *Discourse* (1608), reprinted in *J.V.*, vol. 1, p. 220 and n. 1 (amended for apparent printer's error in original document).

4: WINGFIELD

1. President Wingfield's policy, Paspahegh visits: Symonds (1612), pp. 205–206; Percy, *Observations Gathered Out of a Discourse* (1608?), reprinted in *J.V.*, vol. 1, pp. 139–40.

Although the quoted chapter of Symonds's *Proceedings* is not credited, and the following chapter is credited to colonist Thomas Studley, both chapters appear to have been written by John Smith. See Smith (1986), vol. 1, p. 195.

2. Exploratory trip: Archer, *A Relation* (1607), reprinted in *J.V.*, vol. 1, pp. 80–84.

3. The colonists dined: Archer, *A Relation* (1607), reprinted in *J.V.*, vol. 1, p. 84; Percy, *Observations Gathered Out of a Discourse* (1608?), reprinted in *J.V.*, vol. 1, p. 141; Smith (1608), p. 29; Barbour (1964a), p. 129. Powhatan Empire: Rountree (1990), pp. 9–10, 25; Gleach (1997), pp. 22–25; Strachey (1612), pp. 48, 51–52. Wahunsenacah: Strachey, op. cit., p. 48. Tsenacommacah: Strachey, op. cit., pp. 29, 47; Gleach (1997), p. 23. Trained from early childhood: Wingfield, no title (n.d.), reprinted in *Narratives*, p. 202; Strachey, op. cit., p. 110.

4. A nation would arise: Strachey (1612), p. 101; Rountree (1990), pp. 25–27. As they sat eating: Rountree (1990), p. 33; Archer, *A Relation* (1607), reprinted in *J.V.*, vol. 1, pp. 84–89. "Gifts of divers sorts": Ibid., p. 84. "We trifled": Smith (1608), p. 31.

5. With the Weyanock tribe: Archer, *A Relation* (1607), reprinted in *J.V.*, vol. 1, pp. 94–95; Smith (1608), p. 31. Taken the colony by surprise: Archer, op. cit., p. 95; Smith (1608), p. 31; Symonds (1612), p. 206. "Had it not chanced": Symonds (1612), p. 206.

6. "Hereupon the President": Symonds (1612), p. 206. "The best part thereof": Archer, *A Relation* (1607), reprinted in *J.V.*, vol. 1, p. 95.

7. May 28: Archer, *A Relation* (1607), reprinted in *J.V.*, vol. 1, pp. 95–96.

8. Shot him in the head: Archer, *A Relation* (1607), reprinted in *J.V.*, vol. 1, p. 96. Debate over Smith: Ibid., p. 97; Symonds (1612), p. 207. Wingfield had recruited him: Wingfield, *Discourse* (1608), reprinted in *J.V.*, vol. 1, p. 233.

9. Two native men came unarmed: Archer, *A Relation* (1607), reprinted in *J.V.*, vol. 1, pp. 97–98.

10. Newport asked Wingfield: Wingfield, *Discourse* (1608), reprinted in *J.V.*, vol. 1, p. 214.

11. Newport bid adieu: Percy, *Observations Gathered Out of a Discourse* (1608?),

reprinted in *J.V.*, vol. 1, p. 143. "Within lesse then seaven weekes": Letter from the Council in Virginia (June 22, 1607), reprinted in *J.V.*, vol. 1, p. 78. Brewster: Letter from William Brewster to unknown recipient (May–June 1607), reprinted in *J.V.*, vol. 1, p. 107. "The mayne river": Archer, *Description of the River and Country* (1607), reprinted in *J.V.*, vol. 1, p. 99. "They are proper lusty": Archer, *Description of the People* (1607), reprinted in *J.V.*, vol. 1, p. 103. "The people steale": Ibid. Still living in tents: Smith (1608), p. 35; Smith (1631), p. 295. Springtime deceptively mild: As far as I am aware, this connection was first made in Kelso (1996), vol. 2, p. 14.

12. Powhatan sent a messenger: Wingfield, *Discourse* (1608), reprinted in *J.V.*, vol. 1, pp. 214–15. Percy complained: Percy, *Observations Gathered Out of a Discourse* (1608?), reprinted in *J.V.*, vol. 1, p. 143. Daily rations: Percy, op. cit., p. 144; Symonds (1612), p. 210. "Had we been as free": Symonds (1612), p. 210.

13. Virginia Company had urged: *Instructions Given By Way of Advice* (1606), reprinted in *J.V.*, vol. 1, p. 52. Shortcomings of site: Hatch (1957), p. 3; Axtell (1995), p. 16. increasingly brackish: Earle (1979), p. 102. "Full of slime and filth": Percy, *Observations Gathered Out of a Discourse* (1608?), reprinted in *J.V.*, vol. 1, p. 144. "The sixt of August": Percy, op. cit., pp. 143–44.

14. "Our men were destroyed": Percy, *Observations Gathered Out of a Discourse* (1608?), reprinted in *J.V.*, vol. 1, p. 144. Causes of death: Earle (1979), p. 99. As few as five: Percy, op. cit. Smith says "scarce ten amongst us coulde either goe, or well stand, such extreame weaknes and sicknes oppressed us." Symonds (1612), p. 209. Men groaned and cried out: Percy, op. cit., p. 145. Smith and Ratcliffe ill: Smith (1608), p. 33. Wingfield-Gosnold ties: Gookin (1949), pp. 408–409. "In his sickness time": Wingfield, *Discourse* (1608), reprinted in *J.V.*, vol. 1, p. 215. Gosnold was buried: Percy, op. cit., p. 144. Movement to depose Wingfield: Wingfield, op. cit., p. 218; Percy, op. cit., p. 145; Symonds (1612), p. 210. George Kendall: Smith (1608), pp. 33–35; Percy, op. cit., p. 144. Nearly half of the colonists were dead: Symonds (1612), p. 210; Smith (1608), p. 35; Wingfield, op. cit., p. 215. Began bringing corn: Percy, op. cit., p. 145; Symonds (1612), p. 210.

15. A signed order discharging him: Wingfield, *Discourse* (1608), reprinted in *J.V.*, vol. 1, p. 219. Could remove the president: *Instructions for Government* (Nov. 20, 1606), reprinted in *J.V.*, vol. 1, p. 36. "That they had eased him": Wingfield, op. cit., p. 219. Master Martyn followed: Ibid., p. 220.

16. Wingfield denied any wrongdoing: Wingfield, *Discourse* (1608), reprinted in *J.V.*, vol. 1, pp. 220–23. Crofts: Ibid., p. 222. Power to hold trials: *Instructions for Government* (Nov. 20, 1606), reprinted in *J.V.*, vol. 1, pp. 38–40. Action for slander: Wingfield, op. cit., pp. 223–24; Smith (1624), p. 140 (written by Robert Fenton, Edward Harrington, and John Smith). At this time: Smith (1624), p. 323.

17. Smith's new duties: Symonds (1612), p. 211; Smith (1608), p. 35. Food in the stores: Symonds, op. cit., p. 211.

5: THE RESCUE

1. For Zúñiga's correspondence, see *J.V.*, vol. 1, pp. 114–23. See also Wright (1971), p. 35.

2. Exactly that offense: James Read, the blacksmith, was on the scaffold and

about to swing from a rope, having been convicted of punching President Ratcliffe (after the president struck him first). At the last minute, Read avoided the noose by accusing George Kendall of serving as a spy for Spain. A jury accepted Read's allegation; Kendall was executed by a firing squad. See testimony of Francis Magnel, July 1, 1610, reprinted in *J.V.*, vol. 1, p. 156; Wingfield, *Discourse* (1608), reprinted in *J.V.*, vol. 1, p. 224; Smith (1608), p. 41. As this episode occurred after Kendall's initial arrest and banishment from the council, the unspecified "heinous" activity that led to his arrest was probably distinct from this alleged espionage and remains a mystery.

3. Ajacán: Lewis and Loomie (1953), p. 15. King James received Zúñiga: *J.V.*, vol. 1, pp. 117–19. "I am quite satisfied": Ibid., pp. 122–23.

4. "In such despaire": Smith (1608), p. 35.

5. "Emotional death": Frankl (1959), p. 33.

6. Smith's trading activities: Smith (1608), p. 37. Wingfield also credits Smith for "trad[ing] up and downe the river with the Indyans for corn, which releved the collony well." Wingfield, *Discourse* (1608), reprinted in *J.V.*, vol. 1, pp. 222–23.

A "bushel," at this time, was officially defined according to the capacity of a container in London that served as a reference standard. The container was measured in 1931 and found to have a capacity of 2,148.28 cubic inches—essentially eight gallons. Zupko (1977), pp. 77, 93. Where the colonists wrote of "bushels" of corn, they were obviously writing in approximate terms.

7. Phrases he left behind: Smith (1612), p. 136. Smith was interrogated in English, French, Dutch, and Italian during an episode in his slavery; see Smith (1630), p. 187. He negotiated with French pirates in their language during a later episode in 1615; see Smith (1616), p. 355. Natives' daily lives: Smith (1612), pp. 162–70; see also chapter 5 of Rountree (1989).

8. Approach of winter: Smith (1624), pp. 145–46. "tuftaffaty humorists": Tuftaffaty, or tufted taffeta, was used in fancy attire. *Humorists*, in this context, were persons too much in thrall to their "humors."

9. One can only speculate: For this observation, I am indebted to Barbour (1964a), p. 155.

10. "A tragedie": Smith (1624), p. 146.

11. Smith's party rowed: Ibid.; Smith (1608), pp. 43–45.

12. A most unhappy ending: *Relation of William White*, reprinted in *J.V.*, vol. 1, p. 150; Strachey (1612), p. 52; Smith (1612), p. 175. These accounts came to the English later from the natives.

13. Smith, Emry, and Robinson: Smith (1608), p. 45; Smith (1624), p. 146. The battle with the natives and Smith's subsequent captivity are recounted by Smith in his *True Relation* and *Generall Historie*, among other places. See Smith (1608), pp. 45–57; Smith (1624), pp. 146–52. An abbreviated version is in Smith's contribution to Symonds's *Proceedings*; see Symonds (1612), pp. 212–13.

Apart from the rescue story—still to come—the essential facts of Smith's captivity are not in dispute. For example, Smith's antagonist Edward-Maria Wingfield evidently accepted Smith's account, at least in general outline, and summarized it in his own history. Wingfield, *Discourse* (1608), reprinted in *J.V.*, vol. 1, pp. 226–27.

14. "A man of large stature": Beverly (1705), p. 61. Age: The English thought Opechancanough to be about a hundred years old in 1646. Gleach (1997), p. 177.

15. He had observed: Smith (1612), p. 169.

16. "The roundnesse of the Earth": Smith (1624), p. 147.

17. "no canyballs": Wingfield, *Discourse* (1608), reprinted in *J.V.*, vol. 1, p. 216.

18. Opechancanough visited Smith, messengers, reported in regretful tones: Smith (1608), pp. 49–51.

19. "Presently came skipping": Smith (1624), p. 149.

20. From the ceremony: Ibid., p. 150. Anthropologist Frederic W. Gleach has argued that the purpose of the ceremony was not to divine the intentions of the English, but to "control the way in which the English (represented by sticks) entered from beyond, through the boundaries (the grains of corn), into the Powhatan world itself." Gleach (1997), p. 114.

21. Smith was brought: Smith (1624), p. 150. On the location of Werowocomoco, see Strachey (1612), p. 36. The Virginia Department of Historical Resources and the College of William and Mary announced in May 2003 that an archaeological team had located the probable site of Werowocomoco on the York River.

22. The description of Powhatan's appearance is from Smith (1624), p. 126, and Strachey (1612), p. 49. The estimate of sixty for Powhatan's age is Smith's; the estimate of eighty is reported by Strachey. The portrayal of his subjects' fearfulness is also Strachey's; ibid., p. 51. The description of his countenance at the meeting is from Smith (1608), p. 53.

23. "Little wanton": Strachey (1612), p. 111. Strachey, like Smith, described her as an attractive ("well-featured") girl. Ibid., p. 65. Regarding Powhatan's wives, see Rountree (1990), p. 9. Smith's description of Pocahontas is at Smith (1608), p. 93. The characterization of Pocahontas as her father's "delight and darling" is Ralph Hamor's. See Hamor, *A True Discourse* (1615), reprinted in *Narratives*, p. 802.

24. Came forward with water: Smith (1624), p. 151. "Fat, lusty, manly": Archer, *A Relation* (1607), reprinted in *J.V.*, vol. 1, p. 92.

25. Dialogue with Powhatan: Smith (1608), pp. 53–55. On the beating out of brains as a Powhatan form of execution, see Spelman, *Relation of Virginia* (1609), reprinted in *Narratives*, p. 492; Strachey, (1612), pp. 37, 52, 54; Purchas, *Relation of Tomocomo* (1617), reprinted in *Narratives*, p. 882. Chiefs kept in servitude: Smith (1612), pp. 166, 175. Hostile neighbors: Rountree (1989), p. 120; Gleach (1997), p. 24; Strachey (1612), p. 104.

26. "There he was doomed": Marshall (1804), vol. 1, p. 42.

27. Powhatan sent him home: Smith (1624), p. 151. Smith himself would develop a high estimation of Powhatan's son Nantaquoud, "the most manliest, comeliest, boldest spirit, I ever saw in a salvage." Ibid., p. 258. He is also variously referred to in Smith's writings as Nantaquaus and Naukaquawis; see the editor's note at Smith (1986), vol. 2, p. 151 n. 4.

6: GILDED DIRT

1. "Somewhat too heavie": Smith (1624), p. 152. The depiction of Rawhunt is from Smith (1608), p. 93. On demiculverins and other ordnance of the day, see Smith (1627), p. 109. Smith also showed the men a millstone, which, like the demiculverins, was too heavy to carry away.

2. Regarding Archer's swearing in, the attempt to run off with the *Discovery*, the charges against Smith, and Smith's salvation upon Newport's return, see Smith (1608),

p. 61; Smith (1624), pp. 152–54; and Wingfield, *Discourse* (1608), reprinted in *J.V.*, vol. 1, p. 227. The accounts of Smith and Wingfield are in accord. Archer is not explicitly named as among the gentlemen in the *Discovery* plot (no participants are named), but it is circumstantially likely, making sense of Smith's near execution. See Barbour (1964a), p. 171. On a councilor's status and compensation, see Letter of Francis Perkins (Mar. 28, 1608), reprinted in *J.V.*, vol. 1, p. 158.

3. "Everything my son and I had": Letter of Francis Perkins (Mar. 28, 1608), reprinted in *J.V.*, vol. 1, pp. 160, 161–62. "Lost all his library": Smith (1624), p. 157.

4. "In a short time, it followed": Symonds (1612), p. 215. This section of the *Proceedings* is credited to both Anas Todkill and Thomas Studley; Studley, however, was not present to witness the events described, having died the previous August.

5. Todkill . . . thought: Symonds (1612), p. 216. "Such a majestie": Smith (1608), p. 65. The accounts omit mention of the *Discovery*, referring only to the barge, but it is unlikely that the colonists would have brought only the barge to accommodate thirty to forty men overnight.

6. Powhatan then inquired: Smith (1608), p. 65. Regarding the fond care given the white dog, see Smith (1624), p. 261.

7. Carried out the plan . . . Powhatan rose: Smith (1608), pp. 65–67. The description of the conversation in Smith's lodge is Todkill's. Symonds (1612), p. 216.

8. Savage, Namontack: Smith (1608), p. 69; Symonds (1612), p. 216 (Todkill). Smith's role as interpreter was recorded by Todkill. Symonds (1612), p. 217. The placement of Thomas Savage with Powhatan is also noted by Spelman, *Relation of Virginia* (1609), reprinted in *Narratives*, p. 482. Powhatan apparently liked Savage and treated him well. Ralph Hamor, *A True Discourse* (1615), reprinted in *Narratives*, p. 830.

9. "To beleeve his friendship": Smith (1608), p. 69.

10. "Ostentation of greatnes": Symonds (1612), p. 217 (Todkill).

11. Blue beads: Ibid.; Smith (1608), p. 71; Smith (1624), p. 156.

12. "The countrie is excellent": Letter of Christopher Newport (July 29, 1607), reprinted in *J.V.*, vol. 1, p. 76.

13. "All turned to vapour": Letter of Sir Walter Cope (Aug. 13, 1607), reprinted in *J.V.*, vol. 1, p. 111. Spanish ambassador: Letter of Don Pedro de Zúñiga (Aug. 22, 1607), reprinted in *J.V.*, vol. 1, p. 77. The gold-colored flecks: Smith (1986), vol. 1, p. 218 n. 1. Spiders: Strachey, *A True Reportory* (1625), reprinted in *Narratives*, p. 394. He passed word to the earl: Letter of Sir Thomas Smythe (Aug. 17, 1607), reprinted in *J.V.*, vol. 1, p. 112.

14. Refiners, goldsmiths: Regarding the practice of these crafts during the Jamestown era, see Kelso (2000), vol. 6, pp. 36–38. Materials used by the gold refiners at Jamestown have been recovered by archaeologists of the Jamestown Rediscovery team. Ibid. The council's report: Letter from the Council in Virginia (1607), reprinted in *J.V.*, vol. 1, p. 79. "All their wealth": Smith (1608), p. 67.

15. Riches . . . in more mundane articles: Smith (1612), p. 159. "Our gilded refiners": Symonds (1612), pp. 218–19.

16. "Very oft she came": Symonds (1612), p. 274 (Richard Pots and William Fettiplace). *Kekaten pokahontas:* Smith (1612), p. 139. Rally the boys: Strachey (1612), p. 65. Apronlike deerskin dresses: Rountree (1989), p. 69 & n. From Smith's description of Pocahontas in the *True Relation*, their friendship had evidently begun by the time Thomas Nelson left for England with Smith's manuscript in early June of 1608.

17. "Petitions, admirals": Symonds (1612), p. 219.

7: POWHATAN BECOMES AN ENGLISH PRINCE

1. Turkeys, approach of the *Phoenix:* Smith (1608), pp. 81–85; Symonds (1612), pp. 219–220 (Todkill). "We thought ourselves as well fitted": Smith (1608), p. 85.

2. Reliable and sensible: Smith (1624), p. 154. Spent a week training: Smith (1608), p. 85; Symonds (1612), pp. 219–20 (Todkill).

3. First offensive: Smith (1608), pp. 87–93; Symonds (1612), p. 220 (Todkill). The natives' method for building canoes has been described as follows. (Evans [1957], p. 1).

> A long and thick tree was chosen according to the size of the boat desired, and a fire made on the ground around its base. The fire was kept burning until the tree had fallen. Then burning off the top and boughs, the trunk was raised upon poles laid over crosswise on forked posts so as to work at a comfortable height. The bark was removed with shells; gum and rosin spread on the upper side to the length desired and set on fire. By alternately burning and scraping, the log was hollowed out to the desired depth and width. The ends were scraped off and rounded for smooth navigating.

4. Rawhunt presented: Smith (1608), pp. 91–95; Smith (1624), pp. 159–60 (Todkill).

5. The native attacks: Smith (1624), p. 160 (Todkill).

6. "None was slaine": Ibid.

7. "Desirous to injoy": Ibid.

8. "This Newport brought": Letter of Don Pedro de Zúñiga (June 26, 1608), reprinted in *J.V.*, vol. 1, p. 163.

9. "I hear not": Chamberlain (1965), p. 40.

10. Smith's intentions: The byline on the *True Relation* ultimately read, "Written by Captaine Smith one of the said Collony, to a worshipfull friend of his in England." On that basis, the *True Relation* is universally described nowadays as having been a letter from Smith to a friend. But those words were Healey's, not Smith's, and the reliability of Healey's information about Smith's intentions can only be guessed at. (At the time of the first printing, Healey did not even know who the author was, and so the *True Relation* was wrongly credited at first to a "Thomas Watson.")

On balance, the *True Relation* seems more likely an official or unofficial communication to a member of the Virginia Company, rather than a letter to a "worshipfull friend." This is suggested by the extent of the negative information it contained, which would have put Smith at risk of punishment for violating the colony's censorship rules if it were addressed to a friend outside the company. It is also suggested by the reportorial tone of the *True Relation* as published, which scarcely has the flavor of a personal letter—though, since the verbatim text of the original is lost, it is impossible to say whether Smith's original had more of a personal, familiar aspect that Healey rooted out.

Editor named John Healey: The *True Relation* identifies its editor only as "I.H."; regarding the identification of "I.H." as John Healey, see *J.V.*, vol. 1, p. 168 n. 1. Note that the letter *I* substituted for the letter *J* in certain circumstances at this time, as in "Iones" for "Jones"—hence the seeming lack of congruity in the initials.

The publisher of the *True Relation*, John Tapp, was a leading publisher of books on nautical subjects. Waters (1958), p. 497.

11. "Fit to be private": Smith (1608), p. 24. "Being in good health": Ibid., p. 97. That the latter was added by Healey is reasonably clear from its variance with practically the entire content of the *True Relation*.

12. Took fourteen men: Smith (1624), pp. 162–63. Read avoided the noose for his belligerence only by accusing councilor George Kendall of espionage. See chapter 5 n. 2, above.

13. "Mineralls, rivers, rocks": Smith (1624), p. 168. This portion of the *Generall Historie* is signed by Walter Russell, Anas Todkill, and Thomas Momford, all of whom were members of the exploration party.

14. Place-names, "the best merchants": Ibid., pp. 164–67. Washington, D.C.: One of the villages the party visited, Moyoanes, was near present-day Washington. *J.V.*, vol. 1, p. 239.

15. Stingray, Kecoughtans: Smith (1624), pp. 168–69.

16. "Pallace": Ibid., p. 180. "There we found": Ibid., p. 169.

17. "Not worthy of remembering": Ralph Hamor, *A True Discourse* (1615), reprinted in *Narratives*, p. 806. "All the time": Smith (1624), pp. 174–75. This section of the *Generall Historie* is credited to Anthony Bagnall, surgeon; Nathaniel Powell, gentleman; and Anas Todkill. All three were part of the second Chesapeake expedition.

18. Seven or eight canoes: Smith (1624), pp. 178–79.

19. "The weaknesse of the company": Ibid., p. 169.

20. Respite over: Ibid., pp. 180–81.

21. Seventy colonists, including: Ibid., pp. 190–91. Two hundred . . . men: Ibid., p. 189. There were 130 or so before the second supply arrived, and the second supply added some 70 more. Ibid., p. 181. See also Barbour (1964a), p. 456 n. 1. The two were married: Smith (1624), p. 192.

22. "Ifs and ands": Letter of John Smith to the Treasurer and Virginia Council (1608), reprinted in *J.V.*, vol. 1, p. 241. Made a futile attempt: Smith (1624), pp. 182, 188. Winne and Waldo: Ibid., p. 188. Scrivener: Ibid., p. 182.

23. "Strange coronation": Ibid., p. 181.

24. Three men and two boys: Ibid., pp. 182–83. To provide honored guests with a bedmate: Smith (1612), p. 168; Beverly (1705), p. 189; Rountree (1989), p. 91.

25. "Eight days": Smith (1624), p. 183.

26. Solemn ceremony, too heavy to carry, Monacans: Ibid., pp. 184–85, 188; letter of Peter Winne (Nov. 26, 1608), reprinted in *J.V.*, vol. 1, pp. 245–46. Three barges: Symonds (1612), p. 237. Pair of shoes: Although not separately listed, this gift is to be inferred from the fact that Powhatan reciprocated by giving the English his "old shoes"—his moccasins—together with his deerskin mantle (the latter in exchange for his new scarlet cloak).

27. Twenty good workingmen: Smith (1624), pp. 185–86. On the crafts and backgrounds of the German and Polish tradesmen, see Kelso (2000), vol. 6, pp. 62–66. Archaeologists of the Jamestown Rediscovery project have found glassmaking materials at the site. Ibid., pp. 64–65.

28. "Expresly to follow": Letter of John Smith to the Treasurer and Virginia Council (1608), reprinted in *J.V.*, vol. 1, p. 242.

29. "When you send againe": Ibid., pp. 242–45. For further analysis of the letter, see Hayes (1991b), pp. 142–43.

8: POCAHONTAS SAVES JOHN SMITH AGAIN

1. Another winter, Nansemond village: Symonds (1612), p. 242; Smith (1624), p. 191. Newport had planned: Symonds (1612), p. 235; Smith (1624), p. 182. "Though there be fish in the sea": Letter of John Smith to the Treasurer and Virginia Council (1608), reprinted in *J.V.*, vol. 1, p. 243.

2. Radical plan, cautioned Smith: Symonds (1612), pp. 242–44; Smith (1624), pp. 191–93. (Which were new to Virginia): Henry Spelman, *Relation of Virginia* (1609), reprinted in *Narratives*, p. 487. In calling for swords and guns: For this insight I am indebted to Rountree (1990), p. 49. Friendly relations: Smith (1608), p. 37. To serve as a spy: Symonds (1612), pp. 246–47; Smith (1624), p. 195. Warraskoyack chief, Tackonekintaco: Strachey (1612), p. 58.

3. "We were never more merry," "though I had many courses": Smith (1624), p. 194. This chapter of the *Generall Historie* is credited to William Fettiplace, Jeffrey Abbott, and Anas Todkill, who were part of the voyage, and Richard Wiffin, who apparently was not. Werowocomoco: Ibid., pp. 194–95.

4. "Some doubt," "friendly care": Symonds (1612), pp. 246–48; Smith (1624), pp. 195–97. "Waste ground": Percy, *Observations Gathered Out of a Discourse* (1608?), reprinted in *J.V.*, vol. 1, p. 141.

5. Passing the time, offered to guard: Symonds (1612), pp. 249–50; Smith (1624), pp. 197–98. John Russell: Symonds (1612), p. 245; Smith (1624), p. 194.

6. A visitor appeared: Symonds (1612), p. 274; Smith (1624), pp. 198–99, 259. The account in the *Proceedings* is by Richard Pots and William Fettiplace. Fettiplace was part of the expedition, as was his brother, Michael.

7. Came to fruition, casting their lot: Symonds (1612), pp. 250–51; Smith (1624), pp. 199–200. Matchlock guns: Peterson (1956), pp. 14–15. On the archaeological excavation of gun parts at Jamestown, see Kelso (1998), vol. 4, pp. 13–14, 49–51.

8. Oration: Smith (1612), p. 160; Symonds (1612), pp. 251–52; Smith (1624), pp. 200–201.

9. Challenged Opechancanough, "if I be the marke": Symonds (1612), p. 253; Smith (1624), p. 202.

10. "Men may thinke it strange": Symonds (1612), p. 256; Smith (1624), p. 205.

11. "Pamaunkees king we saw thee captive make": The poem is a dedicatory verse published in the *Generall Historie*, signed by Michael and William Fettiplace and Richard Wiffin, "gentlemen, and souldiers under Captaine Smith's command." Smith (1624), p. 229. As noted, the Fettiplace brothers were members of the expedition. Wiffin linked up with it just after the incident.

12. "I speake not": Symonds (1612), p. 259; Smith (1624), p. 208. This part of the *Proceedings* and the *Generall Historie* was apparently written by Smith.

13. New operating principle, casks were infested: Symonds (1612), pp. 263–64, 265; Smith (1624), p. 212–13, 214; Earle (1979), pp. 106–7. Dispersing into small groups: Smith (1612), p. 162. Smith reduced the risks somewhat: See Rountree (1989), p. 45.

14. Ambitious plans: Craven (1957), pp. 17–19; Rowse (1959), pp. 70–71. Spreading the word from their pulpits: Letter of Don Pedro de Zúñiga (April 12, 1609), reprinted in *J.V.*, vol. 2, p. 259. "They have collected in 20 days": Letter of Don Pedro de Zúñiga (Mar. 15, 1609), reprinted in *J.V.*, vol. 2, p. 256. Stock certificates: Billings (1975), pp. 27–28.

15. "There is no intendment": Gray (1609), pp. C 3, C 4. Gray further argued that if the native priests and rulers resisted the English presence, a war of liberation would be necessary to bring civilization and English liberty to the common people. Such a war, he argued, was within the prerogative of a Christian king—so long as the object was indeed liberation, not "covetousness and crueltie." Ibid., p. D.

Another surviving promotional tract from 1609 is Johnson, *Nova Britannia* (1609), reprinted in *N.A.W.*, pp. 234–48.

16. Sir Thomas Gates: *Narratives*, p. 46; *DNB; Dictionary of American Biography.*

17. Test a new, more direct route: Council of Virginia, *A True and Sincere Declaration* (1609), reprinted in *Narratives*, p. 361. Some generalities: Smith (1624), p. 217. Argall found the colonists: Letter of Gabriel Archer (Aug. 31, 1609), reprinted in *J.V.*, vol. 2, pp. 281–82. Spanish ship: Report of Francisco Fernández de Écija (1609), reprinted in *J.V.*, vol. 2, pp. 293, 307–11. Venetian ambassador: *J.V.*, vol. 2, p. 252.

18. Resupply: Letter of Gabriel Archer (Aug. 31, 1609), reprinted in *J.V.*, vol. 2, pp. 279–81. Would wish the ships had been Spanish attackers: Smith (1624), p. 219 (signed by Richard Pots, William Tankard, and William Fettiplace). "Gave not any due respect": Archer, op. cit., p. 282.

19. Operating under the first charter: Smith (1624), p. 230. Sailors: Letter of Gabriel Archer (Aug. 31, 1609), reprinted in *J.V.*, vol. 2, p. 282. The company's orders: Instructions to Sir Thomas Gates knight Governor of Virginia (1609), reprinted in *Va. Co. Recs.*, vol. 3, pp. 13–14 (council), 18–19 (Smith's command, natives).

20. *Sea Venture:* Letter of John Ratcliffe (Oct. 4, 1609), reprinted in *J.V.*, vol. 2, p. 283. John Martin: Smith (1624), pp. 220–21. "Unruly gallants": Ibid., p. 220. Francis West: Letter of Gabriel Archer (Aug. 31, 1609), reprinted in *J.V.*, vol. 2, p. 282. "ill chance": Smith (1624), p. 218.

9: THE STARVING TIME

1. They would be pardoned: Smith (1624), p. 217. Orapakes: Smith (1612), pp. 147, 173. They told Powhatan: Smith (1624), p. 226 (signed by Richard Pots, William Tankard, and William Fettiplace). At least one German, Samuel by name, held back from accepting the offer of a pardon, preferring to wait and see whether conditions at the colony improved (ibid.). For all their mercenary inclinations, the German glassmakers were considered good workers. So were the Polish tradesmen (ibid., p. 225).

2. A knotty question, problematic from the outset: Smith (1624), pp. 220–21; Percy, *A True Relation* (1612?), reprinted in *Narratives*, pp. 501–502; Rountree (1990), p. 52. Company's desire to build up new outposts: Instructions to Sir Thomas Gates knight Governor of Virginia (1609), reprinted in *Va. Co. Recs.*, vol. 3, pp. 15–17. Ten weeks' worth of rations: Symonds (1612), p. 273 (by Richard Pots and William Fettiplace).

3. When Smith arrived, new arrivals: Smith (1624), pp. 221–23; Percy, *A True Relation* (1612?), reprinted in *Narratives*, p. 502. Spelman would stay: Spelman, *A Relation of Virginia* (1609), reprinted in *Narratives*, p. 482; Smith (1986), vol. 1, p. xlix. Spelman misunderstood and thought he had been "sold" to Parahunt.

4. Seventy-four-mile trip: *J.V.*, vol. 2, p. 465. "Tore the flesh": Smith (1624), p. 223. The mishap was also recorded by George Percy. Percy, *A True Relation* (1612?), reprinted in *Narratives*, p. 502.

5. No doctor, secured a place: Smith (1624), pp. 223–24.

6. Denunciations: Symonds (1612), pp. 273–74; Percy, *A True Relation* (1612?), reprinted in *Narratives*, p. 502. Line of succession: Symonds (1612), p. 247; Smith (1612), p. 174; Rountree (1989), p. 93. That he was dead: Smith (1624), p. 261.

7. A letter for Robert Cecil: Letter of John Ratcliffe (Oct. 9, 1609), reprinted in *J.V.*, vol. 2, pp. 283–84.

8. "What shall I say?": Symonds (1612), p. 273.

9. The council consisted: Letter of John Ratcliffe (Oct. 9, 1609), reprinted in *J.V.*, vol. 2, p. 284. Percy's background: Shirley (1949), p. 228. "Ambitious, unworthy and vainglorious": Percy, *A True Relation* (1612?), reprinted in *Narratives*, p. 502. "A continual and daily table": Letter of George Percy (Aug. 17, 1611), reprinted in *Narratives*, p. 559. In this letter, Percy referred to his practice of keeping a dining table for gentlemen during a subsequent period in 1611 when he was governor. It can be assumed he did the same, for as long as he was able, during his presidency in 1609–1610. New wardrobe: Shirley (1949), pp. 237–38.

10. "all revolted": Symonds (1612), p. 275. Martin had deputized: Percy, *A True Relation* (1612?), reprinted in *Narratives*, p. 503. Pouring molten gold: Benzoni (1565), p. 73.

11. Captured alive: Percy, *A True Relation* (1612?), reprinted in *Narratives*, p. 504; Henry Spelman, *Relation of Virginia* (1609), reprinted in *Narratives*, pp. 483–85; Strachey, *A True Reportory* (1625), reprinted in *Narratives*, p. 441; Smith (1624), p. 232.

12. The natives rarely attacked: Ratcliffe's ship was a pinnace, the same as the 20-ton *Discovery*. West sailed: Percy, *A True Relation* (1612?), reprinted in *Narratives*, pp. 504–505; Symonds (1612), p. 275.

13. "Starving Time": Percy, *A True Relation* (1612?), reprinted in *Narratives*, p. 505; Symonds (1612), p. 275; Smith (1624), p. 232; Strachey, *A True Reportory* (1625), reprinted in *Narratives*, pp. 433, 441; Ancient Planters of Virginia, *A Brief Declaration* (1624), reprinted in *Narratives*, pp. 895–96; Answer of the General Assembly in Virginia (1624), reprinted in *Narratives*, p. 913. Among discarded food bones from the period, Jamestown archaeologists have found "poisonous snake vertebrae" as well as "butchered horse bones and bones of the black rat, dogs, and cats." Kelso (2000), vol. 6, p. 24.

Hog Isle: Smith (1624), p. 212. Ruffs: Pritchard (1999), p. 21. Probably Henry Collins: Henry Collins is listed as arriving in 1608 with the second supply. See Smith (1624), p. 190. He is the only Collins noted for the period. Because the passenger lists are only around 80 percent complete, however, there is some slight chance that a different Collins was involved. Virginia Company propaganda: Council of Virginia [in London], *A True Declaration* (1610), reprinted in *Narratives*, pp. 473–74. William Strachey (who was not present at the time of the incident) accepted the company version. Strachey, *A True Reportory* (1625), reprinted in *Narratives*, p. 440. To the contrary are the reports by Percy (who was certainly present) and by Smith's anonymous correspondent in the *Generall Historie* (who appears to have been).

14. Dug their own graves: Answer of the General Assembly in Virginia (1624), reprinted in *Narratives*, p. 913. Ran away to the natives: Ancient Planters of Virginia, *A Brief Declaration* (1624), reprinted in *Narratives*, p. 896. Hugh Pryse: Percy, *A True Relation* (1612?), reprinted in *Narratives*, p. 507.

15. The men there were hale: Percy, *A True Relation* (1612?), reprinted in *Narratives*, p. 506. "It were too vile to say": Symonds (1612), p. 276.

A rough and ready calculation of the mortality rate is four hundred dead out of five hundred who started, or 80 percent. A more specific calculation of the mortality rate for Jamestown itself should reflect, in the numerator, that there were only sixty survivors at Jamestown proper, not one hundred. Both the numerator and denominator should exclude West and the rest of the absconders in his party (for a total of thirty-seven), as well as those sent to Point Comfort (of whom there were forty). The reported mortality rate at Jamestown was thus (500-60-37-40)/(500-37-40), or 363/423, or 82.5 percent.

Having foisted this arithmetic on the reader, I must point out that the difference in the rates is not really meaningful. As noted in the text, the underlying figures from the chroniclers may be plus or minus a little bit, so it is safer to say simply that the mortality rate was around 80 percent.

Earle arrives at a much lower mortality rate of 44 percent by assuming that there were only 220 or 250 living colonists in the fall, not 500. Earle (1979), pp. 108–109. This would seem to be in error. Both George Percy and an unknown contributor to Symond's *Proceedings* report a population of 500, which is consistent with the arrival of seven ships from the 1609 resupply. Percy, op. cit., p. 507; Symonds (1612), pp. 275–76.

10: RESTORATION

1. *Sea Venture:* Strachey, *A True Reportory* (1625), reprinted in *Narratives,* pp. 383–90; Letter of Sir George Somers (June 15, 1610), reprinted in *Narratives,* p. 445; Letter of Gabriel Archer (Aug. 31, 1609), reprinted in *J.V.,* vol. 2, pp. 279–81. veer north of the West Indies: Waters (1958), p. 259. 300-ton flagship: Strachey, op. cit., p. 415.

2. Ruin of French, Dutch, and Spanish ships: Smith (1624), p. 345 (written by Henry May). "As they would shun the Devil himself": Jourdain, *A Discovery of the Bermudas* (1610), reprinted in Wright (1964), p. 108. Somers background: *DNB*; Crashaw, Epistle Dedicatory [preface] to Alexander Whitaker's *Good News from Virginia* (1613), reprinted in *Narratives,* p. 709. Consistent with the yardstick of the time, Crashaw describes the fifty-five-year-old Somers as having been "in his old age" when he led the expedition. Whom Smith would laud: Smith (1624), pp. 350–51.

3. As Somers approached: Strachey, *A True Reportory* (1625), reprinted in *Narratives,* pp. 390, 395–400; Rich, *News From Virginia* (1610), reprinted in *Narratives,* p. 375; Jourdain, *A Discovery of the Bermudas* (1610), reprinted in Wright (1964), pp. 107–12. "The richest, healthfullest, and pleasing land": Ibid., p. 109.

The wreck of the *Sea Venture* was found in 1958 between two reefs off St. George's Island. Beginning in 1978, a team led by Allan J. Wingood excavated the wreck under the auspices of the Bermuda Maritime Museum. Bass (1988), pp. 111–13.

4. Henry Ravens: *J.V.,* vol. 1, p. 58 n. 1; Strachey, *A True Reportory* (1625), reprinted in *Narratives,* p. 418. Shipbuilding plan, marriage, births: Strachey, op. cit., pp. 403, 413–14; Jourdain, *A Discovery of the Bermudas* (1610), reprinted in Wright (1964), pp. 113–14. Oddly enough, the name of Bermuda Rolfe's mother is not recorded. Eustacius: *Narratives,* p. 54.

5. A handful of dissenters: Strachey, *A True Reportory* (1625), reprinted in *Narratives,* pp. 404–10.

6. Had come to fruition: Strachey, *A True Reportory* (1625), reprinted in *Narra-*

tives, pp. 414–16. Lost only six of the company: Ibid., p. 413. Strachey lists five, but omits Henry Paine. "From morning until night," one bolt: Jourdain, *A Discovery of the Bermudas* (1610), reprinted in Wright (1964), p. 116. Inspiration for *The Tempest*: Wright (1964), pp. x, xviii; Sanders (1949), pp. 119, 123–24.

7. A ghost town, departure: Strachey, *A True Reportory* (1625), reprinted in *Narratives*, pp. 419–20, 423, 426–27; Percy, *A True Relation* (1612?), reprinted in *Narratives*, pp. 506–508; Jourdain, *A Discovery of the Bermudas* (1610), reprinted in Wright (1964), p. 115; Copland (1622), p. 11.

8. Brewster, De La Warr voyage, arrival of Gates and De La Warr: Strachey, *A True Reportory* (1625), reprinted in *Narratives*, pp. 427, 432; letter of the Governor and Council in Virginia to Va. Co. of London (July 7, 1610), reprinted in *Narratives*, pp. 458–59; letter of Thomas West, Lord De La Warr to the Earl of Salisbury (1610), reprinted in *Narratives*, p. 466; Percy, *A True Relation* (1612?), reprinted in *Narratives*, p. 508. "To the great grief": Ancient Planters of Virginia, *A Brief Declaration* (1624), reprinted in *Narratives*, p. 897. "Then I delivered some few words": Letter of the Governor and Council in Virginia, op. cit., pp. 458–59. An open pit: Kelso (1999), vol. 5, pp. 7–9.

The figure of 150 newcomers is West's. Letter of Thomas West, op. cit., p. 465. Other sources put it at 250 (Ancient Planters of Virginia, op. cit., p. 897) or 300 (Percy, op. cit., p. 508). West, having brought the colonists over, would have known better than anyone.

9. "For if God had not sent": Council of Virginia [in London], *A True Declaration* (1610), reprinted in *Narratives*, p. 474.

10. Somers surprised everyone: Jourdain, *A Discovery of the Bermudas* (1610), reprinted in Wright (1964), pp. 115–16. The company had recommended: Instructions to Sir Thomas Gates knight Governor of Virginia (1609), reprinted in *Va. Co. Recs.*, vol. 3, pp. 14 (priests), 18 (chiefs).

11. Humphrey Blunt, attack on Kecoughtans, message to Powhatan: Percy, *A True Relation* (1612?), reprinted in *Narratives*, pp. 508–509; Strachey, *A True Reportory* (1625), reprinted in *Narratives*, pp. 434–36.

12. "To the first I replied": Percy, *A True Relation* (1612?), reprinted in *Narratives*, pp. 508–509; see also Smith (1624), p. 236.

13. Even the natives: Smith (1612), p. 175; Smith (1624), p. 119.

14. "Nor would I have it conceived": Letter of the Governor and Council in Virginia to Va. Co. of London (July 7, 1610), reprinted in *Narratives*, p. 463. See also p. 462 n. 1.

15. Fate of Somers: Symonds (1612), p. 277; Smith (1624), pp. 350–51.

II: THE MARRIAGE

1. "Masts, deals, pitch": Council of Virginia [in London], *A True Declaration* (1610), reprinted in *Narratives*, pp. 475–76. "Only the name of God": Craven (1957), pp. 26–27. To the same effect, see the epistle dedicatory to Robert Johnson's *New Life of Virginea*, bemoaning that "there is no common speech nor publicke name of any thing this day, (except it be the name of God) which is more vildly depraved, traduced and derided by such unhallowed lips, then the name of Virginea." Johnson, *The New Life of Virginea* (1612), p. 4, reprinted in Force (1836), vol. 1. See also Chamberlain

(1965), p. 209. Stock offering the previous year: Craven (1957), pp. 22–23, 26; Johnson, op. cit., p. 20. Lotteries: Ezell (1948), pp. 186–87; *Va. Co. Recs.*, vol. 1, p. 390; *Va. Co. Recs.*, vol. 3, p. 67; Smith (1624), pp. 252–54.

2. West's departure and embarrassment: Craven (1957), p. 26; West, *A Short Relation* (1611), reprinted in *Narratives*, pp. 527–29. Dale's background: Rutman (1960). Laws called for: Provisions referenced in the text are articles 9, 10, 15, 22, 25, 28, and 31 of the laws "divine and morall" and articles 3 and 34 of the martial laws. They are reprinted in Flaherty (1969), pp. 12–21, 27, 35. Emigration had been forbidden: *Va. Co. Recs.*, vol. 3, p. 68. "Some he appointed": Percy, *A True Relation* (1612?), reprinted in *Narratives*, pp. 517–18. See also Ralph Hamor, *A True Discourse* (1615), reprinted in *Narratives*, p. 823. "Continual whippings": Ancient Planters of Virginia, *A Brief Declaration* (1624), reprinted in *Narratives*, p. 900.

3. "Trading place": Rountree (1989), p. 12. Argall who hauled: *DNB*. "Yea, to this pass": Hamor, *A True Discourse* (1615), reprinted in *Narratives*, pp. 801–802. "Whilst I was in this business": Letter of Samuel Argall to Nicholas Hawes (June 1613), reprinted in *Narratives*, p. 754.

4. Pocahontas's abduction: Hamor, *A True Discourse* (1615), reprinted in *Narratives*, pp. 802–804; letter of Samuel Argall to Nicholas Hawes (June 1613), reprinted in *Narratives*, pp. 754–55; Smith (1624), p. 243. Patawomeck god of rain: Spelman, *Relation of Virginia* (1609), reprinted in *Narratives*, p. 486.

5. Communications with Powhatan: Hamor, *A True Discourse* (1615), reprinted in *Narratives*, pp. 804, 806; letter of Samuel Argall to Nicholas Hawes (June 1613), reprinted in *Narratives*, p. 755; Smith (1624), p. 243. "Would fall to the ground of itself": Chamberlain (1965), p. 209. "There is a ship": Ibid., p. 210.

Regarding the response from Powhatan, there is a conflict in the two surviving accounts written by colonists on the scene, Argall and Hamor. Hamor said the English heard nothing at all from Powhatan until several months after Pocahontas's capture, and that he returned the seven Englishmen only at that point. Because Argall was directly involved, had no reason to prevaricate on the subject, and wrote his account closer to the time of the occurrences, his account is probably the more accurate.

6. "Thus they betrayed": Smith (1624), p. 243. Alexander Whitaker: *Narratives*, p. 65. "It was a day or two": Letter of Sir Thomas Dale to "D.M." (1614), reprinted in *Narratives*, p. 843.

7. Matchcot: Hamor, *A True Discourse* (1615), reprinted in *Narratives*, pp. 807–808; Letter of Sir Thomas Dale to "D.M." (1614), reprinted in *Narratives*, pp. 843–44. Smith (1624), p. 258. Sent each of his wives away: Spelman, *Relation of Virginia* (1609), reprinted in *Narratives*, pp. 488–89. A handsome man: Woodward (1969), pp. 160–61. Gentle and devout nature: That Rolfe was pious and unusually mild-mannered is suggested by the tone and substance of his letter to Sir Thomas Dale, reprinted in *Narratives*, pp. 850–56. Manly virtue of superior hunting ability: Rountree (1990), p. 12; Rountree (1989), pp. 38, 90. Married to and divorced: Strachey (1612), p. 54. Divorce: Rountree (1989), p. 91 and n. 25.

It is sometimes suggested that Rolfe's wife may have died in childbirth on Bermuda. If this had happened, however, Strachey would have almost certainly noted it, having been the godfather of Bermuda Rolfe. Strachey, *A True Reportory* (1625), reprinted in *Narratives*, p. 413.

8. Laughingstock, Dale's reaction, Rolfe distracted: This is clear in various passages of Rolfe's letter to Dale. Letter of John Rolfe to Sir Thomas Dale (1613), reprinted in *Narratives*, pp. 850–56. Whitaker's approving eye: Letter of the Rev.

Alexander Whitaker to Master Gouge (n.d.), reprinted in *Narratives*, p. 848. Looks of Powhatan women: Rountree (1989), p. 65. "No way led": Rolfe, op. cit., p. 851. See also Robertson (1996), pp. 569–70.

Pocahontas lived to see the publication of Rolfe's letter in Hamor's *True Discourse* in 1615. If Rolfe had any instinct for self-preservation, he presumably kept the book out of her hands at any cost. Amid his confession of love for her, he argued for the purity of his motives by asserting that if he were merely seeking sensual thrills, "I might satisfy such desire (though not without a seared conscience) yet with Christians more pleasing to the eye and less fearful in the offense unlawfully committed." Rolfe, op. cit., p. 855. Committing that argument to paper, even for the sake of advocacy in a private letter, was not too brilliant.

The authenticity of Rolfe's letter was questioned by some critics, who could not believe that a man in love would write so aridly—until the original letter was located in the Bodleian Library at Oxford. *Narratives*, p. 794 and n. 1.

9. "Oftentimes with fear and trembling": Letter of John Rolfe to Sir Thomas Dale (1613), reprinted in *Narratives*, p. 853. Ezra's warning: Ibid. and Ezra 10:2. That day in Matchcot: Hamor, *A True Discourse* (1615), reprinted in *Narratives*, p. 809. Baptism: Letter of the Rev. Alexander Whitaker to Master Gouge (n.d.), reprinted in *Narratives*, p. 848. Rebecca: Genesis 24.

10. Brother of Pocahontas's mother: Powhatan's only known brothers or half brothers were Kekataugh, Opitchapam, and Opechancanough. Twenty sons: Strachey (1612), p. 54. He may have had more by 1614. English customs of the time: Pearson (1957), pp. 342–44, 347, 351–57. "Tunic of dacca muslin": Woodward (1969), p. 165. Powhatan custom: Rountree (1989), p. 90.

11. "Ever since we have had": Hamor, *A True Discourse* (1615), reprinted in *Narratives*, p. 809. "Golden age": Rountree (1990), p. 61. See also Rolfe, *A True Relation* (1616), reprinted in *Narratives*, p. 869. Chickahominies: Hamor, op. cit., pp. 809–13.

An early historian of colonial America, Robert Beverly, interrupted his 1705 history of Virginia with the comment that the English had missed a crucial opportunity by failing to encourage intermarriage well before Rolfe and Pocahontas's (Beverly [1705], p. 38):

> Intermarriage had been indeed the method proposed very often by the Indians in the beginning, urging it frequently as a certain rule, that the English were not their friends, if they refused it. And I can't but think it wou'd have been happy for the country, had they embraced this proposal: For, the jealousie of the Indians, which I take to be the cause of most of the rapines and murders they committed, wou'd by this means have been altogether prevented, and consequently the abundance of blood that was shed on both sides wou'd have been saved; the great extremities they were so often reduced to, by which so many died, wou'd not have happen'd . . . and, in all likelihood, many, if not most, of the Indians would have been converted to Christianity by this kind method. . . .

12. King James: Willson (1956), pp. 282–83. Hamor and Savage's visit: Hamor, *A True Discourse* (1615), reprinted in *Narratives*, pp. 830–32. Dale was already married: Rutman (1960), p. 292 and n. 34; *Dictionary of American Biography*. Although it was permissible: Pritchard (1999), p. 27; Stone (1977), pp. 40–44, 408.

13. "Who for this purpose": Hamor, *A True Discourse* (1615), reprinted in *Narratives*, p. 833.

14. "Further give him to understand": Ibid., pp. 834–35.

12: POCAHONTAS IN LONDON

1. Within a few months: Letter of Sir Thomas Dale to "D.M." (1614), reprinted in *Narratives*, p. 845. Company's broadsides: Craven (1957), illustrations following p. 28. "Will not give a doit": *The Tempest*, act 2, scene 2.

Regarding the flying squirrels, Henry Wriothesley, earl of Southampton, wrote to Robert Cecil, earl of Salisbury, in late 1609 (*J.V.*, vol. 2, p. 288):

> Talkinge with the King by chance I tould him of the Virginia squirrils which they say will fly, wherof there are now divers brought into England, & hee presently & very earnestly asked mee if none of them was provided for him, & whether your Lordship had none for him, saying hee was sure you would gett one of them. I would not have trobled you with this but that you know so well how hee is affected to these toyes. . . .

Lost all enthusiasm: Willson (1956), pp. 330–31.

2. Arrival: Letter of Sir Thomas Dale to Sir Ralph Winwood (June 3, 1616), reprinted in *Narratives*, p. 878. In the hold: Chamberlain (1965), p. 214; letter of Sir Thomas Dale, op. cit., p. 878. "Safely returned": Letter of Sir Thomas Dale, op. cit. Tomocomo was to count: Purchas (1625), vol. 19, p. 119; Smith (1624), p. 261. Busy port town: Rowse (1971), p. 88. To London by coach: Smith (1986), vol. 3, p. 258 n. 1. Namontack: Purchas, *Relation of Tomocomo* (1617), reprinted in *Narratives*, p. 880.

The priest Tomocomo was also known as Uttamatomakkin.

3. Around a week: An estimate based on progress of thirty miles per day. A coach in 1661 from Oxford to London traveled at this rate; a coach from London to Edinburgh two years later traveled a somewhat faster thirty-three miles a day. Besant (1903), pp. 340–41. Dirt roads: Ibid., p. 83. Tooth-chattering ride: Coaches of this period had no springs. Ibid., p. 338. What the natives saw: Rowse (1971), p. 67. French visitor: Ibid. Southwark: Besant (1903), p. 180. Severed heads: As represented in the C. J. Visscher engraving of London in 1616. Reproduced in Pritchard (1999), p. 155. London Bridge: Pritchard (1999), pp. 154–55. Streets resounded: Ibid., pp. 156, 164–65; Besant (1903), p. 123. City had grown: Pritchard (1999), p. 152; Rowse (1971), p. 69; Bridenbaugh (1968), p. 164. Commerce: Besant (1903), pp. 195–96. houses: Bridenbaugh (1968), p. 182.

4. Wood smoke inoffensive: Rountree (1990), p. 63. Burning coal: Bridenbaugh (1968), pp. 184–85. "Hellish and dismall": Evelyn, *Fumifugium* (1661), reprinted in Lodge (1969), pp. 14–15. Air pollution from coal was noticed in London as early as the thirteenth century. Lodge (1969), p. x. Human waste: Kent (1970), pp. 359, 406; Besant (1903), p. 283. Natives did not have domesticated horses: Rountree (1989), pp. 27, 157 n. 21. The Belle Savage: Kent (1970), pp. 297–98; Woodward (1969), p. 175. Belle Savage Inn background: Matz (1922), pp. 61–68.

5. When Thomas West sailed: Letter of the Governor and Council in Virginia to Va. Co. of London (July 7, 1610), reprinted in *Narratives*, p. 454. "Seeing he cannot

there": Purchas (1625), vol. 19, p. 116. The notes he made: See the introductory message by "T.A.," probably Thomas Abbay, stating "this book may best satisfie the world, because it was penned in the land it treateth of." Smith (1612), p. 135. "Virginia is a country": Smith (1612), p. 143.

6. "Their buildings and habitations": Smith (1612), pp. 161–62, 164, 166, 173.

7. Background of *Map of Virginia* and *Proceedings:* Smith (1986), vol. 1, pp. 122–23, 195–97; *J.V.,* vol. 1, pp. 4–5. Stationers' Company, had invested: Hayes (1991b), p. 127; O'Brien (1960), p. 141. Stationers' Company background: Kent (1970), p. 219.

8. A third of Strachey's book: Smith (1986), vol. 1, p. 124. Give the region its name: Bradford (1952), p. 38 n. 5. Voyage of 1614: Smith (1624), pp. 400–402; Barbour (1964a), pp. 306–13. "I have had six or seven": Smith (1624), p. 405. An engraving of Smith's 1614 map of New England is reproduced in Smith (1616), pp. 320–21.

9. "Accomack": Smith (1616), p. 340. Popham Colony: Brain (2002); Smith (1624), pp. 397–99. 1615 voyage: Smith (1624), pp. 427–35; Smith (1616), pp. 353–59; Barbour (1964a), pp. 315–23. "to keepe my perplexed thoughts": Smith (1616), p. 357. A number of details of the encounter with du Poiron, including the loss of his ship, are also recorded in French archival sources; see Barbour (1964b).

An archaeological effort led by Jeffrey P. Brain at the site of the Popham Colony has excavated remains of its fort, known as Fort St. George, as well as other artifacts of the colony. See Brain (2002).

10. Allowance for expenses: Chamberlain (1965), p. 216. "However this might bee": Smith (1624), pp. 258–60.

11. "Pocahontas had many honours done her": Beverly (1705), pp. 43–44. "Entertained her with festivall state": Purchas (1625), vol. 19, p. 118. "With this savage": Ibid.; Purchas, *Relation of Tomocomo* (1617), reprinted in *Narratives,* pp. 880–82. Theodore Goulston background: *DNB.* Goulston (or Gulston) was a friend of Sir Edwin Sandys, an investor who was later elected treasurer of the company; Sandys had credited Goulston in 1614 with saving his life. See *DNB* entry for Sandys.

12. Masques were a form: Lindley (1995), pp. ix–x. Staged in the Banqueting House: Herford and Simpson (1950), vol. 10, p. 569. January 5: Some sources put the date of the masque as January 6, apparently based on the misconception that Twelfth Night fell on the evening *of* Twelfth Day—January 6. It actually fell on the evening *before* Twelfth Day. See *OED.* Ambassadors, "well placed": Herford and Simpson, op. cit., pp. 568–69. She was accompanied: Ibid.; Smith (1624), pp. 261–62. "Handsome, noble and jovial": Willson (1956), pp. 167–68. Other descriptions of King James: Ibid., pp. 378–79. Disdain for the female sex: Ibid., p. 196; Besant (1903), p. 359. They had no idea: Smith (1624), p. 261.

13. Did not have her husband with her: Neither John Smith nor John Chamberlain includes Rolfe when listing those who accompanied Pocahontas. Repulsed by the tobacco habit: James I (1604), pp. 45, 50. Observed a street scene: B. Jonson, *The Vision of Delight* (1617), reprinted in Orgell (1970), pp. 149–50. Bare-breasted: This is clear from surviving sketches of other Inigo Jones designs for masques of this period. See part 2 of Strong (1967). An hour or so: One of Jonson's characters in the 1612 masque *Love Restored* refers to masques as "the merry madness of one hour." Bevington and Holbrook (1998), p. 1. "Bright Night, I obey thee": Jonson, op. cit., p. 151.

For insights into *The Vision of Delight,* I am indebted to the commentaries in Herford and Simpson (1925), vol. 2, pp. 303–304; Orgell (1970), pp. 34–35; Robertson (1996), pp. 574–75; and Strong (1967) (no page numbering).

14. "Behold a king": B. Jonson, *The Vision of Delight* (1617), reprinted in Orgell (1970), p. 157.

15. "a Virginia maske": Smith (1624), p. 182 (marginal note).

16. Raise investment money: Barbour (1964a), pp. 332–33. Tomocomo, Pocahontas meetings: Smith (1624), pp. 260–61. "With a well set countenance": Ibid., p. 261.

17. "They did tell us always you were dead": Smith (1624), p. 261. Preferred to stay there: Chamberlain (1965), p. 215. Coal smoke disagreed: Stith (1747), p. 143. Pneumonia or tuberculosis: Smith (1986), vol. 1, p. xlv; Woodward (1969), p. 184. A native woman of Pocahontas's retinue who stayed behind in England contracted "consumption"—tuberculosis—several years later. *Va. Co. Recs.*, vol. 1, p. 338.

18. Gravesend, *George:* Smith (1624), p. 262. "All must die": Letter from John Rolfe to Sir Edwin Sandys (June 8, 1617), reprinted in *Va. Co. Recs.*, vol. 3, p. 71. Funeral: Woodward (1969), p. 185. Bells: Rowse (1971), p. 244. Stukely: Rolfe, op. cit. "At my departure from Gravesend": Ibid.

19. "Much lamented": Letter from John Rolfe to Sir Edwin Sandys (June 8, 1617), reprinted in *Va. Co. Recs.*, vol. 3, p. 71. "Goes from place to place": Letter of Samuel Argall to Va. Co. (Mar. 10, 1618), reprinted in *Va. Co. Recs.*, vol. 3, p. 92. "At her returne": Purchas (1625), vol. 19, p. 118. "Tomakin rails": Letter of Samuel Argall (June 9, 1617), reprinted in *Va. Co. Recs.*, vol. 3, p. 73.

Thomas Rolfe did not go to the New World until 1635, long after his father's death there in 1622. He became a successful Virginia planter in his own right with two thousand acres of holdings.

Later generations of the Virginia aristocracy would trace their bloodlines back to Pocahontas's son. To free Virginia's preeminent families from being classified as mixed race—a serious disability in the segregationist South of the nineteenth and twentieth centuries—Virginia's laws against interracial marriages would eventually contain a "Pocahontas exception" for whites with small amounts of native blood in their veins. See Tilton (1994), p. 29.

13: THE FIRST AFRICAN AMERICANS

1. "The greatness and bounds": Strachey (1612), p. 48. When he died: Letter of John Rolfe (June 15, 1618), reprinted in Smith (1624), p. 265. Whitaker . . . had drowned: Smith (1986), vol. 1, p. lii. John Rolfe had married or was about to: The year of this marriage is unknown, but was evidently between 1618 and 1621 (the latter being the year he and Jane Pierce Rolfe had a daughter, Elizabeth). *Narratives*, pp. 55–56. One man, "all our riches": Letter of John Pory (Sept. 30, 1619), reprinted in *Va. Co. Recs.*, vol. 3, p. 221. A newcomer to the colony in 1619: Ancient Planters of Virginia, *A Brief Declaration* (1624), reprinted in *Narratives*, p. 908. Tobacco trade statistics: "Lord Sackville's Papers" (1922), pp. 496–97.

2. King James's opposition: Willson (1956), pp. 303, 331. "We have with great joy": Letter of the Treasurer and Council for Virginia to Sir George Yeardley (June 21, 1619), reprinted in *Va. Co. Recs.*, vol. 3, pp. 146–47.

3. Increased tenfold: Heimann (1960), p. 50. "Because corne was stinted": Smith (1624), p. 327. See also p. 287. Purchas makes the same point, possibly under the influence of Smith (whom he reprints extensively on other matters). "Some thinke that if corne might there be valued (not at two shillinges six pence the bushell) as deere as

that which is brought from hence, there would be lesse feare of famine, or dependance on tobacco." Purchas (1625), vol. 19, p. 150. On the setting of the price of tobacco, see also *Va. Co. Recs.*, vol. 3, p. 162.

4. Assignment of private land ownership: *Instructions to George Yeardley* (Nov. 18, 1618), reprinted in *Va. Co. Recs.*, vol. 3, pp. 100–101, 103. Four "cities or borroughs": Ibid., p. 100. "Particular plantations": Morgan (1975), p. 94. Smythe's Hundred, Martin's Hundred: Hatch (1957), pp. 38–39, 104. By the end of 1619: Letter of John Rolfe to Sir Edwin Sandys (Jan. 1620), reprinted in *Va. Co. Recs.*, vol. 3, p. 245.

Sir Thomas Dale had granted the colonists the use of around three acres apiece to encourage planting, but those rights appear to have been rights of tenancy rather than ownership; there is no indication that the colonists had permanent ownership of their plots or that they could buy and sell them. Hamor, *A True Discourse* (1615), reprinted in *Narratives*, p. 814; Morgan (1975), pp. 93–94.

5. "A forme of government": Treasurer [Sir Edwin Sandys] and Company, *An Ordinance and Constitution for Council and Assembly in Virginia* (July 24, 1621), reprinted in *Va. Co. Recs.*, vol. 3, p. 482. This document is believed to be a copy made by Yeardley of the instructions he received in 1618. See Billings (1975), p. 11. Reflected the growing influence: Davis (1955), pp. 97, 280–82. Sandys background: Rabb (1998), pp. 6–10, 13, 99; *DNB*. Natural rights: Rabb (1998), pp. 30 n. 5, 100 n. 69; Malcolm (1981), p. 301. "There was not any man": Sir Nathaniel Rich, *Captain John Bargrave's Discourse* (May 16, 1623), reprinted in *Va. Co. Recs.*, vol. 4, p. 194. Captain Bargrave's extreme accusation probably overstated Sandys's true intentions, but it indicates that Sandys was seen as having democratic motives in governing the company as well as in the parliamentary sphere. Burgesses: Treasurer and Company, op. cit., p. 483. Census taken in March 1620: McCartney (1999), p. 182; Thorndale (1995), pp. 160, 168.

Much confusion has arisen from the fact that this census was taken "in the begininge of March 1619" (ibid., p. 168). The operation of the "old style" Julian calendar, which has its new year on March 25, is completely counterintuitive in some respects. This is one of them: March 24, 1619, is the *last* day of 1619, and March 25, 1619, is the *first* day of 1619. In other words, March 24, 1619, actually falls a year (minus a day) *after* March 25, 1619. Thus, "the begininge of March 1619"—right up to March 24—corresponds to 1620 in the modern calendar. (The confusing nature of this conversion is the reason I have converted old-style dates to the familiar January 1 new year throughout this book.) Extrinsic historical evidence that confirms the 1620 dating of the census is set out in McCartney (1999).

6. "Council of State," power of veto, "imitate and followe the policy": Treasurer [Sir Edwin Sandys] and Company, *An Ordinance and Constitution for Council and Assembly in Virginia* (July 24, 1621), reprinted in *Va. Co. Recs.*, vol. 3, pp. 483–84. A half dozen men: Smith (1624), p. 266. First session: J. Pory, *A Reporte of the Manner of Proceeding in the General Assembly Convened at James City* (1619), reprinted in *Va. Co. Recs.*, vol. 3, pp. 153–54. Small timber church: McCartney (2000), vol. 1, p. 47. Notorious drunk: Carlton (1972), pp. 98 n., 145, 150, 241 n., 246 n.; Chamberlain (1965), p. 219 and n.

7. The meeting: J. Pory, *A Reporte of the Manner of Proceeding in the General Assembly Convened at James City* (1619), reprinted in *Va. Co. Recs.*, vol. 3, p. 155. Complaint against John Martin: Ibid., pp. 157, 163.

8. Driven the Kecoughtans: See p. 141. Appomattocs: Percy, *A True Relation* (1612?), reprinted in *Narratives*, p. 511; Hamor, *A True Discourse* (1615), reprinted in *Narratives*, p. 826. "Very willingly selling it": Rolfe, *A True Relation of the State of Virginia* (1617), reprinted in *Narratives*, p. 870.

The General Assembly voted on July 31 to ask the council in London to "change the savage name of Kiccowtan." J. Pory, *A Reporte of the Manner of Proceeding in the General Assembly Convened at James City* (1619), reprinted in *Va. Co. Recs.*, vol. 3, p. 161. It was renamed Elizabeth City in honor of King James's daughter. See Hatch (1957), p. 97.

Based on minutes of a July 17, 1622, meeting of the Virginia Company council in London, it has been suggested that the company regarded the natives as "having no right to the land" in Virginia at all. Rountree (1990), p. 72. I believe these minutes are reasonably clear in indicating that the discussion dealt instead with the internal division of powers within the company—that is, whether the governor in Virginia could assign rights to land on his own accord, or whether he could only carry out grants of land authorized by the council in London. The council opted for the latter course. *Va. Co. Recs.*, vol. 2, p. 94.

The specific land grant that was disputed at the meeting had been made by Sir George Yeardley to Sir Edward Barkham, Lord Mayor of London, "upon condition that he compounded for the same with Opachankano"; this in itself indicates that the English assumed native ownership of lands, unless the colonists had validly acquired them (by way of abandonment, purchase, or just conquest). The notion of valid acquisition, of course, would have been radically different for the two peoples. The English did not, however, consider themselves to have free rein at this stage over all native territory regardless of the natives' wishes. See also the Reverend Patrick Copland's sermon to the Virginia Company in 1622: Copland held that it was "a work of wonder" for the Lord to have moved the natives "to sell to the English and their Governor Sir George Yeardley the right and title they had to their possessions." Copland (1622), pp. 25–26.

9. Named a committee: J. Pory, *A Reporte of the Manner of Proceeding in the General Assembly Convened at James City* (1619), reprinted in *Va. Co. Recs.*, vol. 3, p. 159. Eighteen provisions: Ibid., pp. 164–69. Violence between Chickahominies and English: Smith (1624), pp. 257, 264.

10. "Extream heat" and the illnesses: J. Pory, *A Reporte of the Manner of Proceeding in the General Assembly Convened at James City* (1619), reprinted in *Va. Co. Recs.*, vol. 3, pp. 170, 176. Shelley: Ibid., p. 162. Around three hundred: Hatch (1975), p. 21. Typhoid, dysentery, or salt poisoning: Earle (1979), p. 116. Fifty-foot-by-twenty-foot church: McCartney (2000), vol. 1, p. 47. Their lasting effect: Bancroft (1834), vol. 1, p. 120.

11. The *White Lion:* Letter of John Rolfe to Sir Edwin Sandys (Jan. 1620), reprinted in *Va. Co. Recs.*, vol. 3, p. 243; letter of John Pory (Sept. 30, 1619), reprinted in *Va. Co. Recs.*, vol. 3, p. 219; Smith (1624), p. 267. Dutch man-of-war commanded by a Captain Jope: High Court of Admiralty examination of Reinold Booth, HCA 1/48 (1620). Booth was a crewman on the *Treasurer.* His testimony is abstracted in Coldham (1984), p. 182. *São João Bautista* background: Sluiter (1997). "Mett with an Angola shippe": High Court of Admiralty examination of John Martyn in *Warwick v. Brewster,* HCA 13/44 (1623–24). It is clear from his testimony that John Martyn is a different man from John Martin, the 1607 colonist. Martyn left London on the *Neptune* in 1618 as an attendant to Thomas West, Lord De La Warr, who intended to return to Virginia; Lord De La Warr died en route. Martyn's testimony is abstracted in Coldham (1984), pp. 12–13. Estimated overall death rate: McCartney (2000), vol. 1, p. 49. "Some wet and blowing weather": Quoted in Kolchin (1993), p. 21.

It has been argued that the census "taken in the begininge of March 1619" demonstrates that Africans were present in the colony before the arrival of the Dutch man-of-war in August 1619. See Thorndale (1995). As explained in note 5 above, however, the date of this census falls *after* August 1619, and corresponds to early 1620 in the modern calendar. Researchers of Jamestown history are indebted to Mr. Thorndale for highlighting this census and providing extensive historical context.

12. *Treasurer* arrived: Letter of John Rolfe to Sir Edwin Sandys (Jan. 1620), reprinted in *Va. Co. Recs.*, vol. 3, p. 243; minutes of Virginia Company meeting of May 7, 1623, reprinted in *Va. Co. Recs.*, vol. 2, p. 402; McCartney (2000), vol. 1, p. 49. Crewmen of the *Treasurer:* Examination of Reinold Booth (see note 11 above). Passenger John Martyn makes no mention of such a threat from the *White Lion.* Ndongo and Imbangala background: Thornton (1998). "A quasi-religious cult": Ibid., p. 426. Luanda, thirty-six slave ships: Ibid., p. 431. Divided between men and women: See below. Tobacco harvest season: Morgan (1998), pp. 166–68. "It is a culture": Jefferson (1787), p. 166. Africans' status: For a sampling of the positions taken by scholars over the years, compare Hatch (1957), p. 25 (servants), and Vaughan (1972), pp. 470–71 (some were servants, but probably held longer than whites), with Morgan (1998), p. 8 (slaves), and Berlin (1998), pp. 29, 386 n. 2 (holding the evidence to be inconclusive). Until the 1640s: Morgan (1975), p. 154 n. 69. John Smith denounced: Smith (1616), p. 352. John Pory wrote: Letter of John Pory to the Earl of Southampton (Jan. 13, 1623), reprinted in James (1963), p. 11. Disappeared from England: Bancroft (1834), vol. 1, p. 134. Census of 1620: Thorndale (1995), p. 168. Won their freedom: Vaughan (1989), pp. 328–30. John Gowen: Heinegg (2001), vol. 1, pp. 1, 410. Anthony Johnson: Heinegg (2001), vol. 2, pp. 533–34; Berlin (1998), pp. 29–30.

The census of March 1620 records thirty-two Africans in the colony—fifteen men and seventeen women. This number could imply the presence of Africans before those who arrived in August 1619. It seems unlikely, however. The arrival of Africans on the Dutch man-of-war elicited comment from two correspondents (John Rolfe and John Pory); any earlier arrival would probably also have elicited comment in one or more of the extant accounts. The apparent discrepancy between the thirty-two of the census and the number arriving in late August (the "20 and odd" bought from Jope) and early September (the one or more left by the *Treasurer*) might simply be the product of the ambiguous reporting of the August and September arrivals. Alternatively, it could reflect the (unrecorded) appearance of another privateering ship bringing a few Africans between September and early March.

Regarding the sailing history of the *Treasurer,* see Vaughan (1972), p. 474 n. 17.

13. "Mislike me not": *The Merchant of Venice,* act 2, scene 1. No recorded effort to convert: Jordan (1968), pp. 21–22. Exposed to Christianity: Thornton (1998), p. 434. Notions of black racial inferiority: Vaughan (1989), pp. 339, 349 n. 118; Jordan (1968), chapter 1. Analysis of rosters of 1624 and 1625: Vaughan (1972). The rosters are published as appendices to McCartney (2000), vol. 1.

Alexander Whitaker himself was no longer in a position to attend to the religious instruction of the Africans, having drowned in March 1617. The Reverend Richard Buck was still on hand, however. Another minister, Thomas White, joined the colony in 1621. See *Va. Co. Recs.*, vol. 3, pp. 503, 583.

14: MARCH 22, 1622: SKYFALL

1. May 17, 1620, company meeting: *Va. Co. Recs.*, vol. 3, pp. 348, 357. Meeting with King James: Woodnoth (1651), pp. 7–8. Wriothesley elected: Craven (1964), pp. 144–45.

2. Opitchapam was soon displaced: Rountree (1990), p. 66. Various writers have argued that Opechancanough was not a brother of Powhatan and Opitchapam, but the contemporaneous sources are consistent in holding that they were indeed brothers. Ibid., pp. 18–19. Opechancanough assured: *Va. Co. Recs.*, vol. 3, p. 584; Smith (1624), p. 287. "That the best meanes": *Instructions to the Governor and Council of State in Virginia* (July 24, 1621), reprinted in *Va. Co. Recs.*, vol. 3, p. 470.

3. 10,000 acres of land: *Instructions to George Yeardley* (Nov. 18, 1618), reprinted in *Va. Co. Recs.*, vol. 3, p. 102. "Dust and Ashes": Minutes of Va. Co. meeting of Jan. 30, 1621, reprinted in *Va. Co. Recs.*, vol. 1, pp. 585–86. Who arrived in May 1620: Gethyn-Jones (1982), pp. 138–39. Thorpe was officially: Minutes of Va. Co. meeting of April 3, 1620, reprinted in *Va. Co. Recs.*, vol. 1, p. 332; Smith (1624), p. 294. "A violent misper-suasion": Letter of George Thorpe to Sir Edwin Sandys (May 15–16, 1621), reprinted in *Va. Co. Recs.*, vol. 3, p. 446.

4. Georgius Thorp: Gethyn-Jones (1982), pp. 55–60. Free to enter: Waterhouse, *A Declaration* (1622), reprinted in *Va. Co. Recs.*, vol. 3, p. 550. Disciplining any subordi-nates, dogs killed through hanging: Waterhouse, op. cit., p. 552; *Va. Co. Recs.*, vol. 3, p. 118; Smith (1624), p. 395. "He thought nothing too deare": Waterhouse, op. cit., p. 552. Stockham: *Master Stockham's Relation* (May 28, 1621), reprinted in Smith (1624), p. 286. To embrace Thorpe's policy: Waterhouse, op. cit., p. 550; Beverly (1705), p. 50. English-style house: Waterhouse, op. cit., p. 552; Purchas (1625), vol. 19, pp. 153, 160. By the summer: Letter of George Thorpe to Sir Edwin Sandys (June 27, 1621), reprinted in *Va. Co. Recs.*, vol. 3, p. 462.

5. Powhatan leader dropped hints: Letter from Council in Virginia to Va. Co. of London (Jan. 1622), reprinted in *Va. Co. Recs.*, vol. 3, p. 584. See also Smith (1624), p. 287; Waterhouse, *A Declaration* (1622), reprinted in *Va. Co. Recs.*, vol. 3, p. 552. New names: Letter from Council in Virginia to Va. Co. of London, op. cit. In the Powhatan tradition: Gleach (1997), p. 146; Kupperman (2000), p. 186; Rountree (1990), p. 73; Rountree (1989), p. 80.

6. Accomac background: Rountree (1989), p. 141. Hallucinogen, of unknown ori-gin: Percy, *A True Relation* (1612?), reprinted in *Narratives*, p. 515; letter of the Rever-end Alexander Whitaker to the Reverend William Crashaw (Aug. 9, 1611), reprinted in *Narratives*, pp. 549–50. Dotted both sides of the James: Waterhouse, *A Declaration* (1622), reprinted in *Va. Co. Recs.*, vol. 3, p. 554; Hatch (1957), pp. 32–33. Forty-two shiploads: Purchas (1625), vol. 19, p. 149. Requested from the Accomac chief: Water-house, *A Declaration* (1622), reprinted in *Va. Co. Recs.*, vol. 3, p. 556; Smith (1624), p. 298. *Cicuta maculata*: Rountree (1990), p. 302 n. 41. See also Lampe and McCann (1985), p. 56. Yeardley himself went: Letter from Council in Virginia to Va. Co. of London (Jan. 20, 1623), reprinted in *Va. Co. Recs.*, vol. 4, p. 10. Sir Francis Wyatt: *Instructions to the Governor and Council of State in Virginia* (July 24, 1621), reprinted in *Va. Co. Recs.*, vol. 3, p. 471; Smith (1624), pp. 284, 286–87. Presents and a message: Letter from Council in Virginia to Va. Co. of London (Jan. 1622), reprinted in *Va. Co. Recs.*, vol. 3, p. 584.

7. Nemattanew background: Smith (1624), p. 293; Percy, *A True Relation* (1612?), reprinted in *Narratives*, p. 517. Nemattanew incident: Smith, op. cit.; Waterhouse, *A Declaration* (1622), reprinted in *Va. Co. Recs.*, vol. 3, p. 550; letter from Council in Virginia to Va. Co. of London (Jan. 20, 1623), reprinted in *Va. Co. Recs.*, vol. 4, p. 11. "The sky should sooner fall": Smith (1624), p. 294; letter from Council in Virginia to Va. Co. of London, op. cit.; Waterhouse, op. cit.; Purchas (1625), vol. 19, p. 158.

The several accounts are inconsistent as to the timing of Nemattanew's shooting. John Smith, reprinting a relation from a gentleman known only by his surname of Wimp, puts it at the second week of March 1622. Edward Waterhouse similarly puts it at "about the middle of March." Yet the 1623 letter from the council states that it occurred during the regime of Sir George Yeardley—that is, before November 18, 1621.

The Smith and Waterhouse dating deserves precedence, and I have used it here. Although the council letter was signed by both Yeardley and Francis Wyatt, among others, the Smith and Waterhouse accounts in combination are likely more reliable about the time frame. Waterhouse had the benefit of relations from a number of colonists whose words have not otherwise survived, as well as other letters from the governor and council. The shooting of Nemattanew would have been notorious within the colony, and so it seems persuasive that the March time frame was reflected in the reports received by Smith and Waterhouse. The issue was a comparatively small point in the 1623 council letter, which was written some nine months after the fact.

On the other hand, with regard to a conflict between Smith and the council letter on the diplomatic communications between the colony and Opechancanough, the council is more reliable, given that it would have had superior knowledge of their contents. Smith (but not the council) has Opechancanough making threats of revenge, and receiving "terrible answers" from the English. Here, Smith's correspondent seems to be straining to explain the events of March 22 as a reaction to the Nemattanew incident, when it is clear that Opechancanough had been planning a decisive action against the English long before then.

8. March 22 events: Waterhouse, *A Declaration* (1622), reprinted in *Va. Co. Recs.*, vol. 3, pp. 550–55; Pace, Petition to the Governor and Council in Virginia (n.d.), reprinted in *Va. Co. Recs.*, vol. 3, p. 682; Letter from Council in Virginia to Va. Co. of London (April 4, 1623), reprinted in *Va. Co. Recs.*, vol. 4, p. 98; Smith (1624), pp. 294–98, 303; Beverly (1705), p. 51; Johnson (1960); Johnson (1963); Chamberlain (1965), pp. 225–26. Sixteen plantations: In the order listed by Waterhouse, they are Berkeley Plantation, Sheffield's Plantation, Pierce's Plantation, "other plantations next adjoining" Charles City, Berkeley Hundred, Francis West's Plantation, John West's Plantation, Gibbs' Dividend, Macock's Dividend, Flowerdew Hundred, Weyanoke, Powell-brooke, Southampton Hundred, Martin's Brandon, Martin's Hundred, and Bennett's Plantation. "Not being content": Waterhouse, op. cit., p. 551. Martin's Hundred: Ibid., p. 570; Johnson (1963), p. 408; Smith (1624), p. 296.

9. College lands: Waterhouse, *A Declaration* (1622), reprinted in *Va. Co. Recs.*, vol. 3, p. 566. Ironworks: Beverly (1705), pp. 54–55. Thorpe: Ibid., pp. 552–53, 567. Wife, eight-year-old daughter: Gethyn-Jones (1982), p. 56. At least 347 English: Initial reports from the colony put the toll at 329. Johnson (1963), p. 408; Johnson (1960), p. 108. Later enumerations of the dead increased the figure to 347. Waterhouse, op. cit., p. 571; Smith (1624), p. 302. Some colonists put the figure at 400 dead. *Va. Co. Recs.*, vol. 4, pp. 234, 524; see also Bradford (1952), p. 110. Colony's population:

Va. Co. Recs., vol. 4, p. 158. "I thinke the last massacre": Letter of William Capps to Dr. Thomas Wynston (1623), reprinted in *Va. Co. Recs.*, vol. 4, p. 38.

10. Copland delivered a sermon: Copland (1622). Raised money: *Va. Co. Recs.*, vol. 3, pp. 531, 537–40. Company's invitation: Minutes of Va. Co. meeting of April 10, 1622, reprinted in *Va. Co. Recs.*, vol. 1, pp. 628–29. "Blessed be God": Copland (1622), pp. 9–10. *Sea-flower:* Waterhouse, *A Declaration* (1622), reprinted in *Va. Co. Recs.*, vol. 3, p. 554; Davis (1955), p. 127; Chamberlain (1965), p. 225. Donne's sermon: Merchant (1972), p. 452. See also Lim (1998), pp. 73–74.

11. Gentleman investors, members of Parliament, and divines alike: The former two categories overlapped substantially; one in seven members of Parliament was an investor in the Virginia Company. Rabb (1967), p. 128. *Morninge Virginia:* Merchant (1972), p. 441. Next to appear, in August: Brooke (1622), p. 259. Its former secretary: Powell (1958), p. 47. "These beasts": Waterhouse, *A Declaration* (1622), reprinted in *Va. Co. Recs.*, vol. 3, p. 551. "Because our hands": Ibid., pp. 556–57.

12. Praised the mastery: Waterhouse, *A Declaration* (1622), reprinted in *Va. Co. Recs.*, vol. 3, p. 558. "And for certaine howres": Brooke (1622), p. 274. "Those bestiall soules": Ibid., p. 275. "Securitie, the Heaven that holds a Hell": Ibid., pp. 279–80.

Waterhouse predicted that the destruction of the Powhatans would not only benefit English agriculture, but also boost the abundance of wild game. "The deere and other beasts will be in safety, and infinitly increase" with the end of the natives' intense hunting. "There will also be a great increase of wild turkies, and other waighty fowl, for the Indians never put difference of destroying the hen, but kill them whether in season or not, whether in breeding time, or sitting on their egges, or having newly hatched, it is all one to them." Waterhouse, op. cit., p. 557.

13. "Take heart": Brooke (1622), p. 291.

14. "Vacant places": Purchas (1625), vol. 19, p. 222. "These barbarians": Ibid., p. 224. "Seems distempered": Ibid., p. 229. "Amazed": Smith (1624), p. 285. "Labyrinth of melancholy": Ibid., p. 305. Nathaniel Powell: Ibid., p. 295; Hatch (1957), p. 70; Waterhouse, *A Declaration* (1622), reprinted in *Va. Co. Recs.*, vol. 3, p. 569; McCartney (2000), vol. 1, p. 46. "If you please": Smith (1624), pp. 305–306.

15. "Except it be a little corne": Smith (1624), p. 307. Forty-two barrels: Powell (1958), p. 48. Gifts from King James and private donor: Warrant to the Lord Treasurer (Sept. 1622), reprinted in *Va. Co. Recs.*, vol. 3, p. 676; Powell (1958), p. 49. The one thousand light muskets were divided between seven hundred calivers and three hundred harquebuses. Halberds description: Peterson (1956), pp. 93–95. Brigandines description: Ibid., pp. 140, 146. Except for the bows and arrows: Minutes of Va. Co. meeting of Aug. 14, 1622, reprinted in *Va. Co. Recs.*, vol. 2, p. 100. Plantations to be abandoned: Letter from Council in Virginia to Va. Co. of London (April 1622), reprinted in *Va. Co. Recs.*, vol. 3, p. 612; Smith (1624), pp. 302–330 and n. 4. against the Rappahannocks: Powell (1958), p. 53; Letter from Council in Virginia to Va. Co. of London (Jan. 20, 1623), reprinted in *Va. Co. Recs.*, vol. 4, p. 9. "Make warr": Commission to Sir George Yeardley (Sept. 10, 1622), reprinted in *Va. Co. Recs.*, vol. 3, pp. 678–79. "We have to our extreame grief": Letter of Va. Co. of London to Governor and Council in Virginia (Aug. 1, 1622), reprinted in *Va. Co. Recs.*, vol. 3, p. 666.

16. "Perpetual warre": Letter of Va. Co. of London to Governor and Council in Virginia (Aug. 1, 1622), reprinted in *Va. Co. Recs.*, vol. 3, p. 672. "We conceave it": Letter of Va. Co. of London to Governor and Council in Virginia (Oct. 7, 1622), reprinted in *Va. Co. Recs.*, vol. 3, p. 683.

17. "Wee have much anticipated": Letter from Council in Virginia to Va. Co. of London (Jan. 20, 1623), reprinted in *Va. Co. Recs.*, vol. 4, pp. 9–10.

18. "Whereas in the begininge": Letter from Council in Virginia to Va. Co. of London (Jan. 20, 1623), reprinted in *Va. Co. Recs.*, vol. 4, p. 10.

19. Raids, mortality, and causes: Letter from Council in Virginia to Va. Co. of London (April 1622), reprinted in *Va. Co. Recs.*, vol. 3, pp. 613–14; Letter of George Sandys to Sir Miles Sandys (Mar. 30, 1623), reprinted in *Va. Co. Recs.*, vol. 4, pp. 70–71; Letter of Richard Frethorne to Mr. Bateman (Mar. 5, 1623), reprinted in *Va. Co. Recs.*, vol. 4, p. 41; *Va. Co. Recs.*, vol. 3, p. 537. Sharpe, Capps, and Hill letters: *Va. Co. Recs.*, vol. 4, pp. 76, 233–34. "Instead of a plantation": Nathaniel Butler, *The Unmasked Face of Our Colony in Virginia as it was in the Winter of the Yeare 1622*, reprinted in *Va. Co. Recs.*, vol. 2, p. 376. African population figures: Thorndale (1995), p. 168; Quisenberry (1899–1900), p. 364. Promises of ready wealth: *Va. Co. Recs.*, vol. 4, p. 232. "Loveing and kind father and mother": Letter from Richard Frethorne to his father and mother (Mar. 20, 1623), reprinted in *Va. Co. Recs.*, vol. 4, pp. 58–59.

20. Opechancanough sent a messenger, English reaction: Letter from Council in Virginia to Va. Co. of London (April 4, 1623), reprinted in *Va. Co. Recs.*, vol. 4, pp. 98–99. "Trie if wee can": Letter of George Sandys to Sir Miles Sandys (Mar. 30, 1623), reprinted in *Va. Co. Recs.*, vol. 4, p. 71. On May 22, 1623: Letter from Robert Bennett to Edward Bennett (June 9, 1623), reprinted in *Va. Co. Recs.*, vol. 4, pp. 221–22; Commission to Captain William Tucker (May 12, 1623), reprinted in *Va. Co. Recs.*, vol. 4, p. 190; Rountree (1990), p. 77. Released prisoners: Letter from Council in Virginia to Va. Co. of London (after April 4, 1623), reprinted in *Va. Co. Recs.*, vol. 4, p. 102.

21. March 22 holiday: Wyatt, *Order to Keep the 22d of March Holy* (Mar. 4, 1623), reprinted in *Va. Co. Recs.*, vol. 4, p. 40; Council and Assembly, *Laws and Orders* (Mar. 5, 1624), reprinted in *Va. Co. Recs.*, vol. 4, p. 581; Gleach (1997), p. 163. "Before the end of two moons": Smith (1624), p. 308. By the end of 1624: Quisenberry (1899–1900), p. 366. Population in 1629, 1632, 1634: Morgan (1975), p. 404. "The colonye hath worne": Letter from Council in Virginia to Va. Co. of London (Dec. 2, 1624), reprinted in *Va. Co. Recs.*, vol. 4, p. 508. Investigation and dissolution of the Virginia Company: Craven (1964), pp. 266–67, 295; Craven (1957), p. 57; Davis (1955), p. 159; McCartney (2000), vol. 1, p. 65. £200,000: Rabb (1967), pp. 58–59; Woodnoth (1651), p. 2; Smith (1631), pp. 270, 283.

22. Summer of 1624 saw a battle: *Va. Co. Recs.*, vol. 4, pp. 507–508. War continued: Powell (1958), pp. 70–74. 1632 Peace treaty: Ibid., p. 75; Rountree (1990), p. 81. Still observing the date: Gleach (1997), p. 169. Now around eight thousand: Morgan (1975), p. 404. Along all the rivers: Axtell (1995), p. 39. April 18, 1644: Beverly (1705), pp. 60–61; Gleach (1997), pp. 174–75; Rountree (1990), p. 84. Capture and killing of Opechancanough: Beverly (1705), p. 62. "So routed": McCary (1957), p. 80. "The Indians of Virginia": Beverly (1705), p. 232. Numbers dwindled: Rountree (1990), pp. 144, 158–66.

15: SMITH'S VISION FOR AMERICA

1. Attempted voyage of 1617: Smith (1622), p. 427; Smith (1624), p. 440. Living frugally: In his letter to Bacon, he apologized for the "povertie of the author." Smith

(1986), p. 382. Letter to Bacon: Reprinted in Smith (1986), pp. 377–83. "And though I can promise": Ibid., pp. 382–83.

2. King James's dislike: Willson (1956), p. 209. Ban Sabbath day sports: Ibid., pp. 400–401; Besant (1903), pp. 14–15. King James Bible: Daiches (1941), pp. 64, 152, 163. Separatists in Amsterdam and Leiden: Bradford (1952), pp. 11–17. Obtained a patent: Ibid., p. 39 n. 6, p. 60 n. 6. Smith and the Separatists: Smith (1624), p. 221; Smith (1630), p. 221. Take Smith's books and maps: Bradford (1952), pp. 68 n. 7, 82. Fundamental incompatibility: Smith (1631), pp. 285–86; Barbour (1964a), pp. 343–44.

3. *New Englands Trials* background: Smith (1986), pp. 387–89, 411; O'Brien (1960), p. 154; Barbour (1964a), p. 477, n. 5. "For want of experience": Smith (1622), p. 429. Digression on that event: 22: Ibid., pp. 431–32. Virginia Company had considered: Minutes of Va. Co. meeting of April 12, 1621, reprinted in *Va. Co. Recs.*, vol. 1, pp. 451–52. Fully outlined: Smith (1986), vol. 2, p. 6. Commendatory verses: Smith (1624), pp. 51, 228–30. Commissioners posed: Smith (1624), pp. 327–32; Craven (1964), pp. 267, 295. "To rectifie a common-wealth": Smith (1624), p. 330.

In the "Generall Historie" genre, another example is Louis de Mayerne Turquet's *Generall Historie of Spaine*, translated into English by Edward Grimeston and published in London in 1612.

4. Anas Todkill: Hayes (1991b), pp. 136–37. John Russell: Smith (1624), p. 198. Pocahontas and Tomocomo: Ibid., pp. 258–61. Sir Samuel Saltonstall: Smith (1630), pp. 142, 230. "Men of good credit": Smith (1631), p. 270. "So doating": Smith (1631), p. 272. "Onely spending my time": Smith (1631), p. 271.

5. "Now they take not that course": Smith (1631), p. 270. Easy promises of gold: Smith (1631), p. 285. "Here every man": Smith (1616), p. 332. "Who can desire": Smith (1616), p. 343.

6. One of the benefits: Johnson, *The New Life of Virginea* (1612), p. 18, reprinted in Force (1836), vol. 1. "And who is he": Smith (1616), p. 349. "No man will go": Smith (1622), p. 440. "The benefit of libertie": Smith (1624), p. 247 (marginal note). "Glad was he": Smith (1624), p. 247. "Therefore let all men": Smith (1631), p. 287.

Somewhat along the lines of his case for private planting and the freedom to pursue a trade, Smith also argued against heavy customs duties for the colony's shipping. "Therefore use all commers with that respect, courtesie, and libertie is fitting, which in a short time will much increase your trade and shipping . . . now there is nothing more inricheth a common-wealth than much trade, nor no meanes better to increase than small custome [customs duty] . . ." Smith (1631), p. 298.

7. "No silvered idle golden Pharises": Smith (1616), p. 360. "Was it vertue": Smith (1616), p. 361. See also Smith's dedication of the *Map of Virginia*: "Though riches now, be the chief greatnes of the great: when great and little are born, and dye, there is no difference: Vertue onely makes men more than men: Vice, worse than brutes." Smith (1612), p. 133.

8. A half dozen or so: Smith (1631), p. 285 and n. 5. "The Sea Marke": Smith (1631), p. 265.

9. Stricken ill: Barbour (1964a), pp. 393–94. Home of Sir Samuel Saltonstall: Will of John Smith, reprinted in Barbour (1968), p. 627; Rowse (1959), p. 113. Signing of will, death: Barbour (1968), p. 626. Abigail: Smith (1624), pp. 98–99 (map); Barbour (1964a), pp. xi, 485.

Lifelong bachelorhood was unusual in Smith's day, though not an extreme rarity.

During this time, an estimated 15 percent to 20 percent of men in the English upper classes who lived to the age of fifty never married. Stone (1977), pp. 40–41. I have not encountered statistics for Smith's own stratum.

10. "Here the rewards": Crèvecoeur (1782), pp. 44–45. Thomas Jefferson: Sowerby (1952), vol. 1, p. 210; Jefferson (1787), p. 177. Jeremy Belknap: Belknap (1794), pp. 42, 241, 272, 299–300.

See also William Stith's 1747 *History of the First Discovery and Settlement of Virginia*, which credited Smith's "vigor, industry, and undaunted spirit and resolution" for the survival of Jamestown. Stith (1747), p. 108.

11. John Marshall: Marshall (1804), vol. 1, pp. 41, 44, 46. Bancroft's highly successful *History:* Bancroft (1834), vol. 1, pp. 96, 98–99, 105, 124. Noah Webster: Webster (1791), pp. 8, 12. Life itself is the one carrying out the interrogation: The thought is Viktor Frankl's. Frankl (1959), p. 85.

MARGINALIA

1. The papers referenced in the commentary are Brown and Hopkins (1956) and Richards (2002).

2. Modern scholars: See, e.g., Kupperman (2000), p. 114; Gleach (1997), p. 117. "some sort of flank": Adams (1982), vol. 1, p. 287. "No man rejoiced": Belknap (1794), p. 314. John Randolph: Adams (1982), vol. 1, pp. 280, 281 n. 5, 287.

3. "It is true": Smith (1622), p. 432. Purchas: Purchas (1625), vol. 18, p. 472. 1685 biography: Wharton (1685), p. 72. Strachey recommended: Strachey (1612), p. 41. as did William Crashaw: Crashaw, Epistle Dedicatory [preface] to Alexander Whitaker's *Good News from Virginia* (1613), reprinted in *Narratives*, p. 712. John Stow's *Annales:* Gookin (1949), p. 406. 1662 comical biography: Fuller (1662), pp. 75–76. Confirmed obscure details: Barbour (1964a), p. 41; Striker and Smith (1962).

A modern skeptic with regard to the rescue story has downplayed the significance of Purchas's publication, on the ground that Purchas merely quoted Smith "verbatim without comment." Rountree (1990), p. 38. In fact, Purchas inserted a marginal note next to the story in *Purchas His Pilgrimes*, reading "Pocahuntas saveth his life." Purchas did not editorialize further about the rescue, but he repeatedly made positive comments about Smith as an explorer and chronicler.

4. Some researchers: E.g., Gleach (1997), pp. 118–21; Kupperman (2000), pp. 114, 174. In general, these books are replete with valuable insights into Powhatan culture. Adoption procedure comparable: Rountree (1990), p. 39. "The classic pattern of rites of passage": Gleach (1997), p. 120.

5. Ceremony: Relation of William White, reprinted in *J.V.*, vol. 1, pp. 147–49.

6. Smith later witnessed: For Smith's observations of the black boys ceremony, see Smith (1612), pp. 171–72, or Smith (1624), pp. 124–25.

7. Powhatan had referred: See, e.g., Smith (1608), p. 65.

8. Article in *Science:* Stahle (1998). Stormy weather, rain, and snow: Smith (1608), pp. 35, 67; Symonds (1612), p. 255; Smith (1624), pp. 191, 194. "Some times": Smith (1612), p. 144. Native planting cycle: Smith (1612), pp. 156–59. Gabriel Archer: Archer, *Description of the River and Country* (1607), reprinted in *J.V.*, vol. 1, p. 100.

9. Hancock has argued: See, e.g., Alan Flanders, "Theory Suggests Jamestown

Settlers Were Murdered," *Virginian-Pilot* (Norfolk), Aug. 5, 2001, p. 3. The theory figured prominently in the British Broadcasting Corp.–Public Broadcasting Service documentary produced in 2000, *Secrets of the Dead: Death at Jamestown*. Told Zúñiga: *J.V.*, vol. 2, pp. 255, 269.

10. *Junta de Guerra: N.A.W.*, p. 151. Wyatt would write: Wyatt (1926), p. 117.

Bibliography

I have tried to stake out a middle ground in cataloguing primary materials. For brevity's sake, I have generally omitted primary documents from the bibliography if they are available in a published compilation. When citing one of these materials, I have identified it in the chapter notes with a recognizable short form, together with a page reference to a collection in which it can be found.

Adams, Henry. *The Letters of Henry Adams.* Edited by J. C. Levenson et al. 6 vols. Cambridge: Harvard University Press, 1982–1988.

Andrews, K. R. "Christopher Newport of Limehouse, Mariner." *William and Mary Quarterly*, 3d ser., 11, no. 1 (Jan. 1954): 28–41.

Axtell, James. *The Rise and Fall of the Powhatan Empire in Virginia.* Williamsburg, Va.: Colonial Williamsburg Foundation, 1995.

Bancroft, George. *History of the United States from the Discovery of the American Continent to the Declaration of Independence.* 7 vols. 1834. Reprint, Boston: Elibron Classics, 2001.

Barbour, Philip L. *The Three Worlds of Captain John Smith.* Boston: Houghton Mifflin, 1964a.

———. "A French Account of Captain John Smith's Adventures in the Azores, 1615." *Virginia Magazine of History and Biography* 72, no. 3 (July 1964b): 293–303.

———. "A Note on the Discovery of the Original Will of Captain John Smith: With a Verbatim Transcription." *William and Mary Quarterly*, 3d ser., 25, no. 4 (Oct. 1968): 625–28.

———, ed. *The Jamestown Voyages Under the First Charter: 1606–1609.* 2 vols. London: Cambridge University Press, 1969.

Bass, George F., ed. *Ships and Shipwrecks of the Americas: A History Based on Underwater Archeology.* London: Thames and Hudson, 1988.

Belknap, Jeremy. *American Biography.* 2 vols. Boston: Isaiah Thomas and Ebenezer T. Andrews, 1794.

Bell, Hesketh. *Report on the Caribs of Dominica.* London: HMSO, 1902 (Colonial Reports—Misc. No. 21).

Bemiss, Samuel M., ed. *The Three Charters of the Virginia Company of London*. Charlottesville: University Press of Virginia, 1957.

Benzoni, Girolamo. *History of the New World*. 1565. Translated by W. H. Smyth, 1857. Reprint, Boston: Elibron Classics, 2001.

Berlin, Ira. *Many Thousands Gone: The First Two Centuries of Slavery in North America*. Cambridge: Harvard University Press, 1998.

Besant, Walter. *London in the Time of the Stuarts*. London: Adam & Charles Black, 1903.

Beverly, Robert. *The History and Present State of Virginia*. 1705. Reprint, edited by Louis B. Wright. Chapel Hill: University of North Carolina Press, 1947.

Bevington, David, and Peter Holbrook. *The Politics of the Stuart Court Masque*. Cambridge: Cambridge University Press, 1998.

Billings, Warren M. *The Old Dominion in the Seventeenth Century: A Documentary History of Virginia, 1606–1689*. Chapel Hill: University of North Carolina Press, 1975.

Boucher, Philip P. *Cannibal Encounters: Europeans and Island Caribs, 1492–1763*. Baltimore: Johns Hopkins University Press, 1992.

Bradford, William. *Of Plymouth Plantation, 1620–1647*. Edited by Samuel Eliot Morison. New York: Alfred A. Knopf, 1952.

Brain, Jeffrey P. *The Popham Colony: An Historical and Archeological Brief*. Salem, Mass.: Peabody Essex Museum, 2002.

Bridenbaugh, Carl. *Vexed and Troubled Englishmen, 1590–1642*. New York: Oxford University Press, 1968.

Brooke, Christopher. "A Poem on the Late Massacre in Virginia." 1622. Reprint, *Virginia Magazine of History and Biography* 72, no. 3 (July 1964): 259–92.

Brown, E. H. Phelps, and Sheila Hopkins. "Seven Centuries of the Prices of Consumables, Compared with Builders' Wage-rates." *Economica* (Nov. 1956): 296–314.

Carlton, Dudley. *Dudley Carlton to John Chamberlain, 1603–1624: Jacobean Letters*. Edited by Maurice Lee, Jr. New Brunswick, N.J.: Rutgers University Press, 1972.

Chamberlain, John. *The Chamberlain Letters*. Edited by Elizabeth Thomson. New York: Putnam, 1965.

Coldham, Peter Wilson. *English Adventurers and Emigrants, 1609–1660: Abstracts of Examinations in the High Court of Admiralty with Reference to Colonial America*. Baltimore: Genealogical Publishing, 1984.

Copland, Patrick. *Virginia's God Be Thanked, or A Sermon of Thanksgiving for the Happie Successe of the Affayres in Virginia This Last Yeare*. London: I.D., 1622.

Craven, Wesley Frank. *The Virginia Company of London: 1606–1624*. 1957. Reprint, Baltimore: Clearfield, 1993.

———. *Dissolution of the Virginia Company: The Failure of a Colonial Experiment*. Gloucester, Mass.: Peter Smith, 1964.

Crèvecoeur, J. Hector St. John de. *Letters from an American Farmer*. 1782. Reprint, Oxford: Oxford University Press, 1997.

Cuffe, Henry. *The Differences of the Ages of Mans Life: Together with the Originall Causes, Progresse, and End thereof*. London: Martin Clearke, 1607.

Daiches, David. *The King James Version of the English Bible: An Account of the Development and Sources of the English Bible of 1611 with Special Reference to the Hebrew Tradition*. 1941. Reprint, n.p.: Archon, 1968.

Davis, Richard Beale. *George Sandys, Poet-Adventurer*. New York: Columbia University Press, 1955.

Earle, Carville V. "Environment, Disease and Mortality in Early Virginia." In *The Chesapeake in the Seventeenth Century: Essays on Anglo-American Society*. Edited by Thad W. Tate and David L. Ammerman. Chapel Hill: University of North Carolina Press, 1979.

Evans, Cerinda W. *Some Notes on Shipbuilding and Shipping in Colonial Virginia*. Newport News, Va.: Mariners Museum, 1957.

Ezell, John. "The Lottery in Colonial America." *William and Mary Quarterly*, 3d ser., 5, no. 2 (April 1948): 185–200.

Fausz, John Frederick. "The Powhatan Uprising of 1622: A Historical Study of Ethnocentrism and Cultural Conflict." Ph.D. diss., College of William and Mary, 1977.

———. "Opechancanough: Indian Resistance Leader." In *Struggle and Survival in Colonial America*. Edited by David G. Sweet and Gary B. Nash. Berkeley: University of California Press, 1981.

———. "The Invasion of Virginia: Indians, Colonialism, and the Conquest of Cant: A Review Essay on Anglo-Indian Relations in the Chesapeake." *Virginia Magazine of History and Biography* 95, no. 2 (April 1987): 133–56.

———. "An 'Abundance of Blood Shed on Both Sides': England's First Indian War, 1609–1614." *Virginia Magazine of History and Biography* 98, no. 1 (Jan. 1990): 3–56.

Fee, Robert G. C., and Howard H. Faucett, Jr. *The Design, Construction and Sailing of the Jamestown Ships*. Newport News, Va.: Mariners Museum, 1958.

Flaherty, David H., ed. *Lawes Divine, Morall and Martiall, etc.* Charlottesville: University Press of Virginia, 1969.

Force, Peter, ed. *Tracts and Other Papers, Relating Principally to the Origin, Settlement, and Progress of the Colonies in North America, From the Discovery of the Country to the Year 1776*. 4 vols. 1836–1846. Reprint, New York: Peter Smith, 1947.

Foss, Michael. *Undreamed Shores: England's Wasted Empire in America*. New York: Charles Scribner's Sons, 1974.

Frankl, Viktor E. *Man's Search for Meaning*. 1959. Reprint, New York: Simon & Schuster, 1984.

Fuller, Thomas. *The Worthies of England*. 1662. Reprint, edited by John Freeman. London: George Allen & Unwin, 1952.

Gethyn-Jones, Eric. *George Thorpe and the Berkeley Company*. Gloucester, U.K.: Alan Sutton, 1982.

Gleach, Frederic W. *Powhatan's World and Colonial Virginia: A Conflict of Cultures*. Lincoln: University of Nebraska Press, 1997.

Gookin, Warner F. "Who Was Bartholomew Gosnold?" *William and Mary Quarterly*, 3d ser., 6, no. 3 (July 1949): 398–415.

Gray, Robert. *A Good Speed to Virginia*. 1609. Reprint, New York: Scholars' Facsimiles & Reprints, 1937.

Haile, Edward Wright, ed. *Jamestown Narratives: Eyewitness Accounts of the Virginia Colony: The First Decade: 1607–1617*. Champlain, Va.: RoundHouse, 1998.

Haring, C. H. *The Spanish Empire in America*. 1947. Reprint, New York: Harcourt Brace Jovanovich, 1952.

Hatch, Charles E., Jr. *The First Seventeen Years: Virginia, 1607–1624*. Charlottesville: University Press of Virginia, 1957.

Hayes, Kevin J. *Captain John Smith: A Reference Guide*. Boston: G. K. Hall, 1991a.

———. "Defining the Ideal Colonist: Captain John Smith's Revisions from A True

Relation to the Proceedings to the Third Book of the Generall Historie." *Virginia Magazine of History and Biography* 99, no. 2 (April 1991b): 123–44.

Heimann, Robert K. *Tobacco and Americans*. New York: McGraw-Hill, 1960.

Heinegg, Paul. *Free African Americans of North Carolina, Virginia, and South Carolina: From the Colonial Period to About 1820*. 4th edition. 2 vols. Baltimore: Clearfield, 2001.

Herford, C. H., and Evelyn Simpson. *Ben Jonson*. 11 vols. Oxford: Clarendon Press, 1925–52.

Hill, J. W. F. *Tudor and Stuart Lincoln*. Cambridge: Cambridge University Press, 1956.

Horn, James. *Adapting to a New World: English Society in the Seventeenth-Century Chesapeake*. Chapel Hill: University of North Carolina Press, 1994.

Hubbell, Jay B. "The Smith-Pocahontas Literary Legend." In *South and Southwest: Literary Essays and Reminiscences*. Durham, N.C.: Duke University Press, 1965.

James I. *A Counterblaste to Tobacco*. 1604. Reprint, New York: G. P. Putnam's Sons, n.d.

James, Sydney V., Jr., ed. *Three Visitors to Early Plymouth*. Plymouth, Mass.: Plimoth Plantation, 1963.

Jefferson, Thomas. *Notes on the State of Virginia*. 1787. Reprint, edited by William Peden. Chapel Hill: University of North Carolina Press, 1954.

Johnson, Robert C. "Note: The Indian Massacre of 1622." *Virginia Magazine of History and Biography* 68, no. 1 (Jan. 1960): 107–108.

———. "The Indian Massacre of 1622: Some Correspondence of the Reverend Joseph Mead." *Virginia Magazine of History and Biography* 71, no. 4 (Dec. 1963): 408–410.

Jones, H. G. *Sir Walter's Surname*. Chapel Hill, N.C.: University of North Carolina Library, 1987.

Jordan, Winthrop D. *White over Black: American Attitudes Toward the Negro, 1550–1812*. Chapel Hill: University of North Carolina Press, 1968.

Kelso, William M., et al. *Rediscovering Jamestown: The Search for the 1607 James Fort*. 7 vols. Jamestown, Va.: Association for the Preservation of Virginia Antiquities, 1995–2001.

Kent, William. *An Encyclopedia of London*. Rev. ed. London: J. M. Dent & Sons, 1970.

Kingsbury, Susan Myra, ed. *The Records of the Virginia Company of London*. 4 vols. Washington: U.S. Government Printing Office, 1906–1935.

Kolchin, Peter. *American Slavery, 1619–1877*. New York: Hill and Wang, 1993.

Kupperman, Karen Ordahl. *Roanoke: The Abandoned Colony*. Savage, Md.: Rowman & Littlefield, 1984.

———. *Indians and English: Facing Off in Early America*. Ithaca, N.Y.: Cornell University Press, 2000.

Lampe, Kenneth F., and Mary Ann McCann. *AMA Handbook of Poisonous and Injurious Plants*. Chicago: American Medical Association, 1985.

Las Casas, Bartolomé de. *A Short Account of the Destruction of the Indies*. 1542. Reprint, New York: Penguin Classics, 1992.

Lavery, Brian. *The Colonial Merchantman Susan Constant 1605*. London: Conway Maritime Press, 1988.

Lemay, J. A. Leo. *Did Pocahontas Save Captain John Smith?* Athens: University of Georgia Press, 1992.

Lewis, Clifford M., and Albert J. Loomie. *The Spanish Jesuit Mission in Virginia, 1570–1572*. Chapel Hill: University of North Carolina Press, 1953.

Lim, Walter S. H. *The Arts of Empire: The Poetics of Colonialism from Ralegh to Milton.* Newark: University of Delaware Press, 1998.

Lindley, David, ed. *Court Masques: Jacobean and Caroline Entertainments.* Oxford: Oxford University Press, 1995.

Lodge, James P., Jr., ed. *The Smoake of London: Two Prophecies.* Elmsford, N.Y.: Maxwell Reprint Co., 1969.

"Lord Sackville's Papers Respecting Virginia, 1613–1631, I." *American Historical Review* 27, no. 3 (April 1922): 493–538.

Malcolm, Noel. "Hobbes, Sandys, and the Virginia Company." *Historical Journal* 24, no. 2 (1981): 297–321.

Marshall, John. *The Life of George Washington.* 5 vols. 1804. Reprint, Boston: Elibron Classics, 2001.

Matz, B. W. *The Inns and Taverns of "Pickwick."* 1922. Reprint, New York: Haskell House, 1973.

McCartney, Martha W. "An Early Virginia Census Reprised." *Quarterly Bulletin of the Archeological Society of Virginia* 54, no. 4 (Dec. 1999): 178–96.

McCartney, Martha W., et al. *Jamestown Archeological Assessment, 1992–1996: Documentary History of Jamestown Island.* 3 vols. Williamsburg, Va.: National Park Service, 2000.

McCary, Ben C. *Indians in Seventeenth-Century Virginia.* 1957. Reprint, Charlottesville: University Press of Virginia, 1995.

McClusker, John J. *Money and Exchange in Europe and America, 1600–1775: A Handbook.* Chapel Hill: University of North Carolina Press, 1978.

Merchant, W. Moelwyn. "Donne's Sermon to the Virginia Company, 13 November 1622." In *John Donne: Essays in Celebration,* edited by A. J. Smith, pp. 433–52. London: Methuen & Co., 1972.

Morgan, Edmund S. *American Slavery, American Freedom: The Ordeal of Colonial Virginia.* 1975. Reprint, New York: W. W. Norton, 1995.

Morgan, Philip D. *Slave Counterpoint: Black Culture in the Eighteenth-Century Chesapeake and Lowcountry.* Chapel Hill: University of North Carolina Press, 1998.

Morison, Samuel Eliot. *Admiral of the Ocean Sea: A Life of Christopher Columbus.* Boston: Little, Brown, 1942.

———. *Christopher Columbus, Mariner.* 1955. Reprint, New York: Meridian, 1983.

Oakes, A. J., and James O. Butcher. *Poisonous and Injurious Plants of the U.S. Virgin Islands.* Washington: U.S. Government Printing Office, 1962.

O'Brien, Terence H. "The London Livery Companies and the Virginia Company." *Virginia Magazine of History and Biography* 68, no. 2 (April 1960): 137–55.

Oldmixon, John. *The British Empire in America.* 2 vols. 1741. Reprint, New York: Augustus Kelley, 1969.

Orgell, Stephen, ed. *Ben Jonson: Selected Masques.* New Haven, Conn.: Yale University Press, 1970.

Pearson, Lu Emily. *Elizabethans at Home.* Stanford, Calif.: Stanford University Press, 1957.

Peterson, Harold L. *Arms and Armor in Colonial America, 1526–1783.* 1956. Reprint, Mineola, N.Y.: Dover, 2000.

Powell, William S. "Books in the Virginia Colony Before 1624." *William and Mary Quarterly,* 3d ser., 5, no. 2 (April 1958): 177–184.

Pritchard, R. E., ed. *Shakespeare's England: Life in Elizabethan and Jacobean Times.* Phoenix Mill, U.K.: 1999.

Purchas, Samuel. *Hakluytus Posthumus or Purchas His Pilgrimes.* 1625. Reprint, Glasgow: James MacLehose and Sons, 1905–1907. 20 vols.

Quinn, David Beers. *New American World: A Documentary History of North America to 1612.* 5 vols. New York: Arno Press, 1979.

———. *Set Fair for Roanoke: Voyages and Colonies, 1584–1606.* Chapel Hill: University of North Carolina Press, 1985.

Quisenberry, A. C. "The Virginia Census, 1624–25." *Virginia Historical Magazine* [*Virginia Magazine of History and Biography*] 7 (1899–1900): 364–67.

Rabb, Theodore K. *Enterprise and Empire: Merchant and Gentry Investment in the Expansion of England, 1575–1630.* Cambridge: Harvard University Press, 1967.

———. *Jacobean Gentleman: Sir Edwin Sandys, 1561–1629.* Princeton, N.J.: Princeton University Press, 1998.

Richards, Patsy. *Inflation: The Value of the Pound, 1750–2001.* London: House of Commons Library, 2002.

Robertson, Karen. "Pocahontas at the Masque." *Signs: Journal of Women in Culture and Society* 21, no. 3 (Spring 1996): 551–83.

Rountree, Helen C. *The Powhatan Indians of Virginia: Their Traditional Culture.* Norman: University of Oklahoma Press, 1989.

———. *Pocahontas's People: The Powhatan Indians of Virginia Through Four Centuries.* Norman: University of Oklahoma Press, 1990.

Rountree, Helen C., and E. Randolph Turner III. *Before and After Jamestown: Virginia's Powhatans and Their Predecessors.* Gainesville: University Press of Florida, 2002.

Rowse, A. L. *The Elizabethans and America.* New York: Harper & Brothers, 1959.

———. *The Elizabethan Renaissance: The Life of the Society.* 1971. Reprint, Chicago: Ivan R. Dee, 2000.

Rutman, Darrett B. "The Historian and the Marshal: A Note on the Background of Sir Thomas Dale." *Virginia Magazine of History and Biography* 68, no. 3 (July 1960): 284–94.

Sanders, Charles Richard. "William Strachey, the Virginia Colony and Shakespeare." *Virginia Magazine of History and Biography* 57, no. 2 (April 1949): 115–32.

Shirley, John W. "George Percy at Jamestown, 1607–1612." *Virginia Magazine of History and Biography* 57, no. 3 (July 1949): 227–43.

Sluiter, Engel. "New Light on the '20 and Odd Negroes' Arriving in Virginia, August 1619." *William and Mary Quarterly,* 3d ser., 54, no. 2 (April 1997): 395–98.

Smith, Abbott Emerson. *Colonists in Bondage: White Servitude and Convict Labor in America, 1607–1776.* 1947. Reprint, New York: W. W. Norton and Co., 1971.

Smith, John. *A True Relation of Such Occurrences and Accidents of Note, As Hath Hapned in Virginia, Since the First Planting of that Collony.* 1608. Reprinted in Smith (1986), vol. 1, pp. 27–97.

———. *A Map of Virginia. With a Description of the Countrey, the Commodities, People, Government and Religion.* 1612. Reprinted in Smith (1986), vol. 1, pp. 131–77.

———. *A Description of New England.* 1616. Reprinted in Smith (1986), vol. 1, pp. 305–63.

———. *New Englands Trials.* 1620. Reprinted in Smith (1986), vol. 1, pp. 391–406.

———. *New Englands Trials.* 1622. Reprinted in Smith (1986), vol. 1, pp. 419–41.

———. *The Generall Historie of Virginia, New-England, and the Summer Isles.* 1624. Reprinted in Smith (1986), vol. 2, pp. 33–475.

———. *A Sea Grammar.* 1627. Reprinted in Smith (1986), vol. 3, pp. 45–113.

———. *The True Travels, Adventures and Observations of Captaine John Smith.* 1630. Reprinted in Smith (1986), vol. 3, pp. 137–241.

———. *Advertisements for the Unexperienced Planters of New England, or Any Where.* 1631. Reprinted in Smith (1986), vol. 3, pp. 259–302.

———. *The Complete Works of Captain John Smith (1580–1631).* Edited by Philip L. Barbour. 3 vols. Chapel Hill: University of North Carolina Press, 1986.

Sowerby, E. Millicent. *Catalogue of the Library of Thomas Jefferson.* 5 vols. 1952. Reprint, Charlottesville: University Press of Virginia, 1983.

Spencer, Hazelton. *Elizabethan Plays.* Boston: Little, Brown, 1933.

Stahle, David, et al. "The Lost Colony and Jamestown Droughts." *Science,* no. 280 (April 24, 1998): 564–67.

Stith, William. *The History of the First Discovery and Settlement of Virginia.* 1747. Reprint, New York: Johnson Reprint, 1969.

Stone, Lawrence. *The Family, Sex, and Marriage in England 1500–1800.* 1977. Reprint, New York: Harper & Row, 1979.

Strachey, William. *The Historie of Travaile Into Virginia Britannia: Expressing the Cosmographie and Comodities of the Country, togither with the Manners and Customes of the People.* 1612. Reprint, Boston: Elibron Classics, 2001.

Striker, Laura Polanyi, and Bradford Smith. "The Rehabilitation of Captain John Smith." *Journal of Southern History* 28 (1962): 474–81.

Strong, Roy. *Festival Designs by Inigo Jones: An Exhibition of Drawings for Scenery and Costumes for the Court Masques of James I and Charles I.* N.p.: International Exhibitions Foundation, 1967.

Symonds, William, ed. *The Proceedings of the English Colonie in Virginia since their first beginning from England in the yeare of our Lord 1606, till this present 1612, with all their accidents that befell them in their Journeys and Discoveries.* 1612. Reprinted in Smith (1986), vol. 1, pp. 199–279.

Thorndale, William. "The Virginia Census of 1619." *Magazine of Virginia Genealogy* 33, no. 3 (Summer 1995): 155–70.

Thornton, John. "The African Experience of the '20 and Odd Negroes' Arriving in Virginia in 1619." *William and Mary Quarterly,* 3d ser., 55, no. 3 (July 1998): 421–34.

Tilton, Robert S. *Pocahontas: The Evolution of an American Narrative.* Cambridge: Cambridge University Press, 1994.

Vaughan, Alden T. "Blacks in Virginia: A Note on the First Decade." *William and Mary Quarterly,* 3d ser., 29, no. 3 (July 1972): 469–78.

———. " 'Expulsion of the Salvages': English Policy and the Virginia Massacre of 1622." *William and Mary Quarterly,* 3d ser., 35, no. 1 (Jan. 1978): 57–84.

———. "John Smith Satirized: *The Legend of Captaine Iones.*" *William and Mary Quarterly,* 3d ser., 45, no. 4 (Oct. 1988): 712–32.

———. "The Origins Debate: Slavery and Racism in Seventeenth-Century Virginia." *Virginia Magazine of History and Biography* 97, no. 3 (July 1989): 311–54.

Waters, David W. *The Art of Navigation in England in Elizabethan and Early Stuart Times.* London: Hollis and Carter, 1958.

Webster, Noah. *The Little Reader's Assistant.* 2nd ed. Hartford, Conn.: Elisha Babcock, 1791.

Wharton, Henry. *The Life of John Smith, English Soldier.* 1685. Reprint, edited by Laura Polanyi Striker. Chapel Hill: University of North Carolina Press, 1957.

Bibliography

Willson, David Harris. *King James VI and I.* 1956. Reprint, New York: Oxford University Press, 1967.

Wilson, Harold C. *Gosnold's Hope: The Story of Bartholomew Gosnold.* Greensboro, N.C.: Tudor Publishers, 2000.

Woodnoth, Arthur. *A Short Collection of the Most Remarkable Passages from the Originall to the Dissolution of the Virginia Company.* London: Richard Cotes, 1651.

Woodward, Grace Steele. *Pocahontas.* Norman: University of Oklahoma Press, 1969.

Wright, J. Leitch. *Anglo-Spanish Rivalry in North America.* Athens: University of Georgia Press, 1971.

Wright, Louis B., ed. *A Voyage to Virginia in 1609: Two Narratives.* Charlottesville: University Press of Virginia, 1964.

Wyatt, Francis. "Letter of Sir Francis Wyatt, Governor of Virginia, 1621–1626." *William and Mary Quarterly,* 2d ser., 6 (April 1926): 114–21.

Zupko, Ronald Edward. *British Weights and Measures: A History from Antiquity to the Seventeenth Century.* Madison: University of Wisconsin Press, 1977.

Acknowledgments

I have accumulated many debts in writing this book. I am grateful to the Folger Shakespeare Library for allowing me research privileges in its extraordinary collection of Elizabethan and Jacobean books and documents. The Folger's staff was patient and helpful. I am also grateful to the Virginia Historical Society Library and the Archeological Society of Virginia for various kindnesses.

Thanks to Neil Tanner for answering many questions about transatlantic sailing on ships of the period. Thanks to Tim Hashaw for sharing research leads and insights pertaining to the African Americans of 1619. Thanks to Roger E. Nixon for tracking down the High Court of Admiralty examinations of John Martyn and Reinold Booth in the Public Records Office at Kew.

I have drawn on the investigations and interpretations of numerous scholars, whose names appear in the bibliography and the notes. One name I must single out here is that of the late Philip L. Barbour, the dean of John Smith scholars. It is a shame that he did not live to see the publication of his excellent *Complete Works of Captain John Smith*.

For editorial comments on various drafts, I am grateful to Judith Hagley, Jonathan Lawlor, Susan Hagen, Paul Buck, Jerry Cavedo, Dan Saphire, Victoria Edelman, Belle Peterson, and Rick Peterson.

On matters of historical substance, I had the benefit of comments from Nancy Egloff of Jamestown Settlement and an anonymous reviewer, for which I am deeply grateful. All remaining shortcomings are, of course, solely my responsibility.

Thanks to Ashbel Green of Alfred A. Knopf for supporting this book. Thanks to Jane Garrett, my editor, for helping me make it better. Also crucial at Knopf were Kathleen Fridella, Tracy Cabanis, Soonyoung Kwon, Carol Carson, Abby Weintraub, and Susanna Sturgis. Thanks to my agents, Glen Hartley and Lynn Chu, for believing in the book and finding it a wonderful home.

Anyone who knows me already knows the identity of my Abigail. Throughout the writing of this book, my wife, Susan, has been invaluable as an enthusiast, sounding board, kindly critic, and friend. This book is dedicated to her.

David A. Price
January 2003

Index

David A. Price has written for the *Wall Street Journal*, the *Washington Post*, *USA Today*, *Forbes*, and *Business 2.0*. He was formerly a reporter in the Washington, D.C., bureau of *Investor's Business Daily*. He holds degrees from Harvard Law School, Cambridge University, and the College of William and Mary. He was raised in Richmond, Virginia, and now lives with his wife and their two sons in Washington, D.C.

A NOTE ON THE TYPE

This book was set in Janson, a typeface long thought to have been made by the Dutchman Anton Janson, who was a practicing typefounder in Leipzig during the years 1668–1687. However, it has been conclusively demonstrated that these types are actually the work of Nicholas Kis (1650–1702), a Hungarian, who most probably learned his trade from the master Dutch typefounder Dirk Voskens. The type is an excellent example of the influential and sturdy Dutch types that prevailed in England up to the time William Caslon (1692–1766) developed his own incomparable designs from them.

Designed by Soonyoung Kwon